DATE DUE

DEC - 9 1993	NOV 1 7 2003
APR 2 7 1994	DEC 1 2004
NOV - 1 1995	
NOV - 9 1995	
JAN 1 7 1996	
OCT 2 3 1996	
JAN 2 2 1998	
OCT 1 2 1998	
OCT 2 3 1998	
MAR 1 1999	
OCT 2 8 1999	
NOV 2000	
JUN - 3 2003	

BRODART   Cat. No. 23-221

The Maya built one of the great ancient civilizations in the New World, between A.D. 250 and 900. Famed for over 150 years for its cities buried deep in the Central American jungle, the origins of Maya culture have nevertheless remained obscure until quite recently. Over the past two decades, a series of innovative research projects has established the Preclassic origins of complex society in the Maya area.

Among the best known of these is the study of Cuello, the earliest known ancient Maya settlement. Excavations at Cuello over several seasons from 1975 to 1987 have yielded an unmatched picture of a pioneer tropical forest community. In this timely volume, the early origins of Maya civilization 2,500 years ago are documented with detailed evidence on the environment, economy, buildings, crafts, ritual practices, burials, and artistic imagery.

CUELLO

AN EARLY MAYA
COMMUNITY IN
BELIZE

CUELLO

AN EARLY

MAYA

COMMUNITY

IN BELIZE

edited by

Norman Hammond

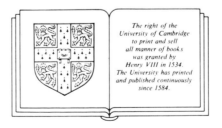

The right of the
University of Cambridge
to print and sell
all manner of books
was granted by
Henry VIII in 1534.
The University has printed
and published continuously
since 1584.

Cambridge University Press

Cambridge
New York   Port Chester
Melbourne   Sydney

Published by the Press Syndicate of the University of Cambridge
The Pitt Building, Trumpington Street, Cambridge CB2 1RP
40 West 20th Street, New York NY 10011, USA
10 Stamford Road, Oakleigh, Melbourne 3166, Australia

© Cambridge University Press 1991

First published 1991

Printed in Great Britain at the Bath Press, Avon

British Library Cataloguing in publication data

Cuello : an early Maya community in Belize.
1. Central America. Maya civilisation
I. Hammond, Norman
972.8004974

Library of Congress cataloguing in publication data

Cuello: an early Maya community in Belize / edited by Norman Hammond.
     p.   cm.
Includes bibliographical references and index.
ISBN 0 521 38422 2
1. Cuello Site (Belize)   2. Mayas – Antiquities.   I. Hammond,
Norman.
F1435.1.C84C84   1991
972.82'2 – dc20   90-1858 CIP

ISBN 0 521 38422 2 hardback

For Gordon Willey

CONTENTS

x   Contents

FIGURES

List of figures

xiv

List of figures

TABLES

ACKNOWLEDGMENTS

During six seasons of excavation at Cuello we have benefited from the help and generosity of numerous people in Belize, in the United States, and in Britain. This book embodies the efforts of many Cuello Project staff other than those who are formal contributors: we thank Michael Walton and Kevin Reiher, who mapped the site, Carl P. Beetz, Amanda Clarke, Michael Davenport, and Mark Horton, who supervised significant areas of the excavation; Karen Bruhns, Jill Mulholland, Priscilla Wegars, and Jim Spriggs, who directed the field laboratory (Spriggs in addition supervised the cleaning, conservation, and lifting of burials); Sheena Howarth, who drew almost all the finds for publication; Susan Bird, Louise Christiansen (now Belanger), Justine Hopkins, and Paul Stempen, who drew pottery sherds and vessels; Bob Erskine, who drew the lithics illustrated in Chapters 8–9; Jan Morrison, who together with Clarke, Davenport, Donaghey, Gerhardt, and Horton was responsible for drafting plans and sections; and Deni Seymour, Lawrence Feldman, and Linda Reynolds, who contributed to the fieldwork and initial description of the work included in Chapters 3 (contextual analysis), 8–9 (shell identification), and 6 respectively. Others who made invaluable contributions were Mark Hodges, Deborah Muyskens, and Ingrid Wuebber, while the excavations themselves could not have taken place without the efforts of several generations of Rutgers University undergraduates, graduate students from the University of Arizona, San Francisco State University, Tulane University and elsewhere, and our team of Belizean workmen.

Assistance and collaboration in post-excavation analyses have been given by many other colleagues: a particular debt is owed to our radiocarbon dating collaborators, who found a simple problem become steadily more complicated as time went on. Rainer Berger and Suzanne de Atley (UCLA), Roy Switsur and Alan Ward (Cambridge), Hans Suess and Timothy Linick (La Jolla), Robert Hedges, John Gowlett, Rupert Housley, and Ian Law (Oxford), and Austin Long (Tucson) deserve our heartfelt thanks. Charles Miksicek acknowledges the assistance of Arthur Gibson, Walter Miller, Lawrence Feldman, and especially the support of Alison Galloway, and Frank and Julie Saul that of numerous colleagues in the Anatomy and Radiology Departments of the Medical College of Ohio at Toledo. Gene Hall and Eric Marshall carried out PIXE analysis of obsidians at Rutgers University, Henry Truebe advised on petrographic identification, and Ronald Bishop and Edward Sayre included Cuello jades in their characterization program at the Brookhaven National Laboratory and subsequently at the Conservation Analytical Laboratory of the Smithsonian Institution. R.E.W. Adams, E. Wyllys Andrews V, and Gordon R. Willey all provided the editor with professional and practical help on many occasions during the Cuello fieldwork and the writing of this book.

Permission to work at Cuello was granted by the Government of Belize, on the advice of successive Archaeological Commissioners, Joseph O. Palacio, Elizabeth Graham, and Harriot W. Topsey, who with their staffs were a constant source of assistance throughout the project. The Cuello Brothers, rum distillers and protectors of the site, allowed us to camp and excavate and provided much logistic help, the latter also given over many years by Belize Sugar Industries Ltd. through Mr. Frank Curtis, Mr. Mickey Browne, and Mr. John Masson. Similar assistance was generously rendered by the British Forces in Belize on a number of occasions.

The investigations at Cuello were funded primarily by the Committee for Research and Exploration of the National Geographic Society (grants 1856-78, 1967-78, 2077-79, 3504-87), the Trustees of the British Museum, and the Research Council of Rutgers University, with generous assistance also from the Society of Antiquaries of London, the Crowther-Beynon Fund of the University Museum of Archaeology and Anthropology at Cambridge, the Center for Archaeological Research of the University of Texas at San Antonio (1976), the Wenner-Gren Foundation for Anthropological Research (1978), and several other institutional and private donors. The 1990 excavations, carried out while this book was in press, some results from which are noted in Chapter 11, were sponsored by the National Geographic Society (grant 4155-89) and Boston University. The laboratory analysis of skeletal material (Chapter 7) was made possible by National Science Foundation grant BNS81-01759, and the radiocarbon and other laboratory analyses acknowledged above were carried out as cost-sharing contributions to the Cuello Project by the respective institutions. Additional cost-sharing in the form of laboratory space, computer time, and other facilities was provided by the authors' own institutions, and we acknowledge with thanks Rutgers University, the University of Arizona, the Florida Museum of Natural History, and the Medical College of Ohio at Toledo.

All of the illustrations used in this book were prepared for the Cuello Project by staff artists and photographers, and are project copyright, but some have previously been used elsewhere: pottery drawings adapted for Laura Kosakowsky's *Prehistoric Maya Pottery at Cuello, Belize* (© University of Arizona Press, Anthropological Papers 47, 1987) and used here in that form are Figs. 3.26–3.32, 3.33–3.35, 3.39–3.42, 10.1–10.2, while Fig. 4.1 appeared previously in Norman Hammond, *Ancient Maya Civilization* (© Rutgers University Press, 1982). Most of the phase plans in Chapter 3, and the architectural illustrations in Chapter 5, were used in Juliette Cartwright Gerhardt's *Preclassic Maya Architecture at Cuello, Belize* (BAR International Series 464, 1988), and Figs. 10.1–10.11 and Tables 10.1–10.2 were used in Cynthia Robin's *Preclassic Maya Burials at Cuello, Belize* (BAR International Series 480, 1989). Figs. 2.8, 3.43, and 10.20 have been used in articles in *American Antiquity* (© Society for American Archaeology, 1979, 1982). We acknowledge the permissions given by these publishers, where necessary. The dustjacket photograph was taken by Michael Hamilton. As is often the case with collective publications such as this, different aspects of the research were carried out and written up at different times over the years; it should be noted that the ideas expressed and conclusions reached in Chapters 1–3 date in their present form to 1987–88; Chapter 4 to 1984; Chapter 5 to 1987; Chapter 6 to 1982; Chapter 7 to 1987; most of Chapters 8 and 9 to 1983; and Chapters 10–11 to 1988–89, although all the authors have had the opportunity to correct them. The small discrepancy in number of burials between Chapters 7 and 10 results from minor phase adjustments and new data, to which the 1990 burials (p. 244) must now be added. Much of the final assembly of this book was carried out during my tenure of a Fellowship in Pre-Columbian Studies at Dumbarton Oaks in Washington, D.C., in 1988.

Chapter 1

THE MAYA AND THEIR CIVILIZATION

Norman Hammond

INTRODUCTION: THE GEOGRAPHY, CHRONOLOGY, AND ACHIEVEMENTS OF THE MAYA

The civilization of the ancient Maya flourished through most of the first millennium A.D. in the tropical lowlands of the Yucatán Peninsula and the adjacent regions of the Petén and Belize (Fig. 1.1), occupying an area now divided among the modern countries of Belize, Guatemala, and Mexico, and extending southeast into the more elevated western fringes of Honduras and El Salvador. While Maya civilization was primarily a lowland phenomenon, it both penetrated and shared its origins with the cultures of the highlands of Guatemala to the south of the Petén, where the Mayan language family has its greatest diversity and perhaps its beginnings.

Thus the Maya Area, as traditionally defined, reaches from the northern tip of Yucatán at sea level, south to the mountain basins of the continental divide, and down into the lowlands of the Pacific coast. On the west it reaches almost to the Isthmus of Tehuantepec, a low saddle permitting easy contact between the Pacific and Gulf Coast regions, beyond which rise up the central highlands of Mexico. To the east is a frontier zone in which Maya and neighboring cultures mixed, but where the basins of the Ulua River, flowing into the Caribbean, and the Lempa, running to the Pacific, seem to have formed the boundaries of Maya cultural expansion.

The highlands and the lowlands form the two major environmental units in this area: the former include the steep slope down to the narrow Pacific coastal plain, the towering volcanic peaks of the continental divide and the basins that lie between them, and the older metamorphic highlands to the north of the Motagua and Grijalva rivers, less dramatic in relief but immensely more complex in their ancient geomorphology. Many of the minerals from these regions, such as obsidian and lava from the volcanic zone, and jade and cinnabar from the metamorphic, are found at ancient sites as far north as Yucatán, underlining the economic unity of the Maya Area in pre-Hispanic times. The subtropical and montane forest vegetation of the highlands has been seriously

Fig 1.1 Map of the Maya Area, showing the location of Cuello and of other important Preclassic sites, together with the geological sources of jade and obsidian traded into the Maya Lowlands.

eroded by centuries of cultivation, although areas of cloud forest remain in the Alta Verapaz (see Hammond 1988, Chapter 3, for a series of maps illustrating the environment of the Maya Area).

The geology of the lowlands is essentially a limestone platform, flat and barely emergent from the sea in the north, interrupted by the range of the Puuc hills in southern Yucatán, and becoming more rolling and then hilly into the Petén region of northern Guatemala, where folding and faulting direct the courses of rivers and form the basins of lakes. In southern Belize the granite and sandstone massif of the Maya Mountains pushes up through the limestone, and formed a valued source of stone in ancient times. Although in many ways an ecological continuum, the lowlands have traditionally been divided into north drier and southern rainforest zones.

The lowlands increase gradually in elevation, rainfall, and luxuriance of vegetation from north to south, with the low scrub of northern Yucatán merging into a mixed woodland that in turn becomes the tropical rain forest of the Petén and Belize; precipitation rises from less than 500 mm a year near Mérida in the arid northwest to 3,400 mm in southern Belize and on the edge of the highlands, where the rain-bearing clouds coming in from the Caribbean meet the land mass. Temperatures are tropical throughout the lowlands, except in the subtropical heights of the Maya Mountains in Belize, and the relative humidity is high.

One of the prime distinctions between the northern and southern lowlands is the existence of rivers: in the north the landscape is karstic, with underground drainage and few surface sources of water except occasional lakes and the *cenotes* or swallow-holes that form when the limestone cap over a subterranean river collapses. The higher rainfall of the rain-forest zone remains largely on the surface, forming major river systems such as that of the Usumacinta, flowing into the Gulf of Mexico, the Belize River, and the Rio Hondo, running to the Caribbean. These are navigable in the rainy season, and in places even in the dry season of January–May, providing a network of highways which were certainly used by the ancient Maya: so many major communities lie along the Usumacinta that it has been dubbed the "river of ruins." The headwaters of the San Pedro Martir, one of its tributaries, and those of the Rio Holmul, part of the Rio Hondo drainage, lie so close together that portage between them would have been easy. It has been suggested that the prosperity of Tikal, a major center on the portage route, was partly due to its strategic location.

South of Tikal, in the area between the Caribbean and Gulf Coast drainages, is a district of lakes, the largest of which is Lake Petén Itzá. Several large sites are known, including Yaxha and Tayasal, but the lakes did not seem to be an especial attraction during the main period of Maya civilization. During the last few centuries before the Spanish Conquest they did support one of the major concentrations of people in the southern lowlands.

This final period is known as the Postclassic, and in the formal division of Maya prehistory lasts from *c*. A.D. 900 down to the Conquest after 1500 (Fig. 1.2). It is preceded by the Classic period, A.D. 250–900, defined as the time during which the rulers of Maya polities erected monuments bearing dates in a calendrical system known as the Long Count. This is a quasi-linear marking of time (actually a very long cycle) with a mythological origin in 3114 B.C., probably representing the last creation of the world. Periods of time within it are divided into *baktunob* of about 400 years, *katunob* of 20 years, *tunob* approximating to a year, *uinalob* or months of 20 days, of which there were 18 to a *tun*, and *kinob* or days. The Classic period fell into the late eighth, ninth, and early tenth *baktunob*.

This book is not the place in which to go into further detail, but descriptions of the workings of the Classic Maya calendar can be found in the standard textbooks on Maya civilization (eg. Morley *et al.* 1983; Coe 1987; Hammond 1988).

The Classic period thus defined was one in which the main Maya cities had their apogee: Tikal, Yaxchilan, Palenque, Copan, Calakmul, and a host of smaller polities flourished in the south, ruled by dynasties which raised temples and inscriptions to themselves and the glory of their ancestors, while in the north centers such as Cobá, Izamal, and Dzibil-chaltun were joined late in the Classic by the Puuc sites such as Uxmal and Sayil, and by the major new polity of Chichén Itzá (Culbert 1991).

Recent studies of the economy and settlement patterns of Classic Maya civilization (Ashmore 1981b; Flannery 1982; Turner and Harrison 1983) have shown that the swidden-farming technique of historic times was augmented in the past by the construction of artificial econiches bringing marginal lands into production. Hillside terracing on steep slopes seems to have been primarily to create extra areas of flat fertile land, while also inhibiting erosion (Turner 1983), but its occurrence on shallower slopes, together with walls running directly downhill, suggests permanent demarcation of the improved land, an assertion of tenure that fits best with short-term fallowing. A second improvement technique, the canalization of wetlands along rivers or in *bajos* to create drained fields, also suggests more intensive cultivation. Both kinds of land improvement are known from at least the beginning of the Classic period, and drained fields appear some centuries earlier at sites such as Cerros and Pulltrouser Swamp. While maize was undoubtedly the principal crop then as now, a wide range of other cultivated plants, orchard crops, and gathered fruits and forest products formed the basis of subsistence. Animal protein came from hunting of deer (some possibly loose-herded), peccary and other forest animals and birds, from the collecting of turtles, fish, and edible mollusks in the rivers (and perhaps in the canals of the drained-field areas), and from domestic dogs. Turkeys were also domesticated, although how early is uncertain.

Maya settlement, long thought to consist of scattered hamlets around sparsely populated ceremonial centers, was shown by the mapping of Tikal in the late 1950s to include more concentrated populations reaching the tens of thousands: it was the perceived imbalance between this raised population density and the accepted swidden-farming economic base that stimulated research into ancient Maya subsistence economics in the 1960s and 1970s (Harrison and Turner 1978). The range of habitation units recorded suggested differential access to resources, and a more stratified society than the simple priest–peasant relationship of rulers and ruled accepted until the 1960s (Becker 1979). The nature of the rulers as secular dynasts became clear with the work of

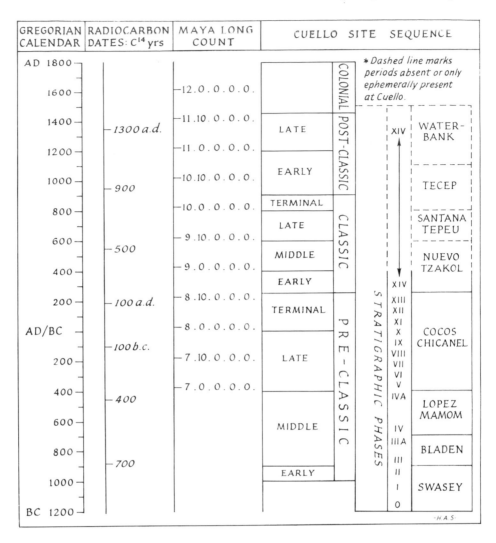

Fig. 1.2 Maya chronology: the Cuello ceramic sequence from the Swasey phase onwards is correlated with stratigraphic phases O–XIV, with the major periods of Maya chronology in general, and with the passage of time in the Maya and Gregorian calendars and in radiocarbon years. For a broad comparison of the Cuello ceramic sequence with those from other Maya lowland sites, see Ashmore (1981b), Fig. 2.2.

Proskouriakoff (1960), and while the "city-state" model of political organization promulgated by Morley (1946) on the basis of Greek parallels still held good, the decipherment of the hieroglyphic inscriptions on dynastic monuments allowed the interactions on those polities and their rulers to be elucidated (for recent summaries of decipherment, see Houston (1988, 1989); for one of political structure and interaction, see Culbert (1988)). The patronage art commissioned by Maya rulers, the relationships with the other-world and underworld deities that it portrayed, and the rituals that linked rulers to their people and their gods have all proved immensely more complex than had been supposed. The changes in understanding are well described by Schele and Miller (1986), a study which in its heavy use of unprovenanced material also illustrates the major problem facing Maya archaeology today: the looting that has removed monuments and burial goods from their contexts and stripped them of much of their value as evidence about Maya society.

Our knowledge of Classic Maya civilization has thus undergone a series of revolutions over the past 30 years: understanding of its economy, social structure, political organization, and ideology has expanded and changed dramatically, and the roots of all of these aspects of Classic society are increasingly recognized as being in the preceding centuries of the Preclassic or Formative period (Adams 1977). This was defined as beginning with the first appearance of forming villages, and ending c. A.D. 250 with the appearance of a writing and calendar system used on public monuments, one of the more striking traits of an emergent complex society. The remainder of this introduction reviews recent developments in our knowledge of the Preclassic, to which the excavations at Cuello have made some contribution.

PRECLASSIC PROBLEMS: THE SITUATION IN 1975

In the mid-1970s, when research began at Cuello, the Maya Preclassic period was widely seen as one of village farming communities, beginning with an initial settlement of the Maya Lowlands in the middle centuries of the first millennium B.C. The chronology of the Preclassic had been first laid out by Robert E. Smith (1955) on the basis of the ceramic sequence established at Uaxactun in the 1930s, and divided into an earlier Mamom and a later Chicanel period, the first beginning c. 500 B.C. and the latter lasting from 300 B.C. to A.D. 300. At this later date the Classic period began, with the inception of vaulted architecture, polychrome ceramics, and dated lapidary inscriptions in the Long Count, three markers of élite culture that were taken to demonstrate the emergence of civilization. Subsequent excavations provided parallel Preclassic sequences at Benque Viejo (Xunantunich) and Barton Ramie in the Belize Valley (Thompson 1940: Figs. 4–5; Willey et al. 1965), with the definition of a slightly earlier period of occupation than Mamom in the Early Jenney Creek phase at Barton Ramie. At Tikal a comparable phase, designated Eb, was recognized, and the appearance of both vaulted construction and a Long Count date (Stela 29) in what was formally the Late Preclassic suggested that the traits of Classic Maya civilization had been of Preclassic origin (W.R. Coe 1965).

The origins of this Formative tradition remained obscure, but in the late 1960s the excavations by Willey at Altar de Sacrificios and Seibal in the Pasión valley showed that another pre-Mamom area of occupation existed. Defined as Xe at Altar (Adams 1971) and Real Xe at Seibal (Willey 1970; Sabloff 1975), the origins of this ceramic tradition were seen as being in the Maya highland zone on the basis of discoveries by Sedat and Sharer (1972) in Verapaz, where pottery with some Xc traits had been recovered. Sharer and Gifford (1970) preferred an origin as far east as El Salvador, seeing close ties with the Chalchuapa sequence; Adams (1972) in contrast proposed a western lowland origin up the Usumacinta drainage from the Gulf Coast, feeling that the lack of early occupation in the Upper Chixoy basin of the western highlands precluded settlement from that region. Such a riverine pattern of settlement, supported by Sisson's (1970) evidence of occupation on the lower Usumacinta by c. 1200 b.c., was also suggested by Puleston and Puleston (1971) for the eastern lowlands.

Radiocarbon dates for the Xe and Real Xe phases of 745 ± 195 b.c. and 660 ± 75 b.c. (GX-172, UCLA 1437) allowed Willey (1970: 318) to place the Xe phase between 800 and 600 B.C.; in the late 1960s calibration of radiocarbon dates as proposed by Suess (1965) had only just begun to make an impact in Old World archaeology, and, since there was no historical chronology that demonstrated the divergence of radiocarbon ages from real time, was not seen as relevant by many working in the New World. Thus radiocarbon ages and solar years were considered to be the same thing, and no formal distinction was made between them in defining chronology. By 1974, however, Berger et al. (1974) noted the difference and proposed a beginning of c. 900 B.C. in calendar years for Real Xe at Seibal based on calibration of the single radiocarbon date to 850 B.C., reflected also in the final Altar de Sacrificios chronological chart (Willey 1973: Fig. 3). This chart embodied the ceramic analyses of Adams, and from its first version in 1968 placed the beginning of the Middle Preclassic ceramic tradition at 1000 B.C. No early Preclassic occupations were known, although a human presence apparently associated with maize was indicated by the pollen and plant remains from the Laguna de Petenxil core (Cowgill et al. 1966) with a radiocarbon date of 2040 ± 160 b.c. (Y-1285), calibrating to > 2500–2310 B.C., and human occupation c. 4000 B.C. was argued by Wiseman (1975) on the basis of the Laguna de Eckixil core.

By the mid-1970s an Early Preclassic phase was well established in other regions of Mesoamerica, including the Pacific Coast of Guatemala and Chiapas, the Gulf Coast, and Oaxaca (summarized in Lowe 1978), and even in the Maya Highlands occupation as far back as 1200 B.C. had been proposed (Sharer 1978, III: 115), as well as in the Chontalpa region of the lower Usumacinta (Sisson 1976: 579–81). The absence of Early Preclassic occupation in the Petén and Yucatán began to look exceptional, especially in a region that had later supported a complex society: all of the other major foci of Mesoamerican civilization had long Preclassic sequences.

Thus, the pre-1000 b.c. dates reported from Cuello (Hammond et al. 1976, 1977; Hammond 1977a: 60 and note 7; 1977b) were not surprising as such, although the earliness of some of the dates occasioned comment, given the Middle Formative appearance of the ceramics illustrated from the newly defined Swasey phase (Hammond 1975c: 206; 1977b: Figs. 7–9; Hammond et al. 1979: Fig. 4), and was remarked on by M.D. Coe (1980: 34–5), followed by Marcus (1983, 1984) and others. These criticisms were entirely justified, as noted in Hammond (1984b: 822), since the ceramics in question were from the end of the Swasey phase as initially defined, which was placed subsequently in the Middle Formative Bladen Xe ceramic complex by Kosakowsky (1983, 1987); in addition, further excavations at Cuello showed that stratigraphic placement of one of the grave groups illustrated (Hammond 1977b: Figs. 8–9; Hammond et al. 1979: Fig. 4, nos. 2, 4) was in fact later still, in the later Middle Formative Lopez Mamom phase.

Ceramics apart, the radiocarbon chronology from Cuello was impressive: where the total number of Formative period dates from the Maya Area was less than two dozen, with no more than five from any one site and not all of those acceptable to the excavators (e.g. Willey 1973: 18), Cuello had 18 dates in good stratigraphic order, together with six other dates considered either far too early (and perhaps run on redeposited charcoal), or far too late. While there were acknowledged gaps in the chronology, especially for the early first millennium b.c. and beginnings of the Middle Formative, the Swasey phase, from which more than a dozen of the dates came, seemed firmly placed in the second millennium b.c. (Berger *et al.* 1979; Hammond *et al.* 1979).

Support for an early beginning to settlement in the Maya Lowlands came from the increasing evidence of social complexity in the Late Preclassic, much of it revealed while the Cuello investigations were in progress. The prescience of W.R. Coe at Tikal (1965) was endorsed by discoveries at Cerros (Freidel 1979; Robertson and Freidel 1986), Edzna (Matheny *et al.* 1983), El Mirador (Matheny 1980, 1986), Komchen (Ringle and Andrews 1988), Lamanai (Pendergast 1981), Seibal (Smith 1982) and elsewhere, showing that massive architecture, sometimes on a scale dwarfing that of the Classic period, had been constructed from perhaps 400 B.C. onwards, in large precincts that argued for substantial and concentrated populations under centralized control. The ideology of the Preclassic and its manifestation in élite iconography began to acquire a coherence of structure and interpretation (Schele and Miller 1986; Freidel and Schele 1988). The beginnings of Maya civilization were placed firmly in the later first millennium B.C., and were increasingly accepted as autochthonous, not the result of direct stimulus from already-advanced societies elsewhere in Mesoamerica. Linkage of the Maya Lowlands with other regions from the early Middle Preclassic onwards was increasingly documented by trace-element analyses of obsidian, recovery of exotic materials such as jade, and recognition of ceramic ties. While the environment, economy, demography and settlement patterns, architecture (apart from a few monumental buildings), mortuary patterns, ceremonial behavior, and ideology of the Maya Preclassic were virtually unknown when work began at Cuello, a decade later there was substantial, if patchy, knowledge of the period which enabled the emergence of Classic civilization to be better comprehended.

To the evidence for early sedentary occupation, with maize agriculture and ceramics, indicated at Cuello and hinted at in other sites where Swasey pottery had been found in small quantities, was added the possibility of a long antecedent preceramic period of gathering and hunting, ending perhaps in a local transition to settled society. Stratigraphic, typological, and/or radiocarbon dating evidence for such preceramic occupation had been found in the highlands at Los Tapiales (Gruhn and Bryan 1977) and the surrounding area of El Quiché (Brown 1980), and in the far north of Yucatán at Loltun Cave (Velasquez 1980). MacNeish *et al.* (1980) then carried out a survey in Belize in which a large number of aceramic sites were recorded; in spite of the lack of stratigraphy and dates, a typological division into six successive phases spanning the period 9000–2000 b.c. was proposed. It began with gatherer–hunters in the tradition of the Clovis manifestation of the southern United States, and proceeded through stages of progressive commitment to localized resources and incipient sedentism until a settled preceramic food-producing society, not unlike the "Pre-pottery Neolithic" of the Near East in conception, was established in the Progreso phase of 3000–2000 b.c. immediately antecedent to the pottery-using Swasey phase. The major problem with this model was that there was no positive evidence that it was valid, as Zeitlin (1984) effectively concedes in a review of the entire Belize Archaic survey program; minor problems included the presence of lithic types designated as early preceramic in Late Formative contexts at both Cuello and Cerros. This is not to say that there is no preceramic in Belize: some of the lithic types do not appear to belong to the inventory of the Formative–Classic–Postclassic Maya continuum, and the Turrialba-variant Clovis point from Ladyville (Hester *et al.* 1981) is as suggestive an indicator of early Holocene human presence as anything from other parts of Mesoamerica. Also, a number of loci in the Maya Area and adjacent Central America have yielded ecofactual evidence, of vegetation disturbance associated with maize pollen, with radiocarbon dates indicating human presence from perhaps the end of the fourth millennium B.C. in calendar years (Rue 1987, 1989). A preceramic phase in Belize antecedent to the first pottery-using villages, whether these were of Swasey date or earlier, is highly likely to have existed, and may have embraced sedentary horticulture in the third and second millennia B.C.

The present situation

The eastern part of the lowlands, and northern Belize in particular, has produced so much information on Preclassic occupations over the past decade that a truly regional research framework has now been built up: the number and distribution of sites has allowed theories about polity and community structure to be proposed (Scarborough 1983, 1985), while the output of the chert-tool workshops at Colha has shown that a Late Formative production economy existed on a regional and not just a local level (Shafer and Hester 1983).

Colha also has a Bladen-equivalent occupation, dubbed Bolay, underlying Mamom and documented with a series of radiocarbon ages that support a calibrated range of 900–500 B.C. and an early Middle Formative position of Bladen, consonant with the Xe links indicated by the initial placing of both Bladen and Bolay in the Xe ceramic sphere (Kosakowsky and Valdez 1982; Kosakowsky 1983; Valdez 1987). I feel that while contemporaneity with Xe is demonstrable, with both modal and some typological equivalences, the Xe sphere itself is a southwestern Petén entity, probably not reaching as far northeast as Tikal, and that both Bladen and Bolay should be placed in a new ceramic sphere, which should probably be dubbed the Swasey or Bladen sphere (see p. 65). A date of 800–550 ± 60 b.c., calibrating to 1000–520 B.C. on that degree of statistical uncertainty and overlapping Mamom in time, would be consonant with the radiocarbon ages obtained at Cuello, Colha, Seibal, and Altar de Sacrificios, with the Cuello dates falling in the later end of the range at *c*. 900–600 B.C. Bladen-like pottery is also known from Lamanai, El Pozito, Nohmul, San Estevan, and Santa Rita Corozal in northern Belize, although some of this could equally well be of Swasey date given the developmental relationship between the two complexes and the resulting subtlety of distinctions (Kosakowsky 1983, 1987), as well as the small sample numbers from these sites. Valdez (1987, personal communication 1989) indeed suggests that Swasey, Bladen, and Bolay should all be placed in a new Swasey ceramic sphere, spanning presumably the first half of the first millennium B.C. and an area centered on, if not confined to, northern Belize.

A definable Swasey complex has so far been found only at Cuello, where the bulk of the 1,900 sherds and the score of whole vessels analyzed by Pring (1977a) in his definition of the complex were excavated. Pring's Swasey complex was later split by Kosakowsky (1983, 1987), using only material from 1980 excavations, into an earlier Swasey complex defined by 371 sherds and no whole vessels, and the later Bladen defined by over 1,300 sherds and 13 whole vessels. The content and relationships of both complexes, together with the succeeding Lopez Mamom and Cocos Chicanel, are discussed in this book.

Mamom pottery was noted by Pring (1977a) at seven sites, including most of those with Bladen ceramics and also Louisville and Caledonia in Corozal District. The large number of radiocarbon ages from Cuello spanning the period 610–350 ± 50 b.c. (with others outside those limits), and suggesting a maximum span of 800–400 B.C., overlaps both the latter part of the Bladen span and the period conventionally assigned to Mamom of 600–300 B.C. in undifferentiated radiocarbon/calendar years. Within this period the first large rectangular substructures were built at Cuello, in stratigraphic phase IVA (Hammond and Gerhardt 1990), matching the architectural differentiation that developed in Group B at Altar de Sacrificios, where Willey (1973: 30) suggests that élite residences may have occupied the enlarged platforms.

As a result of the 1973–1974 Corozal Project surveys, Chicanel occupation was known at all sites in northern Belize with a later history of florescence, and it was suggested that all prime locations had been occupied by this time. Some which appeared to have been subsequently abandoned, such as Kichpanha, have sinced proved to have a Classic occupation in a different part of the site from that investigated initially, but in others the continuation of prosperity through the Classic period presumed on the basis of major architecture has proved to be wrong: at both Cerros and Nohmul the public buildings proved to be of Preclassic, not Classic date, and to have been abandoned for centuries thereafter (Robertson and Freidel 1986; Hammond *et al.* 1988). Cerros seems to have declined earlier than Nohmul, since the latter was at its peak in the early centuries A.D. and was a major producer of pottery in the "Protoclassic" or "Floral Park" tradition. At this period Cuello also attained its maximum degree of prosperity and size, although this does not seem to have exceeded 3,400 people and the public architecture remained modest in scale. The radiocarbon and calibrated chronology for the site falls within the conventionally accepted limits for Chicanel of 400 B.C.–A.D. 250 in undifferentiated radiocarbon/calendar years.

The chapters that follow detail the investigation of the Formative period occupation of Cuello between 1975 and 1980, with further minor excavations in 1987. An account of these excavations, and of the methods used, is followed by a summary of the stratigraphy and chronology of the site, including both radiocarbon dates and the ceramic sequence. These sections are by Juliette Cartwright Gerhardt, Sara Donaghey, Laura Kosakowsky, Richard Wilk, and me. The evidence that archaeobotany and zooarchaeology can bring to bear on questions of environment and economy is then discussed by Charles Miksicek, and by Elizabeth Wing and Sylvia Scudder. The nature of the Cuello settlement is dealt with in two parts: a detailed account of architectural development in the intensively excavated area of Platform 34, the apparent core of the Formative community, by Gerhardt and Hammond; and an analysis of the surrounding settlement based on test excavations by Richard Wilk and Hal Wilhite.

The people of Cuello as a biological population are examined by Frank and Julie Saul, and their craft technology in ceramics and lithics by Rebecca McSwain, Jay Johnson, and Laura Kosakowsky; some of the other artifacts are discussed by myself. External contacts, most visible in the acquisition of exotic materials, involve local, regional, and long-distance contacts, extending certainly as far as the highlands of Guatemala and possibly west to the Olmec heartland of the Gulf Coast. The ideology of the Preclassic people can be discerned to some degree in their patterns of funerary behavior and offerings, discussed by Cynthia Robin, Juliette Gerhardt, and myself, and in the imagery and iconography of their artifacts. Finally, the importance of Cuello as one of the most intensively excavated and best-documented early Maya sites is summarized and assessed.

Chapter 2   ARCHAEOLOGICAL INVESTIGATIONS AT CUELLO, 1975–1987

Norman Hammond

INTRODUCTION

The Cuello site was discovered during the regional survey of northern Belize carried out by the British Museum–Cambridge University Corozal Project in 1973–74 (Fig. 2.1), and was classified as a "large minor ceremonial center" of level 6, in terms of the regional site hierarchy proposed by Hammond (1975a). The main group of mounds was in *ramonal* woodland east of the Cuello Brothers' rum distillery, but extensive settlement was visible in pasture and *huamil* second growth to the north, west, and south of this. On the south the structures included a number of large platforms with smaller mounds on their tops, and a substantial pyramid, Structure 39, which had been partly bulldozed. Sherds from the core of this included abundant Late Preclassic (Chicanel sphere) material, some Middle Preclassic (Mamom sphere) pottery, and other types not immediately recognizable which were thought to be either earlier or exotic, or both. Given the temporal focus of the Corozal Project on the Preclassic (or Formative) period and the antecedents of Classic Maya civilization, the Cuello site appeared to be of some interest, and was scheduled for investigation in the 1975 field season; work there was designated Operation 17 in the regional program, with the 1974 surface collections being Op. 17A(1), and excavations beginning in 1975 with Op. 17B. The research design changed markedly over the period 1975–80, beginning as part of an avowedly regional study and ending as a single large open-area excavation; the considered results of each season set the objectives for the next, and both logistics and techniques evolved in the light of experience (described in detail in the final excavation report: Hammond n.d.).

MAPPING

The main part of the site was mapped, and the structures numbered, in 1975 (Fig. 2.2); the sequence began with Platform 1, underlying the West Plaza of the ceremonial precinct, Structures 2–17 around and north of it, and Platform 18 and Structures 19–30 below and round the East Plaza. (The

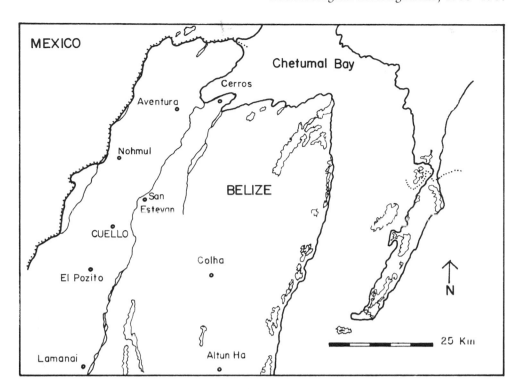

Fig. 2.1 Maya sites in northern Belize, recorded by the Corozal Project regional survey in 1973–74. Cuello is midway between Nohmul and El Pozito, the two major centers on the limestone ridge east of the Rio Hondo.

distinction between Platforms as modifications of the landscape surface and Structures as supports for buildings follows that defined at Lubaantun (Hammond 1975b: 140–1)). The mounds in the area west and south of the main group followed in sequence, and further structures to the north and south were mapped in 1976. The western part of the settlement was mapped in 1980, bringing the total number of structures to 200; the zone east of the ceremonial precinct remained in thick *huamil* throughout the period of investigations at Cuello and was not mapped. Structure numbers above 300 apply to buildings uncovered in excavations on Platform 34.

The known extent of settlement at Cuello runs 1,200 m southwest, 750 m south, 600 m west, and 500 m north from the ceremonial precinct, with the northeast–southwest concentration of mounds that is apparent being the result of local microtopography; areas of lowlying terrain flank Cuello on the other sides, separating the cluster of Platform 90 through Structure 104 from the main body of settlement by some 200 m. The testing program carried out by Wilk and Wilhite (Chapter 6) shows that non-mound occupation also existed, and a rough estimate of population based on the map and test excavations suggests a peak of about 2,600 people in the Late Formative period of maximum occupancy.

Overall site mapping, drafted in the Maudslay convention common in Mesoamerican archaeology (Fig. 2.2), was supplemented for Platform 34 with a contour map at 0.5 m intervals (Fig. 2.3). A site datum at an assumed elevation of 22.00 m above sea level (based on official 1:50,000 maps) and a cardinally oriented grid of 5 × 5 m squares, with an arbitrary origin at 00/00 southwest of Platform 34 and reaching 95 m N/ 75 m E, allowed any point to be fixed in three dimensions, if necessary to the nearest centimeter (Fig. 2.4). The 30 m N and 40 m E grid lines were used to divide the platform into quadrants for logistical purposes, with major baulks running along these lines being left for access to the excavations, although in some areas they were narrowed, and over the pyramid (Structure 35) eventually removed altogether. A Hilger & Watts 10″ Microptic theodolite was used for overall mapping, and a Zeiss level for surveying in the excavation.

EXCAVATION STRATEGY

When excavations began in 1975, Cuello was one of more than 60 sites documented by the Corozal Project regional survey, many of which appeared worth testing by excavation. The Preclassic pottery collected from the bulldozed Structure 39, and the adjacent ancient quarry which appeared to be the source of its fill, suggested that the nearest undisturbed mound, Platform 34, should be investigated. The large area of the platform, and the relatively small size of the pyramidal Structure 35 on its western end, suggested an architectural discontinuity which would repay examination, the more so

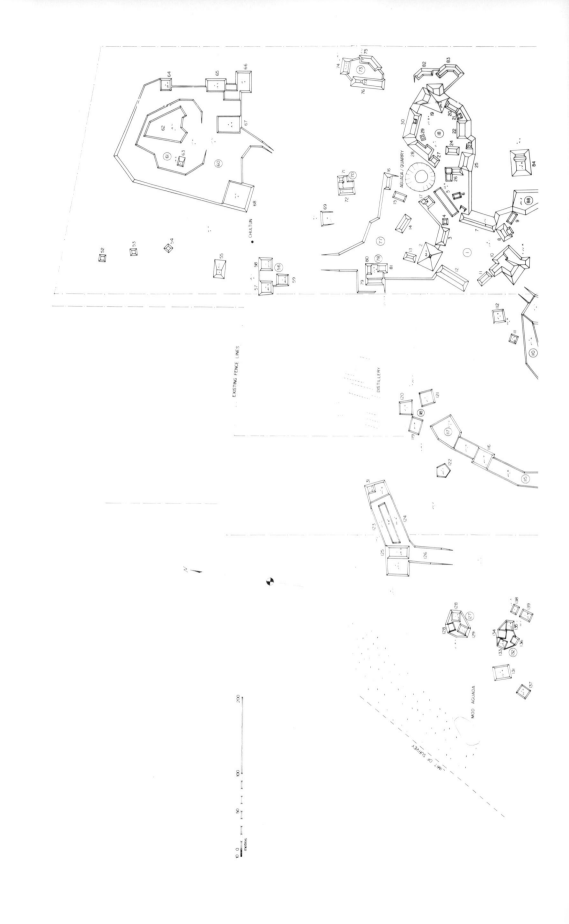

AGUADA / QUARRY

DISTILLERY

CHULTUN

EXISTING FENCE LINES

MOD AGUADA

LIMIT OF SURVEY

N

200

100

50

10 0
metres

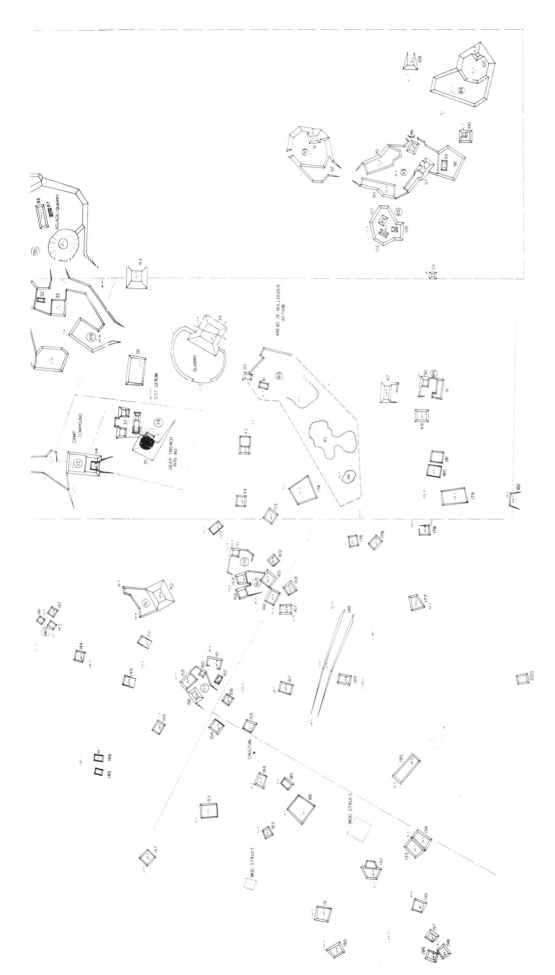

Fig. 2.2 Site map of Cuello, with the Classic period ceremonial precinct to the northeast and Platform 34, the site of the main excavation, towards the south end of the community.

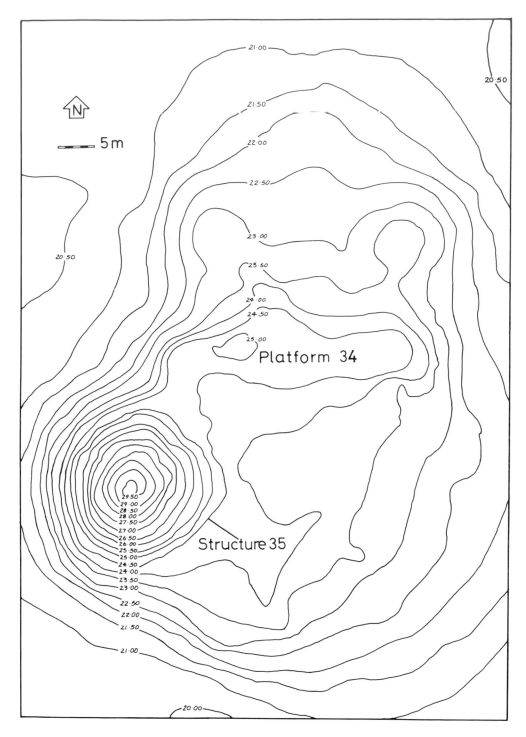

Fig. 2.3 Contour plan of Platform 34 prior to excavation, with the
pyramid Structure 35 at the west end. The 1976–80 Main Trench
lay immediately east of the pyramid (see Fig. 5.27).

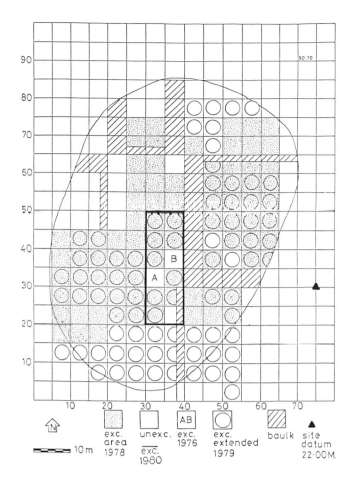

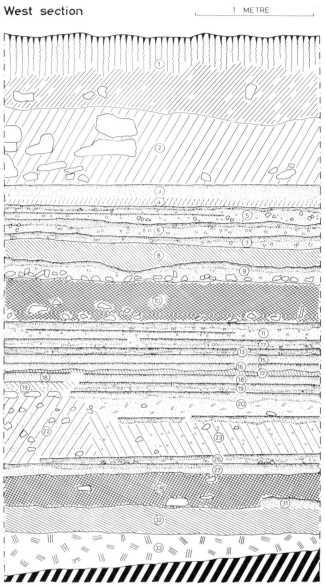

West section

1 METRE

Fig. 2.4 Platform 34, represented as a conventionalized ovoid, with the survey grid of 5-m squares used for three-dimensional recording superimposed and the area of the 1976–80 Main Trench outlined on it. The initial 1975 test, Op. 17B (Fig. 2.5) was in grid square "A" (30/30), and the 1987 excavations were in the northern third (40–50m N) of the Main Trench. Other excavations, covering an area of nearly 3,000 sq. m, took place in all parts of Platform 34 and Structure 35.

Fig. 2.5 Section of the first test pit (Op. 17B), excavated through Platform 34 in 1975 by Duncan Pring. The thick soil levels at the top are erosion from Structure 35, and the upper series of plaster floors are those of the Late Formative Platform 34. The lower floors, thought at the time to be from earlier phases of the platform, were found to be the interior surfaces of buildings on the west side of a buried courtyard.

since similar mound groups at Seibal had proved to be of Preclassic date (Tourtellot 1988b: 277–84). Op. 17B was therefore dug close to the base of the pyramid, and the deep and detailed stratigraphy encountered, and the associated radiocarbon ages obtained from charcoal samples, led to the subsequent seasons of larger-scale excavation at Cuello.

Op. 17B yielded 3.4 m of plaster floors, occupation, and fill deposits (Figs. 2.5, 2.6), together with several burials. The floors appeared to be successive raisings of Platform 34, from a low construction over the buried fossil soil to a final area approaching 90 by 70 m. Charcoal samples assayed by the Cambridge (Q-) and Los Angeles (UCLA-) laboratories gave comparable dates for several parts of the sequence, and suggested that the beginning of the Middle Formative began

as early as 1000 b.c., with an underlying Early Formative going back to 2000 b.c. (Hammond *et al.* 1976). These results were clearly of some interest, since no occupation of the second millennium b.c. had hitherto been confirmed in the Maya Lowlands. There was the wider circumstance that all other areas of Mesoamerica with complex societies – the Valley of Mexico, Oaxaca, the Gulf Coast, etc. – had proved to

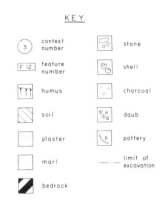

KEY

③	context number		stone
F 12	feature number		shell
	humus		charcoal
	soil		daub
	plaster		pottery
	marl		limit of excavation
	bedrock		

Fig. 2.6 Conventions used on Cuello sections and plans.

have early sedentary occupation. The lack of such occupation in the Maya Lowlands had resulted in hypotheses of immigration and cultural stimulus from these already advanced regions, thus relegating Maya culture to the status of a secondary rather than primary development in Mesoamerican prehistory.

A short season was carried out in 1976 to obtain confirmation (or otherwise) of the results from Op. 17B, the area of which was included within one of two 5 × 5 m squares (30/30 and 35/35 in the grid) that were excavated to bedrock (Fig. 2.7). Set catercornered to each other as the northeast and southwest quarters of a larger 10 by 10 m square, this strategy enabled continuous 10 m-long sections to be obtained on the cardinal axes. By sheer luck square 30/30 came down on the buildings on the west side of a buried courtyard, and 35/35 on those on its north side, so that the pattern of the deposits was clear: Op. 17B had sliced through the successive internal floors of the western building as well as those of Platform 34 above it.

The north side of the stair of Structure 35 was included within 30/30, and the first days of excavation showed that it overlay the final surviving floor of Platform 34, and that the fill of this held numerous caches of the Terminal Late Preclassic (a.d. 150–250). The assessment that Platform 34 was entirely of Preclassic construction was thus confirmed. It had been resurfaced many times during the Late Preclassic, but had initially been constructed in 400–300 b.c. over a very different set of structures. These consisted of low plaster-surfaced platforms set around a patio, those on the west and north sides being encountered in the excavation (see phase plans in Chapter 3). The patio itself had been filled with a meter of rubble, and this had been preceded by a ceremonious destruction of the buildings bordering it, including burning of their superstructures, ripping away façades, and deposition of valedictory offerings in the scars. The penultimate phase of the north building had been a masonry-walled superstructure, the earliest at Cuello. Pottery of the Mamom–Chicanel

transition dated these events (Hammond *et al.* 1979; Hammond 1990).

The slighted structures proved to be the last of a long sequence, with the courtyard layout having begun, so far as the radiocarbon samples from the 1975 season suggested, in the middle of the second millennium b.c. Several burials were found within the buildings. The pottery of the pre-Mamom occupation was placed in the newly defined Swasey ceramic complex (Pring 1977a). The radiocarbon ages obtained on a further 16 samples confirmed the early chronology suggested in 1975 (Hammond, Donaghey, *et al.* 1977), and indicated that the Swasey ceramics dated to between 2000 and 1000 b.c. (*c.* 2500–1300 B.C. in calendar years on the bristlecone pine calibration curve of Clark (1975) then in use). While the beginning suggested for Lopez Mamom was thus much earlier than hitherto thought, its end and the beginning of Cocos Chicanel at *c.* 400 b.c. were in line with radiocarbon and guesstimate dates from other Maya lowland sites, and suggested that the Cuello dates must be taken seriously.

The Cuello Project of 1978–80 was planned as a concentrated attack on the problem of apparent Early Formative occupation: while the chronology seemed fairly secure on the basis of 19 radiocarbon determinations in good stratigraphic order (Fig. 2.8, from Hammond *et al.* 1979: Fig. 1), with a further six assays yielding ages either far too early or far too late (from 3000 b.c. to a.d. 800) to be taken seriously, the samples of Swasey phase architecture, pottery, stone tools, and ecological/economic data were still very small. Several approaches were used to investigate the problem: (1) test excavations around Platform 34 to determine the extent and scale of early settlement, and to see whether any of it was accessible without the removal of thick later constructions; (2) continued exposure of the deep stratified deposits buried by Platform 34; (3) sampling by sieving and flotation of occupation deposits to recover information on the farming, gathering, and hunting practices of the inhabitants and the resulting diet; and (4) calibration, by intensive contextual analysis of sieved samples, of our own inefficiency in data recovery, together with an assessment of site formation processes (Hammond 1985).

All excavation was carried out by natural stratigraphic levels, using hand picks, trowels, and dental tools, with fill deposits recorded horizontally to their 5-m square, occupation layers to the 1-m square, and individual finds of importance to the nearest centimeter in three dimensions. Fifty-liter samples of deposit were taken from randomly selected contexts for contextual analysis, which by analyzing both the sediments and their contents performed the dual function of determining the origin of the context as a deposit (primary refuse, undisturbed secondary refuse, recycled refuse used as fill, freshly quarried fill, a mixture of any of these, etc.), and also, because of the very high rate of recovery from multiple-

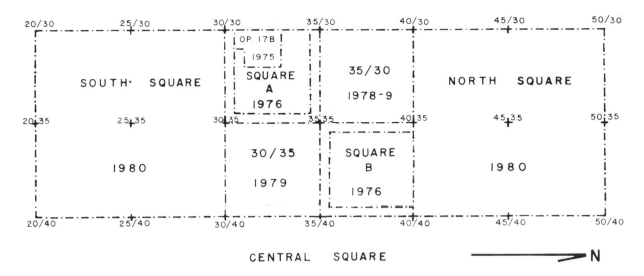

Fig. 2.7 Plan of the Main Trench, showing the Central Square excavated in four 5-m units in 1976–79, and the North and South Squares adjacent to it and dug in 1980 and 1987

sieving, of indicating what sorts of data were under- or over-represented in the areas excavated by more rapid means. The results were such that sieving of all excavated soil was considered unnecessary.

In 1978 the initial question was the extent of early deposits below Platform 34, to gauge whether the platform itself had to be extensively stripped, and whether early material extended beyond the limits of the platform into areas where it was more accessible to excavation. It soon became clear that no *in situ* earlier deposits lay around Platform 34, since the area had been quarried in Late Formative times for the construction of the massive platform, and modern plowing had disturbed any other deposits nearby. The only way in which Swasey and Mamom phase structures could be investigated was to remove the overlying Late Formative layers of Platform 34 first. Consequently, much of the 1978 and part of the 1979 season was spent in determining the limits of early occupation below the later levels. Extensive stripping of the surface of Platform 34 to determine its structure, reaching nearly 3,000 sq. m in 1979, revealed numerous offerings in the final floor. Most of these caches consisted of pairs of lip-to-lip bowls, sometimes containing a jade bead; the largest, Feature 6, comprised 94 vessels. It was found that the northern portion of Platform 34 was an extension of Terminal Late Formative date, itself built on to an earlier Late Formative expansion, and that the core of the earliest occupation lay in the vicinity of the 1975–76 excavations (Donaghey *et al.* 1979).

A third quarter of the 10 × 10 m area marked out in 1976, grid 35/30, was therefore begun in 1978 and completed in 1979, and the fourth quarter, 30/35, was dug completely in the 1979 season to give a total area of 100 sq. m exposed down to

the fossil soil or to bedrock below it (Fig. 2.7). At the same time, a deep exploratory trench in the northeast quadrant of Platform 34 showed that only at its southern end were there early constructions; these were left for future exploration. The final phase of the pyramid, Structure 35, was found to be of Classic date, but with a Terminal Late Preclassic building inside it, which was gradually exposed over three-quarters of its area, and penetrated by a deep trench to bedrock. This showed that early construction did not reach very far west of the main excavation, although the western side of a Middle Formative platform was exposed. A sequence of structures showed low, probably domestic, platforms replaced in the Late Formative by higher platforms and then by three successive pyramids (Hammond 1980a; Hammond and Gerhardt 1990). Although the Late Formative was not the focus of the Cuello Project, the site has become one of the best-documented occupations of that period in the Maya Lowlands, with over 100 burials and 20 excavated buildings in the Platform 34 excavations alone.

The 1980 excavations, two further 10 × 10 m areas north and south of that already completed, yielded further evidence of Late Preclassic ceremonialism (Hammond 1980b): while the North Square had a succession of subcircular buildings, apparently domestic and containing numerous burials, the South Square excavations revealed a plain stela set in front of the pyramid (Hammond 1982a), a large number of caches, and a mass burial of 15 persons, all within the successive floors of Platform 34. Below the earliest floor, and part of the initial construction of the platform, the infill of the Middle Formative courtyard included another mass burial. On the south side of the courtyard a succession of Mamom and Swasey phase buildings matched those found on the west and north sides in earlier seasons; thus, the entire western half of the patio was exposed, with the frontages of the buildings on three of its sides (Hammond 1985).

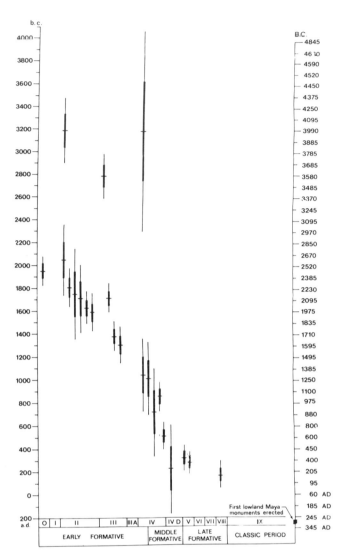

Fig. 2.8 Radiocarbon dates from the 1975 and 1976 excavations, in stratigraphic order by phase. Phases are numbered O–IX and correlated with ceramic complexes. The three very early dates and three very late ones (not shown) were not accepted as part of the chronology. Dates from the 1979, 1980, and 1987 seasons suggest a later beginning for the Cuello sequence (Chapter 3).

After the end of the 1978–80 Cuello Project excavations further radiocarbon assays were made, by the Cambridge (Q-) and La Jolla (LJ-) laboratories. While those for the Late Preclassic continued to match previous ages and expectations, samples from the Swasey levels yielded ages much later than had been obtained from corresponding contexts in 1975 and 1976 (Linick 1984). This supported the views of Coe (1980: 34–5) and Marcus (1983, 1984), that Swasey ceramics appeared to be Middle rather than Early Preclassic (as noted by Hammond (1975c: 138, 206) in accepting the 1975 radio-carbon dates).

There was sufficient of a problem over the dating of both Swasey and Bladen, even though work at the nearby site of

Colha suggested that the latter complex dated to the eighth century b.c. at least (Potter *et al.* 1984), that further excavations at Cuello were desirable. Also, the functions of the buildings around the Early and Middle Formative patio had not been firmly established: Hammond (1980b) had argued for a ceremonial function for some, and Gerhardt (1985, 1988) for a domestic one for all. Excavation of the rear areas of these buildings, where trash dumps might be expected if they were residential, seemed to offer a solution, and completion of the North Square, excavated in 1980 only to the base of the Late Formative deposits, a way to obtain it.

Thus, in 1987 work was resumed on the North Square, with the objectives of establishing the use of the buildings on the north side of the patio, of obtaining further radiocarbon dating samples, especially small ones suited to AMS (accelerator mass spectrometer) dating, a method which had not been available during the previous project, and of enlarging knowledge of the ecology and economy of the earlier periods of occupation at Cuello. In the course of two months' excavation it was found that the rear areas of all phases of the later Middle Formative buildings had been removed in the massive demolition accompanying the construction of Platform 34, and that the process of infill at that time had been extremely complex. The Bladen and Swasey phase deposits were not reached, and will be examined in 1992. The future strategy of excavation will be directed to solving primarily the problems of dating, and secondarily those of function.

DESCRIPTIVE AND ANALYTICAL UNITS
The archaeological deposits thus investigated were described primarily in terms of the *context*, defined as "the minimal unit of archaeological observation useful in the circumstances." A context could be a single layer of deposit, a line of stones or a single stone, the cut for a post hole or its fill: the criterion was that the context could not usefully be subdivided further, a corollary of which was that the context was internally coherent. This does not necessarily mean homogeneous: where numerous small loads of marl or rock fill were dumped to make up a layer, the individual loads could be distinguished in excavation, but there was no point in giving each a separate context number. "Negative contexts" such as the cut for a post hole or grave, or the demolition line where a building had been destroyed, were considered co-equal with accretionary contexts such as fills, floors, and occupation surfaces. In the site records, and in this book, context numbers are enclosed in parentheses, often preceded by the relevant grid designation for clarity, e.g. 35/30(428).

The other major category used was the *Feature*, defined as "a collocation of contexts forming an apparently coherent and meaningful analytical unit." A simple example would be the contexts designating the cut, human remains, grave goods, fill, and capping of a burial; another, the retaining walls, fills, internal floor, post holes, exterior facing, and superstructure remains of a building platform. Features are enclosed in brackets: [F235]. The vital distinction is that while the context is a unit of *observation* and is by definition irreducible, the Feature is a unit of *analysis*, and can be added to, subtracted from, or even dissolved entirely into its constituent contexts if the analysis that defined it turns out to be wrong. Thus post holes can be removed from a Feature to which they were allocated in error, and contexts in a newly excavated area can be added to a Feature already defined in an adjacent area already investigated. Most Features fell into the four categories of building platforms, burials, caches, and firepits (depressions lined with clay/stones/sherds and usually with evidence of burning and/or a fill with ash and charcoal). A few were pits of unknown function, and three [F87, 246, 292] were *chultunob*, bedrock chambers with access shafts dug by the Maya for storage of food or water.

The *Structure* was a term used to define individual free-standing mounds on the Cuello map, and within the excavation to define individual buildings. Such Structures might well comprise either a single Feature, e.g. [F250] = Structure 326, or might include several Features, where these were modifications of an essentially unchanged building, or where a number of firepits formed part of the building's inventory.

RECORDING SYSTEMS
The context number assigned as soon as a new context was recognized was listed in the site notebook, where the context was defined and described, and also entered on a file card on which further information about the context and its contents could be compiled. Labels with the context number accompanied all excavated material throughout processing and into storage, and the number (or, in earlier seasons, a catalog number correlated with the context file) inked on to all objects to be drawn or photographed.

Contexts were drawn on phase plans of the excavated area (single-context plans were not used except in site-book sketches), on plans of each Feature, and on sections. The only standing sections were those around the perimeter of the excavation, although the multi-year nature of the Main Trench excavations meant that sections along most grid lines were drawn. Most sections were drawn cumulatively, as and when needed (Biddle and Kjølbye-Biddle 1969) within the open excavation. Plans and sections used a set of graphic conventions derived from standard British usage and adapted by the Corozal Project to take account of the different kinds of deposit encountered on Maya sites. New conventions were needed for marl and other fills, while the existing plaster floor convention used by the Tikal Project was adopted, and soil tone was expressed by spacing of oblique hatching. All stones over 0.05 m diameter were shown accurately, smaller pebbles conventionally. Final inked plans and sections were drawn in the field laboratory.

Stratigraphic relationships were expressed using a development of the Harris Matrix (Harris 1975, 1977, 1979a, b), in which the vertical and lateral relationships of all contexts must be explicitly defined with a grid of pre-drawn boxes. The Harris–Horton–Hammond (HHH) Matrix used at Cuello removed the boxes from around context numbers, keeping them only for Features to indicate that a separate internal matrix ("mini-matrix") had been drawn (Fig. 2.9). This simplifies the graphic layout considerably, emphasizing the major stratigraphic relationships with no loss in accuracy. Plaster floors, often broad horizon markers and sealing surfaces, have their context number enclosed in an oval cartouche. Structures, often effectively complexes of Features, are defined with a Letraset/Zipatone underlay and heavy inked L-angles at the corners. The only structural change from the original Harris Matrix is the extraction of mini-matrices of Features, but the graphic innovations make the stratigraphic record easier to read direct from the matrix. Separate matrices were drawn for the 1976 excavation of 30/30 and 35/35, for 35/30 and 30/35 in 1978–79, and for the North and South Squares in 1980 and 1987. A master matrix, using only major building platforms, burial/cache Features, and patio/plaza floors to form a framework linking together the North, Central, and South Squares has been assembled and is used for the stratigraphic descriptions in this book (Fig. 3.1)

PROCESSING SYSTEMS
Excavated material was processed in one of three ways: the bulk of it was taken to the field laboratory, cleaned, counted, entered on the context card and the relevant catalog card, and passed to the appropriate specialist for further treatment. The process was rendered much easier by the location of the field laboratory and camp adjacent to the excavation, which also meant that errors in labeling could be corrected swiftly. Ceramics were examined each day, to provide feedback for the excavation supervisors on dating and nature of deposits, and selected for drawing and/or photography to illustrate the typological monograph (Pring 1977a; Kosakowsky 1987). The bulk of the sherds were then bagged by context and shipped for base laboratory analysis. Lithics were also sorted and, like the ceramics, pieces lacking significant information content were tabulated and discarded. Mollusk shells were tabulated by species and context, those of economic significance such as *Pomacea flagellata* sampled and measured, and packed for base laboratory analysis; animal bones were counted and packed, and human remains from burials tabulated and packed, since in both cases the analysis was done off-site. Complete pottery vessels from burials and caches, together with other grave goods and finds of importance, were drawn and photographed; much of this material was taken directly to the Belizean national collection in Belmopan, and not brought out of Belize for further study.

Excavated 50-liter samples for contextual analysis were subjected to multiple-sieving, sediment analysis, tabulation of

2

XIV

3
4
113

34 — 106 — 127

F159
1044 123

XIII
5
130
8
11
1083-4
1052
1075
1020 1022
F16

XII
9 = 1220
139

F151
1089
1271
381
1272
1217
1229

XI
F149
1258
1260
1259 3rd step
121 — 134 — 138
1046

F150
125
1979
111-2 — 114-20

XI
27
1428
1255
1257
1256 2nd step
1252
1253
1254 1st step
1242
1216
1241 = 1218 = 1219
144 — 142 — 129 — 135
1076
1280
1426
264 — 126
162
143
1065
141 — 132 — 137
1080
1232
1299
1226
1273
259
1417
261
1985
1536
1300

X
28
F270
1456
1476
1457
1478
155 — 152
153
154
1231
1458
F193
269 — 1295-8 — 1281-2 — 156-7 — 166-7 — 265
1088
168-9 — 146-7
1279 = 1409
1579 213
1577
1598

IXa
1507
1508
1805-6
1987-9 — 1405-8 — 1411-6
1403

IX
1509
1531
1506
1518
42
1529
266
1459
1432-7 — 1420-1 — 1293-4 — 158 — 163
1292
1569
1459 — 1460
1840
1872
1826

VIII
1533
66 1596
1801-4 1535
1466
1488-95 — 1469-70 — 174 — 176
1461
177
1467
F212

VIII
267 — 214
1583 = 1871
1879
54 F225
1873
1465
1496
1468
1827
1568 — 1477
191
1894-7
1574
1453
1597
1455
1593
1874
195-6
1889

VII
1849-52
1835
1600
F268
1831
1832
1833
1839
1836
1828
1829
1830
1834
1534
222
1519 1530
201
184-5 — 187 — 192
202 — 198 — 194
F242

VI
1925
1582
F235
1853-64
1578
1887
1886
1885
1912
1986
1876
1917
1592
1878
1909
1599
1877
1961
1980
1890
1973
1972

V
1898-9
1906-7 1892
236-8
246-9
F240
239
1883
1882
1940
1919
1884 — 1880
1891
F271
1817-22 — 1807-14
1538
1881 2nd step
1918
1922
1848 — 1847
1867-70
1537
1955
1921
1920 1st step
1823-4 — 1588-9 — 1539-54 — 209-11 — 1983-4
1497
1815-6 — 1913-6
1923
1924
1962-3
1575-6 1594-5
1893
1st step

V
F260
1941-60 — 1928-9
1888 * 1846
99 111
1968
1969
1967
1970

size range, and erosion of cultural material, etc., as described below. Afterwards the material was returned to the main processing sequence, although kept in separately identified bags, and passed to the relevant specialists.

Fifty-liter soil samples for flotation were collected in black plastic sacks, air-dried for several days to deflocculate the soil grains, and passed through a simple water-flotation tank fitted with a mesh-bottomed upper portion which could be lifted out. Charcoal and carbonized seeds were collected from the surface of the water, heavier materials including mollusca and small artifacts from the mesh bottom. Plant remains were passed to the archaeobotanist (working in the field laboratory) for preliminary identification and subsequent packing and shipment; carbon samples collected for possible dating were also examined, and removed for botanical identification instead if they appeared promising. The cultural materials from the float samples were passed into the main processing sequence, although bagged separately from normal excavated material from the same context.

Plaster samples from floors and architectural surfaces were collected initially from the exposed west section of 30/30, by Edwin R. Littmann in 1978 (Littmann 1979), and subsequently from each plaster area excavated; the samples were packed in foil and shipped to Littmann's base laboratory for mechanical and chemical analysis. Littmann's distinction between floor fill, the ballast of aggregate rubble over it, the mortar leveling, and the final plaster and wash coat was one followed in excavation procedure, although usually the last three layers were subsumed under one context number. His conclusion (Littmann 1979: 94–5) that three-element construction, with wash coats made from burnt lime, goes back as far as stratigraphic phase II, and that floor quality declined through the Middle and Late Preclassic, as he had already noted at Barton Ramie, enlarges our knowledge of the date and degree of sophistication of early Maya construction technology.

CONTEXTUAL ANALYSIS

Richard R. Wilk and Laura J. Kosakowsky

This part of the Cuello research, seeking to link archaeological deposits with the environmental and cultural processes that produced them, was based on the premise that what makes a deposit complex is the occurrence of repeated depositional

Fig. 2.9 An example of the Harris–Horton–Hammond Matrix used for recording stratigraphic relationships at Cuello. Derived from the Harris Matrix, this development distinguishes plaster surfaces (oval cartouches), features such as burials (rectangular boxes), and complex features such as buildings (toned underlay). The example spans the Late Preclassic layers (350 B.C.–A.D. 250) of the North Square, excavated in 1980.

acts such as recycling and mixing, and that unscrambling the palimpsest of events enables the origin and nature of deposits to be understood. Formation processes in Maya sites tend to complex, and the typology used to describe the resulting deposits crude, with broad terms such as "fill" or "secondary midden" lumping together very different phenomena. Interest has been concentrated on the artifactual component of any context, which is separated from its matrix at an early stage of the investigation and subjected to exhaustive analysis, while the matrix is usually discarded on-site. A distinction is made between "pure" deposits, containing material from a single period, and therefore useful for chronological and stylistic calibration, and "mixed" ones with material from several phases. Because of the extensive recycling of deposits in architectural construction at Maya sites such "mixed" contexts are predominant, and even "pure" ones are not necessarily representative of a single activity set and may well have been moved from their original locus of deposition. Such processes are not necessarily revealed by typological analysis of artifacts, and must be elucidated by examining other characteristics of the deposit.

The focus of the contextual analysis program at Cuello was the deposit as a whole rather than just its artifact content, although this and other characteristics were used as the data for inference and hypothesis-testing in seeking to dissect depositional history (Wilk and Schiffer 1979; Wilk and Kosakowsky 1979; Seymour 1980). The fieldwork was carried out by Wilk and Kosakowsky in 1978, Kosakowsky and Pamela Ford in 1979 and Kosakowsky and Deni Seymour in 1980. One axiom of the work was that mixed deposits were not a hindrance, but a valuable source of information: when they are "unmixed," refuse disposal patterns can be understood, the significance of radiocarbon dating and archaeobotanical samples appreciated, and locus of deposition tied more firmly to locus of use, allowing firmer definition of activities such as craft specialization. In addition, shifting the focus from the sequential construction of architecture, which embodies so much mixed deposit as fill, to the behavior resulting in the presence of such deposits in the form in which they were finally used, creates a new class of information complementing the fragmentary evidence of the buildings themselves.

The contextual analysis was designed to record detailed information on those aspects of both matrix and artifacts which were *a priori* considered likely to show traces of modes of deposition and subsequent disturbance. *Size* of artifacts, especially sherds, is a major indicator (used informally by excavators) of how much disturbance by trampling or redeposition has occurred. *Condition* and *preservation* of ceramics, lithics, faunal materials, and shell are good indicators of the nature of the post-depositional environment of the context. The total *faunal content* of deposits was taken as evidence of cultural and non-cultural formation processes, with mollusca proving an unexpectedly rich source of data. *Soil texture* (the

ratio of particle sizes comprising the matrix) was also considered a potential indicator of both deposit source and post-
depositional history. A set of computer-compatible coding
forms was used to record data.

PROCEDURES
A total of 163 samples, of minimum 50-liter size, and mostly of
80 liters, was collected and analyzed in 1978–80. They were
chosen to provide wide spatial coverage and good temporal
distribution within the site, and to obtain a wide variety of
deposit types, including control samples from modern contexts. Most samples were excavated by the analysts, who made
detailed observations on the dip, slope, and articulation of
artifacts (potentially useful in reconstructing dumping events)
their condition (eroded, broken, crumbling, etc.), the presence and degree of disturbance by rodents, snails, roots, and
the components and nature of the matrix. The horizontal
location within a 5-m or 1-m square, stratigraphic position,
and damage sustained during excavation (as from the use of
hand picks on a hard matrix) were noted.

In the field laboratory, each sample was divided into 8-liter
lots. Two 1-liter graduated cylinders of soil were removed and
weighed to obtain the average soil weight. The sample was
sieved through graduated screens of *c.* 50-mm, 25-mm and
12-mm mesh mounted in a stack, and half of each also through
a 6-mm screen, dividing artifact and ecofact material into size
categories which were tabulated by number and weight. The
first 8-liter bucket was processed for information on soil
texture: after 50-mm screening the artifact/ecofact content
was removed and saved, the large matrix (stones, etc.) discarded, and a cylinder of soil taken and weighed before being
passed through a 1.5-mm mesh. A sample from this was taken
for texture analysis by the hydrometer method and a Munsell
color reading. The four size-classes of cultural material were
divided into ceramic, lithic, bone, shell, and "other" categories. The results of the processing were entered on the coding
forms, including a master sheet providing a summary of each
sample.

The soil texture form recorded Munsell color, presence of
organic material, mineral composition, and measured texture,
which together allowed determination of the original locus of
the matrix; we concluded that pH would have been a useful
data item also.

The bone form recorded size categories divided into
human, small rodent, and "other" (mainly food remains)
classes. Worked and burnt bone was noted, and the relationship of whole to fragmentary specimens: large pieces of intact
bones were felt to indicate a lack of disturbance of deposits,
although as work progressed it became clear that soil pH,
water infiltration, and age were significant factors in
preservation.

Mollusca were sorted into (1) the edible freshwater snail
Pomacea flagellata, (2) the environmental indicators *Neocyclotus dysoni cookei* and *Euglandina* Sp., (3) other non-economic
species such as *Orthalicus*, *Bulimulus*, and *Helicina*, and
(4) marine shell. Complete and fragmentary shells were
distinguished, and frequencies for each species in each screen-
size category recorded on the shell form.

Lithics, essentially chert and chalcedony with occasional
obsidian fragments, were counted and weighed by size category, then total amounts of fire-cracked and retouched lithics
were recorded. Physical traces of micro-flaking, etc. can
provide clues to post-depositional disturbance, as may the
completeness of debitage assemblages from particular reduction events (e.g. Keeley 1982). Lithic debris was therefore
sorted into types, and the number of whole, broken, and
depleted tools and utilized flakes recorded, as well as the
presence of conjoinable pieces. The size categories of chipping
debris proved useful in differentiating tool retouch and
finishing (which leave small debitage) from tool and preform
manufacture (leaving small and larger flakes) and core preparation (leaving large and cortical flakes).

On the ceramics form, within each size category sherds
were counted by ceramic complex (Swasey, Lopez, etc.: the
Bladen complex had not been split from Swasey at this point).
Each size/period assemblage was classified into unslipped and
slipped (and polychrome for the few Classic samples), and the
conditions of sherds, including edge erosion and rounding,
were noted. All sherds were sorted into vessel form categories
where possible: this may document differential breakage
patterns, the source of refuse, and activities leading to deposition (trash, cache, etc.). We also noted the number of
articulating sherds in a context: a high frequency may be due
to low levels of post-depositional disturbance, with trash at or
near its original locus of use having fragments from the same
vessel, which are likely to become separated if the deposit is
recycled.

RESULTS AND INTERPRETATIONS
When the contextual analysis program began in 1978 the
direct effects of trampling, water percolation, and crushing by
overlying deposits, *inter alia*, on the condition and distribution of artifacts had not been studied, and even now are poorly
understood. These form part of the bridging hypotheses
which Schiffer (1976) terms "c-transforms" and "n-trans-
forms," linking specific environmental or cultural events to
their archaeological residues. An initial typology of deposits
(topsoil, erosion and collapse, subfloor and platform fill, pit
fill, trash, and midden) was refined, with the recognition that
even apparently primary midden could be either *in loco*,
abandoned where it was used, deposited as the result of
normal housekeeping, redeposited, or recycled into construction fill (Fig. 2.10).

Several kinds of deposit fell into the initial category of

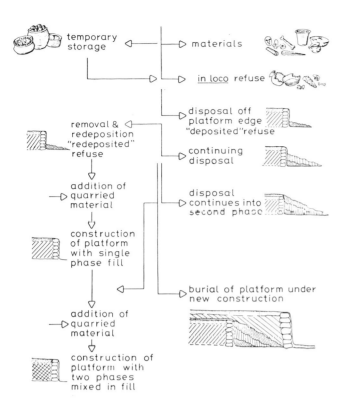

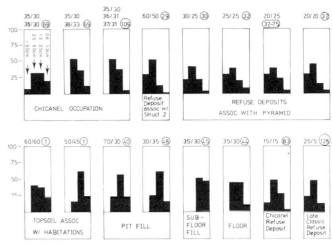

Fig. 2.11 Deposit types at Cuello: sherd weight in each size category as a percentage of the total for 16 selected sample deposits.

Fig 2.10 Some processes in the formation of archaeological deposits at Cuello suggested by the Contextual Analysis Program.

"subfloor fill": while each functioned to level up the surface on which a plaster floor would be laid, the processes that contributed to their character varied. One sample, with much limestone architectural debris, a little soil, and no artifacts, was probably from a demolished structure; another, abutting the base of a platform wall, was rich in complete *Pomacea* shells, charcoal, and sherds from a single ceramic phase, and seemed to be trash dumped off the edge of the platform – "deposited refuse". Such distinctions illustrate the value of contextual analysis, and show how it can be used to make inferences about intra-site variability.

Pottery proved to be a sensitive indicator of the history of a deposit, although it was necessary to determine the rôles of production technology, use wear, and ground pressure on the condition of sherds before the effects of depositional history could be assessed. Certain types of use, such as circular mixing motions responsible for slip erosion at the basal angle of bowls, and the long rim-to-base sherds produced when an upright burial or cache vessel is subjected to vertical ground pressure, are good examples of such deranging factors. Relative age was not an important factor in determining sherd size or surface damage: some of the earliest pottery was among the best-preserved. Technical features such as thickness did, on the other hand, influence breakage patterns much as expected,

with rims and bases yielding larger sherds and the body of the vessel smaller ones (Seymour 1980). Sherd size was shown to reflect differences in the amount of crushing and movement when examined in contexts that were deposited in different ways, while surface damage such as that caused by rootlets enabled a period of exposure before redeposition in fill to be detected. Edge rounding seems to result only from extremely erosive conditions, and is thus a useful index of a high-energy environment. Patterns of variation in sherd size between deposits indicate distinct histories of accumulation: in the 16 examples given in Fig. 2.11, a plot of the weight of sherds in each size category as a percentage of the total, several have very similar size distributions. The four refuse deposits around the base of Structure 35 are similar in spite of spatial separation by up to 10 m; they were dumped in the Middle Postclassic and seem to consist of a recycled midden that had accumulated throughout the Classic period, quarried and placed in several locations around the base of the pyramid. Other deposits with a similar size distribution such as contexts (83) and (128) appeared to be recycled refuse on stratigraphic grounds, and this profile may be definitive of this class of deposit. In contrast, topsoil and the fills of two pits (40) and (48) have a pattern which suggests the latter as root holes. Total sherd densities ranged from 410 gm/m³ to 56,062 gm/m³: absolute values are shown on Fig. 2.12, and again the topsoil and recycled refuse categories are internally consistent. There is a clear distinction between unmixed refuse such as contexts (29) and (28) and those which have been mixed later with non-cultural material.

Mollusca proved to have a very uneven distribution within the sampled contexts: all deposits directly below topsoil had a high frequency of *Neocyclotus*, which local observation showed to live in both cleared bush and *huamil* regrowth, and

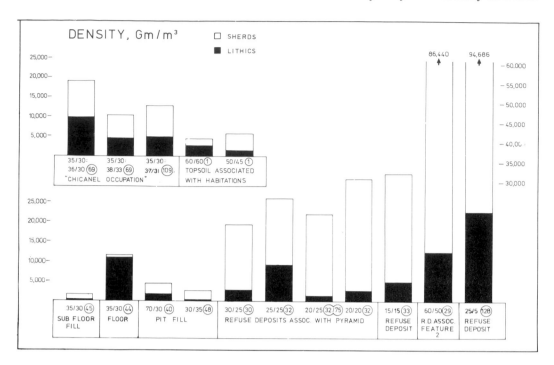

Fig. 2.12 Sherd and lithic densities for select sampled deposits.

to be abundant as shells in burnt *milpa* fields. The species seems thus to be present in archaeological deposits when they have formed part of a surface susceptible to growth of vegetation at some time in their history. Such an environment could be found in a community in unpaved areas, overgrown trash heaps, and abandoned buildings, as well as in the surrounding agricultural area. On the basis of their *Neocyclotus* content, two pits were identified as topsoil-filled root holes rather than cultural features, with important implications for the interpretation of the carbonized plant remains found in them.

The edible snail *Pomacea flagellata*, present in large numbers especially in Cocos Chicanel deposits, was another sensitive indicator. The shell is fragile even when fresh, and becomes more so with age, so that any deposit with a large proportion of unbroken *Pomacea* has probably not been subject to trampling or other post-depositional disturbance. Several contexts were identified as *in loco* or deposited refuse

on this basis, one corroborated by the high proportion of large sherds and the number of those that articulated.

The contextual analysis methods summarized here are easily applied and low in cost. They offer a chance of recovering data from situations often regarded as unprofitable, and of gauging the value of data from contexts which appear to be either undisturbed *in loco* trash, or on the other hand mixed fill of unknown heterogeneity. Artifacts may be as informative taphonomically as they are typologically, and the matrix in which they repose as good a guide to depositional and cultural process as the artifacts themselves. They have the additional value of calibrating the inefficiency of excavation: comparison of the typological and size-range content of a processed sample, intensively sieved and scrutinized, with that of a sample excavated by normal archaeological methods and not subjected to screening, will show how far and in what ways the excavators are failing to recover cultural material. At Cuello the feedback from the contextual analysis, which was carried out only a short distance from the Main Trench, was used to maintain standards of recovery and point up categories of material that were being undernoticed.

Chapter 3

STRATIGRAPHY AND CHRONOLOGY IN THE RECONSTRUCTION OF PRECLASSIC DEVELOPMENTS AT CUELLO

Norman Hammond, Juliette Cartwright
Gerhardt, and Sara Donaghey

The stratigraphy of Cuello is here reconstructed *ex post facto*, from the perspective of the complete excavation, rather than with the incomplete and changing knowledge which accompanies the actual investigation, as described in Chapter 2. This account proceeds from the earliest occupation to the eventual abandonment of the site, describing the cumulative record of deposits; the sequence is divided into stratigraphic phases 0–XIV, which reflect this record and mark salient changes in it (Fig. 3.1). The phases in this relative chronology are independent of any absolute chronology: the stratigraphy is the immutable succession which is calibrated by external forms of dating such as radiocarbon or ceramic sequence, discussions of which follow later in this chapter; raw radiocarbon dates are cited in association with their contexts, but calibrated dates must be taken as more reliable. No hieroglyphic dates in the Maya calendar are available from Cuello: during the Classic period when most such dates were inscribed, the site was of minor status, and the bulk of its period of occupation dates from before the introduction of writing into the Maya Lowlands.

Each phase description is followed by a summary of the ceramic evidence; radiocarbon dates are listed by phase and calibrated on the CALIB program of Stuiver and Reimer (1986) in Table 3.1, with acceptability as assessed at the time: this topic is discussed further in the present chapter. The phases are those on the final 1978–80 master matrix, which differs slightly from the matrices for the individual squares compiled each season. Each phase is illustrated by a plan which brings together data for the entire Main Trench area (North, Central, and South Squares) in summary form: all major features are shown, but minor stratigraphic distinctions in fills have been omitted (the phase plans by square in the final monographs will include all contexts). Each plan shows one "building stage" for the structures on it: a structure may have several successive stages, as modifications such as renewal of floors or the addition of steps occur, and these are noted in the text of this book by lower-case letters attached to

KEY

Floor ⬭ = Equivalent

Feature ▭ 76/ 1976 season

CONSTRUCTION PHASES

PLATFORM FLOORS

STRUCTURES

PYRAMID SEQUENCE

West side of Platform 34   North side of Platform 34   Center of Platform 34

XIV

XIII

XIIB

XIIA

XII

XI

X

IXA

IX

VIII

VII

VI

Structure 35

Structure 350

Structure 301

Structure 300

Structure 303

Structure 302

Structure 305

Structure 304

Structure 307

Structure 308

Structure 306

Structure 309

Structure 310

South side of Platform 34

Structure 313

Structure 312

Structure 311

Structure 351 ?

Structure 351 ?

Structure 351 ?

Structure 352 ?

Structure 352 ?

Structure 352 ?

Structure 352 ?

Structure 352 ?

Structure 353 ?

Structure 354 ?

2
3
4

115
124 — 6
1104
76/8
5
130
8 — 76/9-11
122 — 76/15
11

1130
1137 — 76/14
9 — 1220 — 1139 — 76/12
269 — 76/16
139

128
284 — 1146-7
27 — 1140 — 76/19
1428 — 280 — 76/20
131 — 133 — 136
27
1163 - 72
28 — 1152 — 76/21
355 — 31

1805-6
1507 — 31
1508 — 33
76/38
1173 — 1509
362 — 1174 — 153I — 76/24 — 45
1535 — 1801-4 — 61-4
43
44 — 1533
66 — 1596 — 1358

17
5-5 — 76/29
369 — 76/30 — 76/33 — 1879
22 — 76/31-2
214 — 267 — 1175
76/33 — 1583

1183-4 — 140 — 208
1179
1191
145 — 181
1193
1301
1941-60 — 1928-9
1316 — 1888

16
159
16
151
151
151
4
4
4
150
149
193
270
193
270
193
270
212
225
242
235
242
27
160

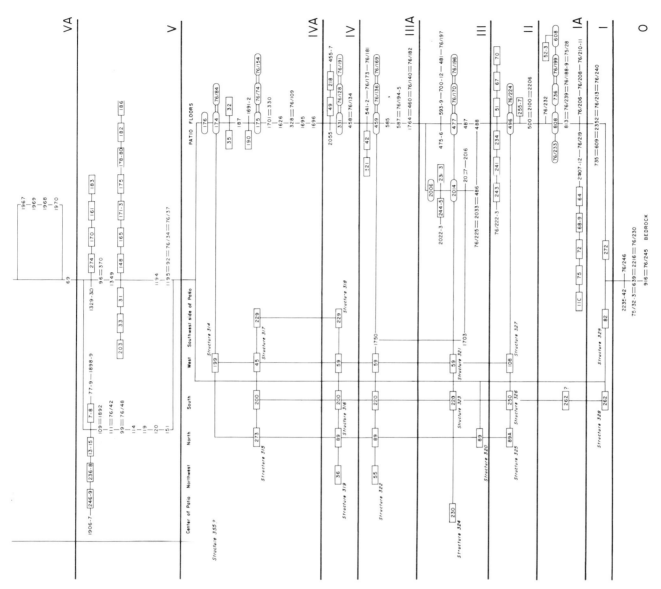

Fig. 3.1 Stratigraphic matrix for the Main Trench at Cuelo.

Table 3.1 *Radiocarbon and obsidian hydration dates from Cuello, organized by phase*

Context	age b.p.	age b.c.	Cal. date B.C. @ 1 sd	lab. no.	value [1]
Phase 0					
76/230	3900 ± 65	1950 ± 65	2478–2305	Q-1571	2
buried land surface with material trodden in					
Phase IA					
1975–76 dates					
75/28	4000 ± 155	2050 ± 155	2868–2330	UCLA-1985e	2
midden adjacent to construction = 76/239					
76/189	3700 ± 200	1750 ± 200	2460–1787	UCLA-2012d	2
midden adjacent to construction					
76/189	3580 ± 70	1630 ± 70	2034–1829	Q-1573	2
midden adjacent to construction					
76/210	5140 ± 145	3190 ± 145	4217–3780	UCLA-2102c	1
firepit contents **unacceptable**					
76/211	3550 ± 85	1600 ± 85	2031–1767	Q-1577	1
firepit contents					
76/219	3660 ± 150	1710 ± 150	2290–1829	Q-1576	1
firepit contents					
76/239	3760 ± 85	1810 ± 85	2329–2040	Q-1572	1
midden adjacent to construction = 75/28					
post–1976 dates					
30/35(616)	2720 ± 50	770 ± 50	916–823	Q-1917	1
[F52] firepit contents					
35/30(813)	2650 ± 130	770 ± 130	920–770	AA-458	1
corn kernels from ?occupation level					
35/30(718)	2420 ± 60	470 ± 60	760–402	LJ-4917	1
[F64] firepit contents					
probably associated:					
35/35(1102)	2460 ± 80	510 ± 80	787–405	OxA-361	1
[F110] collagen date on burial **unacceptable**					
35/35(1102)	3000 ± 60	1050 ± 60	1383–1137	OxA-1649	1
[F110] gelatin date on burial collagen purified					
35/35(1102)	2840 ± 100	890 ± 100	1160–900	OxA-2103	1
[F110] amino-acid date on split ion-exchanged amino-acids					
Phase II					
1975–76 dates					
76/176	3670 ± 65	1720 ± 65	2176–1967	Q-1574	1
post burned *in situ*					
post–76 dates					
30/35(601)	2895 ± 200	945 ± 200	1400–840	Q-1916	1
[F51] firepit contents					
20/30(2219)	2325 ± 60	375 ± 60	406–380	Q-1926	3
[F250] subfloor deposit					
20/35(2218)	2380 ± 60	430 ± 60	524–395	Q-1925	4
[F250] architectural fill					
20/30(2163)	2400 ± 60	450 ± 60	755–398	Q-1924	4
[F250] architectural fill					
20/35(2099)	2480 ± 60	530 ± 60	787–422	Q-1923	4
[F250] architectural fill					
25/30(2096)	2290 ± 60	340 ± 60	400–264	Q-1927	1
[F255] firepit contents					
25/30(2186)	2400 ± 60	450 ± 60	755–398	Q-1928	1
[F256] firepit contents					
Phase III					
1975–76 dates					
76/155	4740 ± 100	2790 ± 100	3640–3370	UCLA-2102b	4
[F59] architectural fill **unacceptable**					

Context	age b.p.	age b.c.	Cal. date B.C. @ 1 sd	lab. no.	value[1]
76/197 firepit contents	3340 ± 65	1390 ± 65	1735–1527	Q-1578	1
76/175 [F59] subfloor deposit	3260 ± 80	1310 ± 80	1670–1444	Q-1579	3
1975–76 dates					
35/30(713) subfloor deposit	2520 ± 70	570 ± 70	799–529	LJ-4922	3
35/30(488) subfloor deposit	2510 ± 60	560 ± 60	795–529	LJ-4923	3
35/30(592) occupation layer	2490 ± 70	540 ± 70	793–422	LJ-4919	2
20/30(2007) subfloor deposit	2300 ± 70	350 ± 70	402–370	Q-1922	3
25/30(2019) [obsidian] in firepit contents	$\sim 980 \pm 30$	1209–1047		165-2019	4
Phase IIIA					
30/35(460) subfloor deposit	2750 ± 110	800 ± 110	1020–810	Q-1918	3
35/30(460) subfloor deposit	2455 ± 45	505 ± 45	765–410	Q-1911	3
35/30(543) [F44] firepit contents	2540 ± 45	590 ± 45	798–603	Q-1914	1
20/35(1764) subfloor deposit	2595 ± 60	645 ± 60	816–781	Q-1920	3
35/35(130) [F89] subfloor deposit	2470 ± 70	520 ± 70	787–408	LJ-4918	3
20/30(2065) [F251] amino-acids from collagen of burial	2390 ± 70	440 ± 70	755–395	OxA-2016	1
35/35(232) amino-acids from collagen of burial	2560 ± 70	610 ± 70	807–599	OxA-2017	1
Phase IV					
1975–76 dates					
75/17 [F321/317] subfloor deposit = 75/17	3000 ± 160	1050 ± 160	1430–1000	UCLA-1985a	3
76/110 [F321/317] subfloor deposit **unacceptable**	5140 ± 445	3190 ± 445	4458–3383	UCLA-2102g	3
post-1976 dates					
76/137 [F89] collagen from burial	2390 ± 90	440 ± 90	760–392	OxA-362	1
35/30(528) [F36] subfloor deposit	2560 ± 40	610 ± 40	801–769	Q-1913	3
35/30(540) occupation buildup below midden	2470 ± 50	520 ± 50	770–422	Q-1912	2
35/30(458) subfloor deposit	2250 ± 45	300 ± 45	392–243	Q-1910	3
25/30(1734) subfloor deposit	2550 ± 60	600 ± 60	803–570	Q-1919	3
Phase IVA					
1975–76 dates					
75/12 subfloor deposit	2680 ± 190	730 ± 190	1040–600	Q-1559	3
75/14 fill of grave	2970 ± 160	1020 ± 160	1420–943	Q-1476	4
75/20 + 22 construction fill **unacceptable**	1140 ± 100	a.d. 810 ± 100	A.D. 780–1000	UCLA-1985bc	4
75/23 construction fill **unacceptable**	1700 ± 60	a.d. 250 ± 60	A.D. 249–412	UCLA-1985d	4

Table 3.1 (*cont.*)

Context	age b.p.	age b.c.	Cal. date B.C. @ 1 sd	lab. no.	value [1]
76/76 subfloor deposit	2470 ± 60	520 ± 60	779–410	UCLA-2102a	3
76/141 construction fill	2190 ± 195	240 ± 195	410–1	UCLA-2102h	4
post–1976 dates					
35/30(333) fill of grave	2420 ± 70	470 ± 70	762–400	LJ-4920	4
35/30(155) subfloor deposit	2195 ± 50	245 ± 50	373–190	Q-1906	3
35/30(187) midden buildup	2345 ± 45	395 ± 45	407–392	Q-1908	2
35/30(187) midden buildup	2315 ± 50	365 ± 50	403–380	Q-1907	2
35/30(161) occupation material recycled as fill?	2195 ± 60	245 ± 60	377–181	Q-1905	4
35/30(152) construction fill	2815 ± 180	865 ± 180	1260–810	Q-1903	4
35/30(146) construction fill	2440 ± 70	490 ± 70	767–403	Q-1902	4
35/30(308) occupation buildup	2420 ± 45	470 ± 45	756–404	Q-1909	2
Q4070 construction fill	2255 ± 55	305 ± 55	405–225	Q-3198	4
76/86 from construction fill	[obsidian]	~880 ± 70	1067–895	JKW-302	4
35/30(114) amino-acid from animal-bone collagen	2700 ± 90	750 ± 90	927–803	OxA-1811	1
35/30(146) amino-acid from animal-bone collagen	2470 ± 80	520 ± 80	791–406	OxA-1810	1
Phase V					
1975–76 dates					
76/34 construction fill	2280 ± 60	330 ± 60	399–258	UCLA-2102f	4
post–1976 dates					
35/30(99 + 111) construction fill	2375 ± 150	425 ± 150	770–261	Q-1901	4
35/30(69) construction fill	2140 ± 150	190 ± 150	390–A.D. 10	Q-1904	4
Q4063 construction fill	2275 ± 50	325 ± 50	405–275	Q-3197	4
Q4059 construction fill	2230 ± 55	280 ± 55	400–200	Q-3210	4
Q4104 construction fill	2235 ± 50	285 ± 50	400–210	Q-3209	4
Q4002 construction fill	2265 ± 36	315 ± 36	405–208	Q-3208	4
35/30 [F7] collagen from burial	2460 ± 70	510 ± 60	778–406	OxA-1653	1
35/30 [F7] gelatin from purified collagen	2520 ± 70	570 ± 70	799–529	OxA-1654	1
35/30 [F7] ion-exchange gelatin from purified collagen	2530 ± 80	580 ± 80	803–529	OxA-1655	1

Context	age b.p.	age b.c.	Cal. date B.C. @ 1 sd	lab. no.	value[1]
Phase VA					
post–76 dates					
Q4073	2280 ± 55	330 ± 55	410–275	Q-3199	4
construction fill					
Q4119	2260 ± 45	310 ± 45	405–270	Q-3200	2
occupation buildup					
Q4092	2250 ± 50	300 ± 50	405–205	Q-3211	2
midden					
45/50(454)	2305 ± 45	355 ± 45	400–378	Q-1915	2
occupation buildup					
25/20(766)	2180 ± 70	230 ± 70	375–123	LJ-4916	4
post hole fill					
Phase VIII					
post–1976 dates					
35/30(47)	2040 ± 40	90 ± 40	106–1	Q-1900	1
[F17] firepit fill					
Phase X					
76/23	[obsidian]	~740 ± 70	952–760	JKW-304	3
subfloor deposit					
Phase XI					
1975–76 dates					
75/6	2125 ± 65	175 ± 65	349–96	Q-1558	3
subfloor deposit					
Not phased					
Dates from outside the main trench					
Ceramic complex: Late Chicanel					
[*VIII* +]					
10/50(1128)	2050 ± 60	100 ± 60	160–A.D. 9	Q-1929	4
fill of *chultun* [F87]					
10/50(1627)	2155 ± 60	205 ± 60	360–112	Q-1930	4
fill of *chultun* [F87]					
Ceramic complex terminal Chicanel					
17C(12)	930 ± 85	a.d. 1020 ± 85	A.D. 1013–1214	UCLA-1985f	4
construction fill **unacceptable**					
Ceramic complex: Bladen Xe					
17C(37)	3180 ± 195	1230 ± 195	1680–1228	UCLA-1985g	4
buried land surface with trampled occupation material					

Note:

[1] explanation of context types: numbers 1–4 classify value for dating.

1 firepit contents burnt material from inside depression within stone/clay/sherd lining and evidence of burning of surrounding soil. Usually a much higher charcoal content than midden, occupation buildup, or fill. Ash not present; animal remains quite common. No reason to doubt contemporaneity of contents and feature.

1 post burnt *in situ* 1 example, specifically noted as such in field book.

1 collagen from burial 10 examples: direct AMS measurement on bone, AMS measurement on corn kernel 1 example.

2 occupation buildup soil with flat-bedded sherds, often trampled, over floor but not as fill; high charcoal content, often high animal bones.

2 midden differs from buildup in having larger and fresher sherds, complete *Pomacea* shells, but still high charcoal and bone content.

3 subfloor deposit differentiated from "fill" because its presence in thin layers over one floor and below another could be due to buildup and covering, rather than deposition as floor padding; the latter explanation has become more likely than the former in the light of actual ^{14}C ages obtained, however.

4 construction/architectural/grave/post hole fill deposits which may have originated as midden or anything else, but which are now in use as part of construction. Any dates from these must be *termini post quem*.

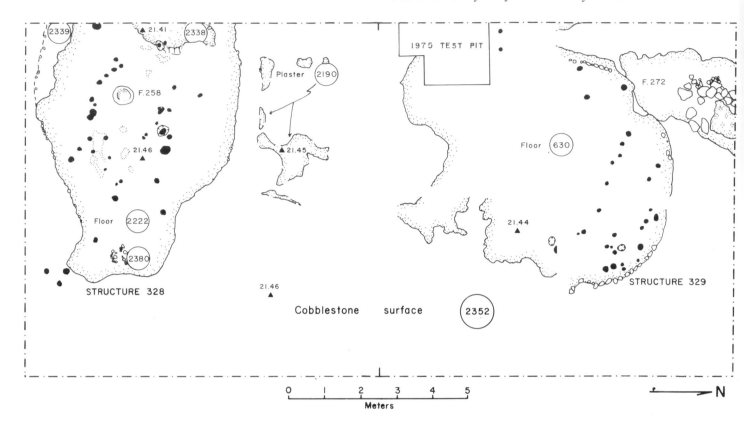

Fig. 3.2 Plan of phase I constructions in the Central and South
Squares.

the structure number, e.g. Structure 315e. The architecture
itself is illustrated in Chapter 5.

Phase 0 The earliest evidence of occupation at Cuello occurred
almost 4 m below the surface of Platform 34 on and in the old
land surface (639), where five post holes were recorded, up to
0.25 m in diameter and depth, not associated with any
subsequent plaster-surfaced platform construction. Pottery,
chert flakes, and charcoal were also found in the soil, trodden
in or mixed down by soil churning.

The pottery was not distinguishable from that in use in the
succeeding phase I, of the Swasey ceramic complex. One
radiocarbon determination on charcoal fragments collected
from the soil was obtained.

Phase I (Fig. 3.2) Over the ancient soil a rough cobbled surface
(2352) was laid, with traces of marl or plaster surfacing.
Several post holes cut it, and the remains of what appeared to
be a demolished structure [F272], large stones, and marl on an
eroded plaster floor ran beyond the northern limit of
excavation.

Two structures (328 and 329) lay in large part within the
excavated area, both consisting of a plaster floor over a ballast

of clay and angular limestone rubble. Structure 329 was
excavated in four quadrants, two in 1976 and the others in
1979, and was in poor condition except at its northern end.
While it was at least 8 m long and 6.5 m wide, the south end
and most of the east side had eroded away, and a section of the
west side had been removed by the 1975 test pit. The north
end was apsidal in plan, with the edge bolstered by small
stones over which the plaster floor (630) beveled down to meet
the exterior surface. The structure was only 0.1 m high. A
number of post and stake holes around the north end suggested a timber superstructure renewed on at least one
occasion, with a line of posts across the chord of the apse,
suggesting either an internal division or a different plan at
some point.

Structure 328 had eroded margins, with no beveled edge
surviving, and was roughly oval in plan, with an eastern
extension, and raised less than 0.1 m above the exterior
surface. Numerous post and stake holes in its interior,
penetrating floor (2222), neither followed the edges of the
platform nor formed any coherent plan, although they
enclosed a clear space in which a baked clay depression [F258]
of 0.56 m diameter and only 0.05 m depth, interpreted as a
hearth, was found. The main floor area was *c.* 5.5 m wide and
at least that long, disappearing into the west section (with an
estimated overall length of 9.6 m).

The two structures seem to have been very low platforms,

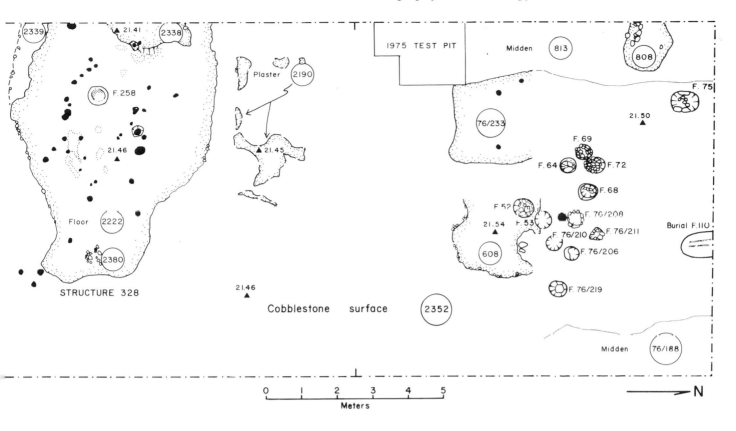

Fig. 3.3 Phase IA constructions overlying Structure 329.

Phase IA (Fig. 3.3) Structure 329 was buried by a thin cobbled layer which seems to have been an expansion of the existing yard surface (2352). This was in turn cut by ten firepits or hearths, clustered over the north end of Structure 329, and overlain by three patches of plaster of ill-defined outline, one cut by three post holes and another by two more firepits of slightly later date. Structure 328 seems to have continued in use at this point, although none of its features can be specifically attributed to phase IA.

The firepits, depressions lined with pottery, clay, or stones, or any combination of these (Fig. 5.3), are the earliest such features known at Cuello [F52, 53, 64, 68, 69, 72, 75, 76/206, 208, 210, 211, 219, 221]. All except [F75] lay within an area 4.5 by 2.8 m in diameter, which does not seem to have been within a building. Their diameters averaged 0.45 m and depths 0.17 m, and all showed evidence of burning, in the hardening of the surrounding area. In some the fill contained charcoal, and five yielded radiocarbon dates, of which two, at *c.* 1600 and 1700 b.c., were held to be acceptable at the time; a third, while

much later, appears to be acceptable with hindsight and a fourth, later still, cannot be discounted (see below). To the west of the floors was a dark brown soil filled with cultural material (76/239), and to the east a similar soil (76/188–189); both yielded radiocarbon ages in the mid-second millennium b.c. (1810 ± 85 b.c., 1750 ± 200 b.c., 1630 ± 70 b.c.); (75/28), which also yielded an early date of 2050 ± 155 b.c., is the same deposit as (76/239).

Of two burials initially associated with this phase, burials 7–8 (76/232) and burial 62 [F110], the former is now placed in phase IIIA, as the pottery style and calibrated radiocarbon date of 793 B.C. suggest. The latter was in a deep bedrock cleft and not recovered in 1976, so that although it appears from the records to be sealed by the edge of 76/199 this is not provable, and a date as late as phase IIIA is also possible. An AMS radiocarbon date of 510 ± 80 b.c. (OxA-361) was obtained, which for technical reasons connected with its low collagen content is probably too recent. The bones had also been heavily coated with PVA preservative: subsequent research has shown this to be a deranging factor in dates based on crude collagen (Law *et al.* n.d.). As a result, a further sample from [F110] was analyzed, splitting part of the collagen into gelatin and then into ion-separated gelatin fractions. While a date on the crude collagen, with its known PVA contamination, yielded an age of 3670 ± 70 b.p. (OxA-1648), the gelatin fraction gave an age of 2920 ± 80 b.p. (OxA-1649), 970 ± 80

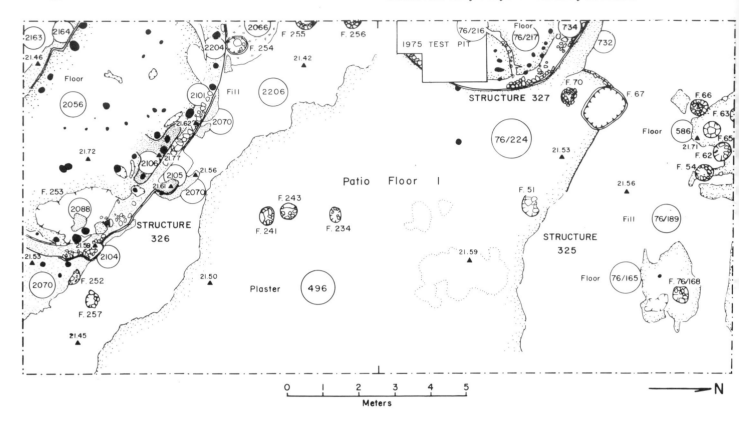

Fig. 3.4 Phase II constructions and Patio Floor I.

b.c. calibrating to 1264–1003 B.C., which is in line with other Swasey phase dates obtained from 1979–80 samples and suggests that the present phase assignment is correct. The amino-acid fraction yielded a similar age of 2840 ± 100 (OxA-2103), 890 ± 100 b.c. calibrating to 1160–900 B.C., suggesting that gelatin separation alone is sufficient to remove even heavy PVA contamination.

The northern part of the excavated area seems to have been used for domestic activities in an outdoor space, with none of the three small plaster areas showing evidence of a coherent structure, while Structure 328 remained in use. The pottery associated with this phase was solely of the Swasey ceramic complex.

Phase II (Fig. 3.4) Soil and rubble ballast (2206) was laid down over the cobbled area and surfaced with Patio Floor I at about 21.6 m elevation, well preserved in its center but eroded at the edges except where it abutted Structure 327, fairly level and with some patches of burning. The northern margin was formed by the edge of the razed Structure 325 [F89A], one of three buildings that stood around this first patio phase (the others being Structure 327 [F108] on the west and Structure 326 [F250] on the south: the east side of the patio area in all phases lay beyond the 40 m E baulk line and remains for future

investigation). From phase II through phase IVA the layout of three or more structures around a courtyard remained constant, with most of the structures undergoing several stages of repair and renewal within each phase.

The fragmentary Structure 325 had four detectable stages of successive internal flooring (736, 76/193, 76/172, 76/165 and 586), all but the second cut by post holes, and the last cut also by five firepits [F168, 54, 62, 63, 66], like those of the previous phase about 0.45 m diameter, 0.2 m deep, and with a stone/clay/sherd lining. Two more firepits [F51, 70] and a clay-lined trough 1 by 0.8 m [F67] cut the patio floor close to its northern margin, three more firepits [F234, 241, 243] the center of the floor, and at least five more the areas in front of Structure 326 and between it and Structure 327 [F252, 254–7]. Of these, [F255–6] were cut by the west section, but clearly sealed by (2059) and [F59] of phase III. [F51, 255, and 256] all yielded charcoal from which radiocarbon ages of 945, 340, and 450 b.c. were obtained (see below). Floor (76/172) of Structure 325 had a number of post holes, of which (76/176) had the apparent remains of a post burnt *in situ*: this yielded a radiocarbon age of 1720 b.c.

Structure 327, of which the western portion lay within the excavated area (but had been partly removed by the 1975 test pit), was estimated to be 5.9 by 5.3 m in area, and increased from 0.2 to 0.3 m in height with reflooring; two building stages each had a perishable superstructure. The later included an

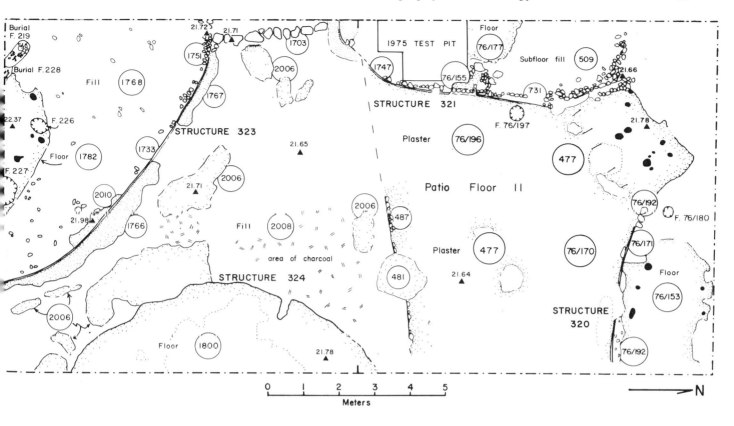

Fig. 3.5 Phase III constructions and Patio Floor II.

unusual reversed-apse plan marked by a plaster turnup, and some refacing of the exterior wall of the substructure.

Substructure 326 was one of the most completely exposed buildings excavated in the early levels at Cuello, with some three-quarters of its surface and all except the apsidal ends lying within the trench. It faced northwards on azimuth 34°, and was *c.* 8.4 by 4.5 m, increasing from 0.1 to 0.2 m in height with four successive building stages. Its earth and stone core (2219) was retained by a wall of large limestone cobbles (2203) and surfaced by a plaster floor (2214), with patches of burning and 23 post holes. Charcoal samples from the fill (2219) and from the fill of one post hole (2218) yielded ages of 375 and 430 b.c. The second and third stages included reflooring, rewalling, and the addition of an axial stepped entry on the north side. Charcoal from soil accumulated behind the structure yielded an age of 450 b.c., while a sample from fill used in the fourth stage refacing of the frontage gave one of 530 b.c. The alterations of this stage are the best preserved, and included renewal of the front step and construction of the entry in an inward-funneling plan flanked by large posts and floored by a T-shaped plaster surface sloping slightly downwards. This elaborate entry could indicate a supra-residential function for the building, although nothing in the associated trash supports this.

Phase II thus saw the beginning of a formal courtyard layout, with a plaster-surfaced patio bordered by low substructures supporting perishable buildings. Structure 326 is the best-known of these, but the evidence from Structures 325 and 327 indicates that they were essentially similar, albeit with idiosyncrasies of internal layout that changed from stage to stage within the phase. Firepits were found within Structure 325, around Structures 326–327, and in the patio. Radiocarbon dates were obtained from these, from soil used as fill in Structure 326 and from an occupation layer behind it. Of eight dates ranging from 1720 to 340 b.c., six lay between 530 and 340 b.c. (calibrated range 767–264 B.C.).

Phase III (Fig. 3.5) Patio Floor II at roughly 21.7 m elevation was laid over the northern half of the courtyard area, ending on a straight edge marked with small stones. South of it floor (2014) survived only in patches, with its fill (486) exposed elsewhere. The patio was bordered by Structure 320 [F89], built over the rear of Structure 325 on the north side, Structure 321 [F59] over Structure 327 on the west, and Structure 323 [F220] over Structure 326 on the south. On the east, part of Structure 324 [F230] was present in the excavated area. The extension of the paved area northwards over the remains of Structure 325 gave the patio a north–south length of 13 meters.

Fills (488) and (713) below the floor contained charcoal

yielding ages of 560 and 570 b.c., and a soil (592) coeval with the floor one of 540 b.c. Floor (477) abutted the frontages of Structures 320 and 321, and extended northwest between them to end in a fairly straight edge; a cluster of stake holes in this area suggests a small enclosure or pen. Floor (2014) extended between Structures 321 and 323 to abut a low wall (1703) forming a western edge to the patio. In front of Structure 321 a pit in the floor (76/197) contained charcoal yielding a radiocarbon age of 1390 b.c.; in the south part of the patio five firepits [F231–233, 244–245] lay in front of and east of Structure 323. The fill of [F231] included the earliest piece of obsidian found at Cuello, a blade section reworked by step-flaking into a neat rectangle and decorated with four incised lines on the ventral face (Fig. 8.13) Analysis showed it to be from the San Martin Jilotepeque source, and hydration dating gave a date of 1128 ± 81 B.C., the equivalent of a radiocarbon date of c. 980 b.c. While this does not date the context in which it was found, it does suggest obsidian imports at Cuello at the end of the second millennium B.C. The southern part of the patio was resurfaced with floor (2006); its fill (2007) contained much charcoal, a sample of which yielded an age of 350 b.c.

Of the buildings around the patio, Structure 320 was both in a new location, and in the worst state of preservation, having been demolished in a further patio extension in phase IV. Nevertheless, six building stages were discerned spanning phases III and IIIA; in the first, the bowed frontage and plaster facing covering its stone framing were clearly coeval with the patio floor; the building was floored with (76/153), cut by post holes and a firepit, and was an estimated 8.1 by 5 m in area.

Structure 321 had its eastern frontal portion within the excavated area, although part of it had been removed by the 1975 test pit. The front was straight, on 7° azimuth and thus facing almost due east, with the ends curving into an apsidal form estimated to have been 8.3 by 5 m, and 0.4 m high initially, rising to a height of 0.6 m by the time it was superseded by Structure 317 at the end of phase IV. In the first of the five building stages, Structure 321 was walled by large rough limestone blocks c. 0.5 m wide; a step (76/155) was inset south of center on the frontage to give access to the platform, its plaster surfacing coterminous with that of the building, but with the tread renewed at some later date. Charcoal from the fill of the step yielded a radiocarbon age of 2790 b.c., judged unacceptable. The internal floor of Structure 321, (76/177), was the first of five, the others belonging to phase IIIA. The floor was eroded in its forward portion, and a deposit of ash, covered by a layer of soil with burnt material (76/175), lay over the fill towards the front wall. Charcoal from (76/175) yielded a radiocarbon age of 1310 b.c.

Structure 323 survived only as a stub, having been cut back for a southward patio extension in phase IV, but sufficient of its base remained to allow an estimate of its area at 11.5 by

6.5 m. It completely covered Structure 326 with 0.6 m of fill, maintaining the same apsidal plan and northeasterly orientation, and with the front wall laid on top of the basal molding of the earlier structure. Six building stages, three each in phases III and IIIA, were discerned, during which the platform rose from 0.45 m to nearly 1 m in height, and the north front was modified, with the long narrow bench attached during the first stage being replaced by a projecting axial step 1.3 m wide and 0.6 m deep in the second, later buried by refacing of the façade. The nature of access during the later stages is unknown because of the demolition of the upper frontal portion of the building. The degree of wear on the floors suggests considerable use between renewals. Two burials, 116 [F219] and 120 [F228], were cut into the third-stage floor: only the first lay entirely within the excavated area, and was of a child 2–4 years old, accompanied by four pottery vessels, a pottery ocarina in the shape of a bird, a pierced shell, and a blue-green jade bead (Fig. 10.1).

Structure 324 consisted of the western chord of a curved 0.15 m high plaster surface, lacking post holes or any other features within the excavated area, which many have been a low oval or circular platform in the center of the patio, or the western frontal portion of a building on its eastern side. The portion within the excavation was 8 m long and 2.5 m wide, and the curvature at the ends suggest an overall length of c. 9 m. The surface of its plaster floor (1800) was heavily burnt. The renewed patio surface (2006) was at the same elevation as this floor, which had been constructed while the earlier patio surface (2014) was in use.

Phase III thus saw the northward extension of the patio area, and its resurfacing in two stages, with the northern part associated with Structures 320 and 321 preceding the southern area towards Structure 323. Existing structures were buried by new ones on the south and west sides, with an increase in size in both cases, while on the north a new location was used, and for the first time a construction, of unknown function, was built apparently in the patio itself. A small stake-built structure stood on the patio floor at the northwest corner, and several firepits were dug into it along the margins. The pottery of phase III is of the Bladen ceramic complex, with external links to the Xe sphere of the southern Petén. Radiocarbon dates for this phase range from 1390 to 350 b.c. (discounting UCLA–2102b), with two between 1390 and 1310 b.c. and three between 570–540 b.c. (799–422 B.C.).

Phase IIIA (Fig. 3.6) Patio Floor III at about 21.9 m elevation was laid over its predecessor on a bed of stones (1764), dark soil with occupation material (460) and plaster rubble (587). Charcoal from (1764) – which may have sifted down from (460) – yielded a radiocarbon age of 645 b.c., and two samples from (460) ages of 800 b.c. and 505 b.c. The floor maintained the same northwest corner between Structures 320 and 321 as

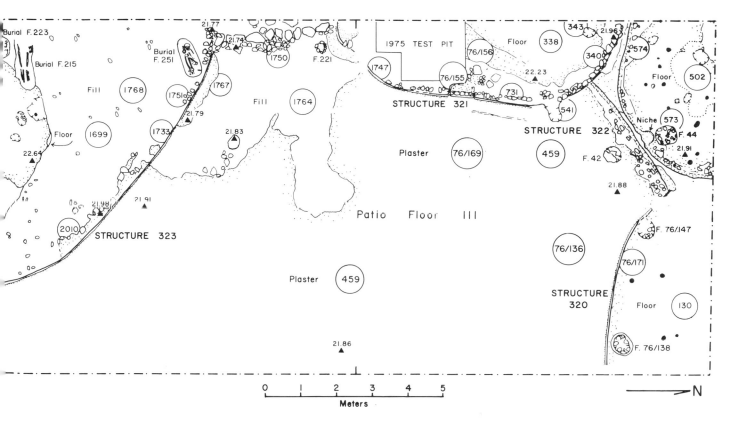

Fig. 3.6 Phase IIIA construction of Structure 322 and Patio Floor III.

in phase III, in this case with a line of stones under the plaster to form a beveled edge. A new building, Structure 322 [F55], was constructed in the gap between the ends of the other buildings, its subcircular plan almost touching their sides; the northern end of Structure 321 had been shortened by this stage, possibly to make room for the new structure in the corner of the courtyard layout. Patio Floor III extended south to span the entire length of the courtyard, abutting Structure 323 at the southern end and burying Structure 324. Between Structures 323 and 321 it ended at a wall (1750) of limestone slabs built directly on that of the previous phase, although worn down to the subfloor fill immediately east of the wall. A small stone-lined pit [F221] lay just inside the boundary wall adjacent to the southeast corner of Structure 321, and a firepit [F42] cut the floor in front of Structure 322.

Somewhat over a quarter (4.5 by 2 m) of the estimated area of this building lay within the excavation. It stood only 0.05 m above patio level, although rising from the lower ground surface outside, and the plaster edging overlay the edge of the patio floor. A small plastered niche was set into the southeastern side, and its floor was cut by a firepit [F44], which contained charcoal yielding an age of 590 b.c., and a number of post and stake holes. In a second stage of construction a raised

floor was built over part of the interior, its curved edge concentric with that of the lower floor, at a smaller radius.

Structure 320b had a new floor (76/130), charcoal from which gave an age of 520 b.c. The most notable features were two pits, c. 0.5 m diameter and 0.15 m deep, just inside the southern wall line, with stone and pottery linings. The subsequent stages, c–e, were floor renewals, of which only the antepenultimate (76/112) and last (76/102) had post holes; Gerhardt (1985, 1988) places stages d–f of Structure 320 in phase IV, however (see Fig. 3.7).

Structure 321b was constructed by the addition of floor (338) over the earlier (177); (338) was itself covered by large fragments of daub from the facing of a perishable super-structure, presumably demolished before the construction of the next floor (337). Burial 2 (75/25), a secondary interment of a young adult female accompanied by three bowls, was apparently intruded through this floor at the south end of the building. The two final stages of Structure 321 belong in phase IV.

At the south end of the patio, Structure 323 received three further floor renewals in stages d–f. The last of these floors (1699) was cut by two burials, 114 [F215] and 118 [F223], and a third, burial 124 [F253], may have been cut into this floor, or from a higher level. The latter was of a 10–12-year-old child, accompanied by two vessels, and like the second was in the south section and only partly excavated. Burial 118 was of an

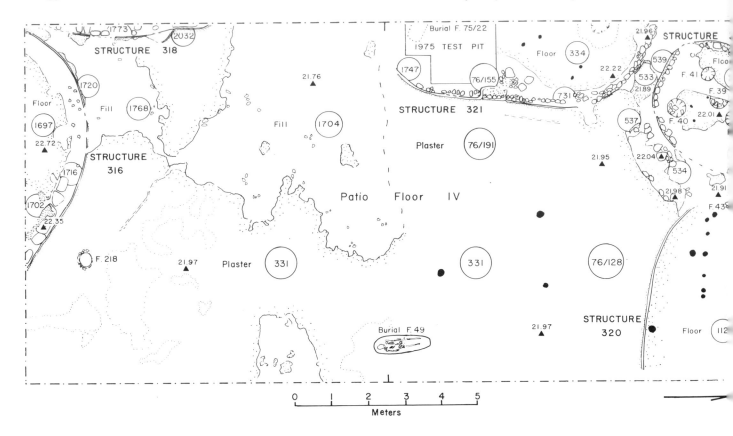

Fig. 3.7 Phase IV constructions and Patio Floor IV in the Central and South Squares (the rear remnant of Structure 320 excavated in the North Square in 1987 has been added).

adult male with a bowl inverted over the skull, and burial 114 of an adult female, with shell bracelets round both wrists and a blue jade pendant of "spangle"form in the pelvic region (Fig. 9.8n). One of the last floors was cut by the shaft for burial 123 [F251], a deep grave penetrating through Structure 326 below into bedrock. The upper part of the shaft was removed by the phase IV demolition of Structure 323, making its precise stage uncertain; the associated pottery is of the Bladen ceramic complex rather than Lopez Mamom (Fig. 10.2c), although a radiocarbon date on collagen from the skeleton yielded an age of 2310 ± 70 b.p. (OxA-2016), 360 ± 70 b.c. calibrating to 408–370 B.C.; the low collagen level (6.4 mg) may have rendered this date later than its true age (R. Housley, personal communication 1989).

Phase IIIA thus saw an increase in the number of buildings clustered around the patio, with the addition of Structure 322 at the northwest corner, although the curious Structure 324 was buried by the new Patio Floor III. The three other buildings continued in use, with reflooring and some remodeling, including shortening of Structure 321 on the north to allow construction of Structure 322. The pottery found in the

occupation levels and burials of this phase was of the Bladen ceramic complex, and five radiocarbon dates on charcoal range from 800 to 505 b.c., with four of them between 645 and 505 b.c. (816–408 B.C.); the single collagen date, possibly younger than actuality, is of 360 b.c.

Phase IV (Fig. 3.7) At the south end of the courtyard, the frontage and northern portion of Structure 323 were ripped away down to patio level; burial 114 was truncated by the demolition, the upper part of the body being removed, while the upper shaft of the deep grave of burial 123 was also cut away. The remaining stub of Structure 323 was used as the core for a new building, Structure 316 [F200], while another, Structure 318 [F229], overlapped the remains of Structure 323 on the western side of the patio, between Structures 316 and 321; only the eastern extremity of this building lay within the excavation. A rubble fill was spread over the previous Patio Floor III, and capped by Patio Floor IV at c. 21.95 m elevation. This floor ran south over the truncated and buried remains of Structure 323 to abut the new Stuctures 316 and 318. It was badly eroded from Structure 318 north to Structure 321, but well preserved in the northern half of the patio. In the northwest corner it met a rectangular area which may have been a front step for Structure 319 [F36], a slightly smaller successor to Structure 322 of which some two-thirds

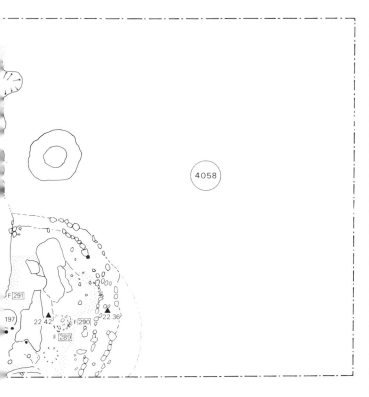

IV; the last, (329) of stage e, was worn almost down to its precursor (334), and was covered with burnt material including daub and plaster, suggesting destruction of the superstructure before Structure 317 was built above it.

Of the three new structures of phase IV, Structure 316 is the most complex, having six building stages running to the end of phase IVA and associated with both Patio Floors IV and V. It faced northeast on 36° azimuth, and is estimated to have been 10.2 by 6 m, raised 0.7 m above the patio and apsidal in plan. It was constructed by cladding the stub of Structure 323 with a retaining wall (1716) of cut limestone blocks with earth packing and plaster facing; the wall was two courses high and then stepped back in a terrace, above which lay the platform surface. Subsequent destruction, and the position of over half the building outside the excavated area, limit the amount of information obtainable.

The same problem limits knowledge of Structure 318, of which only a 3.5m length of the bowed façade (1773), with a few stones of its wall and a trace of the plaster facing, was excavated. There was a small front step, which if axial indicates a building facing north of east on 73° azimuth. The step was buried in phase IVA by Patio Floor V, but the structure seems to have remained in use until the phase V destruction of the courtyard group.

The two final internal floors (334) and (329) of Structure 321 were laid in phase IV, the latter worn, burnt, and covered with burnt material from the demolished superstructure, including daub and plaster. Fragments of several large vessels were found lying on the surface, and it is possible that this destruction was accidental, rather than part of a structured ritual as seems generally to have been the case at Cuello. This layer and the bedding for the succeeding floor (325) of phase IVA, also brown soil with burnt material, were not well separated during the 1975 excavation (as 75/17) or that of 1976 (as 76/110). Two charcoal samples, one from each season, gave ages of 1050 b.c. and 3190 b.c., only the first considered acceptable at the time, and in the light of subsequent dates from the adjacent Structure 319 and associated occupation layers, now considered too early.

Structure 319 was a low platform of ovoid plan, estimated to cover 4 by 3.4 m, and with some two-thirds of its area exposed in the northwest corner of the excavation. It lay between Structures 320 and 321, separated from each by a gap some 0.5 m wide which was paved with plaster, and faced southeast on azimuth 121° onto the patio, where the scar of a front step remained on Patio Floor IV. It was built directly over Structure 322, and had a similar but smaller plan. The internal floor (314) was cut by four firepits [F38–41], and had a fill of soil (528) with charcoal that yielded an age of 610 b.c. An occupation soil (540) accumulating over the plaster surface (539) between Structures 319 and 321 had charcoal giving an age of 520 b.c. The firepit [F38] contained chunks of daub in

lay within the excavated area. At the south end the floor was marked by burning in front of Structure 316, and it had been repaired in places. It was cut by a firepit [F218], in front of Structure 316. Charcoal from the soil layer (458) under the northern part of the patio floor, more likely laid as fill than accumulated as occupation trample, yielded a radiocarbon age of 300 b.c., while a similar layer (1734) under the southern floor yielded one of 600 b.c. The patio floor was cut by burial 22 [F49] at or close to the center of the courtyard, in an extended position with the head to the south, accompanied by a bowl over the face and sealed by a plaster patch in the patio floor.

The final floor of Structure 320f on the north side of the courtyard was cut by two graves, burials 5 and 6, (76/137) and (76/152), which may have been cut from higher up still; the latter was of a child of 5–6 years, flexed and with the head missing, and lacking grave goods, the former of a robust middle adult male accompanied by two pottery vessels and by jade and shell beads. An AMS date on bone collagen yielded an age of 440 b.c., possibly too young because of low collagen content. Several later floors than (76/102), collectively designated (76/59), were seen only in section because their southern parts were removed prior to the construction of Structure 315 in phase IV.

The final two floor renewals of Structure 321 fall into phase

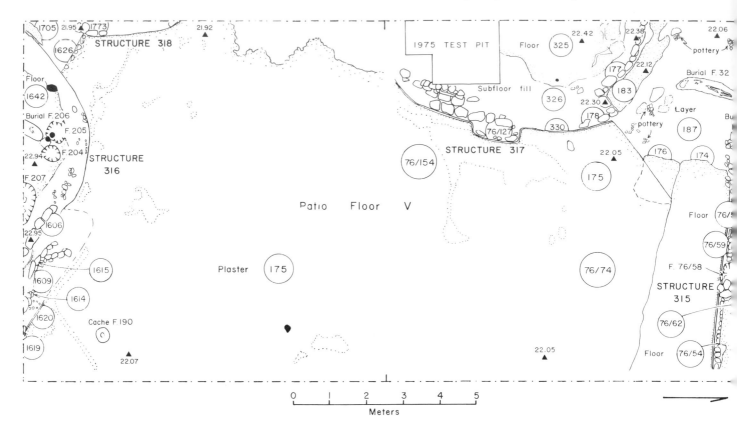

Fig. 3.8 Phase IVA constructions associated with Patio Floor V
(the remnant of Structure 315d excavated in the North Square in
1987 has been added).

its fill which may have come from the superstructure of
Structure 319, if it had one: only three stake holes were found
in the surviving portions of floor.

Phase IV thus saw the extension of the patio to a length of
16 m; if the burial [F49] is indeed central, then a width of *c*. 14 m
and an area of some 225 sq. m are indicated. At least five
buildings stood around the western half of the courtyard: the
final developments of Structures 320 and 321, the new
Structures 316 and 319 overlying the remains of their precursors, Structures 323 and 322, and the southwestern Structure 318. There was room for another small building between
the latter and the south end of Structure 321, but if such
existed, it was set back to the west beyond the limits of
excavation. As in phase IIIA, the patio was almost clear of
firepits, [F218] being the only one in the paved area, and only
Structure 319 had them in its interior. Patio Floor IV was
worn and repaired, indicating a long period of use. Layers
such as (540) and (528) still contained only Bladen complex
pottery, while those that overlay them in phase IVA included
the first Lopez Mamom types. Radiocarbon ages for phase IV
ranged from 1050 to 300 b.c. (apart from UCLA-2102g), with
three of the five lying in the span 610–520 b.c. (801–422 B.C.).

Phase IVA (Fig. 3.8) Patio Floor V, the last in the sequence at
an elevation of *c*. 22.05 m, was laid against Structures 316 and
318 at its south end, with a formal edge bolstered by stones
between the two buildings. On the west it abutted Structure
317, the successor to Structure 321, which extended some 0.8 m
further east, narrowing the patio, while on the north side
Structure 315c was razed, the patio floor extended some 2 m
north over its remains in a second stage of paving, and
Structure 315d built there to give the patio a length of over
18 m. In the northwest corner Structure 319 was buried under
accumulations of trash, and the patio floor ended in a formal
edge with nothing beyond it. The floor itself was marked by
large areas of burning in front of Structures 316 and 317,
including distinguishable marks of large timbers and roof
thatch, dating to the destruction of the buildings at the end of
the phase. A cache of jade beads (Table 9.7) set in a circular
plug of plaster in the floor in front of the center of Structure
316 could have been inserted at any time, but is best seen as
part of the sequence of destruction and burial that marked the
transition to phase V.

The extension of Patio Floor V northwards with the
addition of an extension (174) to the first stage (175), (76/174),
indicates that the first stages of Structure 315 in use at the
beginning of the phase lay further south than stages d–e, and
were coeval with Structure 317 on the west side. The careful
ending of the extension and a patch (176) linking it with the

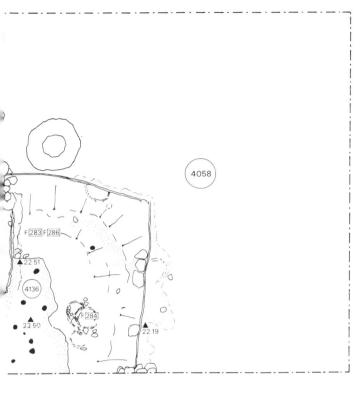

rest of the floor at the northwestern end suggest that the erection of Structure 314 over Structure 317 took place at this time, coeval with the construction of Structure 315. Structure 317 itself had five building stages within phase IVA, in the first of which its apsidal plan, facing south of east on azimuth 98°, was established. It is estimated to have been 7.6 m long and 5.4 m wide at the center, and to have risen from 0.35 to 0.7 m above patio level. The front of its predecessor was used as a foundation for the new façade, and the plaster facing of the latter was abutted by Patio Floor V, laid immediately afterwards. The outline of a projecting axial step remained in the floor after demolition at the end of phase IVA. The four subsequent building stages comprised renewals of the interior floor, with alterations to the timber superstructure, on the substructure of Structure 317a. Burial 1 (75/14), cut into the stage c floor and sealed by its successor, had charcoal in its fill that gave a radiocarbon age of 1020 b.c. Charcoal from the soil below the penultimate floor of stage d yielded a radiocarbon age of 730 (± 190) b.c., and that below the final floor of stage e a radiocarbon age of 245 b.c.; while the two earlier dates, from the 1975 test pit, seemed acceptable at the time, only the later accords with the overall pattern of dates available in 1989. During the existence of Structure 317 the locus of Structure 319 became filled with an occupation and midden soil (187), with much trash, including restorable vessels of early Lopez Mamom types. Two radiocarbon ages on charcoal from (187)

were 395 and 365 b.c. Cut into the deposit were two graves, burial 20 [F35] of a juvenile and burial 18 [F32] of an adult female accompanied by a Lopez Mamom vessel. Charcoal from the soil fill of the grave yielded a radiocarbon age of 470 b.c.

The second through fourth stages of Structure 316 were floor renewals, then the fifth stage saw the addition of a projecting front terrace built over Patio Floor V and hence slightly postdating Structure 317. It was constructed of large limestone blocks retaining a fill of rubble and dark soil, and was stepped in profile. Burial 108 [F206] of a juvenile, lacking grave goods, was inserted into the internal floor of this stage, and sealed by the fills for the final floor of Structure 316f; these were retained by raising the wall of the substructure, and the front terrace was raised at the same time, although subsequent destruction leaves its final form unknown.

The second part of phase IVA saw the transformation of the northwest corner of the patio by the demolition of Structure 315c and Structure 317e, the northward extension of Patio Floor V by the laying of a 2-m broad strip of plaster (174) on to the north end of (175), and the construction of Structure 315d. Only the front of the western portion of this building lay within the excavated area in 1976, although in 1987 the remainder of the west end was uncovered in the North Square (Fig. 3.8).

Structure 315 had five stages of construction and modification, a–e, of which only the last two were associated with the extended patio. The earlier stages (76/57, 59) were cut away by demolition for the extension, and may well have been apsidal structures with timber superstructures; the apsidal rear of the stage c building, uncovered but not excavated in 1987, supports such a view (Fig. 3.7). This structure [F291] had two concentric arcs of stones, the outer at a slightly lower level, framing the north end of a poorly preserved plaster floor with an estimated size of at least 5 by 3.5 m.

Structure 315d was substantially larger, with an estimated length of 11.2 m and a width of c. 5 m. Its straight front possessed a wide step, of two stages, and a terrace running the length of the substructure in front of a stone-walled superstructure, the first known at Cuello (Figs. 5.14–5.15). The walls were of fist-sized limestone cobbles laid in courses, with earth packing and a plaster facing down across the surface and front of the terrace. The door jamb was a separate plaster-faced construction with a rubble and earth packing. Both it and the wall had been demolished to within 0.2 m of their base, so that the original height of the freestanding stone-walled superstructure remains unknown. Hopes that more of the west and north walls might be preserved were dashed in 1987, when it was found that these sides of Structure 315d had been cut back, removing all trace of walls and leaving only a stub of the substructure. Burial 4, of a young adult male accompanied by a Lopez Mamom jar, was inserted into the

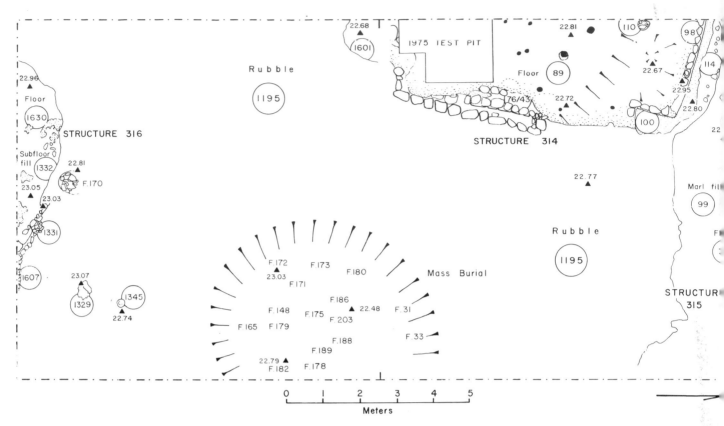

Fig. 3.9 Phase V destruction and infill, with the remains of
Structures 314–316 (the north side of Structure 315e excavated in
1987 has been added).

front step of this stage during construction and sealed by the
plaster tread. An obsidian blade from the fill of the first front
step was sourced to San Martin Jilotepeque and hydration-
dated to 1067–895 B.C., equivalent to a radiocarbon age of
c. 880 b.c. This suggests both that deposits half a millennium
old were being recycled for fill at this point, and that obsidian
was reaching Cuello early in the first millennium b.c.

A final stage, Structure 315e, was built over the demolished
and infilled remains of the walled building, with a timber
superstructure and a floor much reddened by burning (Fig.
3.9); it was demolition of this structure at the transition to
phase V which removed so much of its precursor's substructure on the side and rear, and some of the damage to the front
of the step and terrace may date to this second destructive
episode rather than the first. Charcoal from the infill yielded a
radiocarbon age of 305 b.c.

The straight-fronted plan of Structure 315d was matched
by Structure 314 [F45], built over Structure 317 on the west
side of the patio midway through phase IVA (Fig. 3.9). As on
the north, where Structure 315c had been at least half-razed,
there had been substantial demolition of the front portion of
Structure 317 down to patio level. Of the front step only its

outline on the floor remained, with jade beads scattered in the
scar as part of the valedictory ritual, and the internal floors of
all the precursors of Structure 317e were also torn out as much
as 1.8 m back from the phase IVA frontage, together with any
surviving façades that had been incorporated in the building.
The infill against the vertical scar (75/21–23) yielded charcoal
that gave radiocarbon ages of a.d. 250 and a.d. 810, neither
accepted at the time, and possibly the result of roots penetrating the looser deposits. Substantial fills were added against the
north and south ends of Structure 317, that on the north being
more than 2 m wide, to create a long subrectangular substructure c. 12 m north–south and an estimated 6 m wide, of which
almost half lay within the excavated area. A front section over
5 m long projected slightly, facing south of east on azimuth
105°. The building stood almost 0.7 m above patio level, and
was surfaced by a well-preserved plaster floor (89) with the
remains of a stone-walled superstructure of which only the
basal course at the northeast corner remained, together with a
few blocks at the south end suggesting an overall length of at
least 8 m. The north end of the floor had slumped over the
marl and earth fills beneath, while the central section was
supported by the final floor of Structure 317e below it. Soil
between these floors contained charcoal yielding a radiocarbon age of 520 b.c. The layers of fill dumped to form the
northern extension contained charcoal that yielded radiocarbon ages of 865, 490, and 245 b.c., and animal bone whose

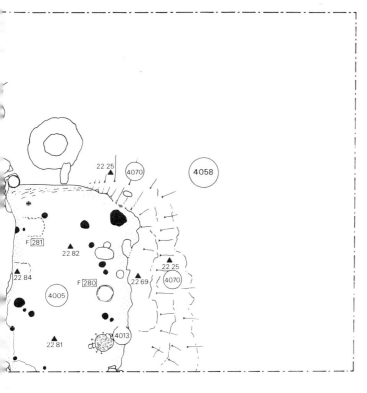

collagen yielded an age of 480 b.c. The north retaining wall, surviving only as a stub in the western section, lined up with the northern edge of the extended Patio Floor V at the base of Structure 315. Two successive plaster floors abutted the north side of Structure 314, and a soil layer between them contained charcoal that yielded a radiocarbon age of 470 b.c. The presence of a few Cocos Chicanel sherds as well as predominant Lopez Mamom suggested that this was a contemporary trash dump and not quarried fill; the fill behind the wall yielding the latest of the three radiocarbon ages (the two other fills contained no pottery) also had some Cocos pottery, suggesting that, when it was dumped, it was contemporary and not earlier material. The front of Structure 314 had in turn been torn away at the beginning of phase V, and a layer of daub, ash, plaster, and soil lay over the scar. A deep pit (76/141) apparently dug from the level of floor (89) contained charcoal yielding a radiocarbon age of 240 b.c.; it may belong to either this phase or to the phase V destruction.

Phase IVA thus saw the successive transformation of almost all the buildings around the north, west, and south sides of the patio, and the creation in Structures 314 and 315d of two substantial rectangular platforms supporting the first stone-walled superstructures known at Cuello. The ceramic evidence from Structure 314 includes a few sherds classed as Cocos Chicanel, in an assemblage predominantly of Lopez Mamom types, while that from Structure 315d (and its

successor 315e) is wholly Mamom. Both the erection and the demolition of these buildings would seem to date close to the time when Chicanel sphere pottery developed out of Mamom. Fourteen radiocarbon samples (excluding UCLA-1985b, c, d) range in age from 1020 to 305 b.c., with eight of them between 520 and 305 b.c. (791–225 B.C.), a span in good agreement with established dates for the latter part of the Mamom ceramic sphere, and a further two of 245 b.c. (377–181 B.C.).

Phase V (Fig. 3.9) This phase spans the most radical transformation of layout, architecture, and stratigraphy in the entire history of Platform 34: the courtyard with surrounding buildings that had existed with successive reconstructions and refloorings since phase II was filled in and paved over to create the broad open space on top of the first stage of Platform 34, in essentially the form that it maintained until the end of the Formative period.

The first set of events in phase V involved the ripping-off of the façades of the buildings around the courtyard: Structures 314, 315e, and 316f were all cut away, and burn marks on the patio floor in front of 314 and 316f suggest that perishable superstructures were burnt and collapsed into the patio; the burning could, in the former instance, have come from the destruction of Structure 317 earlier in phase IVA, however. The only structure where the sides and rear have been excavated, Structure 315e, had been similarly cut away, removing evidence of the superstructures of this and earlier stages. The jade offering [F190] set into the floor in front of Structure 316f on its axis probably belongs to this period also.

The patio was then infilled with a mass of rubble, of limestone and chert (76/34), (1195), up to the tops of ruined substructures, a depth of some 0.7 m. Charcoal in the rubble gave a radiocarbon age of 330 b.c. Between the demolished sides of Structures 314 and 315e a series of white marl and dark soil fills were dumped, from south to north and west to east. The soil was presumably removed in quarrying the marl, probably from areas just west of Platform 34; charcoal from one layer yielded a radiocarbon age of 425 b.c., and animal bone collagen from another one of 740 b.c., suggesting that occupation or midden layers of several periods were gouged up and redeposited as fill. North of this, across the rear of the remains of Structure 315e, a mass of rubble was dumped, much of it freshly quarried, capped with redeposited midden and with further lenses of marl and topsoil; charcoal from one of the latter yielded an age of 285 b.c. Charcoal from the midden that had sifted down among the rubble, or been included with it, yielded radiocarbon ages of 280 and 325 b.c. Charcoal from the redeposited midden in grid 35/30 gave an age of 190 b.c. Two firepits [F170, 274] were dug into the top of the rubble, together with the base of a vessel (1329) apparently also used as an *ad hoc* hearth.

Over the center of the buried patio a 0.3-m-deep depression

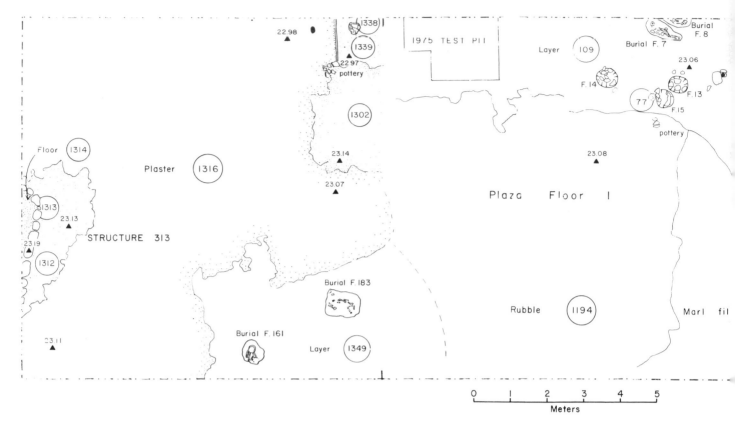

0   1   2   3   4   5
Meters

Fig. 3.10 Phase VA constructions in the North, Central, and South Squares with burials [F7–8] and firepits [F13–15] and plaster surface (1888), ending at (1969), of the preceding phase V also shown. Structure 312 and deposits north of (1969) are of phase VA, together with Structure 313.

5 by more than 4 m (the eastern part unexcavated) was left in the rubble, into which was deposited a mass sacrificial burial, Mass Burial 1, burials 29–60 [F31, 33, 148, 165, 171, 173, 175, 178, 179, 180, 182, 183, 186, 188, 189, 203], including the whole or partial skeletons of at least 32 individuals, 26 males, one female and five uncertain, all adults ranging from the early 20s to one male in his late 50s (with 14 of indeterminate age). Most of the bodies had been butchered and piled in joints, although the first individuals had been buried entire. A number of pottery vessels of early Chicanel types were buried with them, and seven carved bone tubes, five bearing the woven-mat *pop* design that was a symbol of regal power among the Classic Maya, the other two complex designs in a sophisticated style. The sacrifice, the members of which were not necessarily residents of Cuello, was covered by more rubble and this in turn by the redeposited midden layer. Within this layer two more burials were laid, burials 10 and 12 [F7, 8], a young adult male and female, side by side and both decapitated (Fig. 10.7); burial 10 has yielded three radiocarbon dates, on collagen, gelatin, and ion-separated gelatin (OxA-1653–55), the two latter close together in age at 490 and

500 b.c. Three firepits [F13–15] were also dug into the deposit at different levels, showing its accretion in stages; this suggested during earlier seasons that the deposit was an occupation soil built up over a long period, and confirmation of its dumped status was not obtained until the 1987 season, which corroborated the conclusions reached in 1976 and abandoned in 1978. The first stage of Platform 34 was finally finished with a plaster surface (Plaza Floor 1), which on the north side ran down a retaining wall on to the exterior surface, covering a foetal or child burial which seems to have also been part of the ceremonial associated with the construction.

A *chultun* shaft was dug from the surface of the redeposited midden layer, apparently in phase V; the erosion of the plaster surface of Plaza Floor I around its mouth makes it impossible to tell whether it could have been dug subsequently in phase VA, although it may well have been used in that period. The *chultun* [F246] had a circular shaft 1.9 m diameter at the top (although probably eroded back to that size) and 0.76 m diameter where it penetrated bedrock 1.8m below the surface. A subglobular chamber 2.8 by 2.4 m and *c*. 1 m high was cut out of bedrock northwest of the entry from the shaft, which was marked by two steps cut from the rock and a large slab on the floor forming a third step. The shaft fill contained much cultural material.

Phase V thus began with the destruction of the Middle Formative courtyard group, and ended with the creation of an open plaza on top of Platform 34, an estimated 32 m from

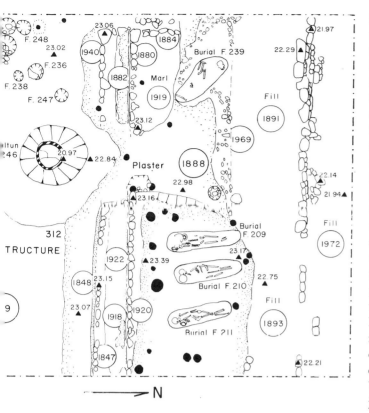

north to south. On its west side stood one of the structures buried within the Early Classic pyramid Structure 35, with Structure 354 being the earliest feasible, given the level of Plaza Floor I at *c.* 23 m elevation (the only earlier building in the pyramid sequence, Structure 355, presumably correlates with the rear of Structure 321, given its pre-Lopez Mamom date on the basis of ceramic content). On the north the surface (1888/Q4001) may have been simply a foundation for Structure 312 of phase VA. All of the radiocarbon dates on charcoal for phase V are from earlier material recycled as fill: they range from 425 to 190 (both extremes being ± 150 yr) b.c., with five of the seven dates falling between 330 and 280 b.c. (400–200 B.C.). The two AMS dates on animal-bone collagen are earlier and also suggest recycling of old deposits. The three AMS dates on human bone collagen fractions fall between 430 and 500 b.c. (770–400 B.C.). The freshness of much of the pottery, and the closeness of most of these dates to that conventionally accepted for the end of Mamom/beginning of Chicanel, *c.* 400 B.C., suggests that the bulk of the fill deposits were probably coeval midden recycled, but that older occupation deposits were quarried in opening marl pits for additional fill.

Phase VA (Fig. 3.10) This phase saw the use of Plaza Floor I at *c.* 23.07 m elevation with the construction on it of buildings at the north and south ends of the open space, and probably a further structure in the pyramid sequence (with Structure 353

the most likely candidate; charcoal from a post hole (766) in the floor of this structure yielded a radiocarbon age of 230 b.c.; comparison of this with the other phase VA ages suggests that Structure 353 could alternatively be placed in phase VI). At the south end of the excavated area the front step or terrace of Structure 313 just extended into the South Square, a single course of stones high, while 22 m to the north the south edge of Structure 312 faced it on a slightly different orientation. This seems to have begun as a single building running completely across the North Square and hence over 10 m long, with a front terrace and a raised main portion, both founded on the phase V floor (1888/Q4001); the northern end of the building required an expansion of Platform 34, which was created by cutting away the retaining wall and some 0.3 m of the fill, adding further masses of fill and constructing a new retaining wall (Q4100) some 1.6 m further north. At the beginning of this construction sequence a double grave was dug into the plaster surface associated with the previous retaining wall, and two children buried in it, burials 126–127 [F 276–277], the latter decapitated and with a small jar over the stump of the neck. An adjacent patch of ash on the plaster floor may be part of the same ritual. Fills were deposited over the area of the extension, and into them was thrown the body of an adult, burial 125 [F274], accompanied by a bowl, lying in the area just behind the new retaining wall. Charcoal from fill (Q4073) yielded a radiocarbon age of 330 b.c. Under the base of the retaining wall was a layer of daub from a demolished building, perhaps removed from floor (1888/Q4001). Over this and in front of the wall layers of occupation material built up, one of which (Q4119) contained charcoal giving a radiocarbon age of 310 b.c., another (Q4092) one of 300 b.c.

Three graves were cut into Structure 312 in the eastern part of the North Square, burials 110–113 [F209–211]; all the individuals were lying semi-prone, facing east and with the head to the south, with two males flanking a female accompanied by an adolescent (Fig. 10.11). *If* the central grave was axial in Structure 312, and the possible west end wall (1884) just inside the west section was indeed such, then the building would have been *c.* 13 m long, and 5.5 m wide to the new north retaining wall.

South of the western end of Structure 312 and west of the *chultun* shaft a cluster of six firepits [F236–238, 247–249] and several post holes may indicate an area of domestic activity, perhaps under a light shelter. Beyond the limits of the Main Trench to the south a sequence of retaining walls of similar construction to (Q4100) were excavated along grid 15 m N, suggesting a length of 34 m for Platform 34 at this phase. In the western trench into the pyramid the retaining wall (216) has been tentatively identified as the western limit of Platform 34, but the latter's extent eastwards beyond the 40 m E grid is unknown. Wall (462), seen in the trench dug at 50–52 m E, is probably the extension of either (Q4100) or its phase V precursor (Q4110): occupation material (454) accumulated

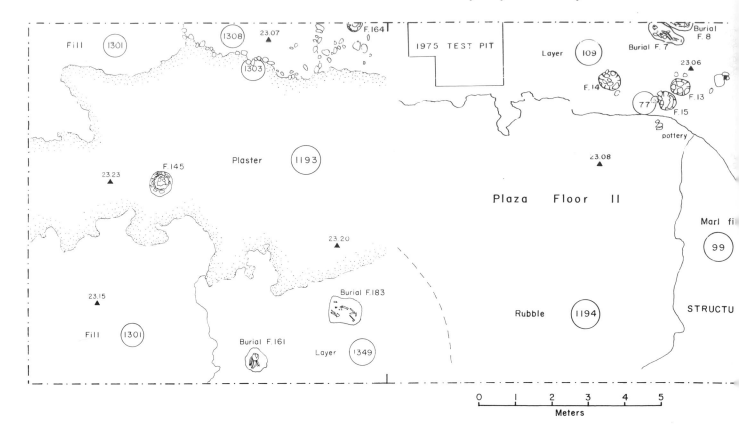

Fig. 3.11 Phase VI construction of Structures 311–312 and Plaza Floor II, with some features of phases V–VA still exposed.

outside the wall contained charcoal yielding a radiocarbon age of 355 b.c. (400–378 B.C.), and pottery of the Cocos Chicanel ceramic complex.

Phase VA therefore comprises the first extension of Platform 34, and the building of structures at its north and south ends. Pottery is of the early facet of the Cocos Chicanel complex, and the two radiocarbon ages are of 330 and 310 b.c.

Phase VI (Fig. 3.11) Platform 34 was surfaced with Plaza Floor II at *c.* 23.20 m elevation, the major constituent of which, (1193), survived only in the South Square, being eroded to its fills further north. A large firepit [F 145], 0.7 m diameter, was set into the floor near the south end, lined with the base of a very large *olla*. A smaller firepit [F164] was cut by the western section.

At the north end of the trench, Structure 312 was cut in half, down to its underlying floor, and the western portion buried beneath an open plaster floor, abutting a subcircular building (Structure 311) set further north and partly beyond the sections. The eastern part was used as the core for another round-sided building, Structure 309, all except the eastern end of which lay within the excavation, also abutted by the

plaster floor on the west. The floor ran back between the two structures to a wall linking them, which stepped down northwards to a lower area behind the buildings, also with a plaster surface, created by infilling the open space behind the north retaining wall of Platform 34 in phase VA. The wall was partly dismantled, and several deep layers of fill dumped over and beyond it, presumably retained by a wall lying beyond the limit of excavation (at the 50 m N grid line).

All that remained of Structure 309 after subsequent demolitions and reconstructions were its western side, with adjacent portions of the rear retaining wall and front step, but the evidence suggests a platform 8.2 m by at least 7.9 m, facing south on 179° azimuth. It had been built by enclosing the stub of Structure 312 in earth fills, and retaining them with a two-course high wall faced with plaster, which at the south end kinked into a straight stretch and then curved east to form the facing of a front step or terrace, seen only as a scar. Two post holes with stone packing appear to have held supports for the front of the superstructure, lying 1.5 m inside the line of the step. No other post holes were found for this building. It is not clear whether the floor of Structure 312 was reused, or whether a new surface was laid down which was subsequently removed.

Somewhat over half of Structure 311 was excavated, and it is estimated to have been 6 by 5.4 m; only a single course of

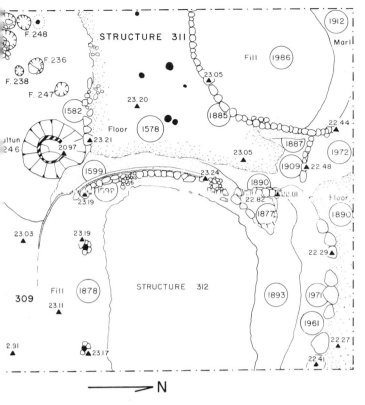

large limestones forming the retaining wall, and part of the fill survived, the internal floor and any features in it having been removed by later construction work. The retaining wall fronting the plaster area south of Structure 311, and the plaster surface abutting Structure 309, both overlay the lip of the *chultun* shaft, but since this is thought to have eroded back there is no stratigraphic import. The shaft may still have been open at this phase, although it was certainly filled in by phase VII. At the south end of the plaza, Structure 313's front step was buried by Plaza Floor II, so any building of this phase must have stood further south. In the pyramid sequence, Structure 353 or the first stage of Structure 352 is the most likely correlate with phase VI.

Phase VI is the first in which two subcircular buildings stood side by side on the north margin of the plaza atop Platform 34, an arrangement that continued until in phase XII a single structure was again built. It is of course possible that more than two buildings stood along the north side of the plaza, with Structure 309 and its successors being central, and Structure 311 and successors flanking them on the west and set slightly back. Phase VI is also the first in which no structure at the south end lies within the excavated area of the Main Trench; although excavations beyond the trench in that direction were limited to superficial deposits, there is no surface or other indication that any building existed there

facing on to the plaza. The pottery from phase VI was of the middle facet of the Cocos Chicanel ceramic complex; there are no radiocarbon dates for this phase (unless Structure 353 belongs here: see phase VA datelist).

Phase VII (Fig. 3.12) Plaza Floor III at 23.28 m elevation, like its predecessor, survived only in the southern part of the trench as (1179), with a cache of two Sierra Red bowls [F181] in the subfloor fill. The floor was cut by a deep vertical-sided pit [F208] of unknown purpose, 1.7 m in depth and 0.78 m diameter, with a smashed pot near the bottom and fragments of human bone from an adult male further up in the sandy fill. The pit lay in the south section, so was only half excavated. Set into the plaza floor over the location of the mass burial of phase V was a cache of 39 deer mandibles and over 300 teeth [F140], laid in a circular area in two strata (see Chapter 10).

The major construction of phase VII was the replacement of Structure 311 by Structure 310, another building on the same site and extending over part of the paved area to the south. Much of the structure had been razed, but the northern side was fairly well preserved, and an apsidal plan 8.15 by 4.7 m, facing southeast onto the remaining paved area, can be proposed. It is also possible that the detached wall fragment (1833) by the western section is not part of Structure 310, in which case the latter would seem to have been a subcircular building similar to its precursor.

The most notable feature of the building was the number of burials packed into its interior at the north end: nine were excavated, none with a clear grave cut, indicating that they might have been laid in the fill when the building was constructed. The floor above and the tops of the graves were removed by later construction, making the point moot. The burials were of both sexes and included several children. The accompanying vessels, almost all of Sierra Red and Society Hall Red types, were of the middle facet of the Cocos Chicanel ceramic complex; there were no radiocarbon dating samples from this phase, in which Structure 309 continued in use.

Phase VIII (Fig. 3.13) Plaza Floor IV at 23.38 m elevation was preserved over much of the excavated area, although worn away in the South Square and with the ballast below showing through in patches elsewhere. On the west, in front of Structure 306, the floor was slightly higher than in front of Structure 308, the two areas being divided by a curving line of stones running southwards from the southwest angle of the latter building. Four firepits lay east of the stones and almost parallel to them: [F17, 22, 214, 267] ranged from 0.3 to 0.7 m diameter and 0.2 to 0.4m deep. The largest, [F17], had two periods of use and infill; from the earlier use charcoal gave a radiocarbon age of 90 b.c.

Both earlier Structures, 309 and 310, were replaced, with Structure 306 on the west directly over the north end of 310

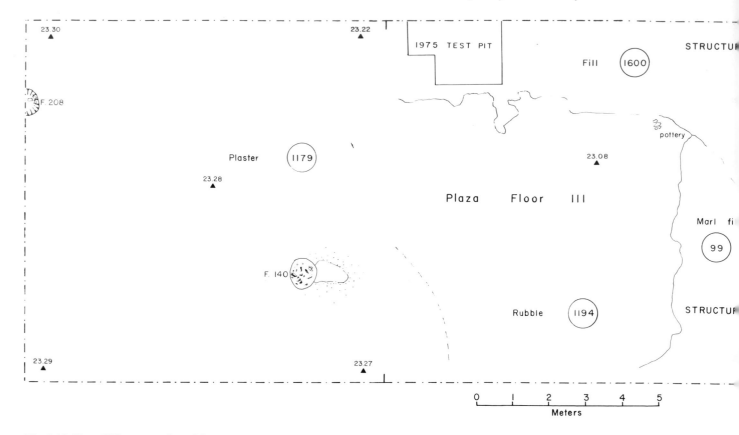

Fig. 3.12 Phase VII construction of Structure 311 and Plaza Floor III.

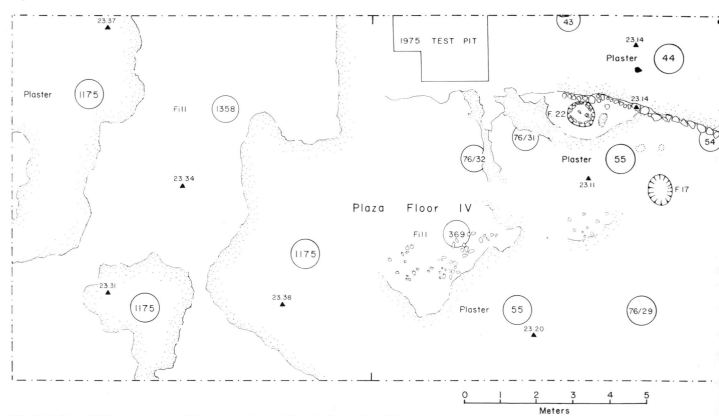

Fig. 3.13 Phase VIII construction of Structures 306 and 308 with Plaza Floor IV.

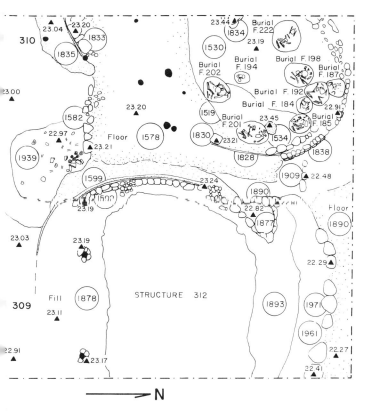

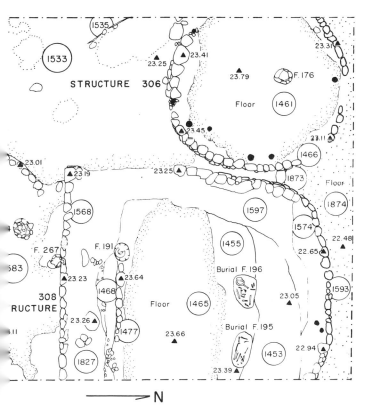

and Structure 308 using most of 309 as its core. The two buildings almost touched, and were linked by a single large stone block forming a step down to a plaster-paved area running behind both of them.

Structure 308 had a straight front facing almost due south on azimuth 177°, turning a right-angle into the west side, which ran back, also straight, before curving into an apsidal rear retaining wall supporting marl fills. Two burials [F195–196] were inserted into these, both of adult males but only one accompanied by a vessel. The internal floor survived only in the center; in its fill was a dedicatory cache [F191], of a single bowl. The overall length of the building from north to south was 7.6 m, and its width at least 6.4 m, with the interior floor 0.5 m above the plaza floor in front and the front terrace about 0.15 m higher than the plaza.

Structure 306 was about 5 m in diameter, almost all of it lying within the excavation and much of the internal floor surviving over a thick fill containing a dedicatory cache [F177] of a bowl. Several post holes around the perimeter suggested a circular superstructure following the line of the wall, with an entry to the south marked by large threshold slabs. Near the center of the floor was a stone-lined pit [F176].

Phase VIII saw the continuation of paired buildings on the north side of the plaza, with the eastern being the larger and set further forward, with a series of firepits in the plaza floor in front of it. Burials were found only in the eastern structure, although both had dedicatory caches. The pottery was of the middle facet of Cocos Chicanel, and firepit [F17] yielded the one radiocarbon determination of 90 b.c. (106–1 B.C.).

Phase IX (Fig. 3.14) Plaza Floor V at *c.* 23.40 m elevation was laid, eroded mostly down to its fill except west of Structure 307, and with no features in its surface. Structure 306 continued in use, with a renewed internal floor and several post holes suggesting a rebuilt superstructure. Structure 307 was laid out over 308, with a similar plan but skewed further to the southwest on azimuth 193° and with a broad squared front terrace 6.2 m wide and 3 m deep. The central portion of the building was also rectangular, 6.2 m wide and *c.* 4.4 m from front to rear, raised about 0.5 m above plaza level. Behind it was an apsidal-walled area of fills dropping almost a meter to the plaster-paved area behind. The three concentric bands of fills detected may have each been walled to form tiered terraces like those on the rear of Structure 350 in a later phase. The overall length of Structure 307 was 10.8 m. The interior floor of the main portion was cut by a cached skull of a 3–4-year-old child between two bowls, and by burial 90 [F158] of a young adult accompanied by two vessels, sealed by a patch in the floor, which continued in use. Adjacent to the east side of the front terrace was a deep pit (76/38) filled with charcoal and sherds, which coincidentally or otherwise was directly over the doorway of the buried Structure 315d.

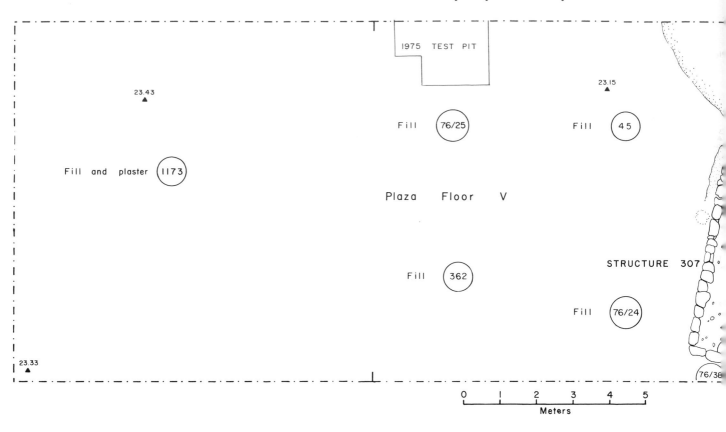

Fig. 3.14 Phase IX construction of Structure 307 and Plaza Floor V.

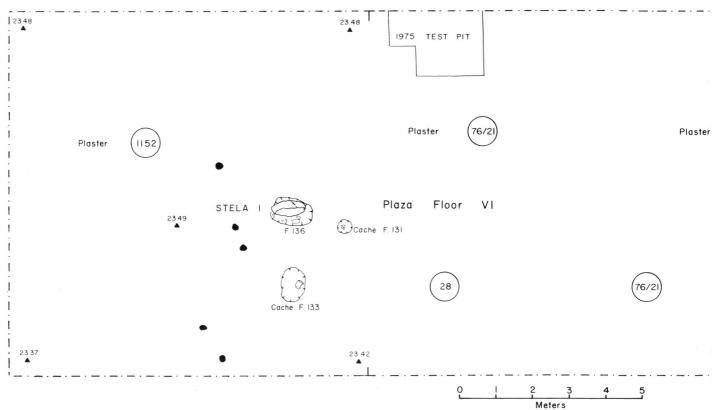

Fig 3.15 Phase X remodeling of Structure 307, with Plaza Floor
VI. The pit for Stela 1, dug into the floor in the following phase, is
shown.

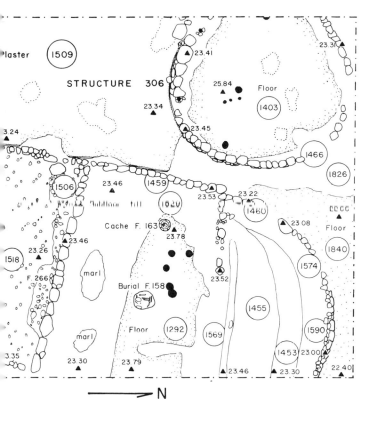

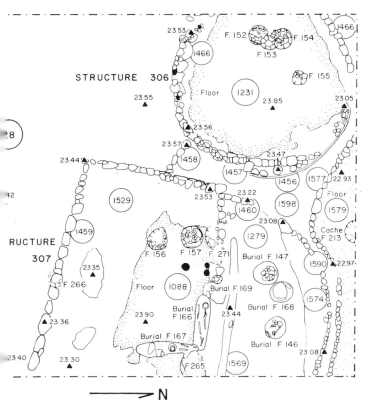

Phase IX saw the reorientation of the building on the east from azimuth 179° to 193°, with the construction of Structure 307 (the threshold of Structure 306 is too broad for a precise orientation to be discerned). The terrace of Structure 307 was the furthest extent that the northern buildings encroached on the plaza area. Structure 306 was refurbished. On the west side of the plaza, Structure 351 may have existed at this phase. Pottery is still of the middle facet of Cocos Chicanel, and no radiocarbon samples were dated.

Phase IXA The northern part of the plaza floor was resurfaced.

Phase X (Fig. 3.15) Plaza Floor VI was laid at *c.* 23.49 m elevation, surviving as a hard surface over most of the excavated area. Within its earth fill was found a cache of deer mandibles [F30] in two layers. An obsidian blade fragment from the fill, from the San Martin Jilotepeque source, yielded a hydration date of 952–760 B.C., equivalent to a radiocarbon date of *c.* 740 b.c., too early for the context and hence presumably redeposited from earlier occupation material (as the mixture of accompanying ceramics going back to Lopez Mamom times suggests). The floor was laid at its northern end against the frontages of Structures 306 and 307, burying both the former surface outside 306 and the front terrace of 307. The floor ended at a row of stones joining the two buildings, behind which the surface stepped down to the north. In the lower area behind the buildings a line of stones, following a sinuous curve that left a narrow gap between it and their rear portions, retained fill surfaced by a plaster floor that continued north beyond the section. The floor was cut by cache [F213], of two bowls containing a jade bead.

Structure 306 was refloored, and the floor cut by four firepits [F152–155], lined with sherds from several vessels instead of the base of a single bowl or jar, as had been usual previously. Structure 307 was also refloored, and cut by three firepits [F156, 157, 271], another pit [F265] sealed with a plaster patch and cut by the east section, which may be the end of a grave, and by six burials, three in the central section and three in the rear fills. They were of adults of both sexes, with one very young child, and included individuals in supine, crouched, and seated positions.

The pottery of phase X is of the middle facet of Cocos Chicanel; the only date, from a redeposited obsidian blade, is not relevant.

Phase XI (Fig. 3.16) At the beginning of this phase several features were cut into Plaza Floor VI, before the laying down of Plaza Floor VII at *c.* 23.60 m elevation. Among these were two caches, [F131] and [F133], one a single vessel, the other a pair containing jade beads. One lay north, the other east of a pit [F136], cut to hold the butt of Cuello Stela 1, a plain stone

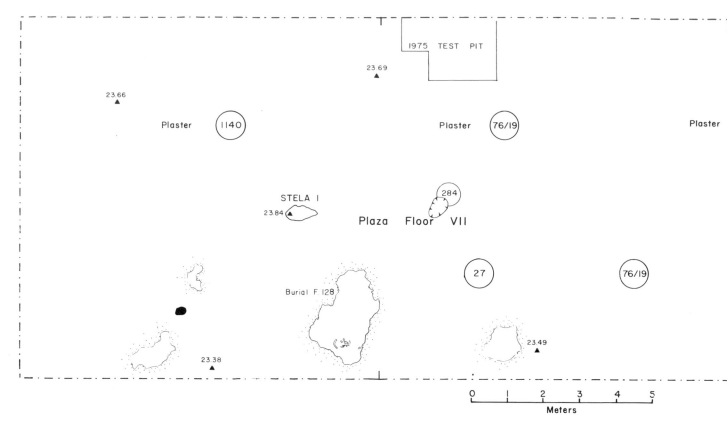

Fig. 3.16 Phase XI construction of Structures 304–305, with Plaza Floor VII coeval with Stela 1 and mass burial [F128].

slab some 0.8 m high. Three vessels and a jade bead were placed into the pit, and the stela was packed around with rubble fill (which did not prevent it from slumping to the south after a short period). Both stela and caches were above the locus of the mass burial of phase V, and [F133] was almost directly above the cache of deer mandibles [F140] of phase VII. A soil layer below the new plaza floor contained charcoal that yielded a radiocarbon age of 175 b.c. Plaza Floor VII included in its fill a dedicatory cache [F27], of three bowls, two containing a jade bead. East of the stela a subrectangular cut into the floor contained Mass Burial 2, burials 68–79 [F128], with a total of 15 individuals represented, most of them fragmentary; 13 were male, two of undetermined sex. The placing of skull/long bones packages in the laps of the completed individuals may indicate the deposition of ancestor bundles. Four large bowls accompanied the burial.

Plaza Floor VII abutted the south side of a new building on the north side of Platform 34, Structure 305 built over 307. A similar orientation, on azimuth 196°, was preserved, but the front terrace of Structure 305 was further north than its precursor, in line with the projecting front entry of Structure 304 to the west; this new building overlay Plaza Floor VII and was thus built slightly later.

The front of Structure 305 was almost straight, but with a slight curve increasing towards the corners; the front terrace extended further out than the sides of the main portion, which also had bowed sides and rounded corners, with an apsidal back, giving total dimensions of 6.2 by 5.6 m. A cache [F162] of two vessels containing a jade bead was put in the core of the step, and another [F143] of a bowl inverted over a child's skull into the southwest corner of the main platform. Structure 305 had two stages, the floor of the first of which was cut by two firepits [F126, 264]. Three burials [F132, 137, 141] in the fill at the rear of the building had no clear grave cuts, and could have been put in at the time of construction, or simply backfilled with the same fill into which they had been dug. One was of a woman, the others of children. The second-stage floor was cut by six firepits [F114–119] used sequentially, two caches [F111, 120] – the latter possibly discarded pottery rather than an offering – and two more interments, burials 63 and 66 [F112, 125]. The former was of a child, the latter a robust male with a large "champagne bucket" deep bowl inverted over his head, and a second, smaller vessel in the extended hand (Fig. 10.9).

Structure 304 had three stages of construction, expanding from 4.7 by 5 m to 6 by 5 m. In the first it had only a small step projecting from the straight south front, while by the third this was as wide as the main part of the building. The first stage had a dedicatory cache of two vessels in the subfloor fill,

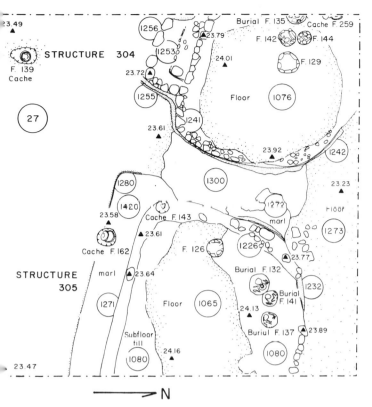

and the floor was cut by three firepits [F129, 142, 144] and burial 83 [F135], of an adult male with severe treponemal infection, seated and with an accompanying vessel. Two of the three firepits had been covered over with marl.

In the second stage the front step of Structure 304 was enlarged out over Plaza Floor VII, to a width of 2.4 m and a depth of 1.1 m. The third stage was a lateral addition of 0.7 m, bringing the side of the step in line with the side wall of the platform. At the same time the internal floor was renewed, to be subsequently cut by three burials, 64, 81, and 85 [F121, 134, 138]; the first was of a child, the last of an adult male, and burial 81 contained the skeletons of two adult females, facing partly towards each other and one with her left arm around the other. Each grave had one pottery vessel.

Phase XI saw more effort put into careful construction than before: Plaza Floor VII was laid at an even 23.6 m, with dedicatory caches and a stela associated with its construction. If Mass Burial 2 is central to Platform 34, in the way that the phase V Mass Burial 1 lay over the center of the courtyard, then Platform 34 would be some 43 m from north to south at this phase (and perhaps retained on the south by walls (672–3) in grids 10/25–30). On the north side of the plaza Structures 304 and 305 were side by side, the former not much smaller than the latter, and with their frontages on the same line by the middle of the phase. The lack of post holes for both means that the possibility of their being unroofed must be entertained,

although nothing else suggests that they are any different from their precursors. The pottery of this phase is now of the late facet of Cocos Chicanel, which persists until the end of the Platform 34 sequence and the construction of Structure 35 after A.D. 250. One radiocarbon age is available to date this period (175 b.c., 349–96 B.C.).

Phase XII (Fig. 3.17) A cache [F139], of a single vessel, was placed in a hole dug into Plaza Floor VII before the laying of Plaza Floor VIII over it at *c.* 23.67 m elevation, in most places directly on the preceding floor, but in the center over a thin ballast. Most of the surface of Plaza Floor VIII was eroded except close to or under later construction. Stela 1 was the only visible feature in the plaza.

A new construction, Structure 303, covered both Structures 304 and 305, with a straight front wall facing south on azimuth 192° spanning the width of the trench and a thick marl fill up to 1.3 m deep at the rear raising its surface 0.4 m above the plaza. The surface has not survived, so the nature of its superstructure, if any, remains unknown, as do its length and breadth.

Phase XII thus involved a simplification of the layout on top of Platform 34, with one large northern structure instead of two smaller ones. Structure 351 was probably in existence on the west side of the plaza by this date, the first building to be of more than modest height; it stood some 4 m higher than its precursor, Structure 352, with a massive fill of limestone blocks. The frontage was removed in the next phase, but post holes on the top surface indicate a perishable superstructure. No burials or caches, except [F139], and [F71] and [F100] as dedicatory offerings in the fill of Structure 351, are associated with phase XII, and there are no radiocarbon dates for it. The pottery is of the late facet of Cocos Chicanel.

Phase XIIA–B Plaza Floor VIII was renewed at the south end of the excavated area by thin floors of 0.04 and 0.02–0.07 m. The major construction, in phase XIIA, was Structure 302, a rectangular platform 5.6 by 5.4 m with a western projection 2.5 m wide and 1.2 m deep, founded on Plaza Floor VIII and abutted by the renewals of phase XIIA and B. On the assumption that the western projection was a stair, the structure faced almost due west on azimuth 280° Total demolition in phase XIV, leaving only the rubble fill and a few blocks of the retaining wall, together with plaster edges turned up against the wall lines, means that little can be said about the structure. The location of Stela 1 in the angle between the main platform and the western stair suggests that this was still visible and respected.

The construction of Structure 302 in the center of the plaza is the first time that any building had stood in that location. It was parallel with Structure 303 to the north, and faced

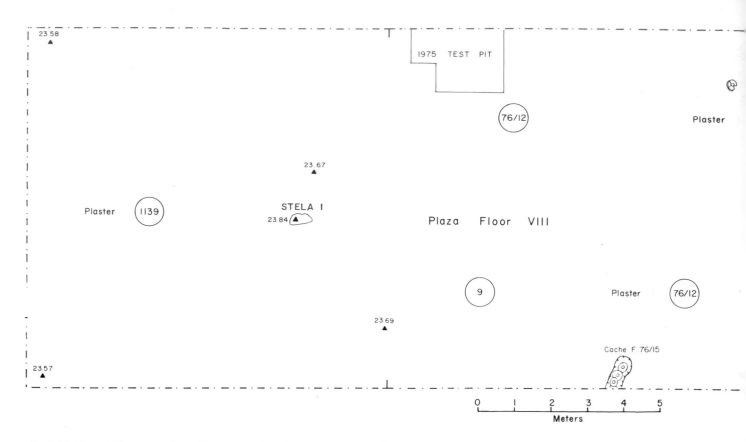

Fig. 3.17 Phase XII construction of Structure 303 and Plaza Floor VIII. Caches dug into the floor before the laying of Plaza Floor IX are shown, as (phases XIII–XIV) dug into Structure 303. Structure 302, built over Plaza Floor VIII in phase XIIA, is shown on the phase XIII plan.

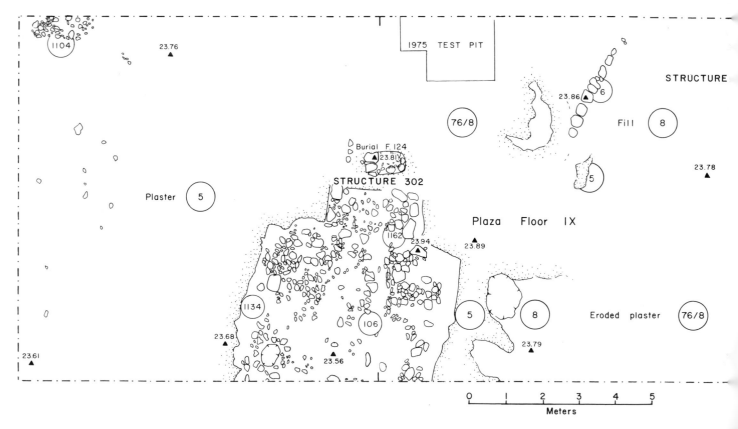

Fig. 3.18 Phase XIII construction of Structures 300–301, with Structure 302 present from the previous phase and adjoined by burial [F124]. Plaza F the pyramid Structure 350 west of the Main Trench.

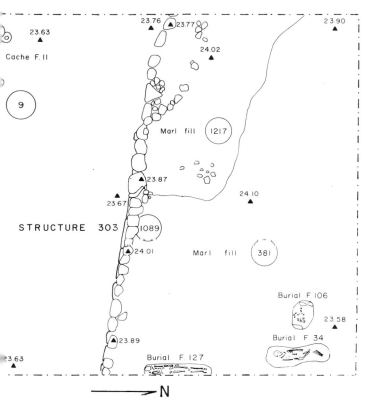

later burials

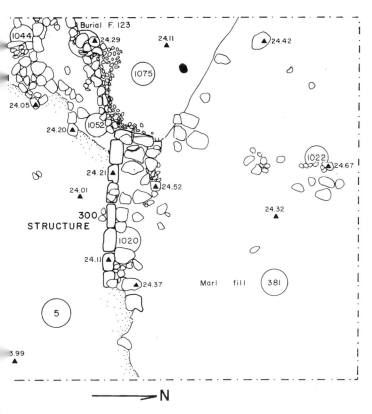

coeval with

towards the pyramid, initially Structure 351 and then in phase XIII Structure 350.

Phase XIII (Fig. 3.18) A cache [F122] was cut through the phase XIIB floor in front of Structure 302 and consisted of two vessels set lip-to-lip. 4.5 m north of Structure 302 and parallel to it another cache (76/15) was set into the floor. A third cache, [F11], to the northwest was not connected with Structure 302, but appeared to be dedicatory to Plaza Floor IX. A firepit [F130] was constructed in the floor fill during the construction process, and Stela 1 was finally buried by the new floor, with its surface at 23.9 m elevation. At the west end of Structure 302 a grave [F221] was cut through the floor and a stone-slab crypt constructed for a crouched burial of an adult male.

Over and in front of Structure 303 was built Structure 300, of which only a short length of wall of well-cut limestone blocks survived, running for 4.3 m almost due east-west. A double row of stones ran south of west from it, broken by burial 65 [F123], which seemed to be associated with a slightly later building, Structure 301. This was a south-facing apse, very similar in plan to [F9] and [F19], excavated outside the Main Trench just to the west; its footings were cut through Plaza Floor IX, and an external projection of flat stones on the southeast may have been a step. All internal features except the burial had vanished. Burial 19 [F34] in the fill of Structure 300 seems to be of this phase.

Plaza Floor IX runs a short distance under the plaster surfacing of the pyramid, Structure 350, and terminates, indicating that pyramid and plaza were part of the same planned construction. Structure 350 consisted of three substantial terraces at the front, flanking an outset stair facing south of east on azimuth 97°, with similar terraces at the sides curving at the rear corners into a set of semicircular concentric terraces on the west. These may have exercised a bracing function, similar to the stepped apsidal rear portions of the earlier Structures 307–309 on the north side of the plaza, but their complete form is unknown because they were partly ripped out when Structure 35 was built. The stone-walled superstructure of Structure 350, visible only as a scar on the top floor, was destroyed at the same time. The walls were only 0.2 m thick, a single course of masonry, and the roof must have been of perishable materials, either a pitched thatch or a flat span of beams with plaster covering. The remains of Structure 351 formed the bulk of the core of Structure 350, with a dedicatory cache [F57] laid in the top of the earlier structure before the later was built.

The appearance of multiple-vessel caches for the first time, with [F11] and (76/15) both containing eight, suggests that some of the other large caches in Platform 34, outside the area of the Main Trench, belong also to phase XIII. The largest of these, [F6] in grid 25/50, contained 94 vessels, set in lip-to-lip

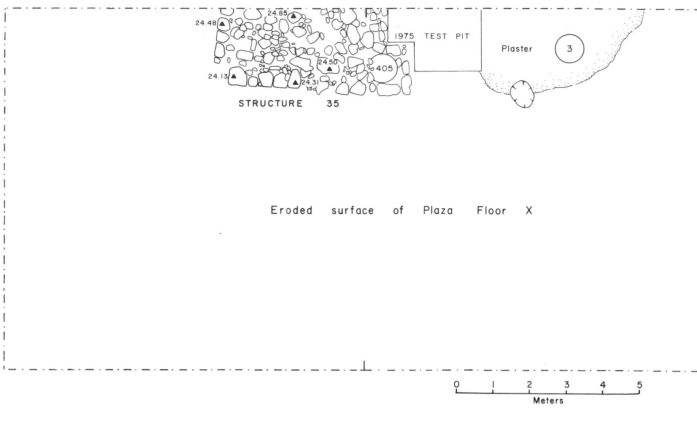

24.48 24.85

1975 TEST PIT

Plaster (3)

24.50

24.13 405

24.31

STRUCTURE 35

Eroded surface of Plaza Floor X

0   1   2   3   4   5
Meters

Fig. 3.19 Phase XIV (Early Classic) construction, with the stair of Structure 35 projecting into the excavation area and abutted by Plaza Floor X, which buries the remains of Structure 302 and abuts Structure 300.

pairs, often in clusters of eight (Figs. 10.13–10.14). The pyramid, Structure 350, was coeval with Plaza Floor IX, and is the first of the pyramid sequence buildings to be known other than in section and as a small area of floor; it is described in the chapter dealing with architecture. North of it the two apsidal structures [F19] and Structure 301 lay parallel, with Structure 300 to the east of them. In front of the stair of the pyramid was Structure 302: the buildings of phase XIII were much more closely packed together than at any previous time in the history of Platform 34. This Terminal Formative phase may well be when the plazuela group on the northern side of Platform 34 came into existence, with the stone substructures [F2] and [F3] facing each other across a patio, and the flimsier [F23] on the south side. The date of the cache [F5] buried below the center of the patio floor would support such a date, or one in either of the preceding phases. Although complex Late Formative activities occurred in the eastern part of Platform 34, including several ephemeral buildings and the digging of a *chultun* [F87], which was then converted into a Puuc-type cistern by the addition of a catchment floor before

being filled with trash (giving a radiocarbon age of 100 b.c.), they cannot be correlated with the stratigraphic sequence in the Main Trench with any precision.

Phase XIV (Fig. 3.19) The final surface of Platform 34, Plaza Floor X, was laid down, with a cache [F113] of two vessels enclosing a jade bead buried in its fill at the north end. Structure 302 was demolished to its foundations, and the few projecting blocks were covered by the floor. This survives in few places, but appears to have been about 0.2 m thick, with a surface at *c.* 24.1 m elevation, rising to the west. The floor buried Structure 301 and abutted Structure 300; west of the main trench [F9], another apsidal building overlay [F19]. Early Classic burials 61 and 67 [F106, 127] were inserted into Structure 300's fill, and a cluster of firepits there (in grid 35/ 45: not on Fig. 3.19) may be of either phase XIII or XIV.

The major construction was of the Early Classic pyramid, Structure 35, over Structure 350, with a long eastern stair projecting into the area of excavation on azimuth 103°. Parts of the stair were sectioned in 1975 and 1976, and the entire construction was removed in 1979 when Structure 35 was dismantled to expose Structure 350 (except in the southwest quadrant, where Structure 35 remains). The pyramid was badly eroded, but in its summit was found a cache [F18], of the skull of a child (burial 13), with a bowl inverted over it, dating it to the beginning of the Early Classic period.

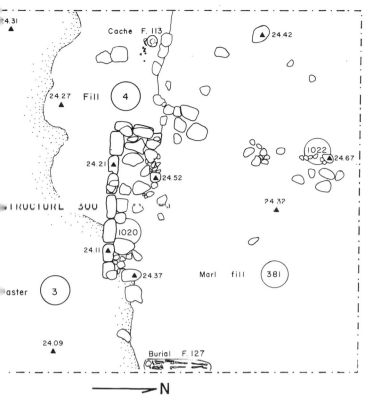

——→N

The Structure 35 sequence While the stratigraphic sequence within Structure 35 (Fig. 3.20) cannot be precisely correlated with that of the Main Trench (Figs. 3.21–3.24), in spite of the short distance separating the excavations (*c.* 6 m from the west section of the Main Trench to the east trench through the pyramid), some possible links have been noted above. The 9 m depth of deposit in the east pyramid trench does, however, constitute a clear stratigraphic succession of seven buildings, of which the latest, Structure 35 of phase XIV and Structure 350 of phase XIII, were almost completely excavated. Those earlier in the sequence are known only in cross-section and in the small areas of floor exposed in the 4 by 2 m east pyramid trench, together with the constructions sectioned in the west trench (most of which belong to Structures 35 and 350).

Structure 355, the earliest in the sequence, stood on the buried land surface, and consisted of a plaster-faced retaining wall, with pre-Lopez Mamom pottery in the fill and a mixture of pre-Lopez and Lopez in the buildup against its western side. On these grounds alone, correlation with Structure 314 of phase IVA is possible, and would indicate that the structures of phases II–IV did not extend this far west. Floor (784), over a fill on the truncated surface of Structure 355, would then equate with Plaza Floor I, and it is possible that the lower tier retaining wall (216) in the western trench is the western boundary of Platform 34. The second tier (216a) is of a height to retain the west side of Structure 354, which is at a markedly

higher elevation than its precursor, consonant with forming part of the new architectural ensemble of Platform 34. The Cocos Chicanel ceramic dating for Structure 354 agrees with this, and the building could be as early as phase VA, coeval with Structure 312 on the north side of the plaza. The single stage of Structure 353 and the three of Structure 352 would then correlate in some way with the succession of remodeled subcircular buildings, Structures 311–307, on the north. The first high stepped pyramidal stage, Structure 351, would be coeval either with a late stage of Structures 306–307 in phase X, with the new pair of buildings, Structures 304–305 of phase XI, and also with Stela 1 in the plaza, or with the construction of a single long building, Structure 303, on the north side in phase XII. For all of these structures in the pyramid sequence, the ripping-out of their eastern frontages for the construction of Structure 351, and the virtual stripping of that building to provide a solid core for Structure 350, creates a stratigraphic breach that renders more detailed estimates otiose. The correlation of Structure 350 with phase XIII and 35 with phase XIV is, however, firm.

Subsequent remodeling of the east front of Structure 35 included the placing of large blocks of fill against the façade; the sherds in these fills, derived from middens, initially indicated that this remodeling took place early in the Late Classic period, *c.* A.D. 600–700. AMS radiocarbon dates on animal bone from these final modifications to the frontage of Structure 35, and from occupation around [F3], place the episode in the twelfth century and the Postclassic, however, and indicate that Cuello was occupied rather than merely visited at this period, although no recognizable Postclassic dwellings or pottery were found apart from the deposition after A.D. 1200 of a Late Postclassic effigy incensario (Hammond 1979: Fig. 1.9), which was either thrown down the back of the pyramid or fell there as the result of erosion.

From *c.* A.D. 400 onwards, however, the Platform 34 locus was not the focus of activity at Cuello, although dwellings may have stood on the convenient elevation and burials taken place, such as [F24] of the late Early Classic. The center of Cuello lay in the Classic period ceremonial precinct some 300 m to the northeast, where occupation persisted from the Early to the Terminal Classic, so far as the results of limited test excavation can show.

RADIOCARBON CHRONOLOGY
Norman Hammond

The radiocarbon chronology for Cuello has undergone several drastic changes over the past 15 years. The initial dates from 1975 Op. 17B, from the Cambridge (Q) and Los Angeles

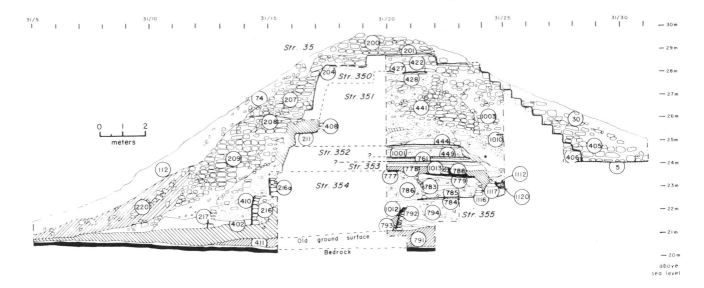

Fig. 3.20 Section through Structure 35 and its precursors: the north sections of the western and central trenches are shown. Although these do not link with the Main Trench, floor (5) is continuous across the hiatus (see Fig. 3.22) and the 24-m elevation is marked on the Main Trench sections (Figs. 3.21–3.24).

(UCLA) laboratories, suggested a span of 2000–200 b.c. (Hammond, Pring, *et al.* 1976), a finding corroborated and amplified by the dates from 1976 (Hammond, Donaghey, *et al.* 1977); while the Middle Preclassic affiliations of even the earliest (Swasey phase) pottery were recognized (Hammond 1975c: 206), the total of 24 dates, 18 of them acceptably correlated with the stratigraphy and between the two laboratories, was so much greater than the sum of dates from all other Maya Lowland Preclassic sites (most of which had produced only a single date) that we felt the radiocarbon chronology had to be given precedence over the conventional guesswork chronology for the Middle Preclassic that had been in place since the excavation of Uaxactun (Smith 1955), and the Swasey phase was thus assigned to the Early Preclassic which conventionally preceded 900 B.C. The clear lack of similarity between Swasey pottery, ancestral to the later lowland Preclassic tradition, and Early Preclassic pottery from the Pacific drainage of Guatemala and Chiapas, and from the Gulf Coast of Mexico to the west, could with some plausibility be ascribed to divergent cultural trajectories and distinct origins for the several second-millennium ceramic traditions documented in eastern Mesoamerica (Pring 1977a).

The 1978–80 excavations, using the same field and laboratory techniques, the same key personnel, and the Cambridge laboratory, but this time with the additon of dating from the La Jolla (LJ) laboratory instead of that at UCLA, yielded an utterly contrasting suite of dates (Linick 1984). The two laboratories still agreed with each other, but the Swasey phase, placed between 2000 and 1000 b.c. on the 1975–76 samples, now yielded dates from 800 to 400 b.c. Some dates were stratigraphically inverted, but in the main they formed a solid block with overlapping standard error margins, statistically inseparable from one another, and also overlapping the conventional dates for the Mamom and even the initial Chicanel periods. No overall explanation for the phenomenon has been forthcoming, although Andrews and Hammond (1990) suggest that recycling of charcoal from older occupations into later deposits could explain some of the dates; this, however, would also entail acceptance of an early second-millennium occupation at Cuello for which no other evidence survives.

The 1978–80 dates together defined, although much less coherently than their predecessors, a "short" chronology for Cuello entirely within the first millennium b.c., in contrast with the "long" chronology of the 1975–76 dates. The "short" chronology, placing Cuello back within the conventional bounds of the Middle Preclassic, agreed with the criticisms of Coe (1980: 34–5) and Marcus (1983, 1984), and, more importantly, with the exhaustive comparative study of Middle Preclassic site sequences carried out by Andrews (1990) in the mid-1980s. Steps had already been taken in 1984 to try and determine which, if either, of the contrasting chronologies was correct, by carrying out direct AMS dating of the inhabitants of Cuello themselves; the first two dates (OxA-361, 362) were run on crude bone collagen and yielded ages in the mid-first millennium b.c. In both cases too recent a date, as the result of low collagen content in the bone, was suspected by the laboratory, although OxA-362 was nevertheless archaeologically acceptable on the "short" chronology. Subsequently it was found that allowance for contamination, especially of OxA-361, by consolidants applied to the bones during excavation, had been inadequate and OxA-361 has been discarded and replaced by OxA-1649 and 2103 (Housley *et al.* n.d.; Law *et al.* n.d.).

A second approach was made by direct AMS dating of a corn kernel, from the phase IA context 35/30(813); this date (AA-458) was archaeologically acceptable on the "short" chronology. Further AMS dating of human skeletal collagen was undertaken at Oxford from 1987 onwards, using gelatin refined from collagen, and also ion-exchanged gelatin and purified amino-acids derived from the gelatin (Housley *et al.* n.d.; Law *et al.* n.d.). These methods allowed the impact of contaminants such as consolidants to be appraised, and yielded several comparable dates from a single bone sample. The AMS dates all support a modified "short" chronology in which the Swasey phase begins *c.* 1000 b.c./1200 B.C.

There are now some 80 radiocarbon dates for Cuello, obtained from five laboratories: three conventional systems (Cambridge (Q), Los Angeles (UCLA), La Jolla (LJ), and the dedicated AMS dating systems at Tucson (AA) and Oxford (OxA). These are listed by stratigraphic phase in Table 3.1, with the distinction between the pre- and post-1977 batches for each phase marked. While the question of cause remains unanswered, this is not the place in which to pursue it further: in this book the modified "short" chronology with a beginning to the documented Cuello occupation *c.* 1000 b.c./1200 B.C. is accepted.

That acceptance is based on the AMS dates and on a number of external factors, including the lack of any corroboration for a "long" chronology from other Preclassic Maya sites excavated since 1976, the clear support for a "short" chronology in the Bolay phase dates from Colha (Valdez 1987), and the overall pattern of Preclassic ceramic sequences documented by Andrews (1990).

Table 3.1 shows all Cuello radiocarbon dates so far obtained: those found unacceptable at the time of processing are thus marked, together with OxA-361, while others, although not archaeologically acceptable in terms of the shortened site chronology adopted here, are cited alongside those now used to date Cuello. These latter, mostly from the post-1976 section for each phase, include the OxA- and AA-AMS dates, the LJ-dates and Q-dates higher than Q-1900. Some 1975–76 dates, especially for phases IVA and later, are also still acceptable: the major impact of the chronological revisions has been on the dating of phases I–IIIA, where a maximum of a millennium in radiocarbon years has had to be subtracted from the age of the Cuello deposits. None of this necessarily excludes some of the older dates from being valid remnants of a pre-sedentary occupation at the site; but they can no longer, especially in evaluation classes 2 to 4, be considered as dating the deposits from which the charcoal was recovered. This leaves a number of early dates in evaluation class 1 in limbo: unacceptable in terms of the new short chronology, but with no *a priori* technical or stratigraphic

reason to doubt them. For the moment we must remark them, and leave them.

The shortened radiocarbon chronology lacks dates for the beginning of the Cuello sequence: for phase 0, there is still only Q-1571, and phase I has never yielded samples for dating. Phase IA has AMS dates on burial 62 [F110] placing it no later than 900 B.C. and possibly as early as 1383 B.C., and an AMS date on corn of 920–770 B.C. These together suggest that the undated earlier phases should probably be placed before 1000 B.C., although pre-1976 charcoal dates for the phase are much earlier and post-1976 charcoal dates somewhat later.

Phases II and III lack AMS dates, although the obsidian date of 1209–1047 B.C. from a phase III redeposited blade fragment again suggests a late second-millennium occupation at Cuello, while two AMS dates from phase IIA indicate that Bladen could begin by 800–750 B.C., in accordance with the suggested beginning of Bolay at Colha. Several of the post-1976 phase II and III dates on charcoal also suggest a beginning after 800 B.C., although others are much later. Many of these dates fall into the mid-first millennium period where the radiocarbon calibration curve is of least use for precise dating.

The single AMS date for phase IV and the two for phase IVA are all within this period, one of them (OxA-1811) earlier than might be expected and the others with a *c.* 800–400 span that encompasses most proposed time brackets for Mamom sphere pottery. The three AMS dates for burial 10 [F7], while in excellent agreement with each other, also suggest a date of death for this sacrificed individual more than a century prior to the charcoal dates associated with the phase V event in which he met his end, although these are all from secondary contexts and the reverse relationship might be more expected. In general, however, all of the Cuello dates, from all seasons and laboratories, from phase IVA onwards tend to agree with each other and with the established conventional chronology for Mamom and Chicanel sphere occupations. We see no reason to propose a span for Lopez Mamom (phases IV–IVA) outside the 650/600–400/300 B.C. range, nor for Cocos Chicanel proper (phases VA–XIII) beginning earlier than 400 B.C. As for the two earlier periods, Bladen (phases III–IIIA) would seem to begin by 800 B.C., and possibly by 900, and to be coeval with Bolay at Colha and with the Xe sphere in the Pasión valley, both with radiocarbon dates suggesting a span from as early as 900 B.C. to as late as 500 B.C. This leaves the earliest of the Cuello ceramic complexes, Swasey (phases 0–II), closely related to Bladen and in the opinion of Andrews (1990) inseparable from it. As noted above, the AMS dates from burial 62 suggest a beginning before 1000 B.C. for phase IA, and it is this combined with the circumstantial evidence of occupation at Cuello in the twelfth century B.C. offered by obsidian date 165–2019 that leads us to propose a date of 1200/1100 B.C. for the beginning of the sedentary village at Cuello.

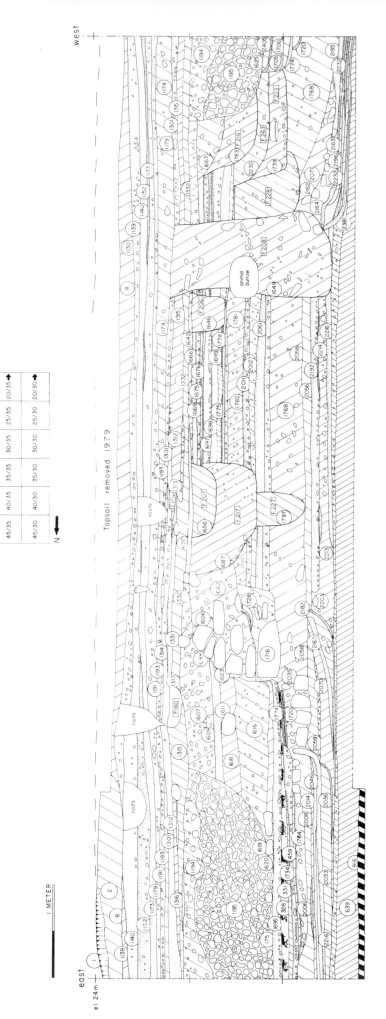

Fig. 3.21 South section of the Main Trench, showing the sequence of deposits from bedrock (916) to topsoil (1). Successive plaster floors (stippled) of phase II–IV structures and patio floors cut by the line of the section can be seen underlying the phase V rubble fill (1195); many of the floors are themselves cut by burials. Above the rubble the continuous platform floors of Platform 34 span the entire width of the section. Fig. 3.22 abuts the west end of this section at right angles.

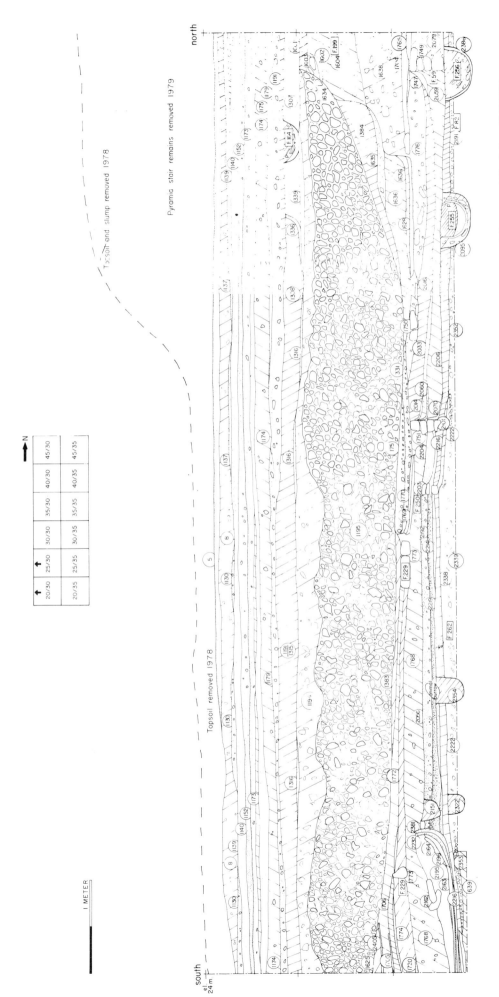

Fig. 3.22 West section of the South Square (1980): early building platforms including Structure 328 of phase I (on section as [F262] and Structure 326 of phase II [F250], and early firepits or hearths [F255–6] underlie the phase V rubble (1195) and the soil fill and plaster surfaces of successive phases of Platform 34. Deposits above floor (5) of phase XIII were excavated in previous seasons. The south end of this section adjoins Fig. 3.20.

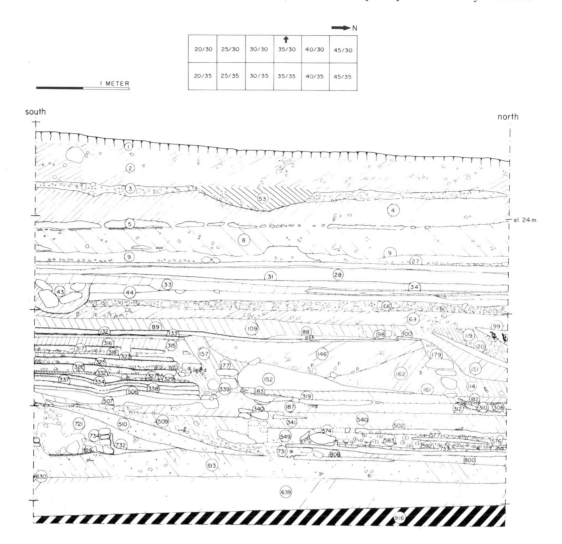

Fig. 3.23 West section of grid 35/30 in the Central Square, excavated in 1979. The successive internal floors of the buildings on the west side of the Middle Preclassic patio ((506) up through (133)) and the phase IVA northern expansion (floor (89) and wall (179)) are apparent, as is the phase V soil fill (69/109) underlying the floors of Platform 34. (43) is a firepit, (3) is a phase XIV surface of Classic period date, and (2) is an erosion deposit from the pyramid, Structure 35, immediately southwest.

CERAMIC CHRONOLOGY AND TYPOLOGY

Laura J. Kosakowsky and Duncan Pring

The Cuello excavations have yielded a ceramic sequence that begins in the late Early Preclassic (Formative) or early Middle Preclassic, and ends in the Classic period nearly two millennia later. The initial analysis of the 1975–76 ceramics by Duncan Pring (1977a), within the framework of a regional sequence for northern Belize, established the basis of the Cuello typology. The larger sample and greater stratigraphic information provided by the 1978–80 excavations allowed refinement of both the Type:variety entities and the succession of ceramic complexes defined by Pring; this work is described in Kosakowsky (1983, 1987). The 1987 sample, almost entirely from the late Middle Preclassic Lopez Mamom ceramic complex, increased understanding of that period, in particular at its transition to the Late Preclassic Cocos Chicanel complex. The Type:variety/mode method of classification commonly used in the Maya Area was employed by both analysts, within a conceptual framework little altered since the work of Sabloff (1975) and Gifford (1976). Only a summary of the ceramic sequence is given here: Pring (1977a) and Kosakowsky (1987) should be consulted for the details of Type: variety designations and descriptions, and for further illustrations of defined ceramic entities, using the same conventions as in Fig. 3.25.

Swasey The earliest ceramic complex identified at Cuello is the Swasey (Fig. 3.26), placed between 1200/1100 and 900 B.C.

Fig. 3.24 East section of the North Square, showing Late Preclassic structures excavated in 1980 and 1987. Floor (4005) is the final surface of Structure 315e of phase IVA, and (4001/1888) above it is part of Plaza Floor I of phase VA. Truncation, infill, and raising of successive structures extended the north side of Platform 34 through phase XII, before the massive deposit (381) of phase XII took the northern margin beyond the limits of excavation. The Early Classic burial 67 [F127] is the latest event visible on the section before the buildup of subsoil (2).

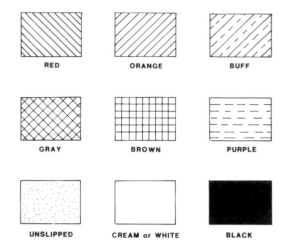

Fig. 3.25 Color conventions used in pottery drawings.

on the basis of the new Cuello chronology proposed by Andrews and Hammond (1990) and used throughout this book. Swasey pottery is found in stratigraphic phases 0–II in the Main Trench at Cuello. The origins of Swasey ceramics, while a millennium later than initially proposed (Hammond *et al.* 1976, 1979), are as obscure as they were then, with no clear derivation from either the Maya Highland zone to the south or from the Gulf Coast of Mexico to the west. Swasey pottery, while clearly ancestral to later Middle Preclassic ceramics, is most likely to have its own ancestry in the Maya Lowlands: more distant origins in lower Central America or South America now seem even more unlikely than they did a decade or so ago (Pring 1977a).

Swasey pottery is fairly simple in design, form, and execution, while being technically accomplished and in no way tentative or experimental in its manufacture. Vessel forms are most commonly bowls with vertical, slightly flaring, or recurved sides, and dishes with direct or thickened rims and squared lips (Fig. 3.27). Jars have medium-to-high outcurving necks, thickened rims, the striking Swasey square lip, and strap handles made of double or triple cylinders of clay (Fig. 3.28). Approximately 58 percent of the ceramic assemblage at any one time is composed of the monochrome red Consejo Group, with a vermilion red slip (Munsell 10R 4/8) and a pinkish, tan, gray, or white underslip. This is followed, in diminishing proportions, by the Chicago Group (orange: 29 percent), the Copetilla Group (unslipped: 9 percent) and the Machaca Group (black: 4 percent). Slips are generally slightly glossy with little crackling or crazing, with occasional fire-clouding and common rootlet erosional marks.

Of the slipped pottery, which comprises some 90 percent of the ceramic assemblage at any one time, approximately 25 percent is decorated in some fashion. This includes groove-

incising and dichrome slips, with a few examples of fine-line incising, modeling, punctation, and black smudging. Pattern-burnishing appears to be present (Fig. 3.29) on unslipped bottles similar to material found at Mani Cenote in Yucatán (Brainerd 1958), and placed by Andrews (1990) in the Middle Preclassic. It is not clear whether Swasey pottery has been identified at other sites in northern Belize, since there is typological overlap with the succeeding Bladen ceramic complex.

Bladen At Cuello the Swasey complex is succeeded by the Bladen, defined at this site and dated to approximately 900–600 B.C. (Fig. 3.30). Bladen was originally the latter part of Pring's Swasey ceramic complex, and is found in stratigraphic phases III–IIIA in the Main Trench. It includes elements closely related to Swasey pottery (Fig. 3.31), together with others paralleled in the Xe ceramic sphere of the southern Petén (Willey 1970; Adams 1971). In northern Belize the Bladen complex is closely matched by the Bolay complex at Colha, 27 km southeast of Cuello (Valdez 1987), and is marked by the appearance of cream-slipped pottery and red-on-cream decoration (Fig. 3.32) that presages the red-on-cream types of the succeeding Lopez Mamom complex. Monochrome red types continue to dominate (56 percent), with the Consejo Group now having a more consistent slip color, achieved in part by a more consistent cream or almost white underslip. Smaller proportions of the Bladen complex are taken up by the orange Chicago Group (24 percent), and the orange-brown Honey Camp Group (15 percent). The remaining 5 percent of the complex is composed of the unslipped Copetilla, black Machaca, and cream Quamina Groups. Slip colors and textures are similar to those of the preceding Swasey phase, being fairly glossy and non-waxy. Vessel forms are also similar, but with the addition of flaring-sided dishes, and the replacement of thickened rims and squared lips with direct or exterior-folded rims and round lips (Fig. 3.31). Although there is some continuation in the use of double- or triple-cylinder strap handles, they are largely replaced by loop handles with incisions, in effect mocking the earlier form. Slipped pottery has a higher (36 percent) decorated proportion, with incising, groove-incising, punctation, modeling, dichrome slips, and resist painting (Fig 3.33).

Bladen-like material has been found at Colha (the Bolay ceramic complex, assigned a span of 900–500 B.C.: Adams and Valdez 1980; Kosakowsky and Valdez 1982; Valdez 1987), Kichpanha (Valdez, personal communication), Nohmul (Hammond *et al.* 1988), El Pozito, Santa Rita Corozal, and San Estevan (Pring 1977a) in northern Belize. Pring originally placed this material in his Swasey complex, now split between Swasey and Bladen, and some of the sherds may indeed be of Swasey date: the sample from all other sites is currently too small to evaluate, and the later dating, immediately prior to

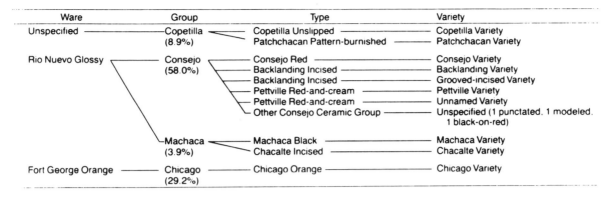

Ware	Group	Type	Variety
Unspecified	Copetilla (8.9%)	Copetilla Unslipped	Copetilla Variety
		Patchchacan Pattern-burnished	Patchchacan Variety
Rio Nuevo Glossy	Consejo (58.0%)	Consejo Red	Consejo Variety
		Backlanding Incised	Backlanding Variety
		Backlanding Incised	Grooved-incised Variety
		Pettville Red-and-cream	Pettville Variety
		Pettville Red-and-cream	Unnamed Variety
		Other Consejo Ceramic Group	Unspecified (1 punctated, 1 modeled, 1 black-on-red)
	Machaca (3.9%)	Machaca Black	Machaca Variety
		Chacalte Incised	Chacalte Variety
Fort George Orange	Chicago (29.2%)	Chicago Orange	Chicago Variety

Fig. 3.26 Pottery types of the Swasey ceramic complex (group frequency based on 360 rim sherds). (Other Consejo Group probably includes a variety of Canquin Black-on-red (Pring 1977a).)

Fig. 3.27 Characteristic bowl and dish forms of the Swasey complex.

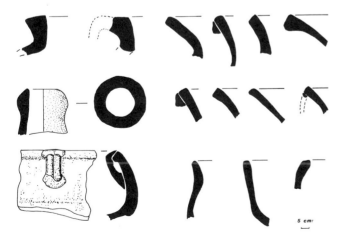

Fig. 3.28 Characteristic jar forms of the Swasey complex.

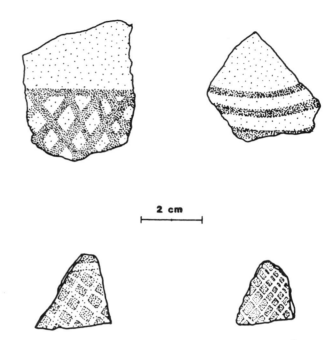

Fig. 3.29 Sherds of Patchchacan Pattern-burnished: variety unspecified, from Swasey phase levels.

the Mamom sphere occupations at all these sites, seems preferable.

The Bladen pottery shows strong parallels with Xe material from Altar de Sacrificios (Adams 1971): Consejo Red is much like Abelino Red, the earliest monochrome red at Altar, and the Huetche White defined by Adams is similar to the underslip found on many Consejo Red sherds at Cuello, which may explain the rarity of white-slipped sherds in northern Belize. The black-slipped Chacalte Incised: Chacalte variety at Cuello, with post-slip incision, is virtually indistinguishable from Chompipi Incised: Chompipi variety at Altar (Kosakowsky, personal observation).

Eb pottery from the earliest contexts at Tikal has further modal similarities with Bladen. Aac Red-on-buff at Tikal is

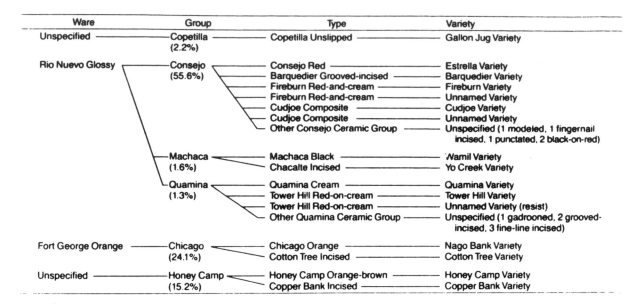

Ware	Group	Type	Variety
Unspecified	Copetilla (2.2%)	Copetilla Unslipped	Gallon Jug Variety
Rio Nuevo Glossy	Consejo (55.6%)	Consejo Red	Estrella Variety
		Barquedier Grooved-incised	Barquedier Variety
		Fireburn Red-and-cream	Fireburn Variety
		Fireburn Red-and-cream	Unnamed Variety
		Cudjoe Composite	Cudjoe Variety
		Cudjoe Composite	Unnamed Variety
		Other Consejo Ceramic Group	Unspecified (1 modeled, 1 fingernail incised, 1 punctated, 2 black-on-red)
	Machaca (1.6%)	Machaca Black	Namil Variety
		Chacalte Incised	Yo Creek Variety
	Quamina (1.3%)	Quamina Cream	Quamina Variety
		Tower Hill Red-on-cream	Tower Hill Variety
		Tower Hill Red-on-cream	Unnamed Variety (resist)
		Other Quamina Ceramic Group	Unspecified (1 gadrooned, 2 grooved-incised, 3 fine-line incised)
Fort George Orange	Chicago (24.1%)	Chicago Orange	Nago Bank Variety
		Cotton Tree Incised	Cotton Tree Variety
Unspecified	Honey Camp (15.2%)	Honey Camp Orange-brown	Honey Camp Variety
		Copper Bank Incised	Copper Bank Variety

Fig. 3.30 Pottery types of the Bladen ceramic complex (group frequency based on 1,302 rim sherds) (Other Consejo Group probably includes a variety of Canquin Black-on-red (Pring 1972a).)

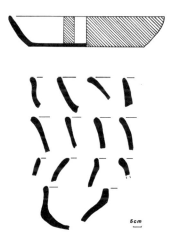

Fig. 3.31 Characteristic bowl/dish forms of the Bladen complex.

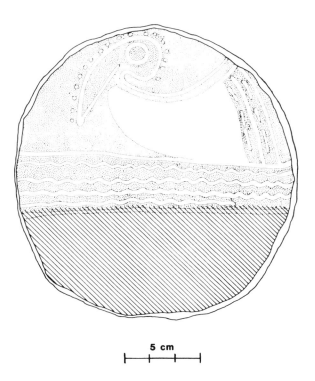

5 cm

Fig. 3.33 Tower Hill Red-on-cream: unspecified organic-resist variety (the stipple represents dark organic resist over a cream slip. This technique may continue into Lopez Mamom times.) Basal diameter 22 cm.

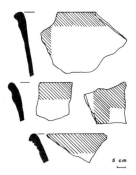

Fig. 3.32 Tower Hill Red-on-cream: Tower Hill variety (Bladen complex).

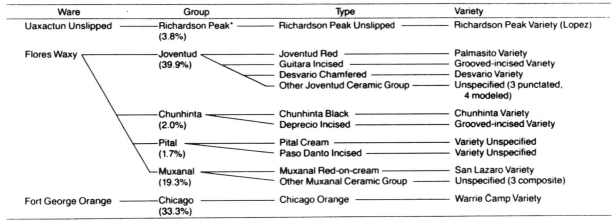

Ware	Group	Type	Variety
Uaxactun Unslipped	Richardson Peak* (3.8%)	Richardson Peak Unslipped	Richardson Peak Variety (Lopez)
Flores Waxy	Joventud (39.9%)	Joventud Red	Palmasito Variety
		Guitara Incised	Grooved-incised Variety
		Desvario Chamfered	Desvario Variety
		Other Joventud Ceramic Group	Unspecified (3 punctated, 4 modeled)
	Chunhinta (2.0%)	Chunhinta Black	Chunhinta Variety
		Deprecio Incised	Grooved-incised Variety
	Pital (1.7%)	Pital Cream	Variety Unspecified
		Paso Danto Incised	Variety Unspecified
	Muxanal (19.3%)	Muxanal Red-on-cream	San Lazaro Variety
		Other Muxanal Ceramic Group	Unspecified (3 composite)
Fort George Orange	Chicago (33.3%)	Chicago Orange	Warrie Camp Variety

*Pending comparisons with other unslipped groups of Uaxactun Unslipped Ware.

Fig. 3.34 Pottery types of the Lopez Mamom ceramic complex (group frequency based on 820 rim sherds). (Other Joventud Group probably includes a variety of Bobo Red-and-unslipped (Pring 1977a).)

similar in vessel form and slip characteristics to Consejo Red, and there is some overlap between Chicago Orange at Cuello and Calam Buff at Tikal (Culbert, personal communication).

The Bladen ceramic complex at Cuello is clearly derived from and closely related to the Swasey complex. While there are similarities to Xe sphere pottery at Altar de Sacrificios and Seibal, we tentatively place the Bladen complex in the already-defined Swasey ceramic sphere. The Bolay complex at Colha would likewise be placed in the Swasey sphere (Valdez, personal communication). The precise relationship between the Swasey and Xe spheres, and between the geographically intermediate northeastern Petén sphere of which the Eb complex at Tikal is a constituent, remains to be established. While close typological similarities are present, so are regional individualities, and the presence of slip and vessel form combinations that overlap into early Mamon sphere pottery complicate matters further. However, the same regional ceramic sphere affiliations that become more apparent in the later Middle and Late Preclassic may now be recognized back into the early Middle or late Early Preclassic.

Mamom Mamom sphere pottery appears at Cuello by *c.* 600 B.C. in the Lopez ceramic complex (Fig. 3.34). There is remarkable standardization of types and even varieties between sites in the late Middle Preclassic, and Cuello is no exception. Monochrome reds, of the Joventud Group (∼40 percent), again dominate the assemblage, with the orange Chicago Group comprising 33 percent, the red-on-cream Muxanal Group 19 percent, the unslipped Richardson Peak Group 4 percent, and the black Chunhinta and cream Pital Groups the remaining 3 percent.

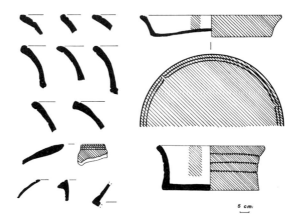

Fig. 3.35 Characteristic dish/plate forms of the Lopez Mamom complex.

Lopez complex slips are generally fairly waxy, non-glossy, thick, and soft. Fire-crackling, crazing, and fireclouding are all common. Of the slipped pottery, some 96 percent of the assemblage, about 44 percent is decorated in some way, either by groove-incising, which predominates, or by chamfering, modeling, or the use of dichrome slips. The dominant vessel form is the dish or plate with outflaring or outcurving sides, and exterior-folded or direct rim and round lip (Fig. 3.35). The dish form often has groove-incising on the interior of the everted rim, with the use of the double-line-break motif. There is an abundance of red-on-cream decoration, with plates or dishes slipped red on the interior, and cream with red dots or vertical/diagonal stripes on the exterior (Fig. 3.36), and further combinations embrace chamfering, modeling, and incision, as for example in a human face-effigy bowl (Fig. 3.37). Other forms include large numbers of thin-walled incurving bowls or *tecomates*, bottle necks (with one restorable vessel: Fig. 3.38) and ovate-sectioned spouts.

There continues to be some regional variation in the

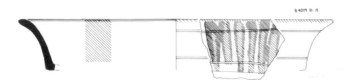

Fig. 3.36 A typical Muxanal Red-on-cream: San Lazaro variety dish of late Lopez Mamom (phase IVA) date, diameter 37 cm.

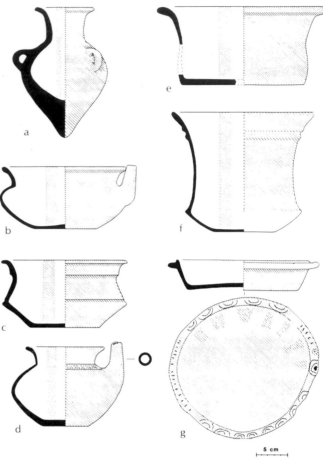

Fig. 3.37 Human effigy bowl fragment showing the use of chamfering, modeling, incision, gouging, and red-on-cream reserved painting (Muxanal Red-on-cream: San Lazaro variety, Lopez Mamom complex). The face has red stripes down the chin and a dotted area across the left forehead and cheek, perhaps reflecting body decoration of the period. Maximum length of sherd *c*. 14 cm.

Fig. 3.39 Vessel forms of the early facet (Mamom–Chicanel transition) of the Cocos Chicanel complex, from the phase V mass burial. Vessels a, b, and e are Sierra Red: Sierra variety; c and d are Sierra Red, Ahuacan variety; f is Ahchab Red-and-buff: variety unspecified, and g is Sierra Group, untyped composite.

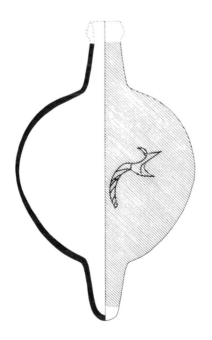

Fig. 3.38 Reconstructed bottle of Joventud Red type with incised graffito; late Lopez Mamom complex. Belly diameter 21 cm.

Mamom sphere in northern Belize: for example, at Barton Ramie in the Belize Valley, ∼100 km south of Cuello, there are different ceramic modes (Gifford 1976), while to the north at Cerros, Robertson-Freidel (1980) reports a complete absence of Mamom pottery. At closer sites such as Colha (Adams and Valdez 1980; Valdez 1987) and Nohmul (Hammond *et al.* 1988), however, the Mamom ceramics are astonishingly similar to those at Cuello.

Lopez Mamom ends at Cuello between 400 and 300 B.C., as the numerous calibrated radiocarbon dates reported earlier in this chapter demonstrate. This Mamom/Chicanel transition at Cuello includes transitional forms that share modes of both Mamom and Chicanel and is also marked by the introduction of Chicanel vessel forms retaining some of the groove-incised decoration and soft, thick, waxy slip of Mamom (Fig. 3.39). This transition, placed in the early facet of Cocos Chicanel between *c*. 350 and 250 B.C. rather than

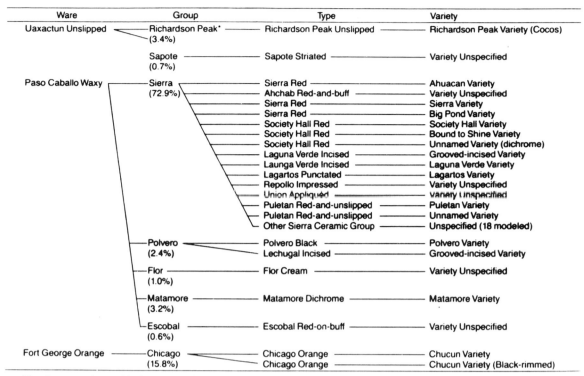

Ware	Group	Type	Variety
Uaxactun Unslipped	Richardson Peak* (3.4%)	Richardson Peak Unslipped	Richardson Peak Variety (Cocos)
	Sapote (0.7%)	Sapote Striated	Variety Unspecified
Paso Caballo Waxy	Sierra (72.9%)	Sierra Red	Ahuacan Variety
		Ahchab Red-and-buff	Variety Unspecified
		Sierra Red	Sierra Variety
		Sierra Red	Big Pond Variety
		Society Hall Red	Society Hall Variety
		Society Hall Red	Bound to Shine Variety
		Society Hall Red	Unnamed Variety (dichrome)
		Laguna Verde Incised	Grooved-incised Variety
		Launga Verde Incised	Laguna Verde Variety
		Lagartos Punctated	Lagartos Variety
		Repollo Impressed	Variety Unspecified
		Union Appliqued	Variety Unspecified
		Puletan Red-and-unslipped	Puletan Variety
		Puletan Red-and-unslipped	Unnamed Variety
		Other Sierra Ceramic Group	Unspecified (18 modeled)
	Polvero (2.4%)	Polvero Black	Polvero Variety
		Lechugal Incised	Grooved-incised Variety
	Flor (1.0%)	Flor Cream	Variety Unspecified
	Matamore (3.2%)	Matamore Dichrome	Matamore Variety
	Escobal (0.6%)	Escobal Red-on-buff	Variety Unspecified
Fort George Orange	Chicago (15.8%)	Chicago Orange	Chucun Variety
		Chicago Orange	Chucun Variety (Black-rimmed)

*Pending comparisons with other unslipped groups of Uaxactun Unslipped Ware.

Fig. 3.40 Pottery types of the Cocos Chicanel ceramic complex (group frequency based on 2,437 rim sherds).

being assigned separate complex status, is similar to the Tzec complex at Tikal, with a single date of *c.* 400 B.C., and to the late facet of the Chiwa Mamom complex at Colha (Adams and Valdez 1980; Kosakowsky and Valdez 1982; Valdez 1987) where, however, this complex, originally assigned a span of 600–250 B.C. (Valdez and Adams 1982), has now been abolished in favor of an expanded Onecimo (Chicanel) complex running from 500 B.C. to A.D. 125 and embracing the Late Middle and most of the Late Formative (Valdez, personal communication 1989). Although Robertson-Freidel (1980) reports the absence of Mamom pottery at Cerros, observation (by LJK) of the earliest Ixtabai (Chicanel) complex pottery shows some Mamom traits. It seems likely that the ceramics of northern Belize over the period from 500 to 250 B.C. are more alike than the classificatory schemes of different analysts initially suggest.

Chicanel Ceramic development continues at Cuello, and by *c.* 250 B.C. the Cocos ceramic complex is marked by the appearance of characteristic Chicanel sphere pottery as found at almost every Preclassic site in the Maya Lowlands, and with a greater standardization from site to site than in previous periods. The dominant monochrome reds of the Sierra Group comprise 73 percent of the assemblage (Fig. 3.40), the orange Chicago Group 16 percent, the unslipped Richardson Peak and striated Sapote Groups 4 percent, with the remaining 7 percent made up of the black Polvero, cream Flor, dichrome Matamore and red-on-buff Escobal Groups. Slips, slightly waxy at the beginning of the phase, become harder and glossier. Fireclouding is common. Slipped pottery comprises 96 percent of the assemblage, with 23 percent decorated; techniques have enlarged to include incising, punctation, impressing, appliqué, modeling, molding, and the use of dichrome, and towards the end even trichrome, slips. Vessel forms (Fig. 3.41–3.43) are highly variable, including bowls and deep buckets with outcurving sides, incurving bowls, composite silhouette vessels with medial and labial flanges, spouted "chocolate pot" jars, and unique forms such as the pointed-base "amphora" found only in the early facet (Fig. 3.39a) and the parrot-effigy bowl from the late facet cache below Stela 1 (Fig. 3.43b). The mammiform tetrapodal supports of the Holmul 1 style, found also at Nohmul in the Freshwater Floral Park ceramic complex (Pring 1977a, b), appear on a Sierra Group bowl (Fig. 3.44); at Cuello, as at Nohmul and in retrospect (Hammond 1984a) at Holmul, this "Protoclassic" ceramic style seems to develop within the local Late Preclassic tradition, drawing in varied decorative modes from as far away as the highland zone and using them in a series of local, usually site-specific, combinations which presage the geometric polychromes of the Early Classic.

One characteristic type that links Cuello with other north-

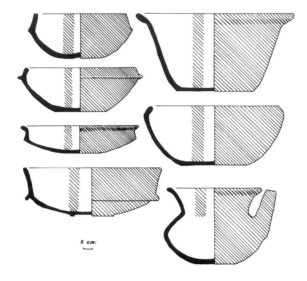

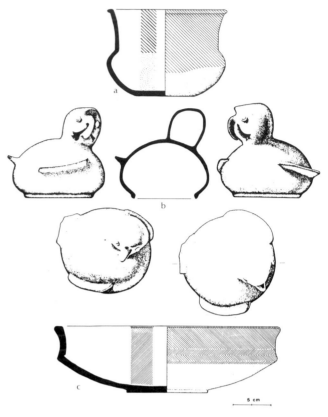

Fig. 3.41 Characteristic vessel forms of the middle and late facets of the Cocos Chicanel complex.

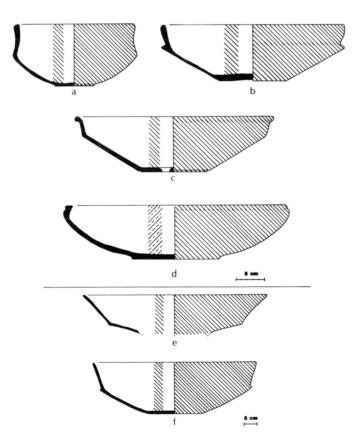

Fig. 3.42 Vessels from the Cocos Chicanel late facet (phase XI) mass burial (burials 68–79: [F128]). All except d (Matamore Dichrome: Matamore variety) are Sierra Red: Sierra variety.

Fig. 3.43 Vessels from the Cocos Chicanel late facet (phase XI) cache below Stela 1 [F136]: (a) Sierra Red: Sierra variety; (b) Sierra Group unspecified (eroded slip) with modeling; (c) Cocos complex unspecified trichrome.

ern Belize sites, and even with the Belize River, the central Petén and the Pasión River sites, is Society Hall Red. Originally designated the Society Hall variety of Sierra Red at Barton Ramie (Gifford 1976) and the Xaibe variety of Sierra Red at Cuello (Pring 1977a), it has since been defined as a type in its own right (Kosakowsky 1983, 1987). The large sample size and variability encountered in the Cuello sample, which persists throughout the Cocos phase, support this. The type is characterized by a semi-glossy streaky finish achieved by successive wipings of slip onto the vessel. Although Society Hall Red is placed in the Sierra Group, the variation of surface color is great, from brown and maroon through red to yellow-orange. By the end of the Cocos phase, c. A.D. 250, the slip colors and textures of this and other ceramic types are approaching the glossiness of Classic period ceramics.

By the end of the Cocos phase at Cuello there is a great deal of experimentation, in the use of the Society Hall wiping technique and in the introduction of dichrome and trichrome slips presaging Classic period polychromes, although technically and stylistically much less sophisticated (Fig. 3.43c). Classic period vessel forms are also introduced, including the

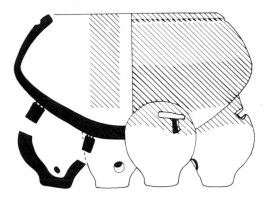

Fig. 3.44 Bowl with mammiform tetrapod supports, Cocos Chicanel late facet (Laguna Verde incised: Grooved-incised variety). Rim diameter 9.2 cm.

basal-flange bowl with ring base still using a Sierra Red slip. It seems possible that at Cuello and other northern Belize sites old traditions died hard, with Chicanel sphere pottery being made into the Classic period, while Petén communities had already embarked on the polychrome tradition. The evidence from Nohmul, Cerros, Santa Rita Corozal, Lamanai, and Colha, all major Late Preclassic centers on established trade routes, suggests that Cuello may have been a cultural backwater at the end of this period.

In sum, the identification of early Swasey sphere pottery of the Swasey ceramic complex is confined to Cuello and dated to *c.* 1200/1100–900 B.C. or slightly later. The later Swasey sphere pottery of the Bladen complex marks the beginning of known affiliations with several other sites in northern Belize, and with the northeast Petén and Pasión regions to the southwest. Broad regionalization in ceramic styles continues through this period, with increasing overall similarities beginning in the Lopez Mamom phase after 600 B.C. By 400–300 B.C., the beginning of the Cocos Chicanel complex, the Chicanel ceramic sphere is virtually homogeneous across the lowlands. By the end of Chicanel, *c.* A.D. 250, some Classic period traditions are being adopted at Cuello, but the community seems to lag behind larger and more strategically placed centers in the region. The ceramic sequence is a continuous one, showing mainly autochthonous development from still-unknown beginnings, with sufficient typological and modal links from the Bladen complex onwards to tie Cuello firmly into the established ceramic chronology of the Maya Lowlands.

Chapter 4

THE ECOLOGY AND ECONOMY OF CUELLO

THE NATURAL AND CULTURAL LANDSCAPE OF PRECLASSIC CUELLO

Charles H. Miksicek

The palaeoecology and archaeobotany research program at Cuello was designed to answer a series of questions about the relationship between environment, agriculture, and Preclassic Maya society, as exemplified by one of the earliest communities so far investigated in the lowland zone. The questions included the nature of the local gathering and farming economy, its impact on the existing biome, and the effect of climatic and environmental variability (such as that proposed by Folan *et al.* 1983 and Dahlin 1983) on that economy. The principal data acquisition methods used were the flotation of soil samples to obtain ancient plant and mollusk remains, and the collection of modern specimens of flora and mollusca to determine their ecological niches and provide comparative material.

METHODS

Over 250 flotation samples were collected for analysis during the 1978–80 seasons. Based on tests of the density of carbonized plant remains in the Cuello deposits in 1978, the sample volume was standardized at 50 liters of soil matrix. All soil samples were processed in the field using a modification of the flotation system described by Minnis and LeBlanc (1976), with a galvanized washtub fitted with a 1.6-mm screen bottom set into the top of a 52-gallon oil drum. Some preliminary sorting was carried out in the Cuello field laboratory to monitor recovery rates (see Chapter 2).

A total of 116 samples was selected for detailed analysis. Each was passed first through a series of graduated geological screens with 4.0, 2.0, and 0.5 mm mesh; this initial size-sorting increases the speed and accuracy of microscopic examination, which was carried out under a compound dissecting microscope at 10X magnification. The 116 samples together yielded over 3,200 charred seeds and >1,300 char-

Table 4.1 *Ecological association of Cuello plant remains*

Common name	Scientific name	Common name	Scientific name
Crop plants		*Forest Trees*	
Maize	*Zea mays* L.	Bribri	*Inga* spp.
Squash	*Curcurbita* sp.	Gombolimbo	*Bursera simaruba* (L.) Sarg.
Beans	*Phaseolus* sp.	Manax, Cherry	*Pseudolmedia oxyphyllaria* Donn. Sm.
Chile	*Capsicum annuum* L.	Allspice	*Pimenta dioica* (L.) Merrill
Cotton	*Gossypium hirsutum* L.	Sapodilla	*Manilkara zapota* (L.) van Royen
		Wild fig	*Ficus* spp.
Weeds and Early Successional Shrubs		Capinol	*Hymenaea courbaril* L.
Passion flower	*Passiflora* sp.		
Virgin grass	*Paspalum* sp.	Guanacaste	*Enterolobium cyclocarpum* Griseb.
Flor amarilla	Compositae	Turtlebone	*Pithecellobium* spp.
Escobilla	*Sida* sp.	Siricote	*Cordia* sp.
Tropical pokeweed	*Rivinia* sp.	Tropical cedar	*Cedrela mexicana* Roem.
Redhead, *Corallilo*	*Hamelia patens* Jacq.	*Escoba* palm	*Crysophilia argentes* Bartlett
Nightshade	*Solanum* app.		
Cojeton	*Stemmadenia* sp.	*Savanna Plants*	
Cockspur	*Acacia* sp.	Sawgrass	*Scleria* spp.
		Caribbean pine	*Pinus caribea* Morelet
Marsh Plants			
Sedge	Cyperaceae	*Economic Trees*	
Tilia	*Corchorus siliquosus* L.	Hogplum	*Spondias* spp.
Razor grass	*Cladium jamaicense* Crantz.	Nance, Crabboe	*Byrsonima* spp.
		Avocado	*Persea americana* Mill.
Early Successional Trees		Soursop	*Annona* spp.
Cordoncillo	*Piper* sp.	Guava	*Psidium guajava* L.
Trumpet tree	*Cecropia peltata* L.	Mamey	*Calocarpum mammosum* (L.) Pierre
Star apple	*Chrysophyllum* sp.	Cashew	*Anacardium occidentale* L.
Hackberry	*Celtis* sp.	Cacao	*Theobroma* spp.
Wild bay cedar	*Guazuma ulmifolia* Lam.	Manioc	*Manihot esculenta* Crantz
Jauacte palm	*Bactris major* Jacq.	*Kinep. Gauya*	*Talisa oliviformis* H.B.K.

coal fragments. Densities ranged from 0.11 seeds/liter in the Swasey phase levels, up to a maximum of 11.6 charred seeds/liter for context 45/35(1597) of Cocos phase date, which alone contained over 400 maize kernels and cob fragments. Samples of representative material were saved, together with material that the author wished to check further; the remainder was discarded and incinerated following U.S. Department of Agriculture guidelines on the importation of soil and soil-contaminated materials.

Seeds and maize remains

All seeds were identified with the aid of a modern comparative collection from northern Belize and elsewhere in Central America (in this report, "seed" is used in the general, and not strict botanical, sense to include both true seeds and other fruit parts). The common and scientific names of Cuello plant remains are listed in Table 4.1 under their strongest ecological associations. These habitat categories are not mutually exclu-

sive: for example, *bribri* and *Hymenaea* are listed in the Forest Tree group, even though they are legumes that produce pods with a sweet edible pulp that may be used similarly to mesquite or carob. *Bribri* and turtlebone are included with Forest Trees, even though they may be found today in older secondary growth, or as protected trees in clearings, pastures, or field edges. Star apple, *sapodilla*, *manax*, and *siricote* all produce edible fruits, and allspice is commonly used as a seasoning in cooking.

Frequency data on Cuello seeds are presented in Table 4.2: frequency in this case is defined as the number of flotation samples that produced a given taxon, divided by the number of samples analyzed from a given stratigraphic phase.

With four exceptions, only carbonized seeds were considered ancient: hackberry (*Celtis* sp.) and sawgrass (*Scleria* sp.) seeds, the former's bony endocarp and the latter's tough seed coat both with high proportions of calcium carbonate, can survive for long periods in the soil uncarbonized. Two other taxa, *Paspalum* and an unidentified member of the

Table 4.2 *Carbonized seeds from Cuello flotation samples (% of samples containing)*

Phase	I	II early	II late	III early	III late	IV	IVA early–late	IVA early–late	IVA early–late	V	VIII	IX–XII
Number of samples	7	13	11	12	7	16	5	8	8	7	14	8
Crop Plants												
Maize	86	92	91	92	57	88	100	88	75	100	93	88
Squash	28		9	33			20			14	14	
Beans		38	18	17		6	20	12	25	28		12
Chile		8							12			
Cotton										14		
Weeds and Early Successional Shrubs												
Passion flower											14	
Paspalum[1]		8	9	8							21	25
Compositae[1]				8							7	
Unknown A											28	12
Escobilla						25	60				14	12
Rivinia												25
Nightshade									12			
Sawgrass[1]	14	15	9							14	93	25
Marsh Plants												
Razor grass		8				6	12					
Corchorus		8										
Sedge						19			12			
Early Successional Trees												
Star apple								12				
Hackberry[1]		8		8								
Jauacte						6	40				36	12
Forest Trees												
Wild fig											14	
Hymenaea		8									28	
Economic Trees												
Hogplum		8									14	
Nance	14	15		25		19	40	25	12	28	21	
Avocado							20			28		
Mamey		8				12		25	38	7		
Kinep				8								

Note:

[1] not all seeds charred

Compositae (possibly *Melampodium*), were also commonly recovered in an uncarbonized state. The *Paspalum* specimens were actually partially decomposed silica skeletons of the glumes surrounding the caryopsis, and the Compositae achenes were dark and papery, but uncharred. Both are quite small, *c.* 1.5 mm long, and could easily have been moved by leaf-harvester ants or other small burrowing animals without leaving much evidence for this in the excavated profiles: although both are reported in Table 4.2, they should be regarded as possibly intrusive. Caches of hackberry seeds were considered intrusive and due to burrowing animals, unless there was a clear association with a ceramic vessel or other cultural feature. Since sawgrass does not grow around Cuello today, and the vast majority of the *Scleria* seeds recovered were from the two *chultunob* (Table 4.7), all were considered as *in situ*.

All intact maize cupules and kernels were measured with an optical micrometer calibrated at 10X. The variables recorded

Table 4.3 *Chronological summary of Cuello maize remains*

Phase	Number of fragments	Mean row number	Mean cupule width (mm)	Mean cupule height (mm)	Mean rachis diameter (mm)	% each maize type					
						SW-1	SW-2	SW-3	MA-1	MA-2	CH-1
IX–XII	10	12.0	3.7	2.3	7.4	0	20	50	10	0	20
VII	18	12.5	4.2	2.0	8.7	0	22	33	17	17	11
V	16	11.0	3.9	2.4	7.2	12	0	44	19	0	25
IVd, e late	8	12.0	3.4	2.2	6.8	0	38	50	12	0	0
IVc	22	11.6	4.2	2.7	8.1	14	14	18	36	18	0
IVb early	33	11.5	3.9	2.4	7.5	3	30	39	21	6	0
IVa	33	11.1	3.4	2.1	6.3	12	30	52	6	0	0
IIIb,c late	8	11.4	3.4	2.2	6.5	0	38	62	0	0	0
IIIa early	9	10.8	2.7	1.8	4.9	33	67	0	0	0	0
IIb,c late	10	11.6	2.6	1.7	5.0	73	9	18	0	0	0
IIa early	22	12.5	3.0	2.0	6.2	14	77	9	0	0	0
I	10	13.5	2.8	1.7	6.2	70	30	0	0	0	0

Note:

All measurements on carbonized cupules, not corrected for shrinkage

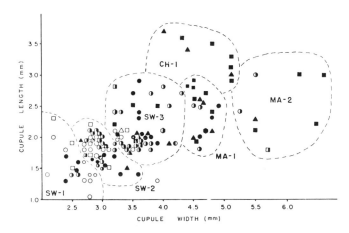

Fig. 4.1 Cupule size and shape for Preclassic maize types at Cuello. Types are named for the phase in which they first occur: SW–1, 2, and 3 indicated initial occurence in the Swasey/Bladen phases, MA1 and 2 appearance in Lopez Mamom and CH–1 in Cocos Chicanel; open symbols indicate specimens recovered from Swasey/Bladen phase contexts, half-filled symbols those from Lopez Mamom, and filled symbols from Cocos Chicanel. Symbol shape denotes cupule shape: circles indicate rectangular or elliptical cupules, squares denote trapezoidal cupules, triangles chevron-shaped cupules, and hexagons "eared" cupules with very broad wings. Symbols smaller than normal indicate cupules intermediate in shape between two types.

for each maize specimen are discussed in Miksicek *et al.* 1981. Summary data for the Cuello maize remains are presented in Table 4.3, while Fig. 4.1 demonstrates the increase in cupule size (and hence kernel size and, arguably, productivity) through time.

Mollusks

All terrestrial, aquatic, and marine mollusks larger than 2 mm recovered from the flotation samples were sorted into recognizable types and counted. The size fraction of shells between 0.5 and 2.0 mm was subsampled and total counts were estimated, based on the proportion of the sample analyzed. The mollusk remains from the flotation samples were identified with the aid of Dr. Walter B. Miller at the University of Arizona, Dr. Alan P. Covich at the University of Oklahoma, and Dr. Lawrence H. Feldman at the University of Missouri-Columbia. Table 4.4 contains data on the average number of valves per flotation sample from each stratigraphic phase. For fragmentary univalves, a complete aperture was counted as a single individual (the columella or apex could have been used with equal validity). If a taxon was represented only by fragments in a sample, all were considered to be from a single individual. For broken bivalves, the presence of a complete hinge was used to indicate one individual.

Table 4.4 *Mollusks from Cuello flotation samples by stratigraphic phase (mean number of valves per sample)*

Phase	I	II		III		IV	IVA			V	VIII	IX–XII
		early	late	early	late		early–late					
MARINE												
Conch							1					
Mussel						1				1		
Marginella			1							1		
FRESHWATER												
Pomacea flagellata	2	5	4	1	1	2	2	2	1	6	19	3
Nephronaias		1	1	1	1	1	1			1	1	1
Pachychilus			1			1	1			1	1	
Pyrgophorus	1	3	1	6	12	6	64	91	11	91	1	
Biomphalaria		1		2			12		1	7		1
Stenophysa		1	1	2	1	7	3	5	10	8	30	2
Gundlachia						1						
Aplexa			1							1		
"Egg"		1	6	12	15	18	42	6	4	44	3	1
TERRESTRIAL												
Practicolella	2		3		1	1			1	2	1	
"Ridged snail"	1	1		2	1		1			1		
Helicina	1	14	13	19	27	7	17	2	11	3	4	1
Neocyclotus dysoni	43	96	128	181	148	176	349	219	161	75	356	132
Bulimulus unicolor	16	23	43	56	16	51	58	72	51	67	134	16
Succinea	1	1	6	11	8	5	9	9	22	6	74	8
Orthalicus		1		1		1	1					
Hawaiia miniscula		14	1	58	55	90	150	14	44	129		
Lamellaxis	76	155	184	687	193	914	983	288	494	941	459	172
Opeas				1	1	24	6		4	3		
Large pupilid			1	8	108	20	26	5	5	49		
Small pupilid		2	1	8	124		58		5			
Unknown A		7	2	27	54	38	96	25	17	28	1	
Euglandina										1	1	

Wood charcoal

A grab sample of charcoal fragments from each flotation sample was selected. Each fragment was fractured to give a fresh transverse section, and examined at 25X magnification.

The identification of wood charcoal from Cuello presented a major methodological challenge. Dwyer and Spellman (1981) estimate that there are over 2,500 species of flowering plants in Belize. At least 65 percent of these are woody plants that could potentially be used for timber, fuel or crafts materials. Over a hundred species of trees and shrubs are common in northern Belize. An archaeobotanist working on materials from sites outside tropical areas usually has only to memorize the anatomy of some 15 common species, and be familiar with another 30 or so. In order to be able to cope with the enormous potential diversity in the Cuello specimens, I devised a numerical code system for unknown charcoal types (Table 4.5), in which each fragment could be described anatomically by a seven-digit code, and thus easily compared to known types. For this comparison, I collected, thin-sectioned, and/or converted to charcoal examples of over 150 ecologically common or economically important woody species from northern Belize and elsewhere in Central America. All anatomical terminology in Table 4.5 is standardized in accord with Esau (1977).

Most taxonomic keys to dicotyledonous woods use as a starting point the difference between ring-porous and diffuse-porous woods: unfortunately, this characteristic is relatively meaningless in tropical areas, where growth is almost continuous and annual rings are poorly defined. I found that the type of axial parenchyma (non-lignified cells found in characteristic patterns in woody stems) was a much more diagnostic feature. Except for the size and density of vessels there seems to be relatively little variation between individuals within a

Table 4.5 *A digital coding system for wood charcoal*

First digit: type of axial parenchyma
0	None apparent or scattered apotracheal
1	Banded apotracheal
2	Unilateral, vascicentric paratracheal
3	Circular, vascicentric paratracheal
4	Flame-like, diagonal, paratracheal bands
5	Aliform paratracheal
6	Confluent bands, narrower than vessel cluster
7	Confluent, paratracheal bands same width as vessels
8	Confluent bands, wider than vessel cluster

Second digit: width of rays
0	Indistinct
1	Uniseriate rays
2	Rays an average of two cells wide etc.

Third digit: vessel density
0	Sparse
1	Medium sparse
2	Medium
3	Medium dense
4	Very dense

Fourth digit: vessel diameter
0	Tiny 20–40 μm
1	Small 40–60 μm
2	Medium small 60–80 μm
3	Medium 80–100 μm
4	Medium large 100–120 μm
5	Large 120–150 μm
6	Very large > 150 μm

Fifth digit: average number of vessels/cluster
1	All or mostly single
2	Mostly double
3	Mostly triple etc.
9	Nine or more vessels per cluster

Sixth digit: fiber area density
0	Large fibers, some libriform fibers
1	Medium dense
2	Dense, non resinous
3	Dense, resinous, appears glossy in charcoal

Seventh digit: annual rings
0	None apparent or no comment
1	Diffuse porous
2	Ring porous

species for the characters I chose. Faster-growing trees, or faster-growing parts of trees, tend to have larger, more widely spaced vessels and a decreased amount of lignification. This digital coding system can be adapted to any part of the world, and is computerizable.

As an example, *Theobroma cacao* (cocoa/chocolate), with scattered apotracheal parenchyma, rays about four cells wide,

an average of 61 vessels/mm², vessels about 67 μm diameter, a mean of two vessels per cluster, large fibers, and indistinct annual rings would code as: 0432200.

Caribbean pine was the only common conifer in the area, so it was easily recognized. The various species of palms could be distinguished from the size and shape of vascular bundles, the degree of sclerification of the bundle sheath, and the number and position of vessel elements within the vascular bundle. Charcoal data from the Cuello site is presented in Table 4.6 as the relative abundance for each taxon from each stratigraphic phase. Relative abundance in this case was defined as the number of fragments of Taxon A divided by the total number of all fragments of identified charcoal recovered from a given phase.

CUELLO 'CHULTUNOB': PALAEOECOLOGY AND EXPERIMENTAL ARCHAEOLOGY
Among the more interesting palaeoecological finds at Cuello were two *chultunob*, subterranean storage chambers cut into bedrock, dating to the beginning and middle of the Late Formative Cocos Chicanel phase, *c.* 300 B.C. [F246] and 150 B.C. [F87] respectively. While most of the plant remains at Cuello were recovered from fill, including recycled trash, that accumulated over a long period of time, the *chultun* fills seem to be refuse deposited quite rapidly, that can be analyzed as discrete lots. They reflect a cross-section of the plants in use during two brief periods, but it must be emphasized that most of the remains represent trash deposited in the chambers when they were no longer in use as storage facilities, and not of material actually stored in them.

[F87] was a two-chambered *chultun* with a collared shaft (see Chapter 2). The northwest chamber was connected to a third chamber by a hole pecked in its wall. Pottery from the fill of [F87] dated to the transition between the middle and late facets of the Cocos Chicanel ceramic complex; charcoal from the fill yielded radiocarbon dates of 205 ± 60 b.c. (Q-1930), calibrating to 360–112 B.C., and 100 ± 60 b.c. (Q1929), calibrating to 160 B.C.–A.D. 9; the calibrated ranges overlap between 160 and 112 B.C. Before [F87] was excavated completely it was described as a "Puuc-type cistern," largely based on the presence of an inward-sloping plaster catchment floor around the mouth of the shaft. I doubt that [F87] was ever used for water storage: the collar at the base of the central shaft was designed to keep water out of the storage chambers, and would also have made it very difficult to draw water from them. In addition, the *chultun* was pecked into very porous limestone bedrock and would not have held water unless the groundwater table was high enough to fill the chambers. To test the porosity of the limestone, I devised a field infiltrometer: although the capacity of [F87] was 12,820 liters, enough water for 50 people for a month, with an infiltration rate of 9 cm/hr it would have emptied completely in 15 hours. It could, instead, have held 423.4 bushels of shelled corn,

Table 4.6 *Wood charcoal from Cuello flotation samples by stratigraphic phase (% of wood charcoal)*

Phase	I	II		III		IV	IVA			V	VIII	IX–XII
		early	late	early	late		early–late					
Number of fragments	24	117	111	106	129	152	121	120	96	193	101	35
Savanna Trees												
Caribbean pine	29	18	35	30	19	26	40	58	34	16	33	34
Early Successional Shrubs												
Nightshade	17	1	15	1	1	1	4	12	5	5	22	8
Redhead		3		6	2							
Cojeton							18					
Cockspur		2		4		35		2		8	1	
Total	17	6	15	11	3	36	22	14	5	13	23	8
Early Successional Trees												
Piper		1						1			1	
Trumpet tree						2	9					6
Star apple						16	3		20	13		
Hackberry		7		7								
Wild bay cedar					1			1				
Jauacte palm				1		1						
Total		8		8	1	19	12	2	20	13	1	6
Forest Trees												
Bribri	4			1	1				3	1		
Gumbolimbo		16	6		35	3			4	5	3	
Manax									1			
Allspice									1			
Sapodilla		2		5	2			5				
Wild fig	4	26	4	10	16	1	2		3	11	3	6
Hymenaea	21	1	10	2			9		3	1	1	11
Guanacaste			1			1				1		14
Turtlebone					1			3		3	5	
Siricote			5		2	1	2	1		2	5	3
Tropical cedar				1								
Escoba palm									1			
Total	29	45	26	19	57	6	13	9	16	24	17	34
Economic Trees												
Chile		4		3	3							3
Hogplum						1			4	5	1	
Nance		1		22		10		2	6	9		
Avocado		2	7	1	2	1		3		8	1	
Soursop	12		11		16				3		3	
Guava		2		7		2	13	10	5	12	21	6
Mamey		4	2									6
Cashew	4	4	4					1	5			
Cacao	8	4		1								3
Manioc										1	1	
Total	24	21	24	34	21	14	13	16	23	35	27	18

Table 4.7 *Importance values for seeds from two Cuello chultunob*

	[F246] Early facet Cocos Chicanel 7 samples 219 seeds 0.62 seeds/liter	[F87] Middle–late facet Cocos Chicanel 14 samples 620 seeds 0.88 seeds/liter
Diversity index =	1.452	2.133
	Maize 89 Nance 16 Beans 15 Avocado 15 Squash 8 Cotton 8 Sawgrass 8	Sawgrass 72 Maize 67 *Jauacte* 18 *Hymenaea* 14 Unknown A 14 Nance 11 *Paspalum* 11 Hogplum 8 Squash 8 Wild fig 8 *Escobilla* 8 Mamey 4 Passion fruit 4 Compositae 4

enough to last 35 people a year. The "catchment" floor may be a drying or other processing feature for harvested grain.

[F246] was a single-chambered *chultun* with a long shaft set to one side of the chamber. Pottery from the fill was of early facet Cocos Chicanel date, as was the stratigraphic position of the shaft cut, and the subsequent covering-over of the infilled shaft. There were traces of a clay or plaster lining, and a low step into the chamber, making it a much more likely candidate for water storage than [F87]. The slightly higher groundwater levels at the beginning of the Late Formative, c. 300 B.C., may even have filled [F246] naturally, and it could have been a domestic well for the inhabitants of the buildings on the north side of Platform 34.

Mollusk and plant data recovered from these two features do suggest differences in the local hydrological regime between 300 and 150 B.C. Flotation samples from [F246] yielded an average 91 *Pyrgophorus* snails (range: 1–192; see Table 4.4), these are aquatic snails found in relatively deep lakes and ponds, which prefers water over 1 or 2 m deep (Covich 1983). In [F246] this species is found with *Biomphalaria*, another aquatic snail preferring slightly shallower water than *Pyrgophorus*; the average density of *Biomphalaria* in [F246] is seven individuals per sample (Table 4.4).

The freshwater snail assemblage from [F87] is dominated

by *Pomacea* and *Stenophysa*. The latter is a shallow-water species, and *Pomacea* has both gills and lungs, and may leave the water for short periods (Covich 1983). No *Biomphalaria* were recovered from [F87] and only a few *Pyrgophorus* (one per sample) were identified. *Pyrgophorus* > *Biomphalaria* > *Stenophysa* > *Pomacea* represents a successional sere from deep water to shallow water. These differences in mollusk assemblages suggest that the low limestone ridge on which the Cuello site is located may have been partially surrounded by shallow lakes at the beginning of the Late Formative. These could perhaps have been formed from the quarry pits dug for the construction fill used to build Platform 34; areas of damp land, flooding temporarily after heavy rains, lie west and north of this locus. Today a small *bajo* lies 1.6 km east of the site and another 2 km northwest, but the area has been drained by modern ditches. Sawgrass seeds were the dominant plant species recovered from [F87] (see Table 4.7), sawgrass is a sedge that grows in savannas and filled-in *bajos* that are only occasionally inundated. Razorgrass (*Cladium*), which was recovered from several Lopez Mamom period samples (Table 4.2) but not [F246] or [F87], is more characteristic of shallow marshy areas at the edge of *bajos* or deeper lakes. [F246] may have been dug during a time of higher groundwater levels and used initially as a well, whereas [F87] was constructed for dry storage during a later period.

The sawgrass seeds from [F87] may represent waste thatching or leafy material used for matting or basketry. The highest densities of sawgrass seeds were from contexts (1201), with 4.48/liter, at the base of the central shaft, (1208) with 0.64/liter at the bottom of the east chamber, and (1202) with 0.46/liter at the bottom of the northwest chamber. These could be *in situ* remains of matting used to line the chambers or a plug for the shaft. Sawgrass seed densities through the rest of the *chultun* fill ranged from 0 to 0.34/liter; the only such seeds recovered from [F246] came from context (1971) at the bottom of the chamber, with a density of 0.02/liter.

The other seeds recovered from the *chultunob* are ranked by Importance Values in Table 4.7. This is a summary statistic commonly used in plant ecology, defined as (Frequency + Relative Abundance)/2, and should be interpreted as "importance in the archaeobotanical record" and not "importance in the diet," because many plant foods are grossly under-represented as charred remains (Hammond and Miksicek 1981: 263, 265).

The other statistic reported in Table 4.7 is the Shannon-Wiener Index (Shannom and Weaver 1949), a measure of species richness or diversity commonly used in ecology. The Shannon-Wiener Index is a much more powerful statistic than a simple count of the number of species recovered, as it is calculated using both the number of taxa and the number of indivuals of each taxon, based on a logarithmic scale. As can be seen from Table 4.7, the archaeobotanical assemblage from [F87], with an SWI of 2.133 is considerably more diverse than that from [F246] at 1.452.

Maize kernels and cupules (cob fragments) were the dominant plant remains from [F246] and the highest-ranked food plant [F87] (sawgrass seeds are inedible). Nance seeds, avocado pits, fragments of squash rind and cotton seeds were also recovered from the earlier *chultun* [F246]; these are among the few cotton seeds recovered at Cuello. The avocado pits were rather small, within the size range of wild avocados or some small-seeded varieties still cultivated in Central America. The beans from [F246] are somewhat of an enigma, as are all of the Cuello beans. They are definitely *Phaseolus*, but are rather small, averaging 4.9 mm long × 3.2 mm wide × 3.3 mm thick: this is larger than most of the wild beans found in northern Belize, but rather small for a cultivated species. Either these are a small variety of common bean (*Phaseolus vulgaris*) similar to types still grown in southern Mexico, or they were immature seeds from the ends of pods that were discarded or tossed into the fire, not saved for food or planting. Because beans are normally prepared by soaking and boiling, they are rarely carbonized and tend to be severely under-represented in the archaeobotanical record (Hammond and Miksicek 1981). *Jauacte* kernels, nance seeds, hogplum pits, mamey seeds, passion fruit seeds, and fragments of squash rind were recovered from [F87] (Table 4.6). Initially the *Hymenaea* seeds from [F87] were misidentified as cacao and reported as such in Hammond (1980b) and Hammond and Miksicek (1981), although the error has now been noted in Adams and Hammond (1982) and Hammond (1984); the late C. Earle Smith (personal communication) made the correct identification. While these *Hymenaea* seeds are the same overall size and shape as cacao beans, *Theobroma* has a tightly folded cotyledon, while *Hymenaea* has a thick flattened cotyledon. Although cacao seeds have thus not been confirmed from Cuello, *Theobroma* charcoal has been identified in a number of flotation samples (Table 4.6), indicating the local presence of cacao trees.

The size distribution of *Pomacea* shells from the two *chultunob* is rather intriguing: a random sample of 100 shells from each was compared with 100 modern shells collected from the banks of the Rio Hondo at San Antonio, Albion Island. The modern population averaged 3.66 ± 1.65 cm long, and included subadults ranging in size from 1.0 to 2.2 cm, adults from 2.2 to 4.8 cm, and very large individuals from 4.8 to 6.8 cm (Fig 4.2). The archaeological shell samples had a much tighter size distribution: the average size from [F87] was 3.37 ± 0.56 cm, with a range from 1.6 to 4.4 cm and from [F246] it was 3.69 ± 0.57, range 2.2 to 5.2 cm (Fig. 4.2).

Individuals in the archaeological size range would normally be called *Pomacea flagellata* form *arata*, while the very large individuals from the Rio Hondo would be classified as *P.*

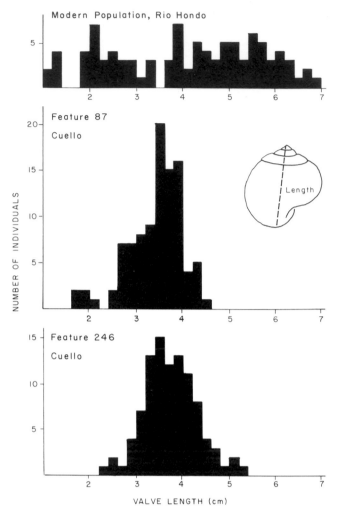

Fig. 4.2 A comparison of the length of *Pomacea* shells recovered from two Cuello *chultunob* with that of a modern population collected from the banks of the Rio Hondo in northern Belize, (n = 100 for each sample).

flagellata form *tristrami* (Moholy-Nagy 1978: 66). These two forms seem to represent ecotypes as opposed to taxonomic varieties. The *arata* type is most commonly found in shallow streams and *bajos*, while *tristrami* is more abundant in deeper lakes. Gastroarchaeological tests suggest that the two forms taste quite different: in 1979 a number of *arata* individuals were purchased on Albion Island, and when boiled and seasoned with garlic were delicious, comparable with *escargots* (*Helix pomatia*). A similar experiment with *tristrami* individuals from New River Lagoon near Lamanai showed the latter to be tough and unpalatable – rather like rubber bands in pond mud. The size distribution from the Cuello *chultunob* (subsequently found to occur at Nohmul also) suggests careful selection for optimal size and taste, and perhaps harvesting rather than casual collection.

A total of 842 complete *Pomacea* shells was recovered from [F246] and 1,274 from [F87]. Modern *Pomacea* contain an average 10 gm of fresh meat, reducing to 7 gm by cooking (data from 1979–80 collection) and 1.05 gm protein (by analogy with *escargots*: Moholy-Nagy 1978: 70–1). The snails in [F246] would have satisfied the complete protein requirements of one person for 22 days, while those from [F87] would have lasted 33 days; this assumes a daily consumption of 38 snails, which may be high. At a more realistic rate of 12 snails/day, the *Pomacea* in [F246] would last one person 70 days, and those from [F87] 106 days, but provide only 32–42 percent of the World Health Organization recommended daily adult protein requirement, and only 2–3 percent of the caloric allotment (Moholy-Nagy 1978). Other freshwater species found at Cuello have slightly lower yields (one *Pachychilus pyramidalis* produces 5 gm meat/4.2 cal/0.32 gm protein: Paul F. Healy, personal communication to Hammond 1989). While this may seem an insignificant amount of food, any supplemental protein may have been critical for a sedentary agricultural population in the past.

After excavation, [F87] was used for an experiment in storage, beginning in February 1980. Following the lead of Puleston (1971) we included unhusked ears of maize, maize kernels in an open container, *ramón* seeds (*Brosimum alicastrum*) both with and without the fleshy pericarp, red kidney beans, black *milpa* beans (*Vigna unguiculata* (L.) Walp., an Old World species commonly grown throughout Belize today), and squash (*Cucurbita moschata* (Duch.) Duch. ex Poir). To test the thesis that smoked maize was stored in *chultunob* (Reina and Hill 1980) we also included unhusked maize ears that had been smoked for one, two, five and ten days respectively. Germination tests on the smoked maize suggested that only those smoked for one day remained viable and could have been used as seed corn. Because of the resemblance of a *chultun* to a traditional "root cellar," we also included several native Central American root crops, including manioc (*Manihot esculenta*), sweet potato or *camote* (*Ipomoea batatas* (L.) Lam.), *jícama* (*Pachyrhizus erosus* (L.) Urb.), cocoyam (*Xanthosoma* sp.), and *macal* or true yam (*Dioscorea* sp.).

After five weeks of experimental storage in the *chultun*, the squash and *ramón* with pericarp had rotted, the *ramón* without pericarp had sprouted but was still edible, both types of beans were covered with a luxuriant growth of fungus, the *camote* showed a little discoloration, and the unsmoked ears of maize had developed a few fungal sporangia, as had those smoked for short periods. Only the maize kernels in a container, and the yam, cocoyam, *jícama*, and manioc were unchanged. After 16 weeks only the cocoyam, *jícama*, and one manioc tuber were in pristine condition. The *macal* and *ramón* seeds without pericarp had sprouted 7 cm etiolated shoots but were still firm and usable. Some mold had developed on the upper layer of

corn kernels in the open container but most were still edible. All of the other specimens, including the maize ears smoked for five and ten days, were either completely decomposed or no longer usable.

The storage experiment was checked again in March 1981 after 13 months, but unfortunately one chamber of the *chultun* had collapsed, and many of the remaining items had been disturbed by human and animal intruders. Only the *ramón* kernels were left, sprouted but edible, and the yam and cocoyam were growing happily in the dark but using up their stored food reserves (Hammond, field notes 1981). I attempted a further check after 16 months in June 1981, but found a coral snake living in the outer chamber, which discouraged enquiry.

The experiment confirmed Puleston's (1971) contention that *ramón* could survive for a year in a *chultun*, and also demonstrated that some root crops could also have been stored for long periods, and other foodstuffs for a short time. In retrospect, some of the results suggest a major flaw in the experimental design: we included only a few examples of each food plant and did not completely fill the available space. The observation that maize kernels could survive in an open container for four months may hold a key to understanding the function of *chultunob*. Although they have a very slow metabolic rate, seeds are living organisms that take in oxygen, give off carbon dioxide, and slowly use up their stored food reserves. Increasing atmospheric concentrations of carbon dioxide can be toxic to rodents and insects that eat stored grain, and will also reduce the growth rates of fungi (Hultin and Milner 1978). Reynolds (1979: 73–6) conducted storage experiments in replications of Iron Age pits at Butser Hill in England, and carbon dioxide levels were monitored throughout the experiment. Grain could be stored in these pits with a loss of only 2 percent of the mass, at seed moisture levels of 16 percent (under modern conditions in grain elevators, seed is dried to 10–14 percent moisture content). Reynolds suggests that the prerequisites for underground pit storage were low (or constant) temperature during the storage period, an impermeable seal, abundant carbon dioxide production, and a subsoil that inhibited lateral water flow. While the temperature regime in Belize is substantially different from that in Britain, other conditions would be similar. If the chambers were completely filled with grain and then tightly sealed, or if the grain was stored in sealed jars so that the internal carbon dioxide level built up rapidly and was held fairly constant, *chultunob* would be suitable features for long-term grain storage. If the chambers were lined with mats or vegetal material, such as the sawgrass identified in the flotation samples, and plugged with the same material, equilibrium carbon dioxide levels would be reached more rapidly. Large plainware jars of the Early Classic period have been found in another *chultun* at Cuello, and could have been used for storage, or perhaps for brewing maize beer (Dahlin and Litzinger 1986).

Building a smoky fire in a *chultun* before storage would seal the walls, sterilize the chamber, and rapidly build up the internal carbon dioxide levels: while the Cuello *chultunob* had no evidence for this, Jim Caldwell (personal communication) suggests that several of those at the neighboring site of Colha had smudging on their walls.

The ability of root crops to survive in *chultunob* for short to medium periods present some intriguing possibilities. Once harvested, root crops are very difficult to store: manioc tubers cannot be stored after harvest unless they are cut into slices and dried (Cobley and Steele 1976), and even today it is difficult to store sweet potatoes for commercial shipment unless they are first "hardened" by keeping them in a well-ventilated room at a constant high humidity and controlled temperature for several weeks. This "hardening" causes a thickening of the periderm, which protects the tubers during prolonged storage (Cobley and Steele 1976). The survival of a fresh manioc tuber for 16 weeks in a *chultun*, along with *jícama*, yam, and cocoyam, is significant. The easiest way to keep root crops for domestic use is to leave them in the ground until needed: bulk storage of tubers, as in a *chultun*, would only be necessary in a socio-economic system with centralized redistribution or well-developed markets, where it would be desirable to have a large supply available at once.

Unfortunately, there is little direct evidence for the use of root crops at Cuello: only a few fragments of manioc stem charcoal were recovered from stratigraphic phases V and VIII, early in the Late Formative (Table 4.6). Roots are usually prepared by boiling, so they are not likely to be charred and preserved in the archaeological record. If charred, roots will survive in the soil as well as some of the softer woods we have identified.

An additional possibility for the use of *chultunob* should be considered: in 1980 a Mopan Maya informant in southern Belize mentioned that a wild custard apple (*Annona* sp.) that grew in the area would be picked while green and buried in pits for several days. He said that fruit ripened this way tasted better than tree-ripened fruits. It is possible that *chultunob* could be used thus: as fruit matures it yields ethylene, a natural growth substance. Increasing the concentration of the gas by trapping it in a closed space makes the fruit ripen faster, something utilized by modern commercial growers. Today many fruits are picked and shipped green to avoid damage: on arrival they are gassed with ethylene to complete the ripening process. Tropical fruit trees tend to bear all at once: either there is no fruit, or there is more ripe than can be used before it spoils. If these same fruits were picked green and stored in a *chultun*, Maya farmers would have been able more easily to control the timing of the supply; fruit could also have been transported green by canoe or porter and ripened on arrival.

Both possibilities have important implications for ancient Maya market economics.

There is some evidence for above-ground storage of corn at Cuello: over 400 cob and kernel fragments were recovered from a flotation sample collected from grid 45/35, context (1597), one of the few examples of "catastrophically preserved *de facto* refuse" (Schiffer 1976) from the site. The sample came from the base of Structure 311, a middle facet Cocos Chicanel building of stratigraphic phase VI, *c.* 300 B.C., and probably represents material from a structure destroyed by fire (the sample is not included in Tables 4.2, 4.3 and 4.6 because a single sample from a phase is inadequate for reliable frequency calculations). The maize remains were concentrated at one end of the platform, and the overall pattern was very similar to that of a modern Kekchi Maya house destroyed by fire, observed in southern Belize. A corn crib had been in one end of the house, and charred maize ears were scattered round that end of the foundation. On this basis of comparison, it seems quite possible that the Cuello structure had a corn crib at one end. Above-ground storage may have been the pattern for short-term domestic usage, with *chultunob* reserved for longer-term or centralized storage. There may also have been a change in storage patterns between middle and late facet Chicanel, *c.* 150 B.C., and if there was also a trend towards increasing dryness in the local hydrological regime, larger food stores may have become important.

So far, this chapter has examined two aspects of Late Formative environment and subsistence in detail, from well-preserved and sealed deposits: it would now be useful to examine these trends over the longer term of the Formative period occupation of Cuello, a period of well over a millennium.

ENVIRONMENTAL AND SUBSISTENCE TRENDS

Phases 0–1 The earliest plant remains from the site were recovered from the buried palaeosol (630) and a small plaster platform (Structure 328) built on it. Eighty-six percent of the flotation samples from this period yielded maize kernels and cupules (Table 4.2). The two most primitive kinds of Cuello maize, SW-1 and SW-2 (Miksicek *et al.* 1981, Table 4.3 and Fig. 4.1), were cultivated at this time. Several nance seeds and fragments of squash rind were also recovered from these samples. Twenty-nine percent of all charcoal from this level was of the Forest Tree category, mostly fig and *Hymenaea* (Table 4.6 and Fig. 4.3), suggesting relatively little disturbance of the natural rainforest.

A surprising amount of pine charcoal (29 percent) was recovered: today the nearest patches of pine savanna are over 10 km southeast and southwest. At Chan Pine Ridge, a village 4.5 km southeast of Cuello, there are no pines today, although the sandy, leached soils support dense sawgrass stands; there may have been pines there in the recent past.

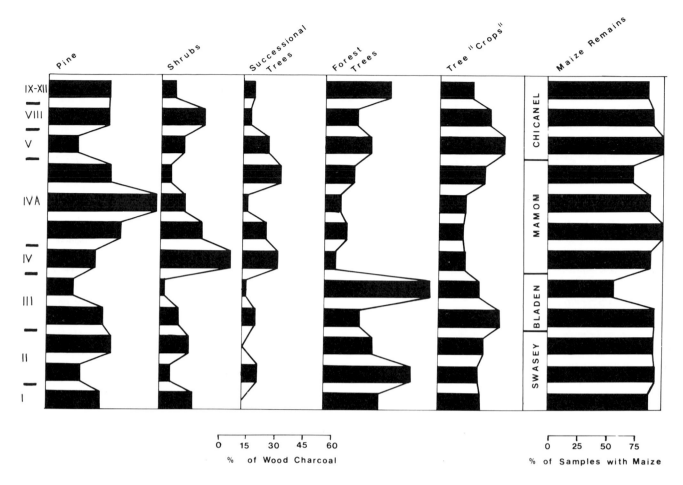

% of Wood Charcoal

% of Samples with Maize

Fig. 4.3 Ecological summary of Cuello plant remains: a summary of charcoal and maize data by stratigraphic phase. Maize data are presented as "Frequency," the percentage of flotation samples from each phase that produced maize cupules or kernels. Charcoal data are presented as "Relative abundance", the number of fragments of a given taxon divided by the total number of identified fragments from that phase.

Nance, represented by seeds (Table 4.2), and cashew, as charcoal (Table 4.6), occur naturally in the savannas of northern Belize, and together with sawgrass are present in these early levels. Several *Practicolella* snails were recovered: although Goodrich and Van der Schalie (1937) list this as a savanna snail, I have collected modern shells from leaf litter in relatively undisturbed broadleaf forest near the Rio Hondo, in association with the unidentified "ridged snail" also found in Swasey phase I samples (Table 4.4). The co-occurrence of pine and cashew charcoal, nance and sawgrass seeds, and *Practicolella* snails may indicate expansion of savanna during phase I, in the late second/early first millennium B.C. As will be discussed later, the ratio of pine to Forest Tree charcoal may have some climatic implications. The two taxa are

significantly, negatively, correlated ($r = -0.588$, $P_{.05} = 0.576$ for 10 degrees of freedom). The climatic signal in the Forest Tree data is not absolute, however, as there is also a strong inverse relationship with the amount of human disturbance. Forest Tree charcoal is negatively correlated with maize ($r = -0.523$, not quite significant), Successional Trees ($r = -0.422$, not significant), and Shrubs ($r = -0.675$, $P_{.02} = 0.658$ for 10 degrees of freedom).

Early phase II The proportions of pine and Forest Trees charcoal suggest some shifts in the local vegetation communities. The high frequency of Forest charcoal (46 percent: Table 4.6 and Fig. 4.3) may reflect a relatively long fallow cycle and a decrease in the reliance on pine imported from nearby savannas for timber or firewood. Forest Trees are found in areas that have not been disturbed by swidden agriculture for over 30 years. The members of the Early Successional Shrubs category are characteristic of *milpas* that have been abandoned for *c.* 1–5 years. Taxa in the Early Successional Trees group are associated with secondary growth found on old fields that have not been cleared for 5–15 years, or more.

Terrestrial snails may also be ranked in a successional sere from little to extensive disturbance. As mentioned above, "ridged snail" and *Practicolella* seem to be most characteristic of relatively undisturbed rain forest. *Helicina*, "large pupilid," and "small pupilid" seem to be most strongly related to older secondary growth. Feldman (n.d.; cf. Hammond *et al.* 1979: 105) has referred to *Neocyclotus* as the "swidden snail," but this relationship may not be as clear-cut as he suggests: while it is true that the ground surface of recently burned *milpas* in northern Belize is usually littered with hundreds of *Neocyclotus* shells, I have collected live individuals from leaf litter under old forest at Altun Ha. Alan Covich and I have also collected live *Neocyclotus dysoni* from piles of chert nodules and limestone boulders in forested areas along Rancho Creek near Colha. *Neocyclotus* seems to be a calciphile that likes to burrow into limestone rubble such as that found around natural outcrops or ancient Maya ruins. While *Neocyclotus* does seem to be associated with disturbance, there may be an even stronger relationship with old sites with masonry architecture. *Hawaiia*, *Lamellaxis*, and Unknown A seem to have the strongest association with recent agricultural disturbance. *Lamellaxis* and Unknown A are highly correlated with *Hawaiia* (r = 0.855 and 0.828 respectively, $P_{.001} = 0.823$ for 10 degrees of freedom). I have collected numerous empty shells of these three taxa from gardens and maize *milpas* in northern Belize. *Orthalicus*, *Bulimulus*, and *Succinea* are tree snails that seem to prefer open, disturbed habitats. *Bulimulus* and *Succinea* are strongly correlated with each other (r = 0.825) and inversely related to Forest Tree charcoal (r = −0.598). I have collected numerous live individuals of these three genera, estivating on fence posts, tree trunks, or palm-thatched roofs on foggy mornings in northern Belize. The relatively high frequencies of *Helicina* and low proportions of *Hawaiia*, *Lamellaxis*, Shrub charcoal and Early Successional Tree charcoal complement the impression of a long fallow cycle suggested by the abundance of Forest Tree charcoal in early Swasey phase II samples.

Maize cupules and kernels were recovered from 92 percent of the samples from this phase; in fact, the abundance of maize is fairly constant from phases I through IIIA, varying by only a few percent (Table 4.2 and Fig. 4.3). The beans recovered from these levels were significantly smaller than those from the later [F246], averaging 3.6 mm long × 2.8 mm wide × 2.9 mm thick. These are more in the size range of wild species of *Phaseolus* found in northern Belize, but they could also represent a very small variety of cultivated bean. The chile seed from early phase II is in the size range of *chile max* or bird pepper (*Capsicum annuum* var. *aviculare*) the small-fruited variety commonly found both growing wild and as a cultivated spice plant in Central America today. It is impossible to determine whether the Cuello seed is from a wild or cultivated chile. Fragments of hogplum, nance, and mamey seeds were

also recovered from this phase; again, it is difficult to distinguish gathered wild fruits from cultivated tree crops, but the question may be moot. A few fruit pits from gathered wild plants would have germinated naturally if discarded in a favorable location such as a midden, and if these seedlings were allowed to mature and bear fruit, stands of productive trees would soon become established around early villages. It is then only a short step, and a matter of semantics, from a few volunteer fruit trees to a planted orchard crop, and since there have been few genetic changes in most Central American tree crops, it is very difficult to determine whether a given seed came from a wild or cultivated plant. A few fragments of cacao charcoal were recovered from the lowest levels at Cuello (Table 4.6): since this taxon disappears after early phase III and is not again recovered until the end of the Late Formative, these early fragments may be wild *Theobroma bicolor* Humb. and Bonpl., which is difficult to tell from the cultivated species by wood anatomy alone.

Late phase II and early phase III Plant remains from these phases were similar: maize continued to be the most conspicuous cultivated plant. Throughout the earliest levels at Cuello there is a general trend towards a decrease in row number and an alternation between the proportions of SW-1, SW-2, and SW-3 maize types. There is also a slight trend toward a decrease in rachis diameter (cob size) but this is probably a geometric effect related to the reduction in row number as the average cupule width is fairly constant (Table 4.3 and Fig. 4.1).

Beans and fragments of squash rind were recovered from both phases, while through the levels there is a trend towards decreasing amounts of pine and forest charcoal (Fig. 4.3) and increases in the per-sample density of *Neocyclotus*, *Bulimulus*, *Lamellaxis*, and *Hawaiia* snails (Table 4.4), suggesting increasing levels of local agricultural disturbance but still a relatively long fallow cycle.

Late phase III Plant and mollusk remains from this period suggest a dramatic shift from previous environmental and subsistence trends. The frequency of maize remains drops to the lowest level in the entire Cuello sequence (57 percent: Table 4.2), and maize was the only kind of "seed" recovered from these samples. At the same time the proportion of Forest charcoal increases to the highest level in the sequence (56 percent: Table 4.6 and Fig. 4.3). The densities of disturbance snails decrease, and the abundance of "ridged snail", *Practicolella*, *Helicina*, and the Pupilidae increases over the late Bladen phase III levels. These data may suggest a slight hiatus in the occupation of the Cuello community area, with decreased population levels and less human disturbance of the natural rainforest environment.

Phase IV Palaeoecological data from the early Lopez phase IV suggest a shift back to pre-late phase III conditions: the abundance of corn increases to 88 percent, with maize type MA-1 recovered for the first time (Table 4.3 and Fig. 4.1). There is a dramatic drop in the proportion of Forest charcoal (6 percent) and significant increases in those of Shrub (36 percent) and Early Succesional Tree (19 percent) charcoal, while at the same time the densities of *Hawaiia* and *Lamellaxis* snails also increase. The relationship between disturbance snails and successional charcoal may reflect a significant reduction in the length of the fallow cycle. The recovery of sedge and razorgrass seeds with *Gundlachia*, *Pyrgophorus*, and *Stenophysa* snails may reflect the beginning of a rise in the local water table, previously discussed in the analysis of [F246].

Early phase IVA Corn was recovered from every sample analyzed from this stratigraphic phase, and maize type MA-2 was added to the Cuello crop inventory (Table. 4.3 and Fig. 4.1). With an average cupule width of 3.9 mm and rachis diameter of 7.5 mm, the early phase IVA cob fragments are significantly larger than any from previous phases. Squash rind, beans, *jauacte* palm, nance, and avocado were recovered also.

The increase in water table level continues in phase IVA: an average 64 *Pyrgophorus* snails were recovered per sample. On dry land, Forest charcoal remained low (12 percent) and large amounts of pine (40 percent of the charcoal) were imported to fulfil the timber and fuel requirements of the inhabitants of the Platform 34 locus. During phase IVA, most of the area around the Cuello site was probably covered by *milpas* or *huamil* fields in the early stages of succession.

Middle phase IVA The highest proportion of pine charcoal in the entire Cuello sequence (58 percent) was recovered from deposits of this phase; it is difficult to see whether this was due to the lack of timber reserves in the immediate vicinity, or if the same climatic factors that caused a raising of the water table also triggered an expansion of pine savanna. The highest densities of the lake snails *Pyrgophorus* and *Biomphalaria* were recovered at this period, as were a few *Cladium* seeds, suggesting that lowlying areas around Cuello may have been open water. The presence of cashew charcoal, and nance seeds and charcoal, may also support the idea of savanna expansion. Flotation samples also yielded maize, beans, star apple seeds, mamey pits, avocado charcoal, and guava charcoal (it is interesting to note that soursop is more common early in the Cuello sequence and guava late: Table 4.6).

Late phase IVA There may have been a slight drop in the groundwater level, since *Pyrgophorus* and *Biomphalaria* are replaced by the shallow-water snail *Stenophysa*. The proportion of pine charcoal decreased (to 34 percent) and the frequencies of Successional Tree, Forest, and Economic charcoal increased. Economic plants recovered from this period include maize, beans, nance, chile, mamey, hogplum, soursop, guava, and cashew.

Phases V and VIII (VI and VII did not yield sufficient remains for analysis.) The apparent rise in water table continues in the early Cocos Chicanel phase V, *c.* 300 B.C., but has reversed itself by phase VIII 150 years later. Maize remains were common in both phase V (100 percent) and VIII (93 percent), with the largest cob fragments in the latter, rachis diameter 8.7 mm, recovered from the *chultun* [F87]. It would be tempting to suggest that the gradual increase in cupule width and rachis diameter throughout the Formative sequence at Cuello reflects an overall increase in productivity (Fig. 4.1), but unfortunately we know too little about cropping practices, the length of the ears, or the number of ears per plant. A corn plant with numerous small ears (which is true of many "primitive" races of maize) could produce almost as much food as a plant with a few larger ears.

Phases IX–XII These late facet Cocos Chicanel stratigraphic phases, between *c.* 100 B.C. and A.D. 250, are the latest part of the Cuello sequence to yield much palaeoecological data. Like the phase VIII samples, those from phases IX–XII produced numerous seeds from disturbance weeds such as *Paspalum*, *flor amarilla*, *escobilla*, tropical pokeweed, and nightshade. The proportions of Shrub, Successional Tree, and tree crop charcoal were relatively low, while pine and Forest charcoal were fairly abundant. Economic species recovered from these phases include maize, beans, *jauacte* palm, guava, mamey, chile, and cacao (Tables 4.2 and 4.6).

PALAEOCLIMATOLOGICAL CORRELATIONS WITH THE CUELLO DATA

A new picture of the vegetation history of the Caribbean Basin is now emerging. Well-dated pollen cores from the Petén (Leyden 1984) and Venezuela (Bradbury *et al.* 1981) suggest that the seasonally deciduous forest of the Central American lowlands may have developed since the Pleistocene (Lewin 1984). Late Pleistocene levels from these cores are dominated by pollen produced by savanna plants (oak, pine, *Bursera*, juniper), or temperate hardwoods, and have only low proportions of pollen from trees characteristic of the semi-evergreen forest found in the region today. These data suggest a cool, dry Pleistocene in the tropical latitudes. Early Holocene levels suggest a completely different picture: pollen from forest trees such as *ramón*, trumpet tree, and *Trema* (*capulin*) dominates the Holocene levels from these cores from approximately

8800 B.P. until about 3000 B.P. (Leyden 1984; Bradbury *et al.* 1981). This seems to represent the establishment of the Central American "rainforest" as we know it today. This pollen spectrum seems to suggest a relatively warm, moist period. Upper-timberline, bristlecone pine dendroclimatic records from the White Mountains of California suggest a relatively warm period for the northern hemisphere from the beginnings of the sequence (5501 B.P./3551 B.C.) until about 3150 B.P./1200 B.C. (LaMarche 1974: 1046). The end of this warm, moist period may be reflected in the early part of the Cuello sequence by the relatively high proportions of Forest Tree charcoal.

Both the Lake Salpeten, Guatemala (Leyden 1984), and Lake Valencia, Venezuela (Bradbury *et al.* 1981), cores suggest slight decreases in forest pollen and minor increases in savanna pollen between around 3000 B.P./1050 B.C. and the late first millennium B.C. The 7.5 m of the Valencia core has seven radiocarbon dates, but events between these points are not precisely dated. This forest-to-savanna shift, of a significantly smaller magnitude than that suggested for the Pleistocene, seems to correlate with the cooler period in the bristlecone pine chronology between 1200 and 300 B.C. (LaMarche 1974). The same shift may be reflected in the Cuello sequence by the increase in pine charcoal between phases III and IVA (*c.* 900–400 B.C.).

The Valencia core suggests an expansion of seasonal forest once again until 1820 ± 70 b.p. (A.D. 118–250) (Bradbury *et al.* 1981), which may correspond with the increase in Forest Tree charcoal during the late facet of Cocos Chicanel, and a return to a warm, moist climate.

A recent article by Folan *et al.* (1983) presented some intriguing climatic patterns that seem to fit quite well with the Formative period palaeoecological sequence from Cuello. They attempted to correlate palaeoclimatic data with Maya settlement patterns. The article included a plot of eustatic sea-level changes for the coastal areas of the Yucatán Peninsula which suggest that during the Early Preclassic sea levels were *c.* 0.75 m above present levels (Folan *et al.* 1983: Fig. 8). The end of this period might correlate well with the abundance of *Pyrgophorus*, *Biomphalaria*, *Pomacea*, *Cladium*, and *Scleria* in early Swasey phase II levels. Sea level then dropped to *c.* 1.5 m below the present level at the end of the Early Preclassic, which could, after some lag, correspond with the hiatus or diminution in activity at Cuello in the middle of Bladen phase III. Since Folan *et al.* are not clear about how the absolute dates for their sea-level changes were obtained – whether from raw radiocarbon dates, calibrated dates, ceramic cross-dating, geology, or just best guesses – a slight shortening of their proposed chronology might be permitted, and would bring the ecological changes at Cuello into line with the sea-level changes on the coast (and the presumably associated changes in river levels on the Hondo and Nuevo in northern Belize).

Folan *et al.* suggest that a dramatic rise in sea level occurred in the Middle Formative, which they place at *c.*1050 B.C. (whether in radiocarbon or calendar years is not clear): this seems to correlate with a peat zone with maize and *Cladium* stems deposited at San Antonio, Albion Island, on the Rio Hondo during a period of increasing water levels and radiocarbon dated to 2626 ± 190 b.p. (990–423 B.C.). It also corresponds well with the local hydrological peak inferred at Cuello for Lopez Mamom phase IV and Cocos Chicanel phase V levels between *c.* 550 and 250 B.C., based on the presence of lacustrine mollusks. In addition, High (1975) identified widespread deposition along the northern coast of Belize that corresponded with a sea-level increase between 1500 and 500 B.C. The higher local water table and the increase in pine charcoal may indicate that the Middle Preclassic was a cool, moist period.

Our understanding of Holocene vegetation change and climatic fluctuations in the Mesoamerican lowlands is only in its most preliminary stages: the palaeoecological data from the Formative sequence at Cuello, spanning the period *c.* 1100 B.C.–A.D. 250, do fit the various reconstructions proposed to date, however, within a modest range of chronological adjustment, and this may well provide a foundation for further investigation of the ecology and economy of the Preclassic period.

THE EXPLOITATION OF ANIMALS

Elizabeth S. Wing and Sylvia J. Scudder

The animal remains from the Preclassic levels at Cuello add to the growing body of data on the use of animals for subsistence and in ceremonial contexts in the Maya Area. One of the central questions that may be answered by the data from this and other sites is the extent to which the Maya controlled their environment, specifically the animal resources in it and the place of hunting and fishing in the pre-Hispanic Maya way of life.

The vertebrate faunal sample considered here was excavated at Cuello in 1976–80, and identified at the Florida Museum of Natural History by Scudder. Some was recovered by trowel excavation, some by screening through 0.63-cm screening, and a small amount from 15 flotation samples. A total of 7,974 bone and tooth fragments were identified to 57 taxa from all vertebrate classes.

The present analysis includes vertebrate samples from early (Swasey and Bladen phases) and late (Lopez Mamom) Middle Preclassic and Late Preclassic (Cocos Chicanel) contexts; the latter included two deer skull caches and the contents of two *chultunob*. There were also contexts of mixed

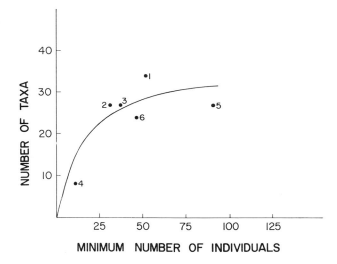

Fig. 4.4 Comparison of number of faunal taxa and minimum numbers of individuals from the successive periods. 1: early Middle Formative (Swasey and Bladen phases); 2: late Middle Formative (Lopez Mamom); 3: Late Formative (Cocos Chicanel); 4: Classic period; 5: *chultun* [F87]; 6: *chultun* [F246].

date, including erosion levels. Classic period remains were too few to be considered an adequate sample for separate analysis (Fig. 4.4).

METHODS

Every bone fragment was identified to the lowest taxon by direct comparison with the reference collection at the Florida Museum of Natural History (Table 4.8). Quantification was by standard zooarchaeological procedures (Wing and Brown 1979). An approximate measure of the number of individuals is obtained by counts of the numbers of fragments, and some of the biases resulting from species with large numbers of identifiable skeletal elements (such as the armadillo) are reduced by calculating minimum numbers of individuals (MNI). MNI were calculated for the animal remains in each cultural unit. A measure of the size of the fragments is provided by the weight (in grams) of the identified material. Each method of quantification is also expressed in relative terms. The resulting data are presented in Tables 4.9–4.15 and Fig. 4.5.

CHARACTERISTICS OF THE FAUNAL SAMPLES

Comparison of the broader classification of these faunal samples reveals both similarities and differences: mammalian remains predominate in all samples except in the *chultun* [F87], where amphibian remains, as measured by fragment count, are overwhelmingly abundant. The contribution of mammals to the weight of each faunal sample is very great,

more than 77 percent: this reflects the greater size of the most important mammals, which are dogs and deer. Second in relative abundance and weight are the reptiles, again with the exception of the sample from *chultun* [F87]. A trend can be seen for the relative increase in the weight of reptile remains and corresponding decrease in the weight of mammalian remains through the Preclassic period. In the late Middle and Late Preclassic fish remains are numerically important, but, as they are small fragments, the contribution of their weight to the samples is insignificant. The most distinctive of the faunal samples is that from *chultun* [F87], which has a great abundance of amphibia, primarily the marine toad *Bufo marinus*, and relatively fewer reptiles than the other samples.

Although fishes do not contribute a great deal to the weight of the samples, the composition of the fish fauna provides unique insight into the fishing practices of the Maya. The total sample includes almost twice the number of freshwater species remains (50) as peripheral and marine species (27) (Miller 1966). Though the sample of fish remains is small, the ratio of freshwater species to peripheral and marine species changes substantially from 2.5 : 1 in the early Middle Formative through 3.8 : 1 in the late Middle Formative to 1 : 3 in the Late Formative.

The predominant species in all these samples are dog (*Canis familiaris*), deer (*Odocoileus virginianus*, and to a far less extent *Mazama* sp.), and turtles. The most abundantly represented of these is the small mud turtle (*Kinosternon* sp.). The other two members of the family Kinosternidae (*Claudius angustatus* and *Staurotypus triporcatus*) are consistently present but in small numbers. The two emydid turtles, the aquatic *Trachemys scripta* and the semiaquatic *Rhinoclemys areolata*, are also abundant. *Rhinoclemys* is the more prevalent of the two in the late Middle Formative samples and in *chultun* [F87]. The large river turtle *Dermatemys mawii* is present in the early Middle and Late Formative samples. The three most abundant turtles, *Kinosternon*, *Trachemys*, and *Rhinoclemys*, show the same increase in their relative contribution to the weight of the sample when they are compared with the combined weights of dog and deer as is seen for reptiles and mammals as a whole. This reflects the importance of these animals in the faunal assemblages.

Evidence that further demonstrates the importance of deer is the Late Preclassic caches of deer skulls [F30] and [F140] (Table 4.15 and Fig. 10.12), which include 329 isolated teeth, 39 upper and lower jaws, and 23 auditory bullae predominantly of white-tailed deer (*Odocoileus virginianus*). Three lower left molars (M_1, M_2, and M_3) are small but worn and are probably attributable to brocket (*Mazama* sp.). In addition, one antler burr is identified to brocket, but otherwise the remains are in the size class for *Odocoileus*. The age distribution as determined from tooth replacement and wear is composed of a majority of subadult individuals (25 MNI) and

Table 4.8 *Species list with common and scientific names*

Family	Scientific name	Common name
Mammals		
Didelphidae	*Didelphis marsupialis*	opossum
Chiroptera		bats
Dasypodidae	*Dasypus novemcinctus*	nine-banded armadillo
Myrmecophagidae[1]	*Tamandua tetradactyla*	four-toed anteater
Leporidae	*Sylvilagus* sp.	rabbit
Sciuridae	*Sciurus* sp.	squirrel
Geomyidae	*Orthogeomys hispidus*	pocket gopher
Cricetidae		mice
	Oryzomys sp.	rice rats
Dasyproctidae	*Agouti paca*	paca
	Dasyprocta punctata	agouti
Canidae	*Canis familiaris*	domestic dog
	Urocyon cinereoargenteus	gray fox
Procyonidae	*Nasua narica*	coati
	Procyon lotor	raccoon
Mustelidae	*Conepatus semistriatus*	hog-nosed skunk
	Galictis probably *G. allamandi*	grison
Felidae[1]	*Felis paradalis*	ocelot
	Felix wiedii	margay
Tayassuidae	*Tayassu pecari*[1]	white-lipped peccary
	Tayassu tajacu[1]	collared peccary
Cervidae	*Mazama* sp.	brocket deer
	Odocoileus virginianus	white-tailed deer
Tapiridae	*Tapirus bairdii*	tapir
Birds		
Phasianidae	*Gallus gallus*[1]	chicken
Meleagrididae	*Meleagris* sp. probably *M. ocellata*	turkey
Psittacidae		parrots
Rhamphastidae[1]	*Rhamphastes* sp.	toucan
Picidae		woodpeckers
Reptiles		
Crocodylidae		crocodile
Boidae	*Constrictor constrictor*	boa
Colubridae	*Drymarchon corais*	indigo snake
	Masticophis probably *M. mentovarius*	coachwhip
Iguanidae	*Ctenosaura similis*	iguana
Dermatemidae	*Dermatemys mawii*	hickety
Emydidae	*Trachemys scripta*	pond turtle
	Rhinoclemys areolata	black-bellied turtle
Kinosternidae	*Claudius angustatus*	mud turtle
	Kinosternon sp.	mud turtle
	Staurotypus triporcatus	loggerhead
Amphibia		
Ranidae	*Rana* sp.	frog
Bufonidae	*Bufo marinus*	marine toad
Rhinophrynidae	*Rhinophrynus dorsalis*	burrowing toad
Plethodontidae		salamander

Family	Scientific name	Common name
Fishes		
Rhinobatidae	*Rhinobatos* sp.	guitarfish
Elopidae	*Megalops atlanticus*	tarpon
Albulidae	*Albula vulpes*	bone fish
Siluriformes		catfishes
Ariidae	*Cathorops* sp.	catfish
Carangidae		jack
Lutjanidae		snapper
Gerreidae[2]		mojarra
Haemulidae		grunt
Sciaenidae		drum
Cichlidae	*Cichlasoma* sp.	mojarra, cichlids
Scaridae	*Sparisoma* sp.	parrotfish
Eleotridae	*Gobiomorus dormitator*	bigmouth sleeper
Acanthuridae[2]	*Acanthurus* sp.	surgeonfish
Scombridae		mackerel

Notes:

[1] May be a modern contaminant

[2] Identified from mixed levels

relatively fewer adults (10 MNI) of the 35 individuals represented.

Several other animals are consistently present but not in large numbers: these are opossum (*Didelphis marsupialis*), armadillo (*Dasypus novemcinctus*), the two large rodents paca (*Agouti paca*) and agouti (*Dasyprocta punctata*), turkey (Meleagrididae), toad (*Bufo* sp.), mojarra (Cichlidae), and catfish (Siluriformes).

The rare species that occur in only one or two lots and are represented by only a few bones are primarily peripheral or marine fishes and a few mammals and birds. The rare species in the *chultun* faunas include tapir (*Tapirus bairdii*), woodpecker (Picidae), parrot (Psittacidae), tarpon (*Megalops atlanticus*), grunt (Haemulidae), and parrotfish (*Sparisoma* sp.). The unusual species represented in the Formative deposits include a squirrel (*Sciurus* sp.), grison (*Galictis* sp.), skunk (*Conepatus semistriatus*), a chicken (*Gallus gallus*) that may be a modern contaminant, a guitarfish (*Rhinobatos* sp.), bonefish (*Albula vulpes*), jack (Carangidae), snapper (Lutjanidae), grunt, drum (Sciaenidae), parrotfish, sleeper (*Gobiomorus dormitator*), and mackerel (Scombridae). The fish remains stand apart from the remains of other classes in their great diversity and at the same time their representation by only a very few identifiable fragments. They differ further by being remains of animals that occur normally in marine and estuarine habitats found at the present day at least 35 km from the Cuello site.

Within the Cuello site the faunal assemblages from distinct cultural contexts have a basic similarity, with the exception of the deer skull caches; despite these basic similarities, the fauna

from *chultun* [F87] are most deviant in terms of the great number of toads and the relatively low ratio of reptiles to mammals. Otherwise the only apparent differences through the sequence are the two trends noted earlier, the increase in reptiles relative to mammals and the increase in peripheral and marine fishes relative to freshwater fishes in the Late Preclassic. These trends may be the result of over-exploitation of the local biome, with a decrease in available mammals, and a resulting broadening of both the catchment area and the spectrum of species utilized.

Comparison of the Cuello fauna with other Maya fauna of the region shows both basic similarities and local variations. The faunal sample from Late Formative deposits at Cerros, studied by Carr (1986), has a similar abundance of dog and deer. It differs from the Cuello sample in the far greater abundance of marine organisms, particularly fishes, as might be anticipated from its coastal location. The Classic period faunas from Colha, southeast of Cuello, and Lubaantun in southern Belize also have abundant deer and dog and a variety of freshwater turtles, but differ from the Cuello fauna in having more marine fishes at Lubaantun (Wing 1975) and more reptiles, including abundant remains of sea turtle and crocodile, at Colha (based on identifications by Scudder of material from the Corozal Project excavations of 1973–75, and on Scott (1982). The Lubaantun and Colha faunas include 41 and 42 percent marine organisms respectively, based on fragment counts, compared with 1 percent at Cuello. A comparison of the abundance of marine with freshwater fish species, as reflected by identified fragment counts, indicates that all the fishes from Colha (as identified by Scudder) and

Table 4.9 *Animal remains from early Middle Formative levels*

Taxa	Number of fragments	Percent of class	Percent of total	Minimum number of individuals	Percent of class	Percent of total	Weight of remains (gm)	Percent of class	Percent of total
Mammals									
Didelphis	13	1		2	10		9.7	tr[1]	
Chiroptera	1	tr		1	5		0.1	tr	
Dasypus	155	14		2	10		42.25	2	
Sylvilagus	7	1		1	5		3.5	tr	
Orthogeomys	3	tr		1	5		1.5	tr	
Cricetidae	3	tr		1	5		0.25	tr	
Agouti	4	tr		1	5		2.2	tr	
Dasyprocta	10	1		1	5		12.15	tr	
Canidae	9	1		—			9.65	tr	
Canis	107	9		3	14		150.65	6	
Procyon	3	tr		1	5		0.5	tr	
Galictis	1	tr		1	5		2.4	tr	
Tayassuidae	19	2		2	10		54.9	2	
Cervidae	129	11		—			290.45	12	
Mazama	24	2		1	5		77.85	3	
Odocoileus	184	16		3	14		966.6	39	
indet. mammal	479	42		—			863.3	35	
Total mammal	1,151		75	21		40	2,487.95		88
Birds									
Meleagris	2			1			2.1		
Gallus	1			1			0.4		
Total birds	3		tr	2		4	2.5		tr
Reptiles									
Constrictor	1	tr		1	6		0.4	tr	
indet. snake	2	1		—			1.5	tr	
Dermatemys	3	1		1	6		2.2	1	
Emydidae	29	8		—			31.8	9	
Trachemys	8	2		2	12		30.2	9	
Rhinoclemys	16	5		1	6		11.7	3	
Kinosternidae	9	3		—			3.75	1	
Claudius	2	1		1	6		0.9	tr	
Kinosternon	152	44		8	47		145.95	43	
Staurotypus	14	4		1	6		27.5	8	
indet. turtle	105	30		—			79.65	24	
Iguanidae	3	1		—			2.3	1	
Ctenosaurus	1	tr		1	6		0.5	tr	
indet. lizard	1	tr		—			0.05	tr	
Crocodylidae	2	1		1	6		1.25	tr	
Total reptile	348		22	17		33	339.65		12
Amphibia									
Rhinophrynus	6	27		2	33		0.45		
Ranidae	4	18		—			0.2		
Rana	1	5		1	17		0.05		

Table 4.9 (*cont.*)

Taxa	Number of fragments	Percent of class	Percent of total	Minimum number of individuals	Percent of class	Percent of total	Weight of remains (gm)	Percent of class	Percent of total
Bufonidae	2	9		1	17		0.1		
Bufo	1	5		1	17		0.2		
Plethodontidae	1	5		1	17		0.05		
indet. anuran	7	32		—			0.3		
Total amphibia	22		1	6		12	1.35		tr
Bony fishes									
Cathorops	2	10		1	17		0.1		
Carangidae	2	10		1	17		1.4		
Cichlidae	7	33		—			0.5		
Cichlasoma	8	38		2	33		0.65		
Gobiomorus	1	5		1	17		0.3		
Scombridae	1	5		1	17		0.2		
Total fish	21		1	6		12	3.15		tr
indet. bone[2]	1,554			—			484.65		
Total vertebrates	1,545			52			2,834.6		
Mollusca									
Strombus	2			2			14.3		

Notes:

[1] trace

[2] not included in total

Table 4.10 *Animal remains from late Middle Formative levels*

Taxa	Number of fragments	Percent of class	Percent of total	Minimum number of individuals	Percent of class	Percent of total	Weight of remains (gm)	Percent of class	Percent of total
Mammals									
Didelphis	2	1		1	7		2.1	1	
Dasypus	108	34		1	7		13.91	4	
Sylvilagus	8	3		1	7		2.3	1	
Sciurus	1	tr		1	7		0.2	tr[1]	
Cricetidae	1	tr		1	7		0.2	tr	
Agouti	1	tr		1	7		1.1	tr	
Dasyprocta	1	tr		1	7		1.2	tr	
Canidae	1	tr		—			0.1	tr	
Canis	66	21		2	14		28.55	9	
Urocyon	1	tr		1	7		0.1	tr	
Tayassuidae	3	1		1	7		6.5	2	

Table 4.10 (*cont.*)

Taxa	Number of fragments	Percent of class	Percent of total	Minimum number of individuals	Percent of class	Percent of total	Weight of remains (gm)	Percent of class	Percent of total
Cervidae	17	5		—			17.6	6	
Mazama	6	2		1	7		15.4	5	
Odocoileus	19	6		2	14		54.9	17	
indet. mammal	87	27		—			175.75	55	
Total mammal	322		47	14		45	319.91		82
Reptiles									
Drymarchon	2	2		1	13		1.2	2	
indet. snake	2	2		—			0.9	1	
indet. lizard	2	2		1	13		0.3	1	
Emydidae	7	6		—			4.3	7	
Trachemys	1	1		1	13		0.4	1	
Rhinoclemys	13	10		1	13		7.8	12	
Claudius	5	4		1	13		4.3	7	
Kinosternon	23	18		2	25		17.3	27	
Staurotypus	7	6		1	13		5.4	8	
indet. turtle	63	50		—			23.0	35	
indet. reptile	2	2		—			0.1	tr	
Total reptile	127		19	8		26	65.0		17
Amphibia									
Bufonidae	2	20		1	33		0.1		
Rhinophrynus	1	10		1	33		0.3		
Plethodontidae	1	10		1	33		0.05		
indet. anuran	6	60		—			0.4		
Total amphibia	10		1	3		10	0.85		tr
Chondrichthyes									
Rhinobatos	1			1			0.2		
Total Chondrichthyes	1		tr	1		3	0.2		tr
Bony fishes									
Albula	3	1		1	20		0.35	6	
Siluriformes	12	5		1	20		0.75	13	
Lutjanidae	1	1		1	20		0.3	5	
Cichlidae	7	3		—			0.4	7	
Cichlasoma	8	4		2	40		0.3	5	
indet. fish	193	86		—			3.85	65	
Total fish	224		33	5		16	5.95		1
indet. bone[2]	1,476			—			245.7		
Total vertebrates	684			31			391.91		

Notes:

[1] trace

[2] not included in total

Table 4.11 *Animal remains from Late Formative levels*

Taxa	Number of fragments	Percent of class	Percent of total	Minimum number of individuals	Percent of class	Percent of total	Weight of remains (gm)	Percent of class	Percent of total
Mammals									
Didelphis	8	1		2	11		7.5	1	
Dasypus	108	19		1	5		22.35	2	
Sylvilagus	2	tr[1]		1	5		0.9	tr	
Orthogeomys	1	tr		1	5		0.5	tr	
Cricetidae	2	tr		1	5		0.1	tr	
Agouti	1	tr		1	5		9.5	1	
Canidae	1	tr		—			0.2	tr	
Canis	98	17		5	26		149.6	12	
Urocyon	2	tr		1	5		4.8	tr	
Procyon	2	tr		1	5		9.1	1	
Conepatus	1	tr		1	5		1.9	tr	
Cervidae	54	9		—			81.5	8	
Mazama	6	1		1	5		29.8	3	
Odocoileus	112	19		3	16		479.9	46	
indet. mammal	183	31		—			246.35	24	
Total mammal	581		63	19		51	1,044.2		74
Birds									
Total indet.	4		tr	1		3	1.05		tr
Reptiles									
Constrictor	2	1		1	10		1.3	tr	
Drymarchon	1	tr		1	10		0.5	tr	
Iguanidae	1	tr		1	10		0.1	tr	
indet. lizard	3	1		—			0.15	tr	
Dermatemys	8	4		1	10		50.6	14	
Emydidae	6	3		—			10.9	3	
Trachemys	19	8		1	10		119.2	33	
Rhinoclemys	2	1		1	10		1.5	tr	
Kinosternidae	2	1		—			0.6	tr	
Kinosternon	86	38		3	30		85.5	24	
Staurotypus	1	tr		1	10		3.1	1	
indet. turtle	94	42		—			87.3	24	
Total reptiles	225		25	10		27	360.75		26
Amphibia									
Bufonidae	1			1			0.1		
Bufo	2			1			0.9		
indet. anuran	1			—			0.1		
Total amphibia	4		tr	2		5	1.1		tr
Bony fishes									
Siluriformes	4	4		1	20		0.2		
Haemulidae	1	1		1	20		0.1		
Sciaenidae	1	1		1	20		0.3		
Cichlidae	1	1		1	20		0.1		

Table 4.11 (*cont.*)

Taxa	Number of fragments	Percent of class	Percent of total	Minimum number of individuals	Percent of class	Percent of total	Weight of remains (gm)	Percent of class	Percent of total
Sparisoma	1	1		1	20		0.1		
indet. fish	96	92		—			3.45		
Total fish	104		11	5		14	4.25		tr
indet. bone[2]	1,912			—			505.25		
Total vertebrates	918			37			1,411.35		
Mollusca									
Strombidae	1			1			51.1		
indet. shell	2			—			1.1		
Total mollusca	3			1			52.2		

Notes:

[1] trace

[2] not included in total

Table 4.12 *Vertebrate remains associated with a Late Formative* chultun *[F87]*

Taxa	Number of fragments	Percent of class	Percent of total	Minimum number of individuals	Percent of class	Percent of total	Weight of remains (gm)	Percent of class	Percent of total
Mammals									
Didelphidae	1	tr[1]		—			0.1	tr	
Didelphis	8	2		5	11		1.6	tr	
Chiroptera	2	tr		1	2		0.2	tr	
Dasypus	106	19		11	23		24.7	4	
Sylvilagus	3	1		3	6		2.1	tr	
Orthogeomys	4	1		4	9		3.6	1	
Cricetidae	55	10		1	2		1.2	tr	
Dasyprocta	2	tr		1	2		2.8	tr	
Canidae	1	tr		—			0.1	tr	
Canis	76	14		14	30		206.5	31	
Urocyon	1	tr		1	2		0.4	tr	
Tayassuidae	1	tr		1	2		0.9	tr	
Cervidae	11	2		—			19.1	3	
Odocoileus	27	5		5	11		246.3	36.7	
indet. mammal	250	46		—			160.7	24	
Total mammal	548		27	47		52	670.3		84

Table 4.12 (*cont.*)

Taxa	Number of fragments	Percent of class	Percent of total	Minimum number of individuals	Percent of class	Percent of total	Weight of remains (gm)	Percent of class	Percent of total
Birds									
Meleagris	2			1			12.1		
Psittacidae	1			1			0.1		
indet. bird	9			—			0.3		
Total bird	12		1	2		2	12.5		2
Reptiles									
indet. snake	4	5		1	6		0.1	tr	
Iguanidae	3	4		1	6		0.1	tr	
indet. lizard	19	24		—			0.1	tr	
Emydidae	1	1		—			0.4	1	
Trachemys	2	3		2	13		16.6	31	
Rhinoclemys	16	20		5	31		16.9	32	
Claudius	2	3		2	13		3.1	6	
Kinosternon	10	13		5	31		9.6	18	
indet. turtle	22	28		—			6.5	12	
Total reptile	79		4	16		18	53.4		7
Amphibia									
Rhinophrynus	16	2		4	19		0.6	1	
Ranidae	2	tr		1	5		0.05	tr	
Bufo	456	44		16	76		31.5	66	
indet. anuran	554	54		—			15.6	33	
Total amphibia	1,028		50	21		23	47.75		6
Bony fishes									
Megalops	1	tr		1	20		3.2	24	
Siluriformes	2	1		—			0.2	2	
Ariidae	6	2		1	20		0.35	3	
Haemulidae	5	1		1	20		0.45	3	
Cichlidae	9	2		1	20		0.5	4	
Sparisoma	1	tr		1	20		0.1	1	
indet. fish	346	94		—			8.35	64	
Total fish	370		18	5		6	13.15		2
indet. bone[2]	2,514						89.7		
Total vertebrates	2,037			91			797.1		

Notes:

[1] trace

[2] not included in total

Table 4.13 *Vertebrate remains associated with a Late Formative* chultun *[F246]*

Taxa	Number of fragments	Percent of class	Percent of total	Minimum number of individuals	Percent of class	Percent of total	Weight of remains (gm)	Percent of class	Percent of total
Mammals									
Didelphis	61	13		6	27		86.6	3	
Dasypus	50	10		2	9		54.8	2	
Sylvilagus	4	1		1	5		4.2	tr[I]	
Oryzomys	1	tr		1	5		0.1	tr	
Agouti	1	tr		1	5		0.9	tr	
Dasyprocta	2	tr		1	5		5.7	tr	
Canidae	2	tr		—			2.1	tr	
Canis	36	7		1	5		127.3	4	
Urocyon	4	1		1	5		11.1	tr	
Tayassuidae	3	1		1	5		17.0	1	
Cervidae	5	1		—			34.85	1	
Mazama	3	1		1	5		10.7	tr	
Odocoileus	129	27		5	23		2,334.4	72	
Tapirus	1	tr		1	5		125.3	4	
indet. mammal	182	38		—			417.1	13	
Total mammal	484		60	22		47	3,232.15		90
Birds									
Meleagris	1			1			1.1		
Picidae	1			1			0.2		
indet. bird	3			—			1.9		
Total bird	5		1	2		4	3.2		tr
Reptiles									
Colubridae	1	tr		—			0.95	tr	
Masticophis	11	4		1	5		4.1	1	
Iguanidae	4	1		1	5		1.15	tr	
indet. lizard	3	1		—			0.5	tr	
Emydidae	1	tr		—			1.4	tr	
Trachemys	19	7		2	11		76.95	21	
Rhinoclemys	16	6		2	11		33.2	9	
Claudius	2	1		1	5		0.6	tr	
Kinosternon	146	50		10	53		214.85	58	
Staurotypus	6	2		2	11		17.7	5	
indet. turtle	79	27		—			16.6	5	
indet. reptile	4	1		—			2.0	1	
Total reptile	292		36	19		40	370.0		10
Amphibia									
Bufo	2			2			0.6		
indet. anuran	1			—			0.5		
Total amphibia	3		tr	2		4	1.1		tr
Bony fishes									
Siluriformes	2			—			0.2		
Ariidae	1			1			0.15		

Table 4.13 (*cont.*)

Taxa	Number of fragments	Percent of class	Percent of total	Minimum number of individuals	Percent of class	Percent of total	Weight of remains (gm)	Percent of class	Percent of total
Cichlidae	10			1			1.6		
indet. fish	5			—			1.3		
Total fish	18		2	2		4	3.25		tr
indet. bone[2]	541			—			127.8		
Total vertebrates	802			47			3,609.7		
Mollusca									
Pomacea	2			2			18.7		
Nephronaias	3			2			13.6		
Total Mollusca	5			4			32.3		

Notes:

[1] trace

[2] not included in total

Table 4.14 *Contribution of the five vertebrate classes to the total Cuello fauna*

Vertebrate Classes	Number of fragments	Percent of total	Minimum number of individuals	Percent of total	Weight of remains (gm)	Percent of total
Mammals	4,933	62	979	73	10,110.39	83
Birds	13	tr	6	1	23.9	tr
Reptiles	1,706	21	247	18	2,028.16	17
Amphibia	1,198	15	56	4	61.65	1
Fishes	124	2	54	4	16.85	tr
Total	7,974		1,342		12,240.95	

Table 4.15 *Cache [F140] of deer skulls from the Late Formative*

	Incisors		Premolars				Molars				Auditory bulla	
			Upper		Lower		Upper		Lower			
	left	right	left	right	left	right	left	right	left	right	left	right
[1]*Subadults*												
Deciduous teeth	3	2	16	21	16	22						
Permanent unworn teeth	5	3	7	10	27	11	23	46	74	34		

Table 4.15 (*cont.*)

	Incisors		Premolars				Molars				Auditory bulla	
			Upper		Lower		Upper		Lower			
	left	right	left	right	left	right	left	right	left	right	left	right
Adults												
Teeth			1	1			1	4	2			
No maturity determined											11	12

	Upper jaws		Lower jaws	
	left	right	left	right
Subadults[1]				
Jaws with deciduous dentition	1	3	10	8
Jaws with permanent unworn teeth			2	1
Adults				
Jaws			6	8

Note:
[1] Subadults under 30 months of age

Lubaantun are marine species, whereas only 35 percent of the fishes from Cuello are marine. Lubaantun and Colha were occupied during the Classic period, later than Cuello, and are slightly closer to the coast. Both of these factors may account for the observed differences in the relative amounts of marine organisms in these faunas; field recovery methods were similar at all three sites and are unlikely to be a deranging factor.

With the exception of the relatively greater abundance of marine organisms, the species compositions of these faunas are similar – deer, dog, and freshwater turtles abound. This does suggest great stability in the pattern of animal use through Preclassic and Classic times. Both deer and dog featured in lowland Maya ritual (Pohl 1981, 1983), but of the faunal remains from Cuello only the two deer skull caches have clear ritual connotations.

The marine toad (*Bufo marinus*) is the other animal that is frequently associated with both Olmec and Maya faunas and may have ritual significance (Furst 1981; Hamblin 1984). Controversy surrounds the toad finds, because they are not a likely food item in view of the poisonous parotid glands, which would require special removal to render the meat harmless. The parotid gland and its poison, bufotenin, would also require special preparation if it were to be used as a psychotropic substance. Whether or not the meat or parotid glands were used, toads feature in the iconography of the Olmec and also the sacred beliefs of the Maya (Furst 1981; Pohl 1983). Thus the large number of toad remains from *chultun* [F87] may be

from intentionally deposited toads; but the chance that the *chultun* acted as a natural trap and that the toads were intrusive should not be dismissed.

All the animals that are abundantly represented at the site could have been procured in the vicinity, and the dogs were undoubtedly reared in the community. The river turtle (*Dermatemys mawei*), as well as some peripheral fishes such as tarpon (*Megalops atlanticus*), would probably have been caught in the Rio Hondo, or the Río Nuevo *c.* 5 km from Cuello. Most of the marine fishes, particularly the surgeonfish (*Acanthurus* sp.) parrotfish, and grunt, would have to come from Chetumal Bay, 35 km north, or the Caribbean coast 50 km east of the site. This is a very extensive catchment area. The faunas from Colha (22 km from the coast) and Lubaantun (25 km) suggest even greater use by Classic Maya of distant marine resources. The marine species at these sites may not be ordinary food items because of the greater transportation distance involved in their procurement; the variety of species represented and the paucity of remains of each also suggest that they were specialty items, and not staples in the way that deer, dog, and freshwater turtles seem to have been.

In summary, the faunal remains are a sample of the animals used by the (probable) élite occupants of Formative period Cuello. As such, they represent a pattern of animal use that continued into the Classic period, with some adaptations to use of local resources. Dogs were reared presumably for food, and their remains do not seem to differ from those of other

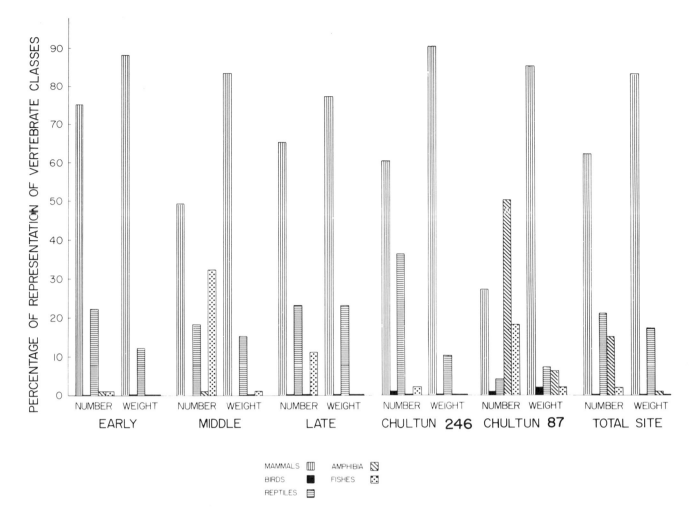

Fig. 4.5 Distribution of fauna in Formative period levels:
Early = Swasey and Bladen, phases O–IIIA; Middle = Lopez
Mamom, phases IV–IVA; Late = Cocos Chicanel, phases V–XIII.
Chultun [F246] is of early Cocos, and *chultun* [F87] of late Cocos
date.

species in any respect, except for modification of some of the
dog teeth. Hunting was based on the primary prey species, the
white-tailed deer, and to a lesser extent on the large rodents,
peccary, other medium-sized mammals, and turkey. Fishing
in small ponds would have been rewarded by catches of

cichlids, and mud and pond turtles. The products of fishing in
more distant marine waters were also used at the site. The
marine resources are scarce commodities in the faunal assemblage but are significant evidence of the distant extent of the
catchment area.

The uses of animals for purposes other than subsistence are
not always as obvious as the deer skull cache, which is clearly
ritual: the toad remains from the *chultun* are problematical,
having as good a chance of being intrusive as of being a
functional deposit, and the marine fishes may also have had a
non-subsistence use because of the costs involved in their
procurement.

Chapter 5   # THE COMMUNITY OF CUELLO: THE CEREMONIAL CORE

Juliette Cartwright Gerhardt and Norman Hammond

Two main periods of architectural development in the core of Formative period Cuello can be defined, prior to and succeeding the transformation which took place at the beginning of the Late Formative period in phase V (Chapter 3; Hammond 1991b; Hammond and Gerhardt 1990). In the early period, spanning stratigraphic phases I–IVA, low platforms were tightly clustered around a patio less than 20 m across, with the boundaries of the patio shifting no more than 2 m in any direction over the entire period. Additional structures were packed into the gaps between the three major buildings on the north, west, and south sides (the east side remaining unexcavated); the patio was surfaced by successive Patio Floors I–V (Figs. 3.2–3.8). This period is dated by pottery of the Swasey, Bladen, and Lopez Mamom ceramic complexes, with a few Cocos Chicanel sherds appearing just before phase V. The late period, spanning stratigraphic phases VA–XIV and dating entirely to the age of Cocos Chicanel ceramics, consisted of the successive open surfaces (Plaza Floors I–X: Figs. 3.10–3.19) of Platform 34, a broad elevation with buildings on its north and west sides, that on the west eventually becoming a 6 m high stepped pyramid. A southern building was present in phase VA, but not thereafter within the excavated area, and with few surface indications outside it. The plaza on top of Platform 34 was 25 percent longer from north to south in phase VA than the phase IVA patio, and enlarged even further southwards from phase VI onwards. The transition from the first to the second of these long periods of development, the architectural transformation of phase V (Fig. 3.9), involved partial demolition of the buildings around the patio, infill of the patio, and the laying of thick fills over the whole courtyard group to support the first surface of Platform 34 (Plaza Floor I), accompanied by offerings ranging from a cache of jade beads to the slaughter and mass burial of 32 individuals (Hammond 1991b). Details of the dimensions and associated features of all buildings are summarized in Table 5.1 at the end of this chapter.

Fig. 5.1 Structure 328 (phase I–IA) from the east, showing the low elevation, irregular outline, and numerous post holes from perishable superstructures. A circular baked-clay hearth (with small scale) is at center rear. The large hole at right rear is the later grave of burial 123 [F251], phase IIIA (Fig. 10.2). (Scale in cm).

Fig. 5.2 Structure 329 (phase I) from the east, as exposed in grids 35/30 and 30/35 in 1979. The other quadrants were excavated to bedrock in 1976 (Hammond *et al.* 1979: Fig. 7). Peripheral and interior post holes and the depressions of later firepits can be seen. (Scale in 0.5 m units).

EARLY PERIOD: PHASES I–IIIA

The initial occupation of this part of the Cuello locality left behind cultural debris mixed and impacted into the old land surface, with several post holes penetrating underlying bed-rock and not associated with subsequent platform architecture. Similar evidence of structures built on the ground surface, noted in the Jenney Creek phase at Barton Ramie (Willey *et al.* 1965: 279) and the Xe phase at Altar de Sacrificios (Smith 1972: 78) in the middle part of the first millennium B.C., is reported in this volume for the area outside Platform 34 by Wilk and Wilhite (Chapter 6), who characterize this class of evidence as "non-mound occupation," and has since been found in Classic period contexts at Nohmul by Pyburn (1987, 1989).

Fig. 5.3 A typical "firepit" ([F64] of phase IA), with a pottery inner lining from the base of a large jar, set in two layers of clay baked hard by fires which have blackened the interior. (Scale in cm).

The first structural remains at Cuello were two eroded low platforms, Structures 328 and 329, built on the old ground surface in phase I (Figs. 3.2, 5.1–5.2). Post holes in their plaster floors indicate several successive timber-framed superstructures; the entire surface of Structure 329 seems likely to have been interior space, judging by the perimeter distribution of the post holes in the better-preserved northern portion, while the concentration of post holes on Structure 328 is in the center, around a shallow basin with hardened clay lining. The area around both structures was a cobbled pavement that may have been surfaced with marl; by phase IA this had covered Structure 329 (Fig. 3.3), and its site became occupied by a number of "firepits," depressions lined with clay, stones, the base of a large pottery vessel with the rim broken off, or any combination of the three (Fig. 5.3). Burning and hardening of the surrounding area shows that fires were lit in these features, and their fills usually contained much charcoal. We took this to be in primary association, and the radiocarbon ages obtained from it to be directly relevant to the dating of the phase with which the firepits are associated; a note of caution is, however, indicated by Wauchope's (1938:138) ethnographic description of Maya wash-bowls:

Clothes are washed in the house or under a shelter outside. Usually a large dug-out wash trough is used, but in many places one sees big bowls of pottery embedded in the ash heaps which are part of the cleansing equipment. These could be readily identified if found at an ancient house site ... The ash heaps were partially solidified by water and in all cases the imprints left by the bowls were still clear. Sometimes the bowls and the rocks which are packed against their rims are found in their original position, especially when the bowls have broken and are of no further use to anyone.

Fig. 5.4 Structure 327 (phase II) from the east, with Patio Floor I in the foreground. Two stages of interior flooring can be seen on Structure 327, the later at center with a curved outline and turnup to a vanished wall. The excavation at left, which has removed much of the structure, is the 1975 test pit Op. 17B. (Scale in 0.5 m units).

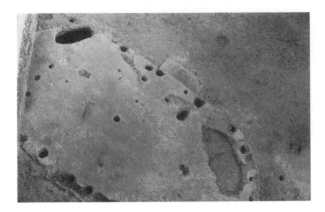

Fig. 5.6 Structure 326 (phase II) from above, with the floor (2056) of the final stage and T-shaped entry flanked by large posts and (?)screen walls visible. The peripheral main post holes and rear outset to the platform (lower left) are also notable. Grave [F251] is at upper left; the depression at right is a repaired worn area.

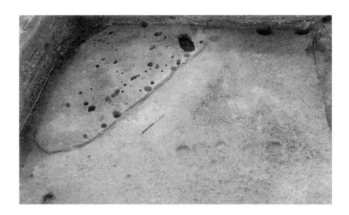

Fig. 5.5 Structure 326 (phase II) from the east, with the floor of building stage "A" exposed. Some of the post holes are from subsequent stages, and the deep grave [F251] is from phase IIIA/IV. The depressions of later firepits can be seen in Patio Floor I and cutting the western section. (Scale in 0.5 m units).

Fig. 5.7 Structure 320 (phase III–IIIA) from the south, seen in the grid 35/35 excavation of 1976 with floor (130) of building stage "b" (phase IIIA) exposed. Two pottery-lined pits lie just inside the south frontage, and burial [76/137], cut from a higher level, can be seen in the northwest corner. The phase V rubble infill is retained by shuttering to east and west, which stands on narrow benches of Patio Floor V left unexcavated to support them. Part of the stone wall and floors of Structure 315d can be seen in the north section, with earlier building floors below and plaza floors of Platform 34 above it. (Scale in 0.5 m units).

Wauchope's Plate 36c, d shows such wash-bowls set among stones and ash. The distinction of the Cuello firepits is that they were carefully constructed, not *ad hoc* collocations, and that hardening demonstrated burning within the containers. The buildup of occupation soil around the firepits indicates persistent or intensive use of the locus; its extent is unknown, although it is likely that other structures lie beyond the excavated area (which at this phase is only 200 sq. m). One interment, burial 62 [F110] may be associated with this phase.

The first courtyard group, with three platforms on the north, west, and south sides of a patio, was constructed in phase II (Fig. 3.4). The platforms were still very low: the four successive stages of reflooring of Structure 325 on the north raised its internal floor to a maximum height of 0.2 m. Each floor had post holes indicating a perishable superstructure,

while Structure 327 on the west side had two stages (Fig. 5.4), and Structure 326 on the south, three (Figs. 5.5–5.6). The latter also rose to a height of only 0.2 m, although acquiring both a projecting axial step and a basal molding on its north front, and having evidence for a funnel-shaped entry with a T-shaped floor sloping slightly inwards (Fig. 5.6). These three buildings were linked by Patio Floor I, running 11 m from

Fig 5.8 Structure 321 (phases III–IIIA) from the east, with Patio Floor I in front penetrated by the firepit [75/197]. The step giving access to the platform lies, partly excavated, behind the large scale and marked by the smaller. Part of the internal floor is visible, but much has been removed by the 1975 pit. (Scale in 0.5 m units).

north to south and at least 8 m east from Structure 327. Firepits, as well as a clay-lined trough [F67], lay in the patio, both close to buildings and out in the center of the space, indicating domestic activities.

The courtyard layout was maintained when Structures 320, 321, and 323 were built directly over these buildings in phase II (at which time pottery of the Bladen ceramic complex replaced that of the antecedent Swasey complex); at the same time the patio was enlarged northwards by 2 m, with Structure 325 being cut back and 320 built only partly over its remains (Fig. 3.5). This building remained in use, with six refloorings that attained a height of 0.4 m, until phase IV, and had a similar orientation, size, and bow-fronted apsidal plan to its predecessor (Fig. 5.7). On the west side of the patio, Structure 321 was larger than 327, rising to a height of 0.6 m by phase IV and needing inset steps to gain access (Fig. 5.8). Structure 323 similarly engulfed 326, with a final height of 1 m; most of its interior floors were destroyed by phase IV remodeling, but sufficient evidence remained to document the existence of perishable superstructures for each of its six stages, of front steps and a possible basal molding (Fig. 5.9). Patio Floor II, raising the level of the courtyard by an average 0.12 m, was laid in two stages, at the north and south ends respectively. The northwest and southwest margins of the patio between the platforms were marked by rows of stones bolstering the edge of the plaster and making a formal limit (Fig. 5.9, far right), with the post holes of a small construction just inside it on the northwest, and several firepits. At the south end Structure 324, a large, flat, very low ovoid/circular

plaster platform was built in front of Structure 323, lacking post holes in the small western portion that lay within the excavation (Fig. 5.10). Resurfacing of the southern part of the patio abutted it.

Patio Floor III in phase IIIA buried Structure 324 and raised the level a mean 0.15 m (Fig. 3.6). Firepits and post holes were confined to its edges, adjacent to the buildings. A new platform, Structure 322, was fitted in between 320 and 321, the northern end of the latter being shortened, perhaps to accommodate the new construction. Structure 322 lay off the edge of the patio floor, so that, although it was 0.15 m high, its surface was level with the patio. A second floor raised it slightly.

The first part of the Early Period of architectural development at Cuello thus spans stratigraphic phases I–IIIA and the Swasey and Bladen ceramic complexes, the latter with modal and typological ties to the Xe sphere that indicate a date in the second quarter of the first millennium B.C., extending back into the first quarter. Radiocarbon ages for Swasey, discussed in Chapter 3 and listed in Table 3.1, range from firepit and midden material dating to the early/mid-second millennium, to firepit contents of the first half of the first millennium B.C. and human bone collagen dating to the same period.

Structure and function

Structural features of architecture in this period, which whatever its lower limits should on general comparative grounds finish before 500 B.C., can be summarized thus: the building platform is the only structure type present, defined as "a substructure component that directly sustains, or appears to sustain, a Building. The building platform duplicates or very closely approximates the Building in its perimeter plan" (Loten and Pendergast 1984: 5). The Swasey/Bladen building

Fig. 5.9 Structure 323 (phase III–IIIA), with the internal floor (1782) of building stage c (phase III) exposed on the remaining stub of the platform, cut back to this line in phase IV. The line of the front, with central step, and the extent of the demolition to extend the patio southwards, are clear, as are the floors of later phases in the south section and the infill of phase V in the west section. Patio Floor II (2014) is in the foreground, and the boundary wall of the patio linking Structures 323 and 321 is at far right. (Scale in 0.1 m units).

Fig. 5.10 The exposed western arc of Structure 324 (phase III), from above, with part of the first stage of Structure 323 at upper left and several firepits in the first period (2006) of Patio Floor II. (Scale in 0.5 m units).

platforms were constructed of a core of small stones and earth within a low retaining wall of limestone cobbles (see Hammond *et al.* 1979: Fig. 6). Over the core an earthen surface was packed and/or a layer of plaster was spread. The plaster was made from burned lime or lime mixed with clay, sand, or some other inert material, applied as a paste or slurry over a rough base or ballast of stones. The floors supported superstructures of perishable materials, of which only post holes and fragments of daub survive. The former can indicate the maximum diameter, and thus the likely height, of principal posts, while the latter preserve impressions of smaller wall posts, poles, or canes infilling between them, vine binders, vegetable matter mixed in as stiffening, and sometimes (if the daub is from the top of the wall) impressions of the leaves used for thatch. The overall appearance of the buildings must have been close to that of traditional Maya houses such as those documented by Wauchope (1938); see also Hammond (1988: Fig. 3.15), and Hammond and Gerhardt (1990), and for a study of daub fragments at Cuello, Dunsmore (n.d.).

The surfaces of the platforms were periodically renewed and the superstructures rebuilt. The two phase I structures had only one stage of flooring, which may account for their worn condition, but from phase II onwards reflooring was the norm. Many factors must have influenced the frequency of rebuilding, including decay or accidental destruction of the superstructure, and burial below the floor, as noted for contact period times by Landa (Tozzer 1941: 130). Reflooring the platforms gradually raised their level relative to the patio; but the patio was itself refloored, and some of the buildings may have been raised to maintain their relative elevation.

Attachments to building platforms, including axial front steps, both inset and projecting, basal moldings, and interior thresholds appear in phase II; by phase III the addition of a mantle of earth and rubble over existing structures to create new, larger, ones had begun, a concomitant of the desire to maintain residence on the same spot. Solid retaining walls, of coursed limestone blocks, shaped or rough, were used instead of the smaller cobbles, but were also faced with plaster. Platforms were now up to 0.6 m high. Those of the Early Period were usually apsidal in plan, with a fairly straight front and rear wall, although both subcircular and ovoid examples occurred. Materials used were local, including limestone cobbles and blocks, lime plaster, clay, and earth. The superstructures could have been of many locally available tree species (Hammond and Miksicek 1981), and where sufficient post holes survive (as with Structure 326) can be seen to follow the perimeter of the building platform.

No overall pattern can be discerned for phase I, with only two structures excavated, although the entire area seems to have been paved. From phase II, the buildings were organized around a central, open, plaster-surfaced patio, with evidence for outdoor activities such as cooking and perhaps washing, which by phase III are confined to the edges of the patio. Any identification of function for these structures must be tentative and based on both internal evidence and external comparanda, including archaeological evidence from other sites and ethnohistoric sources.

Structure 329 may well have been a house platform, given its apparently apsidal superstructure, whereas Structure 328 seems to have been some sort of ancillary building. Erosion of the area between them is such that it is not impossible that they were initially a continuous surface supporting several small buildings. The use of the northern part of the area for firepits in phase IA suggests that other structures probably lie outside the northern and western limits of excavation.

Fig. 5.11 Structure 316 (phases IV–IVA), seen during excavation at building stage e (phase IVA). The frontage was ripped away in phase V: its outline can be seen at right in the edge of the plaster of Patio Floor V. The ramp at center is a "running baulk," and shows part of the destruction deposit banked against the remains of Structure 316.

The creation of the patio group in phase II implies a relationship between the structures reflecting the social organization of the people who built it. All three structures seem to have been house platforms, as they do for phases III and IIIA, although Structure 323 was by this time over 11 m long. Structure 322, fitted into the northwest angle of the group but off the edge of the patio floor, may have served a subsidiary function such as storage or cooking, while Structure 324, in the patio rather than bordering it and lacking any evidence for a superstructure, may have been of ceremonial function. Tourtellot (1970: 414) suggests that later buildings found in patios at Seibal were oratories.

The overall character of the Swasey and Bladen phase buildings, the lack of caches, and the nature of the trash found suggest a residential function for the patio group, perhaps as the residence of an extended family.

EARLY PERIOD: PHASES IV–IVA

In the second part of the Early Period, phases IV and IVA of the stratigraphic sequence, characterized by pottery of the Lopez Mamom ceramic complex (conventionally dated 600–400/300 B.C.), there was significant modification and expansion of the patio group. The northward enlargement of the

patio that had occurred in phase III with the building of Structure 320 was reflected on the south in phase IV when the front of Structure 323 was ripped away down to patio level and its interior cut back for some 2.5 m. The stub was refaced as Structure 316, and Patio Floor IV was laid over the leveled remains of the front portion to abut the new building, giving a space 17 m long (Fig. 3.7). Structure 316 retained the apsidal plan of its precursor; only a small part of it lay inside the excavation, standing 0.7 m high and reached by two steps that were later covered over by a projecting stepped front terrace. All six of the interior floors had post holes from timber superstructures, but destruction of the edges of the building platform in phase V had removed any evidence of their wall plan (Fig. 5.11).

The gap in the southwest corner of the patio opened up by the demolition of Structure 323 was filled by a new platform, Structure 318; so little of the convex frontage of this lay inside the excavation that its presence, and later almost complete demolition, are the only salient facts known. In contrast, in the northeast corner almost all of Structure 319, built over 322, was exposed. At least four firepits lay in its interior, and stake holes in the surviving floor area suggest a light superstructure.

The construction of Patio Floor IV was preceded by the interment of burial 123 [F251] in a very deep grave cutting into bedrock through the truncated fill of Structure 323. It is not certain whether the grave preceded the demolition or not, but interment out in the patio was certainly begun in phase IV: burial 22 [F49], a mature-to-old male, was laid in a grave

Fig. 5.14 Structure 315 (phase IVA) with the front of stage d exposed on the north side of Patio Floor V, excavated in grid 35/35 in the 1976 season. There has been destruction of the platform at its west end, and of the front step, exposing the demolition scar of a precursor. Part of the limestone cobble wall of the stone superstructure can be seen in the north section, with the door jamb separated by a plaster septum, and the doorway blocked by stones lying on the front terrace. The phase V rubble infill of the patio can be seen in the west section. (Scale in 0.5 m units).

Fig. 5.12 Structure 315 (phases IV–IVA) from above, in 1987. The rectangular outline of the demolished north (with remnant blocks) and west sides of building d encloses the stepped apsidal rear portion of stage c. The mouth of the later *chultun* [F246] is adjacent to the west side, and the southern portion was removed by excavation in 1976. (Large scale in 0.5 m units; small scales in cm).

Fig. 5.13 Structures 317 and 314 (phase IVA), from the east in the 1976 grid 30/30, with the 1975 Op. 17B at rear. The fragmentary walls are from Structure 314, overlying Structure 317, of which the outline of the front step and façade, cut away to patio level, can be seen. (Scale in 0.5 m units).

cut into, and sealed by a patch in, the patio floor at or close to the center point (Fig. 10.3). Such burials in Classic times are often regarded as ancestor shrines, and this may be an early example of such cult activity.

Phase IVA saw the complete remodeling of the northern half of the patio, associated with Patio Floor V (Fig. 3.8). Structure 320 was succeeded by Structure 315, of which the first three stages seem to have been rather similar apsidal platforms (judging by the very fragmentary remains: Fig. 5.12), and Structure 321 on the west by 317. The latter extended further east, narrowing the patio slightly, and had a

projecting front terrace with an outset step; its five stages of reflooring raised it from 0.35 to 0.7 m above the patio before it was partly demolished halfway through phase IVA. This followed the familiar pattern of complete removal of the façade down to patio level, and of the platform for up to 2 m back (Fig. 5.13), but the scattering of jade beads in the scar of the step is the first instance at Cuello of this type of termination ritual (noted later in the Late Formative at Cerros: Garber 1983, 1989: 47–50). In the angle between the two platforms the platform of Structure 319, damaged only by removal of its front step, became buried by accumulated trash, into which at least two graves were cut (burials 18 and 20 [F32, 35]).

A second and more drastic remodeling in phase IVA took place when Patio Floor V was extended north by the addition of a long strip of plaster over the demolished front of Structure 315c, to abut stage d of the same building (Fig. 5.14). This was given a straight front, with an axial step leading to a terrace in front of a stone-walled superstructure, the earliest at Cuello (and, from its association with Lopez Mamom pottery, dating to *c.* 400 B.C.). The walls of this had been cut down to their two lowest courses in the following stage (Fig. 5.15), and the side and rear of the platform had been removed in phase V (Fig. 5.16; see also Fig. 3.8), so that the form of this building remains otherwise unknown. On the west side of the patio Structure 314, also with a straight front and with the remains of a masonry superstructure (Figs. 5.13, 5.17), replaced 317, expanding north and south of it by the addition of further masses of fill; it is thought to extend far enough west below the pyramid for Structure 355 at the base of the stratigraphic sequence in the east pyramid trench to be its rear (Fig. 3.20),

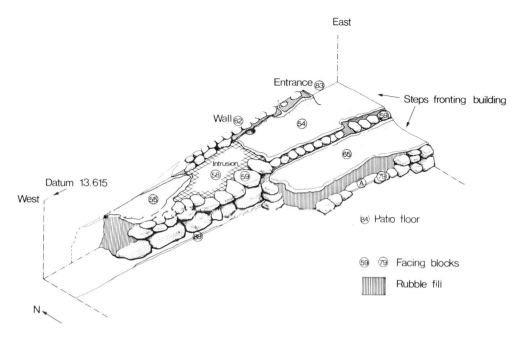

Fig. 5.15 Isometric reconstruction from the southwest of Structure 315 stage d (drawn by Nigel Fradgley). (A) is the scar of a demolished front step antedating that shown (65/79). Context numbers are those of the 1976 excavation. The door jamb flanking the entry (83) and separated by a plaster septum from the wall (62) should be noted.

Fig. 5.16 Structure 315 (phase IVA), with the demolished west side of stage d in the foreground, the north side at left, and the remains of stages b and c buried inside it. (Large scale in 0.5 m units; small scales in cm).

in which case the platform would have been some 13 m deep by 10 m wide. The area between it and Structure 315d was also paved with plaster, the first time that such flooring had extended beyond the patio. The replacement of Structure 315d by stage e (Fig. 5.18), reverting to a perishable superstructure, is the last episode of remodeling before the phase V demolitions.

Structure and function

Structural features of this second half of the Early Period, spanning stratigraphic phases IV and IVA and characterized entirely by Lopez Mamom pottery, continued many of those established in the previous period. Building platforms used the same inventory of materials and the same construction techniques, but were consistently raised further above the patio surface (noted in the Preclassic structures at Barton Ramie also: Willey et al. 1965: 158). All of the Lopez Mamom platforms at Cuello were stepped and had either small axial outset steps for access, or a broad terrace nearly the height of the interior floor with inset or outset steps or a combination of both. Their ground plans were apsidal for most of the period, although Structure 319, like 322 before it, was subcircular due to the small space into which it had to be fitted. Large straight-fronted rectangular platforms were built in the second part of phase IVA, associated with straight-walled masonry superstructures. The walls of these were laid in rows of limestone cobbles packed with earth and faced with plaster, and the one surviving example of a door jamb shows it to have been constructed separately from the wall.

The same locations at the cardinal points (with the axis skewed slightly east of north) were used for the main structures, although the patio was extended first south, then north by a total of 4m, and there was room for an additional building, Structure 318, on the southwest. The patio area was used much less for domestic activities than before: only one firepit [F218] cut Patio Floor IV and none were found in Patio Floor V. Structure 319 had at least four in its interior, and it seems likely that, whatever the functions of the firepits, these

Fig. 5.17 The north end of Structure 314 (phase IVA) in grid 35/ 30, looking west, with the basal course of the stone-walled superstructure abutted by an external plaster floor. On the north is the top of a marl fill dumped against the demolished north side in phase V. (Scale in 0.5 m units).

Fig. 5.18 Structure 315 (phase IVA), from the east, with the internal floor of the final stage e cut back along its west and north sides and the stub abutted by the phase V rubble fill of Platform 34. The phase V north limit of the platform is marked by the edge of the rubble: the soil fill and boundary wall to the north (at far right) are an extension in phase VA. The open area at left was excavated in 1976 and 1979. (Scale in 0.5 m units).

were now carried out in buildings erected for the purpose. As quotidian activity disappeared from the patio, ritual appeared, with the first burial(s) in the open space: their presence outside individual buildings suggests that they were of collective importance to the social group living around the courtyard. The valedictory offering in the remains of Structure 317 is another example of structured ritual not seen before, and the cache of jade beads [F190] inserted into Patio Floor V in front of Structure 316 may extend the principle of the termination ritual to the entire patio if it was deposited, as seems likely, at the initiation of the phase V demolition and burial of the entire Early Period layout (Chapter 10; Hammond 1991b).

Functional interpretation for the later phases of the Early Period suggests that the presence of Structure 319 between 320 and 321, with its series of firepits indicating domestic activities, argues for a residential rôle for the platforms flanking it; Structure 318 to the west of 316 may have had a similar rôle, although too little was exposed to judge. When the large rectangular Structures 315d and 314 were built on the north and west sides of the patio, their new plan and increased size suggest a change in status of their users, if not in the function that they fulfilled. Unfortunately the demolition of even the rear area of Structure 315, the most completely excavated, leaves the nature of this uncertain. The patio group at the close of the Early Period, and the end of the Lopez Mamom phase, may be comparable to Altar de Sacrificios Group B, where the greatly enlarged platforms were judged by Smith (1972: 110) to have developed a ceremonial aspect by the late San Felix Mamom phase.

LATE PERIOD: PHASES V–XIII
This begins with the transformation in phase V, when the frontages of all the buildings around Patio Floor V – Struc-

tures 314, 315e, 316f, and 318 – were ripped away, the superstructures set on fire (witnessed by scorch marks on interior floors and on the patio floor in front of the buildings), and the patio filled in up to the tops of the building platforms (Figs. 3.9, 5.19). This thick rubble deposit was the first stage in the construction of Platform 34, which was marked by the deposition in the rubble of a mass human sacrificial burial of 32 individuals, sealed by an upper rubble mixed with earth which formed a level layer with the tops of the ruined building platforms. Firepits dug into this surface were presumably the temporary facilities of those engaged in construction.

Excavation west and north of Structure 315 showed that outside the patio Platform 34 was built up with loads of white marl and dark topsoil, dumped alternately in bands of contrasting solidity, texture, and color, and with heavy freshly quarried rubble (Fig. 5.18). Above these and the patio area was laid a thick level of soil with much fresh cultural material in it, midden quarried from close by and dumped in such good preservation that it often appeared during excavation to be *in situ*. The presence of several firepits in it reinforced that impression, although the total context given by the larger area excavation showed that these must have been short-term facilities. Two more burials, of a decapitated couple, were placed in this upper fill layer, and Platform 34 was finished with a subfloor ballast of small stones and with Plaza Floor I (Fig. 5.20), which on the north ended by covering the exterior of the platform's retaining wall and running out in an irregular edge on the ground surface north of it. The cutting of a single-

Fig. 5.19 Structure 315 buried by the rubble infill of the patio, up to the terrace level of stage d. The coeval floor (stage e) has been removed and is in section just above the superstructure wall. Flat limestone slabs overlie both the rubble and the front step of Structure 315. (Scale in 0.5 m units).

Fig. 5.21 The North Square, seen from the southwest with several phases of construction exposed. At left is Structure 306, with a plaster-paved area south of it. At center the rectangular front terrace and central portion of Structure 307 (phase IX) have been partly excavated, leaving only their bordering stones, with the remains of Structure 308 (phase VIII) visible within. Structure 308 in turn incorporates the internal floor of Structure 309 (phase VI), reused from Structure 312 of phase VA. The three graves [F209–F211] in the floor may be of phase VA or VI. The marl fill of Structure 303 (phase XII) can be seen in the north section, and the floors and fills of phases X–XIV in the east section. (Scale in 0.5 m units).

Fig. 5.20 The initial surfacing of Platform 34 (Plaza Floor I) in phase V from the east, with post holes antedating the first substructures on the north side of the plaza. The north retaining wall is of the following phase VA, and Plaza Floor I ended close to its extant eroded edge. The *chultun* is of this or the next phase; the narrow trench is part of the excavation process. (Scale in 0.1 m units).

chambered *chultun* [F246] through the fills into bedrock may be as early as this construction phase V, or may date to the succeeding period of occupation on Plaza Floor I, phase VA (Fig. 3.10).

Platform 34 was a raised open plaza some 1.4 m above the surrounding land, supporting a number of smaller building platforms and, later on at the west end, a small stepped pyramid. Such raised constructions are common in the Classic period, and although formally published from only a few sites to date (e.g. Komchen: Ringle and Andrews 1988) seem to be also characteristic of the Late Formative, especially where the scale of the basal platform is larger than the small buildings on it would seem to require. At the beginning of phase VA it is quite possible that Platform 34 supported only perishable

buildings, since a number of post holes survive under Structure 312 (Fig. 5.20), and neither that structure nor Structure 354 in the pyramid sequence (tentatively equated with this phase) are integral with Plaza Floor I, nor indeed does the small portion of Structure 313's front terrace seem to be. All of these building platforms were superimposed on the finished surface of Platform 34, and although their construction may have been part of the overall plan from the beginning, a northward extension of Platform 34 by nearly 2 m was added before the construction of Structure 312 (Figs. 3.10, 5.18, 5.20). The plaza between Structures 312 and 313 was 21 m long.

Structure 312 continued the straight-frontage tradition established in phase IVA, with a 1 m wide front terrace, although the entire substructure was raised only 0.35 m above the plaza. It was over 10 m long, perhaps as much as 14 m, and as much as 5.5 m from front to rear. Three burials in parallel graves cut into its floor (burials 110–113 [F209–211]) may be of phase VA (Figs. 3.10, 5.21), or from phase VI when the internal floor was reused, after the structure had been cut in half and the western part buried by a plaster exterior surface in front of Structure 311 (Fig. 3.11).

In phase VI the eastern half of Structure 312 (or perhaps its central portion, depending on how far east it had extended) was reused as the core of Structure 309 (Figs. 3.11, 5.21), the first of a succession of buildings with plans ranging from bow-sided to rectilinear, but all with apsidal rear ends that may have been terraced in the manner of the later Structure 350, and which seem to have functioned as retaining masses to hold the building platforms over the less solid fills of the extended

Platform 34. By this time Platform 34 had been expanded still further north, and its retaining wall lay beyond the limits of excavation. Part of the newly created area was occupied by a paved space behind Structure 309 at a lower level, but on the west Structure 311 was set back, leaving a paved area in front of it and to the side of Structure 309. In front of this area Plaza Floor II was so eroded that it was not clear whether some of the firepits dated to this phase or to phase V; the *chultun* was apparently still open, although its mouth had eroded back to undercut the floor west of Structure 309. Plaza Floor II buried the front terrace of Structure 313 at the south end of the plaza, and there was no evidence on the surface or in superficial excavations beyond the end of the Main Trench of any successor (but see p. 240). No internal details of either Structure 309 or 311 survived later remodeling, and Structure 353 in the pyramid sequence, the most likely candidate for this phase, was similarly almost obliterated.

No caches were associated with Plaza Floor II, but when its successor was laid an offering of two vessels [F181] was included in its fill, and one of numerous deer mandibles [F140] was set into its surface over the location of the mass burial of phase V (Figs. 3.12, Table 4.15). At the north end of the plaza Structure 309 continued in use, but 311 was replaced by Structure 310, which was either an apsidal platform facing southeast, or a subcircular one directly over its precursor (the former being slightly the more likely on the evidence). The northern part of the building was packed with nine burials, of both sexes and including both adults and children. The grave fill and the platform fill were the same material, and no grave cuts were seen in plan: the floor of Structure 310 had been removed except for one tiny fragment, so that it is not certain whether the bodies were interred at the time of construction or intruded afterwards. In the pyramid sequence, the first of Structure 352's three successive floors is equated with phase VII, standing only a short distance above the truncated remains of Structure 353.

Phase VIII is defined by the construction of Plaza Floor IV (Fig. 3.13), raising the level of Platform 34 by just over 0.1 m, and by Structures 306 and 308 on the north. The former occupied more or less the same area as 310's north end and 311 below it, but lay almost completely within the trench and had both its wall and three stages of floors well preserved (Fig. 5.21); in contrast with the previous phase, there were no burials, although two of the floors had firepits in them. Structure 308 had the same core and rear apsidal line as its precursor, but a straight front with a low terrace, a dedicatory cache, and two burials in its fill. That the two building platforms were planned and constructed together is clear from their positioning, with a narrow passage between bridged by a single-block step, down from the plaza level to a paved area which runs behind both structures. In front, a low wall line running west of south from the corner of Structure 308

Fig. 5.22 Cuello Stela 1 [F136] (phase XI) in its pit, cut into Plaza Floor VI and sealed by Plaza Floor VII. The packing and one of the three vessels of the cache can be seen. (Scale in cm).

separated different levels of plaza in front of each building, with a set of firepits in front of Structure 308. On the west side of the plaza the second stage of Structure 352 is provisionally associated with phase VIII: the burial of a beheaded adolescent in its top (burial 27: Fig. 10.8), with the grave marked by a convex elongated dome of red-painted plaster that was meant to be seen, suggests that the western building may have acquired a non-domestic function, if it did not have one already.

If this correlation of Structure 352 is correct, then its third and final stage, when the floor was raised 0.5 m to give a much more elevated structure, would be coeval with the expansion of Structure 308 into 307, with a broad front terrace extending much further south into the plaza than any previous (or later) structure in this locus (Figs. 3.14, 5.21). Structure 307 can be seen to have three sections: the terrace, a slightly higher central section where the superstructure presumably stood (although the only post holes are clustered in the center of the floor), and the apsidal terraced rear.

Plaza Floor V, poorly preserved except in front of Structure 306, covered Platform 34 in phase IX. In the fill of the succeeding Plaza Floor VI another cache of deer mandibles [F30] was deposited; the floor covered the front terrace of Structure 307, leaving it in phase X as a two-part building only (Fig. 3.15). At least six burials took place in it, three in the main section and three in the rear fills. The first pyramidal substructure on the western side, Structure 351, standing 4 m high but with almost all of its external facing removed subsequently (Fig. 3.20), may be of this phase, which is the last marked by pottery in the middle facet of the Cocos Chicanel ceramic complex.

Phase XI is notable for several developments: two caches [F131, 133] were laid in cuts into Plaza Floor VI before its successor was laid down, and the seating pit for the butt of Stela 1 was also cut (Fig. 3.15). The stela was erected in it,

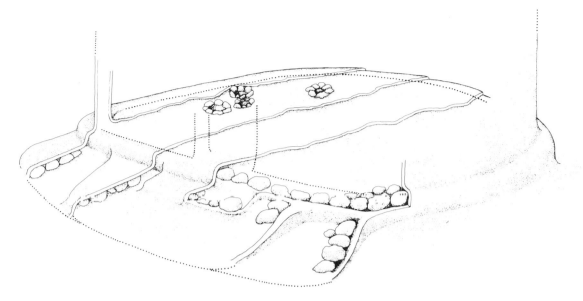

Fig. 5.23 Reconstruction (by Sheena Howarth) of Structure 304, showing the successive modifications of the entry in phase XI.

Fig. 5.24 Structure 302 (phase XIIA–XIII) from the south in 1980, showing the limestone block facing and rubble fill left after demolition in phase XIV. The top of Stela 1 is visible as a bump in the angle between the main platform and its western projection. The north side of Structure 302 was excavated in 1979. (Scale in 0.5 m units).

with a dedicatory cache and packed with boulders, and Plaza Floor VII was laid around it, with a cache in its fill (Fig 5.22). On the north side of the plaza Structure 307 was succeeded by 305 and Structure 306 by 304; by the second stage of Structure 304 they shared a common frontage line (Fig. 3.16). The rectangular central section of Structure 307 was replaced by a platform with rounded corners and a front terrace of similar plan, while the circular Structure 304, on more or less the same locus as its precursor, had a southern entry that grew

from a small step to a feature the full width of the building (Fig. 5.23). Both structures had foundation caches below their floors and burials in their rear portions, and both also had interior firepits. The plaza floor east of Stela 1 was cut by a mass burial [F128], containing the complete remains of three and the partial and excarnate remains of a further 12 individuals. If the first pyramid, Structure 351, had not previously been erected, phase XI, with the stela and mass burial both in front of the pyramid stair and roughly on its axis, would seem a likely time for its erection.

The two buildings on the north side of the plaza, which had in various incarnations persisted from phase VI onwards, were replaced in phase XII with a single large platform, Structure 303, with a straight front going beyond the limits of the trench to both east and west, and with a massive fill extending beyond the north section (Figs. 3.17, 5.21). The top surface had been destroyed by erosion, so the nature of any superstructure is unknown. On Plaza Floor VIII, in the center of the plaza beside Stela 1, the rectangular platform of Structure 302 was built (Fig. 5.24), abutted by the floor renewals of phase XIIA and XIIB, its orientation parallel to the front of Structure 303.

Structure 302 remained in use in phase XIII, when Plaza Floor IX was laid around it, burying the slumped stela (Fig. 3.18), and with a number of multi-vessel caches in its fill. Although not within the main trench stratigraphic sequence, the largest cache at Cuello, [F6] with 94 vessels, seems likely to be part of this pattern. The penultimate building in the pyramid sequence, Structure 350 (Figs. 5.25–5.28), is coeval, with Plaza Floor IX, which on the north abutted Structure 300, another straight-fronted platform of impressive masonry, of which very little survived although it may have been a refacing and southward reorientation of Structure 303.

Fig. 5.25 Structure 350 (phase XIII) from the east after removal of the overlying Structure 35. The upper part of the pyramid is eroded, and the stone-walled superstructure was demolished in phase XIV. (Scale in 0.5 m units).

Structure 301, with its southern apse and central burial (Fig. 5.29), and the similar and parallel [F19] just west of it, belong to the end of this phase, as does the burial [F224] intruded through Plaza Floor IX at the west end of Structure 302.

The final architectural development, at the beginning of the Early Classic period in phase XIV, is the construction of the outer pyramid, Structure 35, over Structure 350 (Figs. 3.19–3.20, 5.30–5.32), following demolition of the latter's superstructure and rear terraces. Structure 302 was also demolished, probably to make way for the stair of Structure 35, and Plaza Floor X was laid over the remains, abutting Structure 300 on the north side of the plaza.

Structure and function

Three architectural types are found in the Late Period: the raised plaza or Platform; the building platform; and the terraced pyramid. The distinction between the first two follows the definitions made by Pendergast (1979: 17) for Altun Ha: the latter defines "platforms as units of construction which do not contain interior space but produce a horizontal surface. Such units are divisible into two classes: those that form part of a structure, and those that are combined with one or more structures to produce a unit comprising building/s plus external space." Pendergast's further subdivision of the latter into classes 1 and 2 approximates to Hammond's (1975b: 140–1) "Structure" and "Platform," where the former is a freestanding substructure and

the latter is a modification of terrain. Pendergast's first class is that of the "building platform" already described for the Early Period, and predominant numerically in the Late Period also. The second class, distinguished here by capitalization (following Hammond 1975b: 140) as a Platform is introduced at the beginning of the Late Period with the construction of Platform 34.

This structure had a core of quarried limestone and chert rubble fill nearly a meter deep, burying the Early Period patio group, with layers of marl and topsoil dumped around the edges, and retained by a wall of limestone boulders, seen on the north as (Q4110) and the succeeding (Q4100), and on the south in one of its phases as the series of walls along grid 15 m N, overlain by a ramp giving access from ground level. Two tiers of walling (216) in the west pyramid trench are also thought to be part of the retaining-wall series of Platform 34, as are several other walls seen in small excavations in the northeast and northwest quadrants of the site. Plaster surfaces, Plaza Floors I–X, raised the elevation of Platform 34 by over 1 m between phases V and XIV, and its dimensions are estimated to have grown from 35 by 30 m to 80 by 70 m, the latter including a Late Formative courtyard group on the northern flank of the main Platform. At no point was the complete layout of any phase of Platform 34 exposed, although for phase XIII c. 40 percent of the area was excavated. No complete cross-section has so far been excavated either, although the combined profiles of the Main Trench and the 1979 northeast quadrant test trench give a combined north–south section over 40 m long.

The *Pyramid* is a type of substructure with steep, often tiered, sides rising from a broad, usually square, base to a small top platform. Three pyramids, Structures 351, 350, and 35, superimposed one over the other, occupied the west side of

Fig. 5.26 Structure 350 from the north, showing the curved
western terraces, and part of Structure 35 in section above them.

the plaza on Platform 34 from perhaps as early as phase X to
after the end of phase XIV. The first of these (Fig. 3.20),
Structure 351, was built on a rubble core raised over a lower
structure, 352, the last stage of which had itself been heightened by 0.5 m. The post holes in the top floor of Structure
351, and fragments of plaster surfacing suggest that it was a
finished construction and not simply a building core for
Structure 350. The latter was the best preserved of the three
pyramids, directly overlying its precursor and faced with
shaped limestone blocks covered with plaster. Three tiers of
terraces, with deeply inset corners, were capped with a
building platform on which stood a thin-walled masonry
superstructure with a flat or thatched roof (Fig. 5.28). The
rear of the pyramid was a cascade of six curved terraces giving
an apsidal western side. The outset eastern stair was placed
north of center; the centers of the risers were painted with
complex designs thought to have been masks (Fig. 10.21), and
the outside edges of the risers and the base of the superstructure were outlined in colors also. The outer pyramid, of
Early Classic date, was badly eroded, with Structure 350
visible through it in places (Fig. 5.31). Only the lowest tier,
with a cornice and inset panels, survived (Fig. 5.32). All three
pyramids faced east: no stair survived for Structure 351, and
that of Structure 35 faced 6° further south than the stair of
Structure 350. Foundation caches of pottery vessels were
buried in the tops of all three pyramids; there had also been
one, of chert macroblades accompanied by a celt and a
stingray spine, in the final stage of Structure 352, and together
with the axial sacrificial burial in the previous stage, these
constitute a continuous succession of dedicatory offerings that

suggest a sacred building on the west side of the plaza from
perhaps as early as phase VIII onwards.

The third architectural type, the *building platform*, was the
most common in the Late Period, as it had been before.
Although the structures on the plaza were less compactly
organized than in the Early Period, they were constructed in
much the same manner as their precursors and were often not
much higher. Instead of a single structure having five or six
episodes of reflooring, with minor remodeling of the frontage,
however, as in phases III–IVA, the entire building platform
tended to be reshaped radically; the three successive floors of
Structure 306, within the same framework of platform walls
(Figs. 3.13–3.15), are the longest Late Period sequence that
compares with the earlier. Axial steps continued to be built
and front terraces became if anything more common as levels
intermediate between the plaza and the interior of the building; post holes suggest that sometimes these were brought
within the covered space.

The ground plans of the Late Period included apsidal,
circular, and rectangular buildings, and combinations such as
the straight front combined with an apsidal rear end. While
formal boundary walls to the patio had existed in the Early
Period, low walls within the open space of the plaza demarcat-
ing separate zones in front of adjacent buildings were an
innovation of the Late Period, as were steps down between
platforms to lower paved rear areas, and small private courtyards beside buildings. This delineation of restricted space
associated with individual structures suggests that the
remainder of the plaza was public, while the lack of such
demarcation in the Early Period indicates equally that the
whole patio was private to the occupants of the buildings
around it.

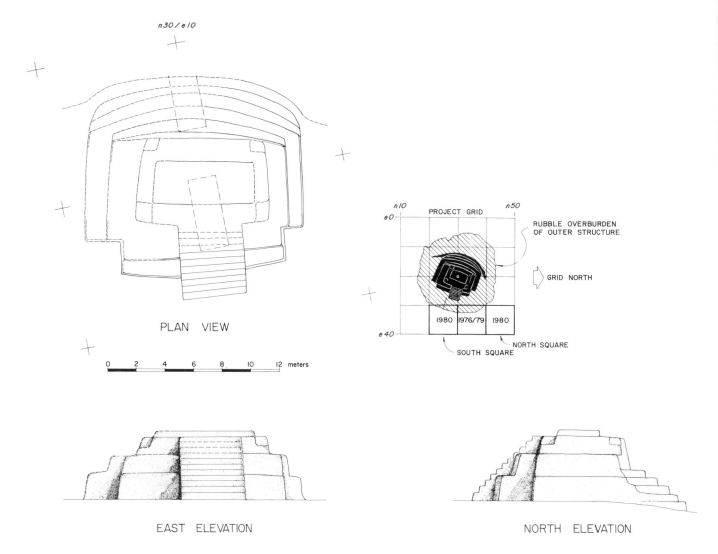

n30/e10

PLAN VIEW

0   2   4   6   8   10   12 meters

PROJECT GRID

n10   n50
e0

RUBBLE OVERBURDEN
OF OUTER STRUCTURE

GRID NORTH

1980 1976/79 1980

e40

NORTH SQUARE

SOUTH SQUARE

EAST ELEVATION   NORTH ELEVATION

Fig. 5.27 Plan and elevations of Structure 350.

The construction of Platform 34 and at least the pyramids, if not any of the other structures on it, was undoubtedly a communal project. Although these structures required a much greater investment of labor and materials than the small building platforms, the techniques involved were not significantly different, and they could, as Erasmus (1965) suggests, have been built cooperatively by the members of local households. Quarries for most raw materials, including limestone, marl, and topsoil (including recycled midden) were in the immediate vicinity. The quality of facing stone used on the pyramids was superior to that on any of the small building platforms, and the only painted decoration was found on them, so that some additional investment clearly was made.

While the general function of Platform 34 as the base for a plaza is obvious, the motive for its construction is not: no single "founder burial" seems to have been the stimulus, and

the large number of young men in the mass burial of phase V could as easily have been captives from some other community, seized for sacrifice at the Cuello dedication, as members of the local community. Some of the excarnate bone bundles could have been from revered ancestors, but this is perhaps more compelling an identification in [F128] than in the mass burial of phase V, where such collections are outnumbered by dismembered but articulated body parts. The burials below the floors or in the fills of the structures on the north side of the plaza show a spread of sex and age that suggests normal domestic sepulture, with no selection for a specific cohort such as is clearly apparent in the two mass burials. The lifelike postures in which some burials were found, kneeling or cross-legged holding a vessel, contrast so dramatically with the more usual extended supine, crouched or tightly flexed burials, that entry of these individuals into the circular grave pit while still alive cannot be ruled out.

The size of most of the north side buildings renders a domestic function plausible; those, such as Structures 312 and

Fig. 5.28 Reconstruction (by Sheena Howarth) of the superstructure of Structure 350, (a) with a thatched roof; a flat roof is also possible (b).

Fig. 5.29 Structure 301 (phase XIII) from above, with a south-pointing apse and an axial burial [F123] at center (small scale, in cm). Part of Structure 300 is marked by the large scale (in 0.5 m units) at upper right.

Fig. 5.30 Structure 35 (phase XIV) during excavation in 1978, from the southeast. The outset stair, frontage with niches and inset corners are visible, and part of Structure 350 can be seen in the northeast quadrant where the Early Classic building has eroded away.

303, which are much larger, could still have supported small perishable superstructures. Since the western building in each pair from phase VI onwards was always the smaller, it may have been an adjunct to the larger residential structure. The west side Structures 354, 353, and the first stage of 352 could all have been houses on the evidence available, although that is effectively only the absence of proof of any other function. The second stage of Structure 352 is the first in which a ceremonial presence on the plaza is strongly indicated, perhaps in phase VIII, but the evidence here is not solely architectural.

The final stage of Structure 352 has some claim to being non-domestic, but only because of the unusual degree (0.5 m) to which its floor was raised. The succeeding Structure 351 is the first which architecturally is unequivocally ceremonial in function, by phase XII at latest and perhaps as early as phase X. The erection of Stela 1 in phase XI with the mass burial [F128] in front of it, and of Structure 302 beside it in phase XII, point to an increased ritual importance of the plaza; their location above the phase V mass burial and the buried patio group of the Early Period may be significant. Structure 303 on the north side of the plaza, parallel to Structure 302, and its successor Structure 300, with fine masonry facing, could as easily be public buildings as private. The small apsidal structures to the west, Structure 301 and [F19], with their central burials, and the latter's successor [F9], all seem to be non-domestic.

SUMMARY OF ARCHITECTURAL EVIDENCE

Thirty-seven Formative period structures were excavated in the main and pyramid trenches at Cuello, of which 19 were interpreted by Gerhardt (1988: 113–18) as house platforms, nine as ancillary domestic platforms, six as ceremonial structures, and three as unknown. The characteristics of these are summarized in Table 5.1.

House platforms

The 19 house platforms included seven of Swasey/Bladen date, five of Lopez Mamom, and seven of Cocos Chicanel, i.e. 12 in the Early Period and seven in the Late. They were defined as such on the basis of a combination of traits: a

Fig. 5.31 Isometric view (by Jan Morrison) from the northeast of Structure 35 as excavated, following the removal of topsoil and erosion deposits. Part of Structure 350 is visible at the top of the stair where Structure 35 has eroded away.

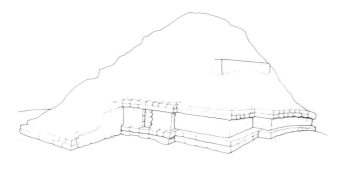

Fig. 5.32 View (by Sheena Howarth) of Structure 35, seen from the northeast with only surviving masonry shown.

platform up to 1 m high, evidence of a superstructure following the plan of the building platform, associated utilitarian artifacts, pits and/or simple graves, and a location facing on to the patio or plaza. The ground plans of these buildings ranged in shape from circular, through apsidal to rectangular, and in area from 5.3 by 5.9 to 7.6 by 11.5 m, with heights of 0.1 to 1.0 m. Addition of a step or terrace was a function of height above the outside surface. The apsidal plan became relatively less frequent in the Late Period but the variety of plans then

was greater. Post holes, a basal course of limestone blocks to hold the wall poles in, or turnups of plaster facing were all that remained of the perishable superstructures that had stood on these platforms. Even where almost the entire ground plan was excavated (Structures 326, 306) there was no evidence for internal partitioning into rooms, although numerous small stake holes could have supported flimsy screens. The superstructures were rebuilt from time to time, and often the floor was renewed at the same time; in only a few instances was the insertion of a burial clearly coincident with reflooring and reconstruction, as observed by Landa (Tozzer 1941: 130). Fragments of red-painted plaster in Lopez Mamom deposits indicate that some buildings may have been decorated.

The floors, where they survived, were generally clean and devoid of *in situ* artifacts, but features such as firepits and unlined pits, used for cooking, washing, storage, and trash disposal, were found in or near the house platforms. Two *chultunob* were excavated, [F246] in front of the north plaza buildings in phases VA–VI and [F87] outside the Main Trench in the southeast quadrant of Platform 34 of a later date.

The Cuello house platforms are comparable with those reported from other Preclassic sites in the Maya Lowlands, including Barton Ramie (Willey *et al.* 1965), Altar de Sacrificios (Smith 1972), Uaxactun (Smith 1937), Seibal (Tourtellot 1970, 1982, 1988b), and Komchen (Ringle and Andrews 1988), and are similar to many of those found in modern Maya villages (cf. Wauchope 1938).

Table 5.1 *Dimensions and other details of the Preclassic structures excavated in the Main Trench*

Major Preclassic periods	Ceramic complexes	Construction phase	Structure number	Feature number	Plan	Building stages	Location in patio/platform group	Dimensions in meters			Features (x = present)			
								Length	Width	Height	Pits	Burials	Caches	Post/stake holes
House platforms														
MIDDLE														
early	Swasey	I	329	82	apsidal	1	—	11.60	7.60	0.10	—	—	—	x
			327	108	circular	2	W	5.90	5.30	0.20–0.30	—	—	—	x
		II	326	250	apsidal	3	SW	8.40	4.50	0.10–0.20	—	—	—	x
			325	89A	apsidal?	4	N	—	—	0.20	6	1	—	x
	Bladen	III	323	220	apsidal	5	SW	11.45	6.50	0.45–1.00	—	4	—	x
			321	59	apsidal	5	W	8.30	4.95	0.40–0.60	—	1	—	x
			320	89	apsidal	5	N	8.10	5.00	0.40	3	2	—	x
late	Lopez Mamom	IV	316	200	apsidal	6	SW	10.20	6.00	0.70–0.90	4	2	—	x
			315	273	rectangular	5	N	11.20	4.40	0.60–1.00	1	1	—	x
			317	45	apsidal	5	W	7.60	5.40	0.35–0.70	—	—	1	x
		IVA	314	199	rectangular	1	W	12.00	6.00	0.70	1	1	—	x
			355	—	—	1	W	—	—	1.00	—	—	—	—
LATE	Cocos Chicanel													
	early	VA	312	271	rectangular	1	N	10.00+	—	0.40	—	4	—	x
			354	—	—	1	W	10.00	—	1.00	—	—	—	—
	middle	VI	309	242	circular	—	NE	8.20	7.20+	—	—	9	—	x
		VII	310	225	apsidal	1	NW	8.15	4.70	0.25	—	—	—	x
		VIII	308	212	rectangular	1	NE	7.60	6.40+	0.50	—	2	1	x
		IX	307	193	rectangular	2	NE	10.80	6.20	0.50	4	7	1	x
	late	XII	303	151	rectangular	—	N	10.00	—	0.40+	—	3	—	—
Ceremonial structures														
MIDDLE														
early	Bladen	III	324	230	oval	2	C	9.00	6.40	0.05	—	—	—	—
LATE														
	Middle	VII	352	—	—	3	W	—	—	1.00–1.50	—	1	1	x
	Cocos Chicanel	X	351	—	pyramid	1	W	11.00	11.00	4.00	—	—	2	x
	Late	XII	302	4	square	—	C	5.60	5.40	—	—	—	—	—
	Cocos	XIII	350	—	pyramid	1	W	15.50	15.50	5.00	—	1	1	—
	Chicanel	XIV	35	—	pyramid	1	W	20.00	20.00	6.00	—	1	1	—
Ancillary platforms														
MIDDLE														
early	Swasey	I	328	262	irregular	1	—	9.60–11.90	5.80	0.10	1	—	—	x
	Bladen	IIIA	322	55	oval	2	NW	5.10	5.00	0.15	1	—	—	x
late	Lopez	IV	319	36	oval	1	NW	4.00	3.40	0.05–0.10	4	—	—	x
	Mamom		318	229	—	—	SW	—	—	—	—	—	—	—
LATE														
	Middle	VI	311	235	circular	—	NW	6.00	5.40	—	—	—	1	x
	Cocos Chicanel	VIII	306	270	circular	3	NW	5.10	5.00	0.50	6	—	1	x
	Late	XI	305	150	circular	2	NE	5.60	5.40	0.50–0.60	8	5	4	x
	Cocos		304	149	circular	3	NW	4.70–6.00	5.00	0.40–0.50	3	4	1	—
	Chicanel	XIII	301	159	circular	—	NW	5.30	5.30	—	—	1	—	—

Ancillary platforms

Of the nine structures interpreted as ancillary platforms, two were of Swasey/Bladen date, two of Lopez Mamom and five of Cocos Chicanel, i.e. four of Early Period and five of Late date. Platforms found at the corners of the patio between house platforms, as well as those set back from or linked to a house platform, were defined as ancillary. They were platform substructures built in the same manner as house platforms, but were smaller and lower; where their dimensions overlapped with the lower end of the house platform range, location was the deciding factor in classification. Ancillary platforms were circular or oval in plan, from 3.4 by 4 m to 5.8 by 9.6 m, and from 0.1 to 0.6 m high. In the four cases where there was evidence for pole-and-thatch superstructures, two held buildings of small size on otherwise open platforms. These buildings could have functioned as kitchens, storehouses, or other domestic outbuildings. Their surfaces were cut by one or more, usually lined, pits and occasional graves. Ancillary platforms have been identified in domestic contexts at Barton Ramie (Willey *et al.* 1965), Seibal (Tourtellot 1970, 1983, 1988b), Mayapan (Smith 1962), Dzibilchaltun (Kurjack 1974), and Komchen (Ringle and Andrews 1988).

Ceremonial structures

Of the six structures defined as ceremonial, one was of Swasey date and the other five Cocos Chicanel, i.e. one Early Period and five Late Period. Structures in this category were either more than 1 m high, located in the center of the patio/plaza, and/or associated with an elaborate burial or cache. Three of the six examples were platforms and three pyramids: the platforms were oval or square in plan and ranged in height from 0.05 to 1.5 m, two being in the center of the open area and perhaps used as "oratories" (Tourtellot 1970). The third supported a series of superstructures and was located on the west side of the plaza facing east. While it may initially have supported a house, the increase in height following the placement of an elaborate burial on the axis, with a ceremonial cache as a dedicatory offering, suggests that it had by then become a sacred building. The subsequent superimposition of the three pyramids over it supports this interpretation.

The three pyramids that stood successively on the west side of the Late Period plaza towered over the other buildings on Platform 34. They rose from quasi-square bases in tiered terraces to small top platforms, reached by eastern outset stairs. The bases ranged from *c.* 15 m to *c.* 20 m on a side, and the height from 4 to 6 m. The first had a perishable superstructure, the second a masonry-walled building with a thatched or flat roof; the final phase was too badly eroded for the nature of the superstructure to be known. The second and third buildings had painted decoration, including elaborate designs on the stair risers of the former. Stela 1 may be associated with the earliest of the three pyramids, and all three had dedicatory caches in their cores.

Single pyramid–platform complexes are widely reported in the Maya Lowlands, although the pyramid is most often on the east or north side (Becker 1971); the Group E layout at Uaxactun has the pyramid on the west side. Tourtellot (1988b: 277–84) shows that many of those known are of Preclassic date.

Unknown

Three structures have been put into this category because too little of them was exposed for any function to be ascribed. All are of Cocos Chicanel date in the Late Period.

SUMMARY

From the above it would seem that the Early Period buildings are wholly or predominantly domestic in function (*pace* Hammond 1980b) and that the ceremonial architecture of the Late Period evolved out of a household tradition. Implicit in this is the inference that the patio group was the domain of an extended family, and that its structures and space were the loci of domestic activity. From the beginning of Lopez Mamom, the growth in exterior space with the enlargement of the patio and the later plaza corresponds with a trend away from a solely domestic function, towards an increasing ceremonial rôle. The earliest structure imputed a ceremonial function is Structure 324, in the phase III patio; the only ceremonial behavior (apart from burials) found in the Swasey and Bladen phases I–IIIA was the careful demolition of frontages before subsequent construction, something that continued in phases IV–IVA. By the end of the Early Period the deposition of valedictory caches in structures and in the patio indicated increased ritual activity, followed by the massive architectural transformation of phase V. This could have been triggered by a number of events, including the death of a leading personage; the presence of bone tubes carved with the woven-mat *pop* motif, of possible ancestor bundles of excarnate bones, and of numerous sacrificial victims in the accompanying mass burial would be consonant with such an explanation.

The initial phases of Platform 34 (VA–VIII) had no discernible ceremonial structures; the first such was the second stage of Structure 352, with its axial burial, followed by the third stage with a dedicatory cache including a stingray spine, an object used in bloodletting and linked to ancestor veneration. The west side of the plaza thus became occupied by a succession of ceremonial structures. On the north the subcircular buildings seem to have been domestic in function, their pattern of burials of all ages and both sexes consistent with this, and the marking off of private space around them suggesting public use of the plaza in front, presumably in connexion with the use of the shrine on the west side. Ceremonial use of the plaza included erection of the stela and the deposition of offerings, including dedicatory caches in the floor fill, the mass burial [F128] and the two caches of deer mandibles. Finally, Structure 302 was erected in the center of the plaza, associated with the existing stela, and with a burial [F224] later placed in front of its west end. The occurrence of these activities above the locus of the phase V mass burial may not be coincidental, and may further support the model of an atavistic cult.

The excavation of Platform 34 has shown how a residential patio group grew into an élite compound with its own ceremonial precinct. The large rectangular platforms and caches at the end of the Early Period indicate changes in status, as does the human and material investment in the raising of Platform 34 at the beginning of the Late Period. Jade, *Spondylus* shells, and other goods reflect the increased access to exotic goods of the occupants of the final patio and plaza buildings.

Chapter 6

THE COMMUNITY OF CUELLO: PATTERNS OF HOUSEHOLD AND SETTLEMENT CHANGE

Richard R. Wilk and Harold L. Wilhite, Jr.

INTRODUCTION

The 1980 Settlement Area Sampling Program was designed to widen our knowledge of the Preclassic community at Cuello, and to find out how it changed through time until the abandonment of the site at the end of the Classic period. In designing this program we found it necessary to question some of the assumptions in previous studies of lowland Maya settlement patterns.

It had been accepted for many years that the numerous small mounds scattered throughout Maya sites are the remains of the dwellings of the "common people" (Ashmore 1981c). We accept that these "housemounds" supported dwellings, but we believe that they do not represent *all* Maya houses from all periods. Here we present ethnographic and archaeological evidence that in the Preclassic period at Cuello a majority of the "common people" lived in perishable dwellings which did not leave behind surface features in the form of mounds; we also suggest that throughout this period and the succeeding Classic and Postclassic periods substantial numbers of Maya throughout the lowlands occupied similar perishable dwellings.

By depending on samples of mounds, Maya archaeologists have generated a skewed picture of settlement patterns and population sizes. This reliance on visible traces of houses is also the most probable explanation of the failure to find, recognize, or recover early Formative habitations in previous Maya lowland research. Because the earlier Formative inhabitants did not construct permanent dwellings (which would eventually become surface features), they are effectively invisible when only mounds are sampled.

Ethnographic evidence

Changes in the economic and political order of a society have been systematically linked to changes in household organization (Wilk and Rathje 1982; Wilk and Netting 1984; Ashmore and Wilk 1988). In the course of cultural evolution, households are transformed, and vary in the kinds of archaeological traces they leave behind, as well as the absolute visibility of those traces (Cohen 1975: 472). We can draw both general and specific analogies between the households of modern swidden agriculturalists and those households we should expect to find in the early Middle Preclassic in the Maya Lowlands.

The Kekchi Maya of southern Belize are a suitable source of analogy: like their pre-Late Preclassic period ancestors, they practice extensive agriculture of a wide variety of crops, depend heavily on wild resources, have very low population densities, and have no supra-village political organization. As with most swidden agriculturalists, Kekchi households may be large, but they are also highly mobile with little generational continuity. While Kekchi households frequently move between villages, and villages fluctuate in size in response to man–land ratios, villages themselves are fairly permanent. Cultural values of egalitarianism enforce a uniformity of house construction, preventing anyone from having a house which is more substantial than others (Wilk 1983, 1984). The main reason why Kekchi households are so mobile (and therefore build temporary and perishable houses) is the absence of a system of individual land ownership. With shifting agriculture and low population densities, land is held by the village, not the household, and there is little incentive for locational permanence. Inter-village mobility of individuals and households allows balancing of man–land relationships over time, and relates closely to the sharing of labor within and between domestic groups.

With increasing population densities and increasingly intensive agricultural practices, Kekchi households become locationally stable. The extended household group becomes an important property-holding and productive unit, and it is more prone to invest resources in improved – and more archaeologically visible – housing. At the same time, households tend to become more differentiated, and they begin to use houses as social symbols to express that differentiation. Having more property, the households of the rich tend to be larger (Netting 1982), more stable, and much more archaeologically visible. Poor and landless households remain small, mobile, and less visible, investing little in their dwellings (Selby and Murphy 1981).

In villages which remain outside the market system with low population densities, high household mobility is reflected in temporary housing. In the study village of Aguacate, none of the 30 households present in 1979 had occupied the same house site for more than 25 years, though the village has been occupied for nearly a century. Houses last from six to 12 years, depending on maintenance, and house sites are unimproved except for drainage ditches. The only relatively permanent buildings in the village are those which constitute its "ceremonial center," including the church, school, and *cabildo*. Because no earth or stone is used in house construction, there

is no need to dig borrow-pits. Refuse therefore rarely ends up concentrated in a single locale, and is instead scattered in a "toss zone" around each house site. Hayden and Cannon (1983) found that among the highland Maya refuse was thrown in toss zones around the house, though pits were often used as well if they had been dug for some other purpose; this suggests that concentrated midden-like deposits will only be found where permanent constructions requiring quarried fill are present, or where refuse production rates are so high that some formalized means of disposal is required (Wilk and Schiffer 1979). With no substantial houses, and few concentrated refuse deposits, the only features of the village which are visible to conventional archaeological methods are the civic structures and a nearby cemetery. A clear analogy can be drawn between this situation and that at Middle Preclassic Cuello, with a highly visible ceremonial core, the Platform 34 Group, and a relatively ephemeral habitation zone.

Archaeological evidence

If pre-Late Preclassic houses were indeed less substantial than Classic period dwellings, we would expect that most settlement would leave behind no more than an artifact scatter. Only in exceptional cases would more traces remain, as with the densely nucleated Late Preclassic village at Cerros, capped and preserved by later expansion of the ceremonial precinct (Cliff 1988). When extensive excavation has been done in "vacant" areas of sites (i.e. between the mounds), as at Tikal (Bronson n.d.; Haviland n.d.), quantities of Preclassic sherds have been found. In addition, two patterns of post holes in bedrock were found, the remains of Late Formative perishable houses built directly on the ground surface (Haviland n. d., units 2G-61, 6C-5). Late Formative sherds were found scattered over large areas, away from mounds, in sites around Pulltrouser Swamp in northern Belize (Turner and Harrison 1983). At Barton Ramie, although 18 of 65 excavations recovered Middle Preclassic (Jenney Creek complex) refuse, only three had even inconclusive evidence for construction of that period. Willey *et al.* (1965: 279) concluded that most if not all buildings of that phase were perishable, and built directly on the ground surface. A similar lack of evidence for permanent Preclassic period habitations resulted from settlement area excavations at Seibal and Altar de Sacrificios (Willey 1973; Tourtellot 1988b).

There is archaeological evidence that, long after the rise of complex societies in the lowlands, a substantial portion of the population *continued* to live in perishable dwellings on the ground surface. Archaeologists working in the northern lowlands have long suspected that a large number of dwellings fall under the threshold of archaeological visibility at southern lowland sites (Andrews 1965; Kurjack 1974). This "invisible housemound" hypothesis is, however, more concerned with the possibility that house platforms have been missed in site surveys, and does not directly address the problem that some houses may have created no mounds at all. Yet it is quite possible that only substantial, property-owning or politically important households constructed houses on platforms, while landless classes of slaves, tenants, servants, and workers continued to live in pole-and-thatch houses built on the ground surface. Certainly by the Postclassic period a majority of households was again living at ground level, much as they do today (see, for example, the evidence from Harrison's (1979) Lobil phase in southern Quintana Roo).

Vacant terrain excavations at Seibal (Tourtellot 1988b) and Tikal (Bronson n.d.; Haviland n.d.) have found abundant evidence of Classic activity. More than 250 sherds per cubic meter were found in a test at Seibal which was placed more than 80 m from the nearest mound. Bronson's non-mound excavations averaged over 50 ounces of sherds per 1-m square, many of them Early Classic in date. In one Tikal locus (7C-62) a midden and unpaved ground-level "occupation surface" were found, and post hole patterns in bedrock at locus 6C-5 (Haviland n.d.: 567) were also of Early Classic date. Haviland feels that these perishable structures were kitchens and other outbuildings, rather than residences, but it seems strange that kitchens would be located so far from other structures.

This evidence from other sites, and the analogy with modern Kekchi, were used in designing a sampling strategy for Cuello in 1980. We reasoned that a program confined to mound excavations would provide evidence for only a part, perhaps a small part, of the Formative community. Pyburn (1987, 1989) has subsequently found evidence of several platformless houses in the Late Classic and Terminal Classic/ Early Postclassic (Tecep) phases at Nohmul, a short distance north of Cuello on the same ridge.

RESEARCH DESIGN AND METHODS
Two hypotheses guided our research design: first, that the archaeological traces of the Swasey and Bladen phase communities would consist of no more than sherd and/or lithic scatters, and perhaps the remnants of patio floors; second, that the Platform 34 Group was the ritual core and possibly the cemetery of the early community.

The sample area for the settlement study was a 1-km square centered on Platform 34 (Fig. 6.1), from which we excluded a small portion (9.25 ha) at the northwestern margin that had been leveled and planted in cane. The sample area did not include all visible structures in the vicinity of Cuello, but it did include the most dense clusters of mounds and platforms and the Classic period ceremonial precinct.

We used a random sampling technique to locate our test trenches, but our desire to test a significant number of mounds led us to stratify the sample into mound and non-mound areas; since the mound area of the site constitutes less than 6.4

percent of the terrain, a straight random sample would clearly have included few if any mounds. We wanted to test mounds for two reasons: to compare the results of mound and non-mound tests, and to gather information on the later inhabitants of the site, some of whom certainly did live in houses raised on platforms.

We calculated that with our resources (two graduate students and six workers) we could complete excavation of 80 test trenches, 1.5m² into mounds and 1.25m² in non-mound tests, in the time available; we decided to place 60 tests in non-mound areas, and 20 (later expanded to 21) into visible structures.

Test locations were selected by placing a 50-m grid over the sample square kilometer, and making the northeast coordinates of each cell the sampling universe. For the non-mound sample, 30 of the 363 cells were selected, and two locations within each cell chosen by randomly selecting polar coordinates from the northeast corner. In those cells selected for mound sampling, the nearest mound to the northeast corner was chosen. This method eased the mapper's task: for both samples he needed only to locate the appropriate cell corners, and then the nearest mound, and the coordinates of the non-mound tests. Fig. 6.1 shows the locations of all 81 test units in the Cuello settlement area.

Linda Reynolds and Hal Wilhite supervised two excavations at a time, using one or two workers on each. Excavation followed natural stratigraphy, with deep layers divided into 20-cm levels: the intent was to detect chronological subdivisions within homogeneous strata which might have accumulated over long periods, especially in slopewash and colluvial deposits. All excavations penetrated at least 40 cm into sterile subsoil or bedrock.

Excavation results

The locations for flat tests generated by the sampling program fell in a variety of topographic situations: of the 60 flat (non-mound) tests, 23 were located on low ridges and 30 on slopes or in depressions (*bajos*), while the remaining seven hit previously undetected platforms, a point to which we shall return below. Many of the tests in *bajos* encountered unusual mixes of lenses and pockets of dark colluvial clay with gray/white marl (Fig. 6.2a–c), the proportion of marl increasing with depth to a pure sterile marl underlying the mixture at depths of 1–3 m. Artifacts were often found in these colluvial lenses, suggesting that the mixing process took place partly during the period of human occupation, but we do not believe that all the pedoturbation results from human activity; it also comes from natural shrink–swell action in the clays, root penetration, and surface cracking during the dry season.

Many of the flat tests encountered high sherd densities. Sterile soil or marl was not encountered until about 0.5 m

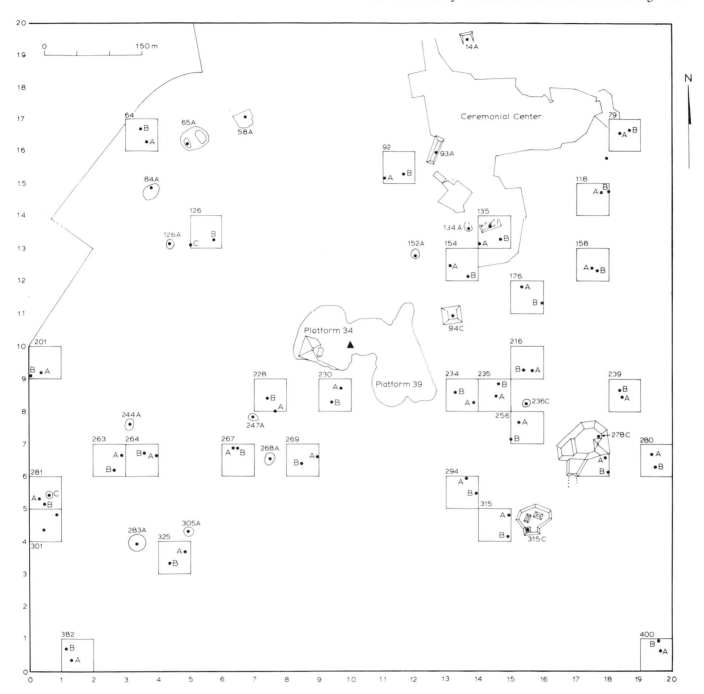

Fig 6.1 Conventionalized map of the Cuello settlement, showing locations of flat tests and mound excavations.

depth on elevations and as much as 3 m in *bajos*. Seven of the tests struck low platform constructions that had not been detected by survey; the confusion of these platforms with low ridges supports Tourtellot's (1988b) finding at Seibal that a certain proportion of low platforms is likely to escape the most thorough surface survey. Our results suggest that the problem

of undetected structures may be of greater magnitude than previously thought, since 12 percent of our tests found them, and most of the site is in pasture, with easily mappable terrain, rather than in forest.

Tests placed in mounds usually uncovered a very thin layer of topsoil above a stratum of mixed topsoil and limestone/marl construction material; this is a destruction layer caused by modern plowing and decades of cane farming. In most mounds the destruction layer rests on a poorly preserved marl, a ▶   ◀

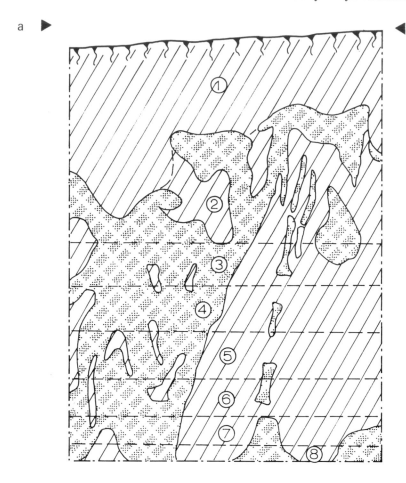

b ▶   ◀

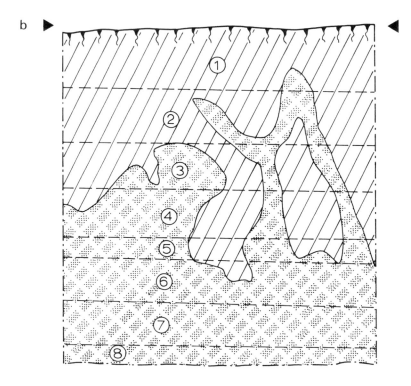

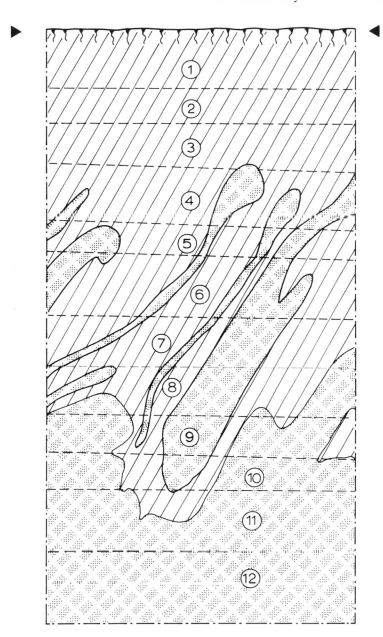

Fig. 6.2 Sections of flat test excavations (a–c). These three sections (tests 269A, 126C, 92B) show the extensive mixing of colluvial clays (oblique lines) and marl (stippling) which characterized many of the flat tests. These mixture patterns are probably the result of natural processes of soil disturbance through shrink–swell action, tree falls, and cracking during the dry season.

limestone, or plaster substructure, which stands in turn on the palaeosol (Fig. 6.3). No middens were found in any of the tests, though their past presence on or around structures is attested by the inclusion of dark, refuse-rich soil in the fill of many structures.

Refuse distribution and density

One of the immediate findings of our sampling program was that sherd density for all flat tests was an impressive 283 sherds/m^3, raising the question of how these high densities can be explained. One possibility is the traditional explanation that sherds and other cultural materials were either eroded or tossed from houses placed on platforms; to test this, we plotted sherd density by topographic location, comparing densities on the tops of natural ridges with those on slopes or in *bajos*. In the upper layers of topsoil on ridges densities averaged 437 sherds/m^3, while in lower areas and slopes they averaged 192 sherds/m^3. If sherd density were a product only

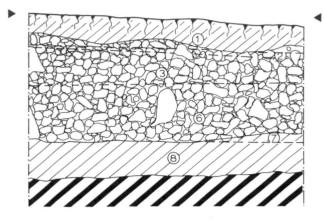

Fig. 6.3 Section of a mound excavation. This is the west section of a 1.5-m square trench in Structure 126A. Below a layer of topsoil and rubble, an Early Classic rubble, marl, and soil platform rests on a buried ground surface (8). A Late Preclassic burial had been made in the ground surface, and a post hole was also cut into that surface. The uppermost levels of the old soil contain a few Early Classic sherds, showing some occupation (perhaps associated with the perishable structure represented by the post hole). The platform, of which little remains, was built later in the Early Classic.

Table 6.1 *Depth of sherds in flat tests as a percentage of the depth of soil*

Distance from nearest mound	Mean depth of colluvium	Maximum depth of sherds	Sherd depth as % of colluvium depth
0–10 m	0.70 m	0.63 m	90
10–20 m	1.19 m	1.10 m	92
20–25 m	0.76 m	0.64 m	84
25–30 m	1.24 m	1.11 m	89
40–50 m	1.05 m	0.98 m	93
50–60 m	1.00 m	0.73 m	73
60–100 m	1.24 m	1.01 m	82
>100 m	1.42 m	1.35 m	95

Note:

If the distribution of sherds in colluvium is purely the result of erosion, we expect to find sherds higher in the soil column at increasing distance from the mounds. This figure shows that there is no clear relationship between distance from mounds and maximum sherd depth in the soil, as measured as a percentage of total soil depth. This implies that sherds are derived from other sources than erosion from mounds.

of erosion we would expect the opposite pattern, with higher densities in low spots where sediment accumulates.

Another pattern expected from the gradual movement of sherds off mounds is a concentration of sherd material at shallower depths as distance from the mound increases, assuming deposition to be a time-dependent phenomenon. Table 6.1 shows that for a sample of 35 tests at various distances from mounds there is only a slight decrease in the maximum depth at which sherds are found as distance from the mound increases (depth of sherds is here plotted as a percentage of total soil depth). We conclude that erosion is actively moving sherds from mounds to surrounding areas, but that this makes only a very minor contribution to the overall sherd distribution.

If toss zones around mounds are responsible for the non-mound material, one would expect the sherd density in the topsoil around mounds to decrease gradually with the distance from mounds. Our data show elevated densities within 20 m of mounds and platform groups, but outside this, sherd density does not decline consistently (Table 6.2). The presence of sherds at great depths in locations distant from mounds (e.g. 1.6 m down at 45 m distance, 1.55 m at 85 m), occasionally in dense concentrations, casts doubt on the toss-zone hypothesis; with the erosion thesis, it may have an effect on artifact distribution, but neither singly nor together do they provide a complete explanation.

Another possible reason for the density and distribution of non-mound artifacts is that sherds and other refuse may have been deliberately disposed of by scattering them in compound areas between houses, in the way that modern highland Maya sometimes do in nucleated villages (Hayden and Cannon 1983), but this is not done in more dispersed villages, since the Maya want to keep hard refuse out of their kitchen gardens where it can damage tools. Since Cuello was always a fairly dispersed settlement which probably included garden plots, it is unlikely that refuse was widely scattered on purpose; instead, we have evidence that it was broadcast in restricted zones around houses, and that by Late Formative times some refuse was collected and reused as construction fill.

Refuse could have been deposited in these non-mound areas during non-habitation activities such as food processing, craft production, or storage. Tourtellot (1988b) found evidence of such activity at Seibal, and Haviland (n.d.: 799) seems to believe that most of the small insubstantial structures found in Tikal vacant terrain excavations were outbuildings associated with regular platform-type residences. This leaves unanswered the question of their function: were they storage areas, kitchens, and specialized activity areas such as workshops, or just the residences of poor dependents? Our data offer no conclusive answers, but we think it unlikely that the majority of vacant terrain remains can be explained as kitchens or specialized activity areas: only one possible lithic workshop was found in a flat test at Cuello, and this unit also yielded numerous sherds from Swasey through Tzakol times. For kitchens to be the answer they must have been built in large numbers at great distances from their associated houses,

Table 6.2 *Sherd density in flat tests and distance from nearest mound*

Distance from nearest mound	Number of sample units	Mean sherd count per m³	Maximum density	Minimum density
0–10 m	3	280.2	315.4	171.8
10–20 m	2	194.8	339.5	50.0
20–25 m	7	120.3	349.5	0
25–30 m	5	87.4	258.5	6.6
40–50 m	5	135.8	354.3	9.5

Note:

Flat test sherd density is averaged for each distance category. Uncounted lots prevent calculations for the tests at distances between 30 and 40 m. Nevertheless a clear pattern of initial fall-off followed by independent fluctuation is found.

Table 6.3 *Recovery of dated materials from Settlement Area Sampling Project excavations[1]*

Measure	Swasey	Mamom	Chicanel	Tzakol	Tepeu
Present in flat tests	3	5	36	26	8
Mounds with dated construction levels	0	0	10	18	5
Mounds with dated construction or refuse	10	12	26	19	6
Total, all tests	13	17	62	45	14
Ratio of mounds with dated construction to total tests with dated refuse	0.00	0.00	0.19	0.67	0.56

Note:

[1] Figures show the number of flat test excavations and mound excavations which produced identifiable sherds of each ceramic phase. Fifty-three tests were placed in non-mound areas, while 28 encountered prehistoric construction. The second row records the number of mounds which had construction levels (floors or platform fill) which could be securely dated to each phase. The third row lists the number of mound excavations with sherds of that phase in either mixed fill, subsoil, or topsoil. The last row gives an index of the quantity of construction per phase in relation to the number of tests which found only refuse. Swasey/Bladen is shown as an undivided Swasey phase.

an arrangement not supported by the ethnographic evidence: if modern Maya kitchens are separate structures (common in Yucatec and Chorti areas but unknown among the Kekchi, Mopan, and Manche Chol), they tend to be very close to the house. Further doubt is cast on this hypothesis by the fact that many of the sherds recovered in flat tests are from serving rather than cooking vessels.

Having rejected the explanations of erosion, garden scatter, and non-habitation activity for the high density of inter-mound sherds at Cuello, we must consider the possibility that they may be refuse left by the inhabitants of temporary and perishable structures. It is likely that traces of such buildings have been seriously disturbed at Cuello by erosion, roots, and modern cultivation, although some may remain; at sites with a different history of disturbance their discovery may be more likely (cf. Pyburn 1989).

SETTLEMENT PATTERNS

Our analysis of the changing settlement at Cuello over time had two objectives: tracing the changes of the locations and arrangement of buildings, and analyzing the changing shapes of structures in light of changes in household organization over the long period of site occupation.

The Middle Preclassic community

Swasey and Bladen complex ceramics were found in 13 of the 81 test trenches (see Table 6.3), ten mound tests and three flat tests. This is undoubtedly an underestimate of the total distribution of early Middle Formative ceramics in our sample, as many of the sherds that were identifiable as Formative were too eroded to be assigned to a specific phase. Several of the mound excavations yielded Swasey/Bladen

ceramics in more than one level, but in no case were they recovered unmixed from later pottery.

As with Middle Formative contexts elsewhere, much of the Swasey/Bladen material came from old organic soils that had been capped by later platform construction. Six of the 13 tests were of this nature, while a further four had Swasey/Bladen sherds mixed with later material in Late Formative platform fill, and the remaining three were flat tests where early ceramics were found in the lower levels of topsoil or colluvium.

In the ancient soils where Swasey/Bladen ceramics were found, they were mixed with Lopez Mamom and/or Cocos Chicanel material, suggesting long accumulation *in situ* before the superimposed construction began. By excavating these deposits in spits (the only time at Cuello that natural stratigraphy was not used) we demonstrated that the relative abundance of early sherds increased towards the base of the deposit. The absence of living floors or other surfaces within the deposits, which tended to be dark with many organic inclusions and much lithic debitage, suggests that they are areas of refuse toss zones around the intermittently occupied sites of temporary housing.

The Cocos Chicanel constructions containing Swasey/

Bladen sherds in their fill all rested on ancient land surfaces in which early sherds were found. The platform fill in these cases was a crumbly dark earth closely resembling topsoil, perhaps scraped up from nearby areas where Swasey/Bladen (and often Lopez Mamom) temporary houses had existed. A pattern of sporadic reuse of particular building sites over long periods is clear. In these mixed contexts it is unlikely that an excavator would be able to isolate Swasey or Bladen ceramics as an early phenomenon on the basis of stratigraphy.

We were at first surprised to find that most of the tests yielding evidence of Swasey/Bladen activities were in the mound excavations rather than the flat tests. One possible explanation is that the same sites were preferentially reoccupied and built over in the Late Preclassic. Most of the locations in question are on rises or ridges, which would have been preferred as drier house sites. An alternative explanation is that the later constructions have protected the early remains from erosion, while elsewhere the diagnostic pottery has eroded beyond recognition. There were clear differences in the degree of slip preservation between sherds found in flat tests and those found in or beneath later construction, suggesting that the second answer may be valid, and that at least a portion of the early settlement has left traces that fall below the level of archaeological recognition. In drawing these conclusions, we should also consider the possibility that ceramic use-life was longer, and ceramics had a more limited range of functions in early Middle Preclassic society, leading to lower breakage and discard rates and much lower archaeological visibility (Schiffer 1975, 1976).

The result is somewhat ironic in view of our original thesis: though Swasey/Bladen houses are not visible on the surface of the site, surface traces of later habitations are good indicators of where the recoverable remains of early occupation are located. On the other hand, our results confirm the hypothesis that there was settlement outside the Platform 34 Group in the earlier Formative, and that this surrounding settlement was different from the plastered platforms found in the Platform 34 excavations. The results are also consistent with our model of how this Swasey/Bladen community looked: a dispersed scatter of temporary dwellings. Unfortunately our sample size was clearly not large enough to inspire a confident claim that no permanent Swasey or Bladen platform constructions exist outside the Platform 34 Group.

The Lopez Mamom settlement was similar to that of the preceding period. Lopez ceramics were found in 17 excavations (Table 6.3), three of which contained fewer than five identifiable sherds. Lopez pottery was mixed with Swasey/Bladen sherds in 11 of the 17 contexts, and nowhere was Lopez pottery unmixed with later materials. No Lopez constructions were found, although Lopez pottery was incorporated in the fill of three Cocos Chicanel platforms. In each of these cases, Lopez material was also recovered from nearby flat tests, suggesting that refuse scatters were being scraped up as fill for platform construction nearby.

The consistent collocation of Swasey/Bladen and Lopez Mamom material suggests that there was continuity in the use of eminences and ridges as locations for dwellings. This is consistent with the ceramic evidence for continuity and overlap between the ceramic complexes, and a gradual development of Swasey into Bladen and then into Lopez (Chapter 3). Though we must again exercise caution in making inferences from our small sample, we find no suggestion of a change in the organization of the Cuello community or its component households during the two periods. This is consistent with the evidence presented elsewhere for continuity in subsistence techniques in the Preclassic (Hammond and Miksicek 1981; this volume, Chapter 4).

Late Preclassic settlement

Of all periods, the most abundant archaeological traces in flat tests and mound excavations come from the Late Preclassic: 62 tests yielded Cocos Chicanel ceramics (Table 6.3), including 26 of 28 mound excavations, and in flat tests, Cocos ceramics were found in both topsoil and subsoil to depths exceeding 2 m. At times they occurred in high densities, although no recognizable activity areas or living surfaces were found; we believe that two millennia of natural soil mixing have obscured any such features.

While Cocos sherds were found in almost every mound, construction levels of this period were encountered in only ten places; in the other 16 mounds the Cocos sherds were either in buried topsoil beneath Nuevo Tzakol (Early Classic) construction (eight cases), mixed into the construction fill of later periods (three cases), or both under and mixed into later buildings (five cases).

Cocos Chicanel constructions were simple platforms of undetermined plan (though one appears to have been round), built with earth fill and capped with thick plaster or plaster/gravel floors that were sometimes very finely finished. In one case a line of small blocks was found on a floor, perhaps the foundation brace for a dividing wall. Most of these platforms do not have complex histories of remodeling: six of the ten show only one construction event, while the rest have two, and in one case four, construction phases (Table 6.4). Individual construction levels vary in thickness from 0.03 m (a floor) to 1.63 m, with a mean of 0.675 m.

Maximum accumulation of construction in any single mound during Cocos times was 2.26 m, where four construction phases were found superimposed. This structure (Platform 90) is one of the large open platforms supporting several small pyramidal structures in the southeast quadrant of Cuello. Looters' pits show it to have been of purely Cocos

Table 6.4 *Number and thickness of construction episodes in platforms*

Measure	Chicanel	Tzakol	Tepeu
No. of mounds with construction	10	18	5
Mean dated construction levels per mound with construction	1.6	1.9	1.0
Total construction levels (all mounds summed)	16	34	5
Mean thickness of construction levels	0.68	0.58	0.36
Mean height of total construction per mound (m)	1.08	1.10	0.36

Note:
The figures record the number, average thickness, and total accumulation per mound of platform, fill, and floor construction layers. There is a consistent trend towards thinner (less massive) construction layers through time. The peak in number of constructions is during the Tzakol phase.

construction, with a stone-walled chamber or tomb in its core. We infer that the Platform 90 Group, like Platform 34 and perhaps also Platforms 102, 152, and the East Plaza of the main ceremonial precinct of Cuello, was functionally different from Late Formative residential structures. Such platforms, with plastered plazas on their tops, small pyramids, multiple burials, numerous caches, *and* evidence for residence in the form of food remains, tools, and other refuse, have been found at Nohmul (Platform 109 Group: Wilk *et al.* 1975) and on a larger scale at Cerros (Cliff 1988). We suggest that the dispersed Late Formative villages were dotted with small numbers of ritual/residential centers of this nature, as Tourtellot (1988b) has observed at Seibal. They can be seen as small-scale versions of the massive "acropolis" structures built at El Mirador and other Petén sites at this period. In early Chicanel times they may have been élite residences at which lineage heads resided and carried out rituals oriented towards lineage ancestors, but by the end of the Chicanel phase they appear to have made the transition to being foci of community-level ritual, reflecting the greater temporal power of their élite residents.

What did the rest of the Cocos Chicanel period community of Cuello look like? Considering the large quantities of Cocos ceramics found at the site and the size of ceremonial construction of this phase, very few dwelling platforms were found. The bulk of Chicanel activity has left its traces in a particularly dense and widespread scatter of sherds and other items of material culture over a large portion of the site. We find this to be most congruent with a pattern of dispersed residence in temporary, perishable buildings that have left behind only refuse scatters. A minority of the population lived in equally perishable buildings raised on small earth-and-plaster platforms. A few of these platforms were larger and more elaborate than the rest, and were foci for ritual activity and élite burial.

It is only fortuitously that traces of a pole-and-thatch building could survive over 500 years of human activity and disturbance, followed by a millennium of natural disturbance and agriculture. Yet, at the base of one of our excavations into an Early Classic platform, in a heavily refuse-laden old soil layer with mainly Cocos ceramics, two distinct postholes were found – evidence of a perishable structure providentially preserved by a platform built very shortly after its abandonment.

Further evidence for non-platform habitation comes from a burial: only two Cocos burials were found in the settlement excavations (there seems to have been a predilection for burial in large platforms such as Platform 34), and only one of these was in a domestic structure. The other (126A 9–12) was found in a pit cut through the old land surface into the marl subsoil, accompanied by a Sierra Red vessel. The burial lay below an Early Classic platform and could not be associated with any nearby Cocos construction, the nearest lying over 60 m away. We conclude that it was buried beneath the floor of a perishable house which has left no other traces: the burial in its shallow pit would probably not have survived without the protection of the later construction over it.

Early Classic settlement

Settlement and household patterns do not depart radically from those of the preceding Late Formative. There is more mound construction, but surface-level residential activity does not cease: 26 of the flat tests yielded sherds and other refuse that could be dated to the Early Classic. Where Nuevo Tzakol sherds are found in flat tests, they are almost always mixed with Cocos material, which argues for continuity of use in many areas of the community rather than a complete shift in residential pattern.

Nineteen mound excavations produced Nuevo Tzakol material, and in all but one case (where the Early Classic sherds were in Late Classic fill) this included coeval construction. We had expected to find reuse and remodeling of Preclassic platforms by Early Classic architects who continued to use preexisting platforms for house construction, but this was not the case. Fourteen of the 18 Nuevo Tzakol platforms were on sites that had not been built on before, and eight of ten Cocos platforms were not covered by Tzakol or later construction. The implication is that there was a change in the identity of the households which enjoyed enough material security to invest in a residential platform.

Nuevo Tzakol buildings were often erected in places where

both Chicanel and Tzakol *temporary* structures had existed: Cocos ceramics were found in the top soil under every Nuevo platform, and in six cases Nuevo sherds were in the topsoil as well, suggesting that perishable Nuevo Tzakol buildings often preceded permanent ones. One Early Classic burial and one small pit were also found below the first Nuevo constructions, again indicating non-mound habitation.

While burial in domestic platforms was not common during the Late Preclassic, when burial in large complex platforms was preferred, in the Early Classic burial below the house floor seems to have become the norm: 18 burials were found in the 18 platforms, with a maximum of five in a single 1.5 m² test. Although burial had become "decentralized," ceremonial architecture was apparently concentrated in a single area of the site in the Early Classic; this suggests the advent of community-level rather than kin-group ritual. At the same time, residential architecture becomes highly differentiated, with some people living on elaborately built plastered platforms with cut stone wall-facings and bases, others on simple earth and marl platforms, and yet others continuing to use simple perishable houses built at ground level.

Early Classic platforms are often organized in the familiar plazuela pattern, with several platforms on a substructure around a small paved patio. This is a change from the Late Formative practice of building several perishable houses on a single raised substructure, a trend paralleled at other Maya lowland sites (Kurjack 1974; Ringle and Andrews 1988).

As shown in Table 6.5, there are more single platforms than plazuelas during the Early Classic. If we assume that the latter represent extended kin groups, it appears that only a portion of the population lived in such groups. Wealth differentials are cross-culturally the strongest determinant of household size and degree of extension (Netting 1982). We suggest that the heterogeneity of housing arrangements reflects differences in access to resources, most likely farmland. Households with control of property (and/or trade) became the cores of localized extended groups, which may or may not have been lineages, with permanent dwellings set around private patios (cf. Wilk 1988).

Late Classic settlement

In the Late Classic the quantity of evidence for construction and occupation at Cuello declined markedly. Late Classic ceramics of the Tepeu sphere (as yet unassigned to a ceramic complex) were recovered in only 14 tests, about the same number as in the Middle Preclassic. The clearest inference is that the community had shrunk from its Early Classic peak, but it is also clear that it was organized in quite a different way from those of the Middle Preclassic. A high proportion of the Late Classic material recovered was from construction. Five mound excavations yielded evidence of Late Classic construc-

Table 6.5 *Plazuela units at Cuello during the Late Formative, Early and Late Classic periods*

Measure	Chicanel	Tzakol	Tepeu
Single platforms	3	7	3
Plazuelas with 2 platforms	0	2	0
Plazuelas with 3 platforms	0	4	0
Plazuelas with 4 platforms	0	1	0

Note:
These figures give very conservative estimates of the sizes of plazuela units during three periods. The only units tallied in each period were those in which the terminal occupation took place during that particular period, in order to minimise the possibility that additional platforms were added to the group after that period.

tion, while one mound and eight flat tests produced refuse (Table 6.3). Preservation of Late Classic structures was very poor: the most substantial encountered (in test 79B: a small low addition at the east end of the main ceremonial precinct) was 0.80 m high, and built directly on the old land surface. The other four were on Early Classic platforms, and range in height from 0.15 to 0.43 m (Table 6.4). These figures underestimate the size of the platforms, since they were the last construction episode in each case and have been subjected to greater erosion than those from earlier phases. Even so, they were less substantial than the average Late Preclassic or Early Classic platform.

In one case (test 65A), a thin topsoil with Late Classic pottery was found on top of an Early Classic plastered platform; a Late Classic burial was intruded into this, but no trace of a Late Classic structure was found. This kind of deposit, reminiscent of the New Town phase occupation at Barton Ramie (Willey *et al.* 1965), seems to result from perishable houses that were occupied for some time, using preexisting mounds as substructures. It is likely that the eight other loci of Late Classic activity in the flat tests are the result of similar kinds of occupation which *did not* reuse earlier platforms.

The Late Classic was apparently a time of population decline at Cuello, but it was also one when that population became archaeologically less visible, turning out less refuse and building fewer permanent structures than before. The Late Classic remains may tell us more about the relative wealth and power of the community than its size.

We were surprised that no Postclassic material was recovered: a well-preserved effigy *incensario* (Chen Mul Modeled) was found behind Structure 35, and a few other Postclassic sherds in the main precinct, so it seems that the site was used at this period, as the two Postclassic radiocarbon dates from

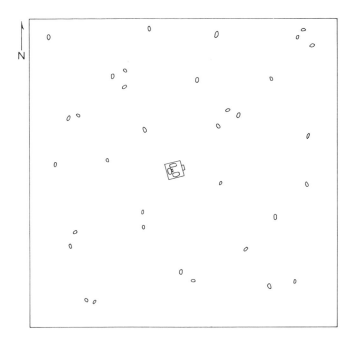

Fig. 6.4 Reconstructed Swasey/Bladen (early Middle Formative) settlement pattern. Figures 6.4–6.8 reconstruct the Cuello settlement pattern at five successive periods: perishable houses are represented by ovals, platforms by squares, and pyramids by triangles. The numbers of structures depicted are lower than our predictions for most phases, but the proportions of the different structure types are correct for each period. The relative locations of each type have been made as accurate as possible, given the stylized nature of the reconstruction.

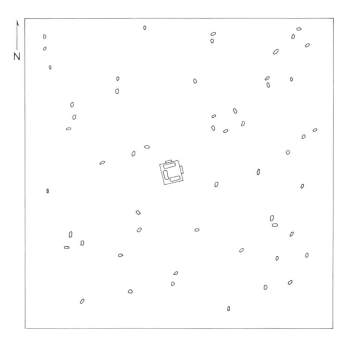

Fig. 6.5 Reconstructed Lopez Mamom (late Middle Formative) settlement pattern.

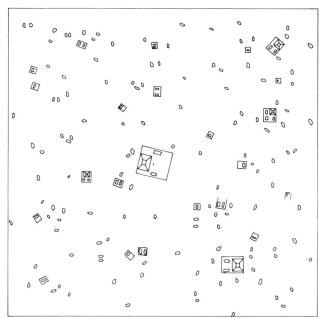

Fig. 6.6 Reconstructed Cocos Chicanel (Late Formative) settlement pattern.

Platform 34 and Structure 35 also indicate. Evidence from Barton Ramie (Willey *et al.* 1965), Altar de Sacrificios (Willey 1973: 57), and southern Quintana Roo (Harrison 1979) suggests that a common pattern in the Postclassic was to reuse earlier mounds for erecting temporary buildings, but we have no evidence for this at Cuello.

COMMUNITY PATTERNING AT CUELLO
We will now offer a speculative reconstruction of social evolution at Cuello based on our knowledge of changes in household organization and settlement patterns. Our information for the Middle and Late Preclassic suggests a dispersed village community with an egalitarian social organization (Figs. 6.4–6.6). Through this period the Platform 34 excavations show the gradual development of a central sacred place, in which community-level rituals were transacted in small public buildings on low plastered platforms. We do not know why this spot was chosen for sanctification. One of the functions of the area was disposal of the dead, and it probably also served as a meeting-place for the adjudication of disputes and community-level decision making.

During the transition from Middle to Late Preclassic the village grew greatly in size, and by the end of the Formative had attained the status of a small town (Fig. 6.6). We find evidence for social ranking: some households lived on large plastered platforms which represented a considerable investment in labor, while most households continued to occupy

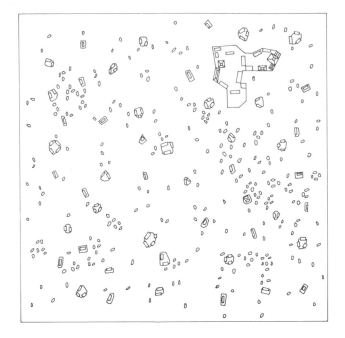

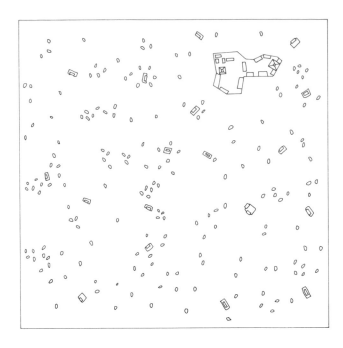

Fig. 6.7 Reconstructed Nuevo Tzakol (Early Classic) settlement pattern.

Fig. 6.8 Reconstructed Santana Tepeu (Late Classic) settlement pattern (no ceramic complex).

perishable dwellings built directly on the ground surface. A few members of the community lived on even larger complex platforms, on which they built pyramidal shrines containing tombs which sanctified ancestors. A larger kin group may have attended rituals at these shrines, and were entitled to bury at least some of their dead in less prominent parts of the platform. There may have been as many as four of these proto-ceremonial precincts or miniature acropoleis, of which Platform 34 is the only excavated example to date. The evidence is consonant with a society in which access to land, and perhaps participation in long-distance trade, were regulated by kin-group membership, though more than one such group existed in the town. Heads of kin-groups sanctified and justified their power through ancestral cults, and solidified their secular control by manipulating ties of kinship. The bulk of the community would be only distantly related to the powerful lineage heads, and may have moved freely between several villages where they had affinal or consanguineal ties.

Early Classic social patterns were more complex: the previous three or four identical kin-based units broke down into much more differentiated and specialized groups, unified by a central administrative authority. A single large ceremonial precinct was built, in which were centralized the administrative and religious functions previously dispersed among lineages (Fig. 6.7). At the same time, a larger proportion of the population became settled property-holding members of the community, building their own plazuela groups which formed

the foci of small-scale communal enterprises. Individuals were now buried below the floors of their own houses: the functions of the lineage had either been taken over by central authority, or had devolved onto the individual household unit.

Plazuelas show a gradation in scale which may imply differences in wealth and the duration of a particular family's continuity and good fortune, but still a large part of the population were mobile, propertyless clients or employees of the more fortunate. Many would have been involved in craft production, hunting, fishing, and gathering, specializations which require no capital or property.

For reasons connected with regional economic and political processes beyond the bounds of the community, Cuello went into a marked decline during the Late Classic (Fig. 6.8). It is possible that a large portion of the population was siphoned off to the expanding regional centers of Nohmul, El Pozito, and Lamanai. Cuello's location away from wetlands exploitable for intensive farming may have been a factor in this stagnation.

The local political power and religious importance of Cuello seem to have declined more drastically than its population size. With political control no longer entirely held at the community level, household organization was affected: there were still divisions between those living on platforms and those at ground level, but the upper stratum (at least outside the courtyards of the ceremonial precinct) no longer had the resources to support an extended household.

POPULATION SIZE IN REGIONAL CONTEXT

The prevailing method of counting housemounds and multiplying by an estimated household size is obviously problematic at Cuello, where only a fraction of the population ever lived on mounds. The major trace of the non-mound-dwelling population is a refuse scatter, and we have developed a method for using the area covered by refuse to produce a population estimate.

Previous methods for arriving at population size from refuse areas are clearly flawed: the Basin of Mexico surveys (Parsons 1971; Sanders et al. 1979) converted the density of surface refuse into "community types" and the area covered by refuse into population using Sanders's (1965) ethnographic data. Disregarding the problems of using surface artifact densities to predict subsurface remains (Tolstoy and Fish 1975), for reasons we will detail below we find that total refuse area is a more accurate predictor of population than the density of refuse.

The relationship between population size and refuse area is not a simple one: occupation span, settlement type, refuse disposal patterns, and the discard rates of artifacts will all affect the size of the area covered by refuse (Schacht 1981: 128; Schiffer 1975, 1976; Schiffer and McGuire 1982: 224–9). Roosevelt (1980) has clearly disregarded all of these factors by deriving a conversion factor of 0.0075 people per m² of refuse from a small sample of Yanoama Villages, and errs further in applying this conversion uniformly to a 3,600-year sequence.

Our conversion method is based on ethnoarchaeological work in the Kekchi village of Aguacate, in southern Belize. These Kekchi houses vary in size from 25 to 110 m² (Wilk 1983), and each house is centered in a house-site or "toft" (Hayden and Cannon 1983) of about 250 m²; Hayden's Coxoh project found that highland toft sizes were about the same as those of the Kekchi (personal communication). This toft accumulates a thin scatter of refuse during the occupation of the house, growing in density but not in size through time.

The number of house-sites in a village always exceeds the number of occupied houses because houses are rebuilt at least every ten years, and many people choose to rebuild them in new locations. As time goes on, and more houses are built in new locations, the number of house-sites in the village increases. Thus, refuse area is a product of both occupation span and population size.

The history of Aguacate provides the starting point for generalizing the relationship between these three variables (occupation span, refuse area, and village population). Over the 90 years of its history the village has averaged about 30 households (range 5–50). About 30 percent of households move their house to a new site each decade, but this does not lead to linear growth in the number of house-sites, and therefore refuse area: instead, a certain proportion of the "new" sites are actually old ones which have been abandoned

for a time. Over time this "redundancy rate" will increase, as the supply of potential housing sites is used up. In other words, the rate of increase in refuse area, with a constant population, will tend to decrease.

Unfortunately, more detailed data would be needed from Aguacate to plot the increase in house sites over time, and the shape of the resultant curve. In any case, this curve would probably vary in different kinds of terrain (if for example there were fewer or more potential house sites in the area). The best that we can do at present is to draw a straight line between the endpoints of our Aguacate data: 30 house-sites at the beginning of occupation and 50 ninety years later. The number of house-sites predicted by this linear function at any time is:

$$H = 0.223t + 30, \text{ where } H = \text{total number of house-sites and } t = \text{number of years elapsed.}$$

Generalizing this rate to villages of differing sizes, we arrive at:

$$H = (0.00778 \times B \times t) + B, \text{ where } B = \text{average number of resident households.}$$

To work backwards from the archaeological record to an estimate of the number of resident households, we solve for B:

$$B = \frac{H}{(0.00778 \times t) + 1}$$

The total amount of refuse at the site (R) is simply the number of house-sites multiplied by 250 m², producing the following conversion equation:

$$B = \frac{R}{250 \times (0.00778 \times t + 1)}$$

This equation does not account for the redundancy rate, which would, over time, cause the population to produce less refuse area per household: it thus gives a minimum population estimate for a particular community.

To apply this equation to Swasey/Bladen-phase Cuello, we begin with an estimate of the fraction of the sample area which was covered with early Middle Formative refuse. To ensure that we include only actual house-site (toft) refuse, we include only those sample units which encountered five or more identifiable Swasey/Bladen sherds. This excludes isolated sherds and allows for the overlap of some pottery types between Swasey/Bladen and succeeding ceramic complexes. From the remaining sample, we estimate that 70,008 m² of the site are covered with Swasey/Bladen refuse, which translates to a village size of 53 households. Treating this as a minimum, and adding a 25 percent margin of error, we arrive at a range of 53–66 households. Using Smith's (1962) admittedly imperfect household size of 5.6 persons this leads to a total of 296–370 people. This seems reasonable for a village of subsistence farmers who have access to a fairly large catchment area.

Using the same method we find only a small population

Table 6.6 *Population estimates for five phases*[1]

Measure	Swasey	Mamom	Chicanel	Tzakol	Tepeu
Non-mound households	53–66	102–27	335–419	394–493	137–171
Non-mound population	296–370	571–711	1876–2346	2206–2761	767–958
Mound households	0	0	45	107	27
Mound population	0	0	252	600	151
Total population	296–370	571–711	2128–2598	2806–3361	918–1109

Note:
[1] This table gives population estimates, based on both mound counts and refuse area. Figures should be taken as averages for the entire phase, and do not imply a stable population for the whole time period.

Table 6.7 *Ratios of non-mound to mound-dwelling populations*[1]

Phase	Ratio of mound to non-mound population
Chicanel	1:7.44
Tzakol	1:3.67
Tepeu	1:5.08

Note:
[1] This table shows minimum ratios of people living in perishable dwellings on ground surface to those living in houses on mounds. The numbers suggest multiplication factors for converting conventionally derived site populations to more realistic figures which take into account the poorer populace.

increase (Table 6.6) in the Lopez Mamom phase. The refuse area is only slightly larger (75,390 sq. m), but the period of time is much shorter than Swasey/Bladen (250 years against 550), so the formula yields an estimate of 102–127 households.

For later periods a simple refuse-area method for population estimation is no longer adequate, because a part of the population began to live in houses on plastered platforms. We continue to use our refuse-area formula for the population which continued to live in perishable dwellings, but add to this figure an estimate derived by traditional structure-counting methods.

In the Late Formative about 507,000 m² of the site were covered with refuse. With an occupation span of 650 years this translates to 335–419 households. Based on our mound sample, we estimate that 45 of the 125 platforms at Cuello were occupied during this time; though it is probable that more than one household lived on each of these platforms (Ringle and Andrews 1988), it is also probable that not all platforms were occupied at the same time. It is therefore safest to count a single household per platform. Even doubling this figure leaves the great majority of the population living in perishable dwellings at ground level. The total community would be between 2,128 and 2,598 people, a great increase over Middle Formative times.

The population of Cuello continued to increase into the Early Classic: 43 percent of the flat tests yielded Nuevo Tzakol phase sherds, which converts to an estimated 366,329 m² of refuse. Though this is less than the area in the Late Preclassic, the length of the Early Classic (350 years) is much shorter, and the Kekchi formula yields a minimum of 394 perishable dwellings. Allowing one household per occupied mound adds a further 107 households for a total of 501–600 households. The ratio of non-mound dwellers to those with houses on platforms is about 4:1 in the Early Classic, compared with 7.5:1 in the Late Preclassic.

The Late Classic population decline was drastic, with an estimated 137–171 households in perishable dwellings and another 27 living on platforms, or a ratio of about 5:1. Table

6.7 plots this relative decrease in the number of people living on mound structures.

What does this method of population estimation imply for other areas of the Maya Lowlands? As Ringle and Andrews (1988) point out, archaeologists have long ignored the possibility of large populations living on "invisible housemounds" at sites such as Tikal. Our method strictly applied to Tikal would swell Haviland's (1970) estimate of 39,000 in the Late Classic to 156,000 or even 200,000.

While we think that there were indeed large numbers of relatively "invisible" people at sites like Tikal, we are not yet prepared to propose an increase of this magnitude. We are aware of the imperfections in our methods for converting refuse area into population, and expect that refuse disposal and house construction in a large urban area would be different from those prevailing in hamlets. It is possibly that at Tikal a smaller proportion of the Classic period population lived in the relative poverty of ground-level perishable housing. On the other hand, it may be that large numbers of perishable houses were concentrated in areas far from the site center, giving the illusion of population "fall-off" away from the center. Failure to find concentric zonation in wealth or status at the site on the basis of architectural evidence (Arnold and Ford 1980) may be due to the exclusion of the truly poor from the sample. If modern urbanism is any guide to the past, we would expect to find *more* poor people in perishable housing in the larger urban centers than in smaller communities.

REGIONAL POPULATION TRENDS

The volume of recent research in northern Belize has produced evidence of Swasey/Bladen settlement at other sites apart from those noted by Pring (1977a), especially the Bolay (=Bladen) complex at Colha (Valdez 1987). The Swasey inhabitants may have had settled or more mobile predecessors in the region, the evidence for whom is summarized by Zeitlin (1984).

The fluctuations in Cuello's population after the beginning of the Late Formative are very similar to those observed at a number of sites in the region, but are different from several others. The population explosion during the Late Formative is an area-wide phenomenon, with almost every excavated site producing abundant remains. In the Classic period, however, sites fall into two distinct groups: a number of small ceremonial centers including San Estevan (Bullard 1965; Hammond *et al.* 1973), Xaman Kiwik (Mitchum 1982), Caledonia, Chowacol and perhaps Aventura (Hammond *et al.* 1973), and San Antonio Rio Hondo (Dahlin 1977) show population peaks in the Early Classic. Other larger sites, including Nohmul (possibly a special and late case: Hammond *et al.* 1988), El Pozito, and Colha have a small Early Classic population but expand in the Late and Terminal Classic.

It seems that during the Early Classic the area was dotted with a number of small centers each serving a small area and with no clear hierarchical ranking. At the beginning of the Late Classic a few of these small centers expanded at the expense of others to establish larger territories, in a process of political consolidation which may parallel that of the Terminal Formative. The Late Classic major centers tended to be fairly evenly spaced along the interfluvial ridges (Hammond 1974: 181), each with access to alluvial soils, drainable wetlands, and river transport. Communities like Cuello which failed to succeed in this competition were not abandoned, but there was a dramatic decline in construction activity, both in ceremonial precincts and in domestic areas. A larger proportion of the population at Cuello lived in ground-level perishable dwellings in the Late than in the Early Classic. Those who continued to live in houses built on platforms did not have extended family households (no Late Classic plazuelas were found), suggesting reduced wealth and status (Netting 1982).

CONCLUSIONS

The Cuello Settlement Area Sampling Project has not provided all the answers we originally hoped for, but we think that we are at least asking the right questions. A major problem that remains relates to the contrast between the dispersed Formative community pattern of Cuello and that of the highly nucleated Late Formative settlement, also of perishable ground-level houses, at Cerros (Cliff 1988). When more is known about subsistence and regional exchange in the Middle and Late Formative this dichotomy in community structures may be more explicable.

Though we have provided evidence that a substantial part of the Cuello population lived in perishable houses at ground level, and have linked changes in residence patterns to the social evolution of the community, more archaeological and ethnographic research is needed. It may well be that actual traces of perishable dwellings can be found, as they have been for the Terminal Classic period at Nohmul (Hammond *et al.* 1988; Pyburn 1989). In retrospect, larger excavation units, post hole tests over long distances at close intervals, or even backhoe trenches might have proved a better sampling strategy than we employed in 1980. Such new tools must be added to Maya settlement studies to ensure that the poor become as well represented in our studies as those who could afford to raise their dwellings into archaeological visibility.

Chapter 7 THE PRECLASSIC
POPULATION OF CUELLO

Frank P. Saul and Julie Mather Saul

INTRODUCTION

Approximately 122 Preclassic human burials were recovered in the Cuello excavations: three in the 1975 test pits, seven in 1976, two in 1978, 15 in 1979, and 95 in 1980, the last including two mass interments with approximately 15 and 32 individuals represented (Chapter 10; see also Robin 1989). A number of Classic period burials were found and partially recovered during the settlement area test excavations of 1980 (Chapter 6), but are not considered here. They are described by Robin (1989), whose burial numbering system is used throughout this book.

The 1976 burials were excavated by us, allowing a direct perspective on problems of preservation, recovery, and conservation. These included root penetration throughout the stratigraphy (even at a depth of 4.7 m below the surface), with pencil-thick roots sometimes traversing the medullary canals of long bones and rootlet acid scouring dental enamel, even on burials that appeared when uncovered to be in ''good' condition. Where the interment was fragmentary, as with many of the remains in the two mass burials, analysis was impeded and some categories of data were not present. Some fragile and small bones and most articular surfaces were rarely present, even in relatively well-preserved skeletons, and bones such as ribs, scapulae, and pelves, while recordable in the ground, were often too decayed to be recoverable for laboratory analysis. The normal crushing by overburden made such premortem cultural modifications as head-shaping more difficult to detect, and post-interment erosion of bone surface may have removed some pathological lesions.

Nevertheless, the Cuello burial population appears to be one of the largest known skeletal samples from the Preclassic period. This is of special significance because it is from a tropical lowland area where preservation is often poor and it has the advantage of good stratigraphic documentation. The Cocos Chicanel sample of 102 individuals, many demonstrably contemporaries, as in the mass burials, and others buried within a fairly short span of time within buildings that were probably family residences, is large enough for some general as well as specific judgments to be made.

Throughout, wherever possible, the Cuello findings are compared with two smaller Preclassic lowland Maya groups from Guatemala whose skeletal remains we have previously studied using comparable methods. These are the remains from Altar de Sacrificios (13 adults, eight subadults; see Saul 1972) and Seibal (six adults, unpublished). In addition, we will reference data from later periods at these and other sites, as appropriate.

POPULATION COMPOSITION: SEX AND AGE

Methods

All determinations were made by both authors independently, with little disagreement, using the standard techniques (Brothwell 1965: 51–65; Bass 1971; Ubelaker 1978: 41–67; Saul and Saul 1989) integrated with knowledge derived from our previous studies of large numbers of Maya skeletons (e.g. Saul 1972; Saul and Saul 1984), other ancient skeletons, and smaller numbers of modern skeletons from forensic cases, etc. The condition of the Cuello remains has forced us to assign some individuals to the unknown or uncertain (or ?) category for sex. All subadults were designated unknown or uncertain as to sex because sexual dimorphism usually becomes distinct only in late adolescence. Most individuals have been assigned to very general age categories (Table 7.1). Not to do so would imply a greater accuracy in age determination than is possible with these poorly preserved and fragmentary remains. These categories are: subadult (immature – dental remains and skeletal changes may enable us to give more specific age ranges), YA or young adult (20–34 years), MA or middle adult (35–54 years), OA or old adult (55+ years) and the more general A or "unspecified" adult. In those cases where our age estimation falls between two ranges, we have added the categories Y/MA or young/middle adult (30–40 years) and M/OA or middle/old adult (45–55 years).

While children as young as 2–4 years were recovered from early (Bladen phase) levels, it is possible that the more fragile juvenile skeletons could have decayed with age, and be under-represented in the earlier sample, although the proportion (subadults are 20 percent of Mamom and earlier remains, 22 percent of Chicanel excluding the mass burials) does not suggest that this is a serious deranging factor.

Sample

The total of 122 burials (103 adults, 19 subadults) can be divided into five groups:

Early Middle Formative (Swasey and Bladen phases)	12 individuals
Late Middle Formative (Lopez Mamom phase)	8 individuals
Early Chicanel mass burial (*c*. 400 B.C.)	32 individuals
Late Formative (Cocos Chicanel phase)	55 individuals
Late Chicanel mass burial (*c*. A.D. 100)	15 individuals

The ratio of adults:subadults in the Swasey/Bladen sample is 11:1, with the former comprising three or four young adults, four or three middle adults and three adults of unspecified age. The certain young adults and those of unspecified maturity are all female, the certain middle adults all male; the one young/middle adult is male, giving a M:F:? ratio of 4:6:0. Only one, burial 62 ([F110], a young adult female) is of possibly Swasey date, so that the roughly 300-year period of the Bladen burials (900–600 B.C.) can be compared with the slightly smaller sample of nine from the 200 years (600–400 B.C.) of the Lopez Mamom phase.

The Lopez sample has a 5:3 adult:subadult ratio, with the latter being 5–6, 10–12, and 12–14 years respectively. Of the six adults, two are young (one male, one uncertain sex), one young/middle (female), one middle (male), one middle/old (male) and one adult of unspecified age (male), for a total M:F:? ratio of 4:1:1.

The phase V (early Cocos Chicanel) Mass Burial 1 (burials 29–60) includes the entire or partial skeletons of approximately 32 individuals, with an adult:subadult ratio of 32:0. The M:F:? ratio is 26:1:5. The single female (who could possibly be an abnormally small male – there is, however, no evidence of dwarfism) is an adult of unspecified age, and 11 of the males and three of those of unknown sex are also in this category. Two of those of unknown sex are respectively a young adult and a young/middle adult. The males comprise six young adults, five young/middle and three middle adults. One male was an old adult of 55–59 years.

The Cocos Chicanel burials, excluding both the phase V and the phase XI Mass Burials 1 and 2, have an adult:subadult ratio of 40:15 and a M:F:? sex ratio of 24:12:4. This skewing towards male burial in Platform 34, when considered with the almost entirely male content of the two mass burials (26:1:5 and 13:0:2) suggests that either death selected males preferentially (by natural or cultural means), that burial in the Platform 34 locus was allowed to males more than females, that the population of Platform 34 was heavily male-dominated, or that more than one of these factors combined. The roughly 2:1 ratio of M:F follows on from the 4:1 Lopez sample (although this is too small to be significant). The mixture of both sexes and all ages in single-phase sets of burials in individual buildings suggests normal family interment, however, while the mass burials, in their lack of subadults as well as females, indicate selection for adult males. The careful manner in which the burials were arranged, in combination

Table 7.1 *Summary of population composition by phase and age cohort*

Culture phase	B-4	5-9	10-14	15-19	YA (20-34) M	F	?	Y/MA M	F	?	MA (35-54) M	F	?	M/OA M	F	?	OA 55+ M	F	?	A M	F	?	All Ages M	F	?	Both sexes
Swasey												1												1		1
Bladen	1					2		1			3			1							3		5	5	1	11
Mamom		1	2		1		1		1		1									1			3	1	4	8
Transitional																										
Mass Burial 1					6		1	5		1	3						1			11	1	3	26	1	5	32
Chicanel	6	6	2	1	10	1	2	4	5	1	6	4	1				1			4		1	25	10	20	55
Chicanel [F128]																										
Mass Burial 2					7			3			2		1							1		1	13	0	2	15
Subtotals all phases	7	7	4	1	24	3	4	13	6	2	15	5	2	1			2			17	4	5	72	18	32	
All totals	19				31			21			22			1			2			26						122

with the skewed age and sex distribution, makes it seem likely that the mass burials were sacrificial events (most epidemic disease would not be age/sex specific), in which case the males present may have been captives from another community and not part of the Cuello biological population at all. If this were the case, 47 male adults would be removed from the Cocos phase sample of Cuello inhabitants, and would form a comparative group of unknown (although probably not distant) origin.

Mass Burial 2 of phase XI (burials 68–79 [F128]), in the latter part of the Cocos Chicanel phase, consisted of approximately 15 adults (ratio 15:0), with a sex ratio of 13:0:2; seven were young adults, three young/middle adults, three middle adult, all of these being male, and two adults of unspecified age/sex.

Comparative The Altar de Sacrificios Preclassic group consisted of eight subadults (six between birth and 4 years, one between 5 and 9 years, one between 10 and 14 years) and 13 adults (seven young, five middle, one old). Only two certain females were present (one young, one middle). A definite sex assignment could not be made for eight subadults, two young adults, and one middle adult.

The Seibal Preclassic group consisted of six adults (three young, two middle, and one unspecified). The two adult females who were present were classified as one young and one unspecified.

HEALTH

General The difficulties inherent in diagnosing disease in living patients are increased when they are dead, excarnate,

and often fragmented, especially since most diseases do not leave recognizable scars on bone. At Cuello the post-burial erosion of skeletal remains by root action has made detection particularly difficult, but some data on the prevalence of potentially significant lesions and the presence of a variety of other disorders has been obtained. The diagnoses that follow are a mixture of obvious categories such as fractures and dental caries together with lesions of uncertain origin such as spongy or porotic hyperostosis cranii and saber-shin tibiae. For these we use descriptive categories with brief discussions of potential disease associations. Some lesions – linear enamel hypoplasia, spongy or porotic hyperostosis cranii – may provide insights regarding population energy levels, and deserve special note. Tables 7.2–7.4 list all individuals together with associated pathology as appropriate.

Saber-shin tibia (S-ST) (Figs. 7.1–7.4 and Table 7.5) This category is essentially the same as osteitis (bone inflammation) as the term has previously been used, but is focused specifically on tibiae, since these were frequently available for many individuals when other bones were not (Saul 1972). Furthermore, many tibiae were apparently abnormal in that they manifested varying amounts of anterior–posterior bowing that was usually (but not always) accompanied by swelling or apparent inflammation. This configuration is often referred to as "saber-shin tibia" (S-ST), so named for its resemblance to a cavalry saber. This is a condition that has been most frequently associated with a group of treponemal infections that include syphilis and yaws.

The origin of syphilis remains controversial after centuries of discussion, although a pre-Columbian origin in the Americas is now seen as likely (Baker and Armelagos 1988). The

Table 7.2 Osteobiographical data on individual burials

Burial Number (Robin 1989)	Feature Number	Sex	Age	Tibial bowing A-P	Tibial swelling	Linear enamel hypoplasia	Spongy/porotic hyperostosis cranii	Ossified subperiosteal hemorrhages	Periodontoclasia	Caries[1]	Calculus	LSAMAT	Head shaping	Dental decoration	Other
Smasey/Bladen															
62	F110	F	YA	+	+	+	0		+		+		+/LF tump?		enameloma
7	76/232a[2]	F	YA	0	0	0	0	+	+			0	tump?	0	
8	76/232b	F	A	+	+										
2	75/25	F	YA	+	+	0	0	+	+	0	+	++	0	0	
9	76/247	M	MA	++	+	+				1	++	++		0	old cut marks, red ocher
3	75/38	M	MA	+	+										
116	F219		2–4												
120	F228	F	A	+	++	0	0								
114	F215	F	A	++	0	0	0								
118	F223	M	MA		++	0			++	2	++	0	++/TO	0	dental abscesses (max)
123	F251	M	Y/MA	++	++	0			++		+++	++	0	0	neurofibroma healed groove and "hole" in frontal bone
22	F49	M	M/OA	+		0	0				+	++	++/T?	0	
Lopez Mamom															
5	76/137	M	MA	++	+	0	0	0	+++	2		+++	+/LF		
6	76/152		5–6												
1	75/14		YA	0	0										
18	F32	F	Y/MA	+	+	+		0	++	4	+	+	0	0	"decapitated"
20	F35		12–14			0	0							0	
4	76/104	M	YA			0	0		+	3		+	0	0	
115	F216		10–12			+	0					0		0	
124	F263	M	A											0	
Cocos Chicanel															
10	F7	M	Y/MA	++	+	+		+		1		++		0	"decapitated"
11	F7a	M	Y/MA			+				1		++			7 teeth only
12	F8	F	Y/MA			0	0		+	1	0	++	++/TO?	0	"decapitated"
110	F209	M	YA			0	0		0	0	+	+++		0	osteoid-osteoma
112	F210 (1561)	F	YA	+	+	0		0		1	+	+++	+/LF	F4?	
111	F210 (1825)		10–14			0						0		0	
113	F211	M	MA	+++	++	0	0	0		0	+	0	++/TE	0	cranial erosion
121	F239a	M	YA	+++	++	0	0	0		0	+	++		0	fracture (femur)
122	F239b		MA			0		0			+	0			
117	F222	F	MA	+	+		0	0	+++	2	+		0		arthritis (hands and neck)

Table 7.2 (cont.)

Burial Number (Robin 1989)	Feature Number	Sex	Age	Tibial bowing A–P	Tibial swelling	Linear enamel hypoplasia	Spongy/porotic hyperostosis cranii	Ossified subperiosteal hemorrhages	Periodontoclasia	Caries[1]	Calculus	LSAMAT	Head shaping	Dental decoration	Other
106	F201	M	Y/MA	+	+	+	0	0		4		0	0		non-linear EH
97	F184	F	5–7	0	0	++	0	0	+	2	++	0	0		
98	F185	M	Y/MA	0	0	++	0	0	0	1	+++	0	0		enameloma
99	F187a		20–24			++	0				+++	0			
100	F187b		2–4			0						0			
101	F192	M	A	+		0	0	0	+++	1	+	+		0	cranial erosion; dental abscess (max)
102	F194		1–2	+		0			+	0					
105	F198	M	YA	+		0	+	0	+		++	++	+/T?	F4?	fracture (tibia); arthritis (hand)
107	F202	M	23–24	++		+	0	0	+	2	+++	++	+/LF	0	dental abscess (max)
103	F195	M	YA	0		0	0	0	+++	12	+++				dental abscess (mand)
104	F196	M	Y/MA			+	0		+++	5	++		+/LF		
119	F224	M	YA	0		+	0	0				0	0	0	enameloma
90	F158		YA												
92	F163		3–4									0			
89	F147	F	MA	++	+	++		0	++				+/LF		arthritis (hand)
88	F146	F	MA		++	++			+++						
96	F169		NB–1					+							
95	F168	M	MA	+	+	+	0	0	+	18	+	0	0		arthritis (hand); dental abscess (max)
94	F167		A	+	++	0	0		+				+/LF		
93	F166	F	MA		++	+	0		+++						
87	F143		5–9		+++										
83	F135	M	A	+	++	0	0		+	3	0	0	0	0	
86	F141		8–9		+++	+	0		++						
80	F132	F	Y/MA	+	+	0	0		+	2	0	0	++/LF		
84	F137		5–7		++	+	0	+	++	1		0	+/LF		
82	F134/1225	F	Y/MA	++	+	+	0		+++	2	+	0	0		spur on metatarsal II
81	F134/1212	F	Y/MA	++	+++	0		0	+	2		0		0	
63	F112		10–11	+	+	0						0			
64	F121		5–7		++	+						0			
85	F138	M	MA	++	++	+	0	0	+++		+	++	0		arthritis (cervical)
66	F125	M	MA	0		0	0	0	+++	3	++	++	0		"hole" in parietal??

No.	Feature	Sex	Age									Notes
28	F84	M	MA	+	+++	0	0	+++	3	+		+++/TE
23	F50	F	6–9	0	0	0	0	++	2	+	0	
25	F73#5	F	YA			+		++		+	0	
26	F73#19	M	A	0		0						
16	F25/256	M	MA	0	0	0	0		2		0	
15	F25/293	F	Y/MA		0		0			++		
109	F208	M	A	0	+++	+++	0			+		cut marks pinkish stain,
27	F79		15–19	0	+	+++	+++	+++		+	0	"decapitated" very small
21	F48	M	YA	0	+	+++	0	+++	1	++		+/LF
61	F106	M	YA	0		+++	0	+++		++		
91	F161	M	18–25	0	+				1	+		+/LF
125	F274	M	Y/MA	0	+							
126	F276		0.5–1.5	0	0							"decapitated"
127	F277		1.5–2.5	0	0							"decapitated"

Note:

[1] Due to missing and/or extremely worn teeth this is a minimum count of carious teeth observable.

[2] Secondary burials in lower case

Table 7.3 Osteobiographical data on the phase V (early Cocos Chicanel) Mass Burial 1 of 400–300 B.C.

Burial Number (Robin 1989)	Feature Number	Sex	Age	Tibial A–P bowing	Tibial swelling	Linear enamel hypoplasia	Spongy/porotic hyperostosis crani	Ossified subperiosteal hemorrhages	Periodontoclasia	Caries[1]	Calculus	LSAMAT	Head shaping	Dental decoration	Other
Cocos Chicanel (early)															
29	F31	M	Y/MA			0					+	0			very small
30	F33	F	A								+				
31	F33a[2]	M	A												
32	F148	M	MA			++	0				+		0		
33	F165	M	Y/MA								+	+	0		
34	F171	M	55–59	++	++		0	0	+++	4	+	+	0		arthritis (entire vertebral column), "parry" fracture, abscess, sinusitis, grooved tooth (max)
35	F172	M	A												
36	F173	F	Y/MA			0						+			
37	F175	M	A												
38	F178	M	A	0	0										
39	F179a	M	YA	0	0	+					((+))[3]				
40	F179b	M	YA							((5))	((+))				
41	F180a	M	A												
42	F180b	M	A												
43	F180c	M	YA												
44	F180d	M	A	((+))	((+))	((+))									
45	F182a	M	YA			0					+	0		C2 or C6	
46	F182b	M	MA			0			+++		((+ +))	++			
47	F183a	M	YA	((0	0))	((+))		((+))		((3))	((+))	((0))			((arthritis, neck, hands))
48	F186b	M	Y/MA												
49	F186c	M	Y/MA												
50	F188	M	Y/MA			+	0		+	1	++	++			
51	F189	M	YA			+	0		+		++	+		0	
52	F203a	M	YA	((+	0))	((+))				((6))					((arthritis of thorax))
53	F203b	M	MA	((+	+))					1					"trephination"
54	F203c	M	A	((+	+))					((1))					((Spondylolisthesis))
55	F203d	M	A												((fracture: toe))
56	F203e	M	A												
57	F203f	M	A												
58	F203g	M	A												
59	F203h	M	A												
60	F203i	M	A												

Note:

1 Number of carious teeth observable (minimum number)

2 Secondary burials indicated by lower case

3 Data in (()) cannot be assigned to a specific individual within the subgroup.

Table 7.4 Osteobiographical detail on the phase XI ([F128]: Cocos Chicanel) Mass Burial 2 of c. A.D. 100

Burial Number (Robin 1989)	Feature Number	Sex	Age	Tibial A–P bowing	Tibial swelling	Linear enamel hypoplasia	Spongy/porotic hyperostosis cranii	Ossified subperiosteal hemorrhages	Periodontoclasia	Caries[1]	Calculus	LSAMAT	Head shaping	Dental decoration	Other
Cocos Chicanel (late)															
	F128														
70	C1318	M	YA	+	+	+			+	1	+	0			arthritis (toes), sinusitus
71	C1318a[2]	M	MA			+									
79	C1352	M	YA			+++				3	++	0			fractures ("Colles" & carpals)
75	C1352a	M	YA							1		0			
76	C1352b		Y/MA			+									
72	C1319a	M	YA			+			+	1	+				
73	C1319b	M	Y/MA			+									
74	C1319c	M	Y/MA						((+++))[3]						((dental abscess: max))
77	C1320a	M	YA			+				2					((osteoid osteoma))
78	C1320b	M	MA			+			++	1		+++			LSAMAT opening to root canal
68	C1143a	M	YA						+++						
69	C1143b	M	MA								++	++			
—	C1187a	M	YA			+					++				
—	C1187b	M	YA												
—	C1187c	M	Y/MA												((arthritis toes))

Note:
[1] Number of carious teeth observable (a minimum number)
[2] Secondary burials indicated by lower case
[3] Data in (()) cannot be assigned to a specific individual within the subgroup.

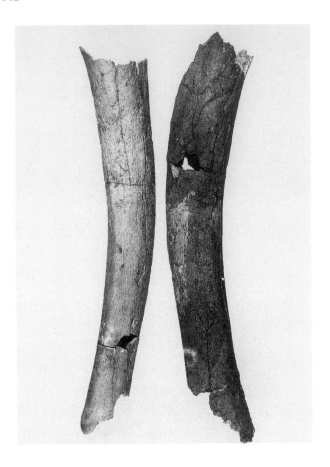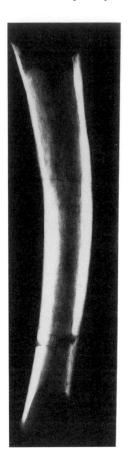

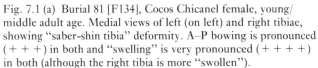

Fig. 7.1 (a) Burial 81 [F134], Cocos Chicanel female, young/
middle adult age. Medial views of left (on left) and right tibiae,
showing "saber-shin tibia" deformity. A–P bowing is pronounced
(+ + +) in both and "swelling" is very pronounced (+ + + +)
in both (although the right tibia is more "swollen").

(b) Burial 81, lateral (on left) and A–P radiographs of left tibia
showing "sabering" and also medullary stenosis or internal
narrowing due to cortical expansion often associated with
treponemal infection.

situation is complicated by the continuities between syphilis
(both venereal and endemic) and yaws and other treponemal
infections (e.g. pinta), all caused by the same organisms
(*Treponema pallidum*), as well as the possibility of change
(evolution) of the organism and its associated diseases over
time.

Additional complications are of course inherent in
diagnoses from ancient dry bone. For instance, we are not
certain that all of these tibiae represent different stages of the
same disease, inasmuch as it is possible that different disease
entities were involved, and perhaps interacted. Several, for
example, show pronounced curvature with little or no apparent swelling, whereas several others show the same amount of
curvature with pronounced swelling (Figs. 7.1 a–c; 7.2); yet
others have only slight curvature but pronounced swelling
(Figs. 7.3–7.4). Therefore, we have evaluated bowing and
swelling separately (Tables 7.2–7.4) and together (Table 7.5).
Of particular note, however, is Cocos burial 83, an adult male

with the usual attrition, caries, and periodontoclasia. His
tibiae (Fig. 7.2) and femora are so misshapen and diseased as
to be difficult to differentiate one from another. Fragments of
clavicle, humerus, and what appears to be either radius or ulna
are similarly affected. The skull suffered from severe post-
mortem damage, but the remnants available certainly are not
"normal." Histological studies have been done in order to rule
out Paget's disease, a disorder that might cause similar
changes, and at the moment the most likely diagnosis is the
advanced stage of a treponemal disease, such as syphilis or
yaws.

In view of the above uncertainties, at this time, it can only
be said that a group (at least 33 individuals) of very pre-
Columbian Maya (from early Middle through Late Formative) manifests tibial lesions that are very similar to those seen
in modern-day syphilis and yaws. As the bony lesions of
treponemal diseases appear during advanced stages, their
presence may indicate a larger number of individuals who

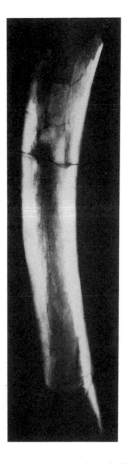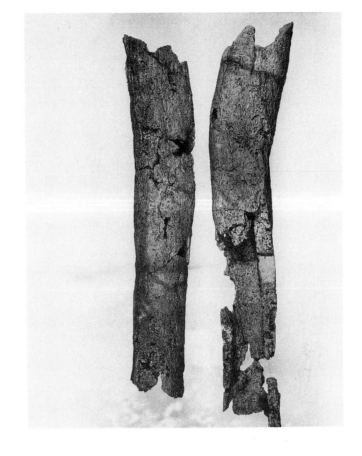

(c) Burial 81, lateral (on left) and A–P radiographs of right tibia showing "sabering" and medullary stenosis.

Fig. 7.2 Burial 83 [F135], Cocos Chicanel male, adult age. Medial views of left (to the left) and right tibiae showing "saber-shin tibia" deformity A–P bowing is pronounced (+ + +) in both (although slightly less marked in the left tibia) and "swelling" extremely pronounced (+ + + + +). Treponemal disease seems to be the most likely diagnosis as radiographic and histologic studies have ruled out Paget's disease.

suffered from the disease but died before the bones were affected.

Comparative Saber-shin tibia was definitely not present in two out of 13 Preclassic adults at Altar de Sacrificios but its presence or absence could not be ascertained in the others. It was, however, present in six later individuals, definitely not present in two others, and could not be evaluated in 42 other Classic or Postclassic adults.

The presence or absence of S-ST could not be determined in six Preclassic adults at Seibal but it was present in seven later individuals (including one child). It could not be evaluated in 48 other Classic or Postclassic adults or children.

Linear enamel hypoplasia (LEH) (Table 7.6 and Fig. 7.5a) Tooth crown formation proceeds gradually from what will eventually be the occlusal or chewing surface on through to the crown-root junction (the roots will form gradually in similar fashion). Linear enamel hypoplasia (LEH) represents a developmental arrest of enamel or underlying tissue forma-

tion during the process of crown formation (Tables 7.2, 7.6 and Fig. 7.5a). Such arrests have been related to a wide range of systemic disturbances including malnutrition and various other disease processes occurring during childhood. The location of the arrest line serves as a clue to the timing of the disturbance, since the timing of enamel formation has been studied in modern populations.

The location of most of the lesions seen in the permanent teeth of the Maya indicate that they occurred at about 3–4 years of age. This is about the age of weaning among the Maya as recorded by Landa at the time of European contact (Tozzer 1941: 125). Weaning has long been considered a critical period from many points of view, with recent investigations among modern highland Maya emphasizing this:

Weanling diarrhea was established by these studies as a classical example of synergistic interaction of malnutrition and infectious disease and, in developing countries, as probably the most important

Fig. 7.3 Burial 85 [F138], Cocos Chicanel male, middle adult age. Medial views of left (on left) and right tibiae showing "sabering" deformity with medium (+ +) A–P bowing and pronounced (+ + +) "swelling" of the sort associated with treponemal disease.

Fig. 7.4 Burial 28 [F84], Cocos Chicanel male, middle adult age. Lateral view of right tibia showing only slight (+) A–P bowing but pronounced (+ + +) "swelling." Although not a true "saber-shin tibia," the general configuration is suggestive of treponemal infection.

single factor in growth and development of children in their most formative years. (Scrimshaw, Behar, Guzman, and Gordon 1969: 55)

The negative consequences of weaning might be reduced in 3 to 4-year-old ancient Maya as compared with the 25-month-old (median age of completed weaning) modern Maya cited above, but the possibility remains that there is a relationship between at least some of the ancient Maya lesions and the rigors of weaning that are heightened by malnutrition and infectious disease (Saul 1972).

At Cuello the earliest time period (Swasey/Bladen) appears to have a lower incidence (29 percent) of evaluable individuals whose permanent teeth bear the lesions of linear enamel hypoplasia, compared to Lopez Mamom (40 percent) and Cocos Chicanel (57 percent excluding the two mass burials). Mass Burial 1 shows a 60 percent presence of this lesion (20 percent higher than Lopez Mamom) while the incidence in Mass Burial 2 is much higher (100 percent). (All percentages refer to percent of evaluable individuals. The permanent teeth of both mature and immature individuals have been included together, as they are a permanent record of "stress" during the

period of enamel formation of the individual – early childhood.)

These figures suggest that overall nutritional and health conditions were better during the Swasey/Bladen and Lopez occupations of Cuello than the Chicanel period. It is interesting to note that the mass burials contained higher percentages of individuals with enamel hypoplasia – individuals who may not be derived from the Cuello population. The mass burial towards the end of Chicanel had a particularly high rate, 100 percent, comparable to the Early Classic Altar rate of 100 percent of evaluable adults. The Preclassic Altar population was perhaps in "better shape" (80 percent) than those of the Early Classic period, although still not as "well off" as the Preclassic Cuello group as a whole (50 percent presence of LEH excluding the mass burials, 58 percent including mass burials).

Although most times of stress marked by linear enamel hypoplasia were typically at around the usual time of weaning

Table 7.5 *Occurrence of saber-shin tibia, A–P bowing and swelling, combined (evaluable adults and sub-adults only)*[1]

	O/?	+/N
Swasey/Bladen	+ +	8
Mamom		2
Chicanel	+ + +	18
Mass Burial 1	+ + + +	6
Mass Burial 2		1
All periods		35

Note:

[1] Except as noted below
+ + No swelling: 1, bowing could not be evaluated: 1
+ + + No swelling: 2
+ + + + No swelling: 1

Table 7.6 *Incidence of enamel hypoplasia among evaluable adults and subadults (permanent teeth only)*

	O	+	N
Swasey/Bladen	5	2	7
Mamom	3	2	5
Chicanel	16	21	37
Mass Burial 1	4	6	10
Mass Burial 2	0	9	9
All periods	28	40	68

(between 3 and 4 years of age), the location of non-linear lesions on the permanent teeth of one Cocos child of 5–7 years (burial 97) indicates problems at the much earlier age of about 9–18 months.

Comparative Linear enamel hypoplasia was present in the permanent teeth of eight Preclassic Altar de Sacrificios adults, not present in two, and could not be evaluated in three others. This lesion was also present in 29 Classic and Postclassic adults, not present in only one, and could not be evaluated in 20 others.

Preclassic Seibal yielded an even higher frequency of LEH, present in five and could not be evaluated in one. Later periods show its presence in 28 adult dentitions and its absence in only one. It could not be evaluated in 11 others.

Spongy or porotic hyperostosis cranii (S/PHC) This lesion is characterized by expansion of the diploe (and reorientation of its trabeculae) between the inner and outer tables of the skull,

Fig. 7.5 (a) Burial 107 [F202], Cocos Chicanel male, 23–24 years old. Anterior view of maxilla: left and right central incisors show medium (+ +) linear enamel hypoplasia or enamel growth interruption suggestive of childhood illness (infection, malnutrition, etc), only medium (+ +) periodontoclasia is present. The large defect visible above the root of the left lateral incisor is a large abscess cavity that may be associated with a pinhole-sized channel running between the tooth's much worn occlusal surface and the apex of the root (see (b)).

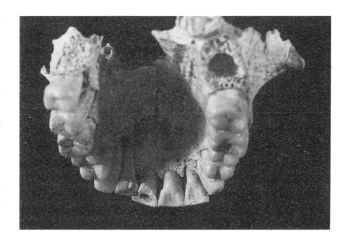

(b) Burial 107: the opening in the occlusal surface and abscess cavity are visible; also shown is a large occlusal caries cavity in the equally worn left central incisor. Both teeth show medium (+ +) oblique or LSAMAT attrition (see also fig. 7.6).

followed by erosion of the outer table in a sieve-like or coral pattern.

Elsewhere (Saul 1972, 1977) we have reviewed the history of this lesion and its location in regard to the marrow tissue and its possible association with several varieties of anemia, especially iron deficiency anemia (perhaps in conjunction with the anemia of protein deficiency and/or scurvy). We have also speculated upon the various factors that might have contributed to the presence of iron deficiency anemia in the Maya

Area. These range from dietary absorption problems to cultural practices such as the use of grinding stones resulting in the introduction of chelating agents into the gut (and more dramatic still – the Maya were very enthusiastic ceremonial bleeders). Actual iron intake varies with the availability of iron-rich foods, which in part is dependent on the iron content of the soil. All of this is compounded by increased iron requirements in the tropics.

However, this lesion, which appears to be quite common elsewhere in the Maya area, is virtually absent in the cranial materials that could be studied (Tables 7.2–7.4). Only two Cocos individuals, burial 27 (severe condition) and burial 105 (moderate condition), manifest the outer table porosity and diploic thickening of S/PHC, whereas 38 (including four from Mass Burial 1) show no signs of disease, suggesting the possibility of nutritional and/or cultural as well as environmental differences at Cuello.

Comparative Spongy or porotic hyperostosis cranii was present in five Preclassic subadults and adults at Altar de Sacrificios, not present in two, and could not be evaluated in 14 others. It was also present in 27 Classic and Postclassic adults and subadults, not present in two, and could not be evaluated in 40 others.

At Seibal, S/PHC was present in two individuals, but could not be evaluated in the four others (all adults) that made up the Preclassic group. It was also present in 20 Classic and Postclassic adults and subadults, not present in one adult, and could not be evaulated in the remaining 22 adults and subadults.

Ossified subperiosteal hemorrhages (OSPH) and periodontoclasia (PDC) Ossified subperiosteal hemorrhages (OSPH) are blood flows outside of the normal channels, in this case just below the fibrous membrane surrounding bone in life, that become calcified or eventually ossified and are thus preserved after death. The initial impetus for such a flow would probably be trauma or injury of some sort (such as a blow), but the possibility of hemorrhaging is enhanced by previous soft tissue (especially capillary wall) structural weakness due, for instance, to inadequate vitamin C in the diet. The perhaps unexpected cultural and environmental bases for vitamin C deficiency in the Maya area are discussed in Saul (1972).

Periodontoclasia (PDC) is a common form of bone inflammation followed by degeneration of the tooth sockets and tooth loss, and may involve a number of factors including mechanical irritation, infection, and tissue breakdown due to vitamin C deficiency. When periodontoclasia occurs in conjunction with ossified subperiosteal hemorrhages, then vitamin C deficiency should be suspected.

Due to post-mortem destruction and erosion at Cuello, very few individuals could be evaluated for ossified subperiosteal hemorrhages (Tables. 7.2–7.4). Only six examples of OSPH were found out of a total of 27 evaluable individuals (22 percent), including the mass burials where one presence and one absence of OSPH were noted in the earlier burial. Of these six, those whose dental remains permitted the determination of presence or absence of periodontoclasia did indeed show this combination (two Swasey/Bladen and two Cocos).

In four cases (Swasey/Bladen burials 7 and 2, Cocos burials 10 and 80) the OSPH appears to be quite small and insignificant. The two others are of more interest. The left fibula of Cocos burial 27, an unsexable 15–19 year old further described in the section on "decapitations," has a "barklike" probable ossified subperiosteal hemorrhage partially covering the cortex of the shaft. The right fibula is missing, but other long bones appear to be unaffected. Burials 47–49 (containing at least three individuals altogether) found in the early Cocos mass burial were linked together by the presence of two femora, one in each section, of the same size and configuration and bearing identical lesions. Some additional long bone fragments bear similar lesions, while others do not.

Periodontoclasia was much more evident (and more evaluable), its presence being noted in the following evaluable individuals: five of seven Swasey/Bladen, three of three Lopez, 21 of 22 Cocos (excluding mass burials), as well as four individuals in the first mass burial and four in the second. Of these, 15 individuals showed no signs of OSPH, 19 could not be evaluated for OSPH, and as noted above, four displayed both lesions.

Comparative Ossified subperiosteal hemorrhages were present in three Preclassic adults at Altar. In addition, all three manifested periodontoclasia which was also present in five other individuals. OSPH was not present in three individuals and PDC was not present in one. Seven individuals could not be evaluated for OSPH and four for PDC. Classic and Postclassic Altar included 14 adults with OSPH and 37 with PDC, of whom 12 individuals had both lesions. Thirty-one others could not be evaluated for OSPH and 13 could not be evaluated for PDC.

Seibal yields fewer instances of OSPH. One Preclassic adult shows both OSPH and PDC whereas five others could not be evaluated. PDC was present in five (including one with OSPH) but could not be evaluated in one individual. Classic and Postclassic Seibal provides only four examples of OSPH (three of them in association with PDC). Twenty other adults show various degrees of PDC with only one showing no signs of PDC and 15 who could not evaluated.

DENTAL ABNORMALITIES

Dental disease in general

A detailed genetic and pathologic analysis of the Cuello teeth in collaboration with Richard Harrington is in process. While

Table 7.7 *Incidence of dental caries among adults*

	?	O	+	N
Swasey/Bladen	8	1	2	11
Mamom	2	0	3	5
Chicanel	16	4	20	40
Mass Burial 1	24	2	6	32
Mass Burial 2	8	0	7	15
All periods	58	7	38	103

Table 7.8 *Incidence of periodontoclasia among adults*

	?	O	+	N
Swasey/Bladen	6	0	5	11
Mamom	2	0	3	5
Chicanel	17	2	21	40
Mass Burial 1	28	0	4	32
Mass Burial 2	11	0	4	15
All periods	64	2	37	103

Table 7.9 *Incidence of LSAMAT among adults*

	?			O			+			N
	M	F	?	M	F	?	M	F	?	
Swasey/Bladen	1	4	0	1	1	0	3	1	0	11
Mamom	0	1	0	0	0	0	2	1	1	5
Chicanel	11	6	2	5	4	1	8	2	1	40
Mass Burial 1	19	1	4	3	0	0	4	0	1	32
Mass Burial 2	8	0	1	3	0	1	2	0	0	15
All periods	39	12	7	12	5	2	19	4	3	103
		58			19			26		

final results are not yet available, it can be said that no real surprises occur. Caries was present from the beginning (Tables 7.2–7.4, 7.7 and Fig. 7.5b), as was periodontoclasia or pyorrhea (Tables 7.2–7.4, 7.8 and Fig. 7.5a), a breakdown of the alveolus or tooth socket ridge (discussed above) and dental calculus, an accretion associated with the chemistry of high carbohydrate diets and a lack of actual or involuntary "brushing" (meat in the diet sometimes automatically "brushes" the teeth). Both problems were as common among the ancient Maya as among modern populations. They may be interrelated in instances where loss of teeth due to decay, followed by initial resorption of empty sockets, is succeeded by disuse atrophy or wasting of the entire jaw as individuals eat less or softer foods in response to tooth loss. Dental decay may be linked to consumption of carbohydrates such as maize, although the situation remains a complex one involving timing of consumption, genetic factors, and dental hygiene. Periodontoclasia may occur in the absence of dental decay as a consequence of soft tissue inflammation due to mechanical irritation or perhaps a vitamin C deficiency. Dental abscesses (frequently linked to caries) were present in the maxillae of six individuals and the mandible of one (Table 7.2, Fig. 7.5a).

Dental attrition (LSAMAT) Dental attrition (or wear) should perhaps be classified as a cultural trait, since it is much enhanced by practices such as the grinding of maize between two stones, producing grit that is then present in the food. At Cuello we have noted a type of wear not, to our knowledge, previously described in the Maya Area. It involves heavy diagonal attrition of the lingual surface of the anterior maxil-

lary teeth with no corresponding diagonal wear of the mandibular teeth (Tables 7.2–7.4, 7.9, Fig. 7.6). Although found only in adults, a YA male aged 23–24 in burial 107 demonstrates fairly severe attrition, suggesting that the predominantly adult population of Cuello (19 subadult (14 under 10 years): 103 adult) gives us a skewed distribution of a trait requiring a certain amount of time to produce and probably present to a lesser degree in younger individuals.

This wear appears to be similar to the LSAMAT (lingual surface attrition of the maxillary anterior teeth) as described by Irish and Turner (1987) in prehistoric Panama and by Turner and Machado (1983) in an Archaic Brazilian site. LSAMAT was found in combination with a high incidence of caries, as is the case at Cuello (76 percent of evaluable individuals). They theorize that use of the upper anterior teeth and tongue to manipulate (much as we eat artichokes) a gritty, high carbohydrate cariogenic food such as manioc roots may have produced this unusual wear coupled with caries. Cuello attrition, and that noted by Turner, Irish and Machado, should not be confused with the attrition described by Anderson (1967) in material from the Tehuacan Valley that severely affected the lower teeth as well. Anderson postulated that it related to the stripping of reeds, an activity involving both upper and lower teeth and producing a unique wear pattern.

LSAMAT is found in four of six Bladen, four of four Lopez Mamom and 11 of 21 Cocos Chicanel individuals (those evaluable) not counting the two Chicanel mass burials. Of those evaluable, Mass Burial 1 contains five of eight and Mass Burial 2, two of six individuals with LSAMAT. Combining time periods and looking only at sex, LSAMAT is found in four of nine females (44 percent) and 19 of 31 males (61 percent). This wear persisted over a long period of time and does not appear to be related to a sexually limited activity – further support for the possibility that a basic local food item was the cause.

In addition to the unusual lingual attrition of the anterior maxillary teeth described above, three individuals show

Fig. 7.6 Burial 123 [F251], Bladen male, young/middle adult. View of occlusal surfaces of mandibular teeth (above) showing absence of oblique wear and maxillary teeth (below) showing medium (+ +) LSAMAT attrition on central and left lateral incisors.

Fig. 7.7 Burial 34 [F171], early Cocos Chicanel Mass Burial 1 (400–300 B.C.), male, 55–59 years old. Right upper canine tooth showing a labial-lingual groove with marked wear and "wear polish" suggestive of unusual usage.

unique variations. Only the upper left mesial and lateral incisors of Chicanel burial 107 are lingually worn – wear on the right upper incisors is flat. The left mesial incisor is worn to such an extreme that the pulp cavity is completely exposed and open into the root, and the left lateral incisor has a pinhole-sized opening culminating in a large maxillary abscess surrounding the root tip (Fig. 7.5). The lower incisors are only slightly worn in normal fashion (flat). Such severe wear involving only two teeth suggests a different tool-like activity by this man, or at least an individualistic technique. A somewhat similar situation was found in Mass Burial 2. One right mesial maxillary incisor is lingually worn (as in burial 107) to the point of resembling a preparation for a root canal procedure. Inasmuch as it is one of a handful of loose teeth, we unfortunately cannot know the wear pattern of its neighbors. The early Cocos mass burial contained an older adult (55–59 years) male (burial 34) whose other characterisics are described in the section on fractures. Although his teeth are so worn, carious, broken or missing as to preclude analysis of the type of wear (diagonal or flat), the right upper canine shows a definite grooving of the occlusal surface (in a labial-lingual direction) with extreme wear and "wear polish" (Fig. 7.7). This would suggest repeated use of at least this tooth (and presumably its mandibular counterpart or the tongue) in a "tool-like" manner.

Comparative Marked attrition is a constant presence in both ancient and modern Maya teeth, owing to the previously mentioned practice of grinding maize or other foods between two stones (*mano* and *metate*), introducing stone grit into the diet as the stones grind each other as well as the food between them. Gann (1918: 71) quotes a modern Maya from Belize as

saying that "an old man eats two rubbing stones [*metates*] and six rubbers [*manos*] during his life."

Gritty and abrasive foods typically produce a relatively even, flat wear on the occlusal surfaces of all teeth, especially molars, and such wear is extremely common in the Maya Area. However, we have not previously (to our knowledge) encountered the unusual type of attrition described above as LSAMAT.

Enamelomas Enamelomas, or enamel pearls, were found on three individuals (Table 7.2): the young adult female in burial 62 of Swasey/Bladen date and two Chicanel young adult males, burials 100 and 119. These "pearls" of dental enamel are typically located near the cemento-enamel junction or further down on the root of the tooth, usually a molar.

Comparative An essentially normal variation of no apparent functional significance, thought by some (e.g. Coon 1985: 151) to be more prevalent in Asiatics and Northern Europeans, enamel pearls have been found at Altar de Sacrifcios and Seibal.

TRAUMA

Fractures Healed fractures were present in at least five individuals (Tables 7.2–7.4):

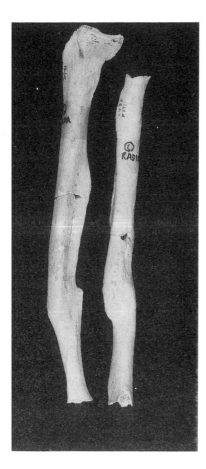

Fig. 7.8 Burial 34. Left ulna (to the left) and radius showing well-healed but malaligned fractures of both bones. This type of fracture usually involves the ulna alone and is called a "parry" fracture. The presence of a fracture in the radius as well suggests an unusually forceful blow or other injury.

(1) A malaligned "parry" (or "nightstick") fracture involving the left radius and ulna of the old adult male in burial 34 of Mass Burial 1 (Fig. 7.8). This injury was a thing of the past, as healing is complete and the fracture callus has been remodeled away. As the name implies, this sort of fracture is apt to be the result of flinging the forearm over the head to deflect a blow. It would have taken a fairly hefty blow to fracture both radius and ulna. This 55 to 59-year-old man suffered from arthritis, including the atlas and axis, sacroiliac joint, and several vertebrae in between. Other joints were not preserved, and may or may not have also been arthritic. As might be expected in a Maya of his years, he had severe dental problems: caries, periodontoclasia, pre-mortem tooth loss, extreme attrition, a dental abscess communicating with a related inflammation of the right maxillary sinus, and the peculiar grooving of the right upper canine described in the section on dental attrition (Fig. 7.7). Tibial curvature (+ +) and swelling (+ +) were also present.

(2) A healed fractured toe phalanx from the same early Chicanel mass burial. The section of the mass burial that this bone is from [F203] consists of the commingled bits and pieces of at least nine adult males.

(3) A malaligned but well-healed Colles fracture of the left distal radius and well-healed fractures of two left carpal (wrist) bones (capitate and lunate) were found in burial 79 of Mass Burial 2. These may have come from the same (male) individual as all are quite robust. A Colles fracture usually occurs when a falling individual catches him or herself on an outstretched hand. It is conceivable that the capitate, lunate, and perhaps other carpal bones could also suffer damage on impact.

(4) A healed malaligned midshaft fracture of the left femur accompanied by what appears to be an "exuberant" fracture callus was found in a young adult male of the Chicanel phase in burial 121. The formation of a fracture callus is a normal part of the healing process, serving as a "bridge" uniting the fractured bones which is then remodeled into a more normal shape. At times the mechanism "goes wild," producing an excessive or "exuberant" callus. LSAMAT (+ +) was present on his maxillary incisors, but not much other tooth wear was evident although he had moderately heavy calculus deposits and periodontoclasia. His tibiae showed a trace (+) of the bowing and a bit more of the swelling (+ +) described in the section on saber-shin tibiae.

(5) An old well-healed fracture of the right distal tibia of a Cocos phase young adult male in burial 105. Like many Cuello individuals he shows a slight (+) bowing of the tibiae (no swelling), lingual wear (LSAMAT + +) of the upper incisors, calculus, pre-mortem tooth loss, and periodontoclasia (+). Arthritic lipping of the distal joint of his left thumb, not present on the right thumb, leads one to speculate on left-handed activity of some sort. Unlike other Cuello people, he may have suffered from iron deficiency anemia, showing a trace (+) of spongy or porotic hyperostosis cranii at lambda (found in only one other evaluable individual). His Tabular cranial shaping of an uncertain variety and Romero type F3 or F4 dental decoration also set him apart from other Cuello burials.

Comparative Preclassic Altar provides one example of a well-healed and remodeled midclavicular fracture (with normal residual deformity) in a 20 to 24-year-old male. Classic Altar yields only a healed (but not yet remodeled) "parry" fracture of the ulna of an old adult male. No fractures were seen at Seibal.

Cranial erosions We have often puzzled over shallow lesions about the size and shape of a thumbprint pressed into the skull. These lesions in general affect only the outer table and show signs of osseous regeneration. Campillo (1977: 229–89) describes similar lesions, noting that they are located in the most vulnerable areas of the skull and predominantly in males.

He concludes that they may represent a healed osseous reaction secondary to traumatic injury to the periosteum. A practicing neurosurgeon, he describes a patient whose radiographs showed a ring of osseous condensation not noted clinically. This patient recalled having been struck on the head in that same spot when a child, with a resultant hematoma.

Two Cocos skulls bear such evidence of "mild" trauma. Burial 101 is a gracile adult male with a "dent" on the right parietal, a very accessible area. Its appearance is similar to those described by Campillo, and is well healed. This individual suffered from the usual dental problems, a maxillary abscess and severe (+ + +) periodontoclasia in particular, plus slight (+) bowing and swelling (+) of his tibiae. Of more interest is the "strange" shape of his asymmetrical skull, which does not appear to have been artificially shaped. Although all long bone fragments are small and gracile, the muscle attachments of the skull (mastoids, supramastoid ridge, nuchal ridges) are all quite pronounced and the mandible abnormally narrow and stocky. Whether his appearance had anything to do with receiving a "rap" on the head is pure conjecture.

The nicely shaped (Tabular Erect) skull of burial 113 [F211] received its injury on the upper part of the frontal bone – again a vulnerable area. The cranial erosion of this middle adult male shows a ring of osseous condensation, well healed. His tibiae are slightly (+) swollen and more severely (+ + +) bowed. Both of these individuals could have been either deliberately or accidentally (as in a fall) struck on the head.

Comparative Possibly overlooked elsewhere, a "dent" in the left lambdoid area of the skull was noted in the earliest Maya burial (no. 135) at Altar de Sacrificios.

Other cranial trauma The skull of burial 123, a Y/MA Bladen male whose neurofibroma (Fig. 7.11) will be described later, has a "healed" groove approximately 15 mm in length above the right orbit (Fig. 7.9). Additionally, there is a small circular (6 mm diameter) opening or perforation with healed edges in the outer table of bone just lateral to and below the groove. As the inner table of bone is missing in this area, we cannot determine how far this opening penetrated. In any event, both injuries are well healed and may have occurred either together or separately and presumably were unrelated to the cause of his death.

A skull in the [F203] section of the early Cocos mass burial was described in the field notes as having "a traumatic hole punched in the right parietal. This does not appear to be a trepanation since grinding holes or cut marks are not readily visible, but seems to have been punched by a pointed instrument." The partially reconstructed hole measures about 25 mm in diameter on the outer table, tapering to about

Fig. 7.9 Burial 123, fragmentary right supraorbital ridge area showing small circular (*c.* 6 mm diameter) opening and "healed" groove (*c.* 15 mm long) above and medial to the circular opening. The groove is directly above the supraorbital notch and the circular opening is lateral to the notch.

20 mm diameter on the inner table. Although the edges appear to be sharp, with little or no healing, and no additional cuts or scrape marks are readily visible, a layer of dirt and preservative remains from the excavation and consolidation process, and therefore we will not attempt to guess at the tool or weapon used. No conclusions should be drawn as to the cause of death of this middle adult male, as the injury could have been inflicted before (without healing time), at the time of, or after death.

Another hole was described in the right parietal of Cocos burial 66, a robust middle adult male (Fig. 10.9). The skull had been freshly fragmented in passage between Belize and Ohio, and the outer surface that could be seen had suffered much post-mortem damage. Again, we set out to reconstruct the hole, but unfortunately this time we were unable to do so, and therefore cannot discuss it.

"Decapitations" Several Cuello individuals have been described as "decapitated" in the excavators' reports, mainly because of the unnatural location of the skull relative to the skeleton. We have found none of the cut marks that one would expect to find on bony remains after decapitation, but due to the condition of this skeletal material that is not at all surprising. Post-mortem destruction of the base of the skull and cervical vertebrae was severe at this site.

Lopez Mamom burial 1 (75/14), a slightly robust female or small male young adult, consisted solely of postcranial fragments, plus three loose teeth: these maxillary incisors show slight lingual wear (LSAMAT +), but may not be associated with this individual, since a block of tabular chert was found in place of the skull.

The mid-late Cocos burial 27 in the pyramid, a gracile, unsexable 15 to 19-year-old, was described in the excavators' reports as having been extended on its back with the skull "placed upright on top of the right humerus, facing north" (Fig. 10.8). This is one of the two individuals who may have been suffering from iron deficiency anemia, as cranial fragments show signs of spongy or porotic hyperostosis cranii. The left fibula (right not present) is partially covered with a "bark-like" ossified subperiosteal hemorrhage. There is no lingual incisal wear, linear enamel hypoplasia is present, and both tibiae appear normal.

The early Cocos burials 10 and 12 were found together (Fig. 10.7). Burial 10, a Y/MA male, was "supine and slightly on its right side" with the head "on the stump of the neck a short distance west of its expected position" (Donaghey et al. 1979: 40). He was one of the individuals whose teeth bore the lesions of linear enamel hypoplasia, and his maxillary incisors were moderately (+ +) worn on the lingual surface (LSA-MAT). Both tibiae were moderately (+ +) bowed and swollen. His companion in burial 12, a female Y/MA, was described as "lying on the right side and apparently flexed. The skull had been detached and stood upright . . . the mandible dislocated by pressure of deposit" (Donaghey et al. 1979: 41). Her skull had been artificially shaped – Tabular of uncertain variety. Maxillary incisors are lingually worn (+ +LSAMAT), periodontoclasia is present, and no signs of linear enamel hypoplasia are evident. Found with burial 10 were seven teeth from an unsexable Y/MA, burial 11 [F7a] (LSAMAT, LEH, and caries present). It is impossible to know whether these teeth were a tooth offering, happened to be present in the fill of the grave, or represent another burial, although the last seems unlikely owing to the absence of other remains. None of the three individuals had decorated teeth.

The early Cocos burial 126–127 of two small children is very confusing. Based on femoral and tibial diaphysial measurements (admittedly only approximations due to the condition of the bones), burial 127 is about 1.5 to 2.5 years of age, and burial 126 about 0.5 to 1.5 years. The skull of burial 127 had been replaced by a pot. Burial 126 had been placed to the left and below the legs of burial 127, and the back portion of a skull (minus frontal, maxilla, and mandible) was in an anatomically correct position for burial 126. A frontal bone and part of a maxilla were located to the right and below the feet of burial 127. The left hand of burial 127 was resting on top of and inside the back portion of the skull. Both cranial portions are consistent (size, thickness) with being parts of one skull, and there does not appear to be any duplication of cranial fragments. The maxilla and teeth yield an age of approximately 1.5 to 2.5 years, and the almost complete closure of the

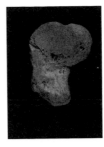

Fig. 7.10 Burial 52–60 [F203], early Cocos Chicanel Mass Burial 1 (400–300 B.C.), adult of indeterminate sex. Vertebral right superior articular process exhibiting spondylolysis (a dissolution of the bony bond between the superior and inferior articular processes) followed by spondylolisthesis (forward slippage of the vertebral body).

metopic suture of the frontal is consistent with an age of 1.5 to 2 years. However, as the approximate bone ages of the two children overlap (at around 1.5), the maxilla, frontal, and back portion of the skull (which may be different parts of one skull) could (by dental age, size, and suture closure) belong to either child.

OTHER DISEASES

Spondylolisthesis Occasionally one encounters a disorder so distinctive that even a small fragment may yield the diagnosis: a bit of bone smaller than a small fingertip from Mass Burial 1 is identifiable as the right superior articular process of a lower lumbar vertebra from a mature individual (sex could not be determined but all "sexable" bones in this burial appear to be male) (Fig. 7.10). Although fragmentary, enough bone is present to indicate that the bony bridge between the superior and inferior articular processes had "dissolved" in life ("spondylolysis") resulting in the anterior slippage of the vertebral body and the upper articular processes known as spondylolisthesis. Fortunately, the low level of the slippage does not ordinarily cause nerve damage but can be painful in some individuals. This condition was fairly common in certain groups of ancient Eskimos and is also well known among professional football players and other athletes. Although once suspected of having genetic overtones due to its preponderance in Eskimos, it is now believed to be due to accumulated stress fractures at the *pars interarticularis* (the place between the superior and inferior articular processes) that result from frequent flexion and especially extension of the lower back of the sort involved in athletics, heavy lifting, and also sitting in kayaks (Merbs 1983: 120–8, 172–6). No other bone fragments can be definitely linked to this individual, therefore we cannot associate this lesion with a specific activity.

Arthritis Arthritis or joint disease, specifically osteoarthritis or degenerative joint disease (as distinct from rheumatoid arthritis), is a standard topic of discussion in studies of ancient material inasmuch as joint changes can provide clues to individual and population activity patterns. Unfortunately, while well-preserved bones of ancient Eskimos (Merbs 1983) and others provide a basis for this type of analysis, the fragmentary bones of the Maya typically yield only a few isolated examples (one exception being the Postclassic site of Playa del Carmen, where elbows, knees, and the lumbosacral area of the vertebral column are most severely affected, possibly the result of fishing, hunting, and agricultural activities (Marquez Morfin 1982: 131–48). Bone preservation at the Cuello site is so poor that few articular surfaces remain. Therefore, we note the presence of arthritic lesions in a handful of individuals (Tables 7.2–7.4) but can say nothing about its absence, and certainly can draw no conclusions regarding the incidence and location of arthritis on a populational level.

The early Cocos Mass Burial 1 yielded these examples: burial 34, the old adult male whose "parry" fractures of ulna and radius are described above (Fig. 7.8), was afflicted with arthritis of the vertebral column, beginning with the atlas and axis and ending in the sacroiliac joint and including a few bits of vertebrae in between. As noted before, other articular surfaces have been destroyed, so the true extent of his arthritis is unknown. [F183–186] consists of bits and pieces of at least three male adults, and contains cervical vertebrae and foot phalanges with arthritic lesions. [F203], consisting of at least nine male adults or parts thereof, also has a thoracic vertebra with arthritic lipping.

In the late Cocos Mass Burial 2, we found toe phalanges whose articular surfaces showed signs of arthritis in sections (1318) and (1187). These may or may not be from one individual, as "bundles" of bones from assorted individuals were included in the burial (see Appendix).

Five other Cocos individuals had arthritic hands and/or vertebral columns. Two middle adult females had arthritic hands, burial 88 in unsided hand phalanges, and burial 117 in right hand phalanges as well as cervical vertebrae. Burial 105, a young adult male described earlier in relation to a fracture of the distal tibia, may have been involved in some sort of left-handed activity, as the distal joint of his left thumb has arthritic lipping, whereas the right thumb does not. The hand phalanges of one male middle adult (burial 95) also appear to have arthritic articular surfaces. Burial 66, a middle adult male, suffered from what may have been fairly severe arthritis of at least one cervical vertebra.

Comparative Arthritis could not be examined for in the 13 Preclassic adults at Altar but was found in various locations in 18 Classic and Postclassic individuals although 32 individuals could not be evaluated.

One Preclassic adult at Seibal did show signs of cervical

Fig. 7.11 (a) Burial 123, medial (internal) view of left ascending ramus and body of mandible showing an open and enlarged mandibular canal with an elliptical perforation in the lateral wall of the ramus; note the V-shaped mandibular notch that indicates changed function probably associated with the neurofibroma of the inferior alveolar nerve that probably produced the other defects.

osteoarthritis but five others could not be evaluated. Only one additional Classic or Postclassic individual showed signs of arthritis, whereas 38 others could not be evaluated.

Neurofibroma The mandible of burial 123 (Fig. 10.2), a Y/MA (30–40 years) Bladen male, bears an interesting lesion with no signs of inflammation (Fig. 7.11 a,b). The localization of the destruction in the left mandibular (nerve) canal allowed us (in cooperation with Robert A. Burns, DDS at the Medical College of Ohio) to diagnose it as a neurofibroma – a tumor, usually benign, which grows slowly along the nerve (in this case, the inferior alveolar nerve, a branch of the mandibular nerve, itself a branch of the trigeminal nerve).

The growth and pressure of the tumor has resulted in an open mandibular canal (medially, from the former mandibular foramen to the root of the third molar), lacking a mylohyoid groove but retaining the lingula, that has more than doubled in diameter (to 7 mm) and has also produced an

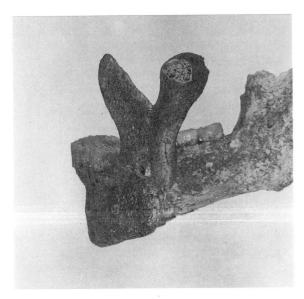

(b) Burial 123, lateral (external) view of the left mandible showing the elliptical perforation and mandibular notch.

elliptical perforation (6 × 7 mm diameter) in the lateral wall of the ramus (about 10 mm below the former mandibular foramen). The shape of the mandibular notch (now V-shaped) and a reduction in width of the ramus indicate changed function in response to this tumor of the nerve that supplies the lower teeth and some muscles associated with mastication.

Periodontal degeneration and calculus are more extreme on the left side of both mandible and maxilla and the lower left second molar is missing (pre-mortem) – more signs of chewing problems on the left side. This individual's maxillary incisors are worn on the lingual surface (+ +LSAMAT), while mandibular incisors show flat wear (Fig. 7.6).

Osteoid-osteomas Osteoid-osteomas are benign bone tumors most commonly found in the femur and tibia, and less commonly the fibula, humerus, vertebrae, and bones of the feet. Although probably of no functional significance, but perhaps of interest to some, we noted two possible osteoid-osteomas at Cuello. One was found on the proximal portion of the left femur of burial 110, a young adult Cocos male, and the other on the right humerus of a male in Mass Burial 2, context (1320).

Sinusitis Inflammation of the maxillary sinuses is present in two Chicanel individuals, one from each mass burial. The floor of the right maxillary sinus of burial 34, the old adult male from the earliest mass burial whose "parry" fractures were described earlier, has the appearance of "foamy mud" typically produced by a sinus infection of long standing. An opening can be seen communicating to a dental abscess, the probable cause of his sinusitis.

A male young adult in the later mass burial (context 1318) also may have suffered from a long siege of sinusitis. Fragments of his maxillary sinuses show the foam-like bony thickening found in burial 34. Because of the fragmentary nature of this specimen, we cannot determine whether dental abscesses were responsible. However, sinus infections can spring from other sources, such as prolonged inhalation of smoky air, allergies etc. It should be noted that the recognition of the presence of sinusitis or similar "within-bone" conditions is usually related to the fragmentary nature of the specimen, as we have not routinely X-rayed in this area.

Comparative Sinusitis was apparently not present at Altar, but was noted in one Preclassic and three Postclassic adults at Seibal.

STATURE (Table 7.10)
Stature or height (standing body length) in the living must be measured very carefully and even then is subject to variation due to intervertebral disc compression during our "upright" hours. Estimating stature from individual bones of unknowns is obviously an even more uncertain process involving selection of an appropriate statistical formula, sex and age adjustments, etc.

At Cuello, the problem was further compounded by the fact that only one male femur and one female tibia could be measured directly. We therefore decided to estimate femoral length by comparing sufficiently intact femora with the complete Cuello femur (and femora from other Maya samples that were complete) thus arriving at statural estimates based on the complete femora. (We chose not to use Steele's (1970) formulae for fragmentary long bones because previous experience had demonstrated that some of his landmarks were difficult to determine with sufficient reliability.)

In spite of all these limitations and permutations we have attempted to estimate stature because stature is a polygenic and multifactorial trait that is probably very much affected by nutrition and disease within both an ontogenetic (life cycle) and phylogenetic (generation to generation) context. Furthermore, previous studies at Altar de Sacrificios (Saul 1972) had suggested a decrease in male (and possibly female) stature over time, from the Preclassic onwards, resulting in the very short Maya of modern times.

Estimates based on nine females and 11 males (Table 7.10) do hint at a similar situation at Cuello but the abovementioned uncertainties of our estimation procedure preclude our making a definitive statement.

CULTURAL MODIFICATIONS

Head shaping Modification of the normal shape of the skull was common in the Maya Area. Some varieties were probably

Table 7.10 *Estimated stature of adults (Genoves formula, 1967)*

	Mean	Range	N
Cuello male stature estimates			
Pre-Chicanel	163.66	161.25–167.13	4
Early Chicanel mass burial[1]	162.58	158.75–164.50	3
Chicanel (minus mass burial)	158.44	151.50–164.50	4
Cuello female stature estimates			
Pre-Chicanel	161.54	159.82–163.25	2
Early Chicanel mass burial[1]	146.50	146.50	1
Chicanel (minus mass burial)	152.25	146.50–159.82	6
Altar de Sacrificios and Cuello Preclassic male stature estimates[2]			
Altar	166.63	163.50–173.00	4
Cuello (minus mass burial)	161.15	151.50–167.25	8
Early Chicanel mass burial[1]	162.58	158.75–164.50	3
Altar de Sacrificios and Cuello Preclassic female stature estimates[2]			
Altar	148.25	147.50–149.00	2
Cuello (minus mass burial)	154.56	146.50–163.25	8
Early Chicanel mass burial[1]	146.50	146.50	1

Note:

[1] The Early Chicanel mass burial (400 B.C.) is listed separately from other Chicanel burials, as it may not be part of the Cuello biological population. Male Early Chicanel mass burial stature appears to resemble more closely that of the pre-Chicanel population than that of other Chicanel males. The possible female [F33] in the mass burial is abnormally small. (Stature estimates were unobtainable for Late Chicanel mass burial [F128].)

[2] It is of interest (albeit baffling) to note that the Preclassic Altar males were considerably taller (mean = 166.63) than either the Cuello mass burial males (mean = 162.58) or the other Cuello males (mean = 161.15), whereas Preclassic Altar females were shorter (mean = 148.25) than their Cuello female counterparts (mean = 154.56, disregarding the mass burial possible female [F33] who is abnormally small). It should also be noted that the Altar estimates are based on *intact* long bones, while Cuello estimates are based on *fragmentary* long bones.

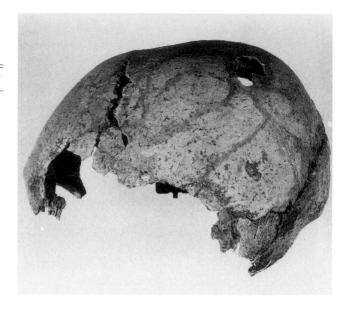

Fig. 7.12 Burial 62 [F110], Swasey female, young adult age. Left lateral view of fragmentary skull showing slight (+) lambdoid flattening with probable presence of "tumpline" deformity (suggested by the postcoronal depression).

unintentional. For instance, the use of a cradleboard in infancy might flatten the back of the head or the use of tumpline or haulage band in later years might groove or depress the upper forehead. Such unintentional "deformation" may have provided the impetus for deliberate shaping using boards and/or bindings.

Several head shaping (we prefer to use the neutral term "shaping" rather than the often used but pejorative term "deformation") classifications have been established based on shapes and/or presumed shaping devices. We have followed Imbelloni's and Dembo's 1938 classification as presented by Comas (1960: 391–5) because it seemed to be the most frequently used classification in Latin America. It consists of a "Tabular" category produced by fronto-occipital compres-

sion between thin boards and an "Orbicular" (sometimes called "Annular") category produced by compressing the head circumferentially with the aid of bandages or elastic bands. Each category is further subdivided into Erect and Oblique varieties according to the inclination of the occipital area upon the Frankfort plane. In the Erect Variety, pressure was confined to the upper portion of the occipital and adjacent portions of the parietalia (the lambdoid area), resulting in an essentially vertical orientation or occasionally an anterior inclination of the occipital bone. The Oblique variety was subjected to overall pressure on the occipital bone to such an extent that the entire occipital was flattened and tilted posteriorly.

Most (14) of the 32 Cuello cranial remains that could be examined for head shaping (Tables 7.2–7.4) were apparently normal in that there were no indications of modification. Two individuals (both female) showed possible signs of tumpline use. One of these (Fig. 7.12), plus ten others, had lambdoid areas with varying degrees of flattening that might have been related to the use of a cradleboard in infancy (Fig. 7.13) although one female in burial 80 shows such pronounced flattening that intentional shaping must be suspected.

Only six individuals (five males and one female) could be classified with certainty as being intentionally shaped. Two were classified as pronounced Tabular Erect (Cocos burials 113 and 28), one as pronounced Tabular Oblique (Swasey/Bladen burial 118), one as probable Tabular Oblique (the female, Cocos burial 12), and two as Tabular of uncertain variety (Swasey/Bladen burial 22, Cocos burial 105).

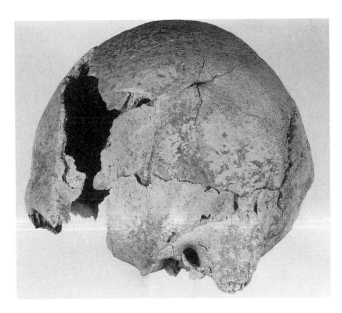

Fig. 7.13 Burial 5 (76/137), Lopez Mamom male, middle adult age. Left lateral view of fragmentary skull showing slight (+) lambdoid flattening with no indication of "tumpline" deformity.

Comparative Preclassic Altar manifested little that could be considered head shaping, with the exception of two individuals with pronounced flattening of the lambdoid region. Three others were considered "normal" although two of these showed slight lambdoid flattening. Sixteen others could not be evaluated. Classic and Postclassic Altar included nine individuals with Tabular Oblique shape, six with Tabular Erect shape, and one had Tabular shaping of an uncertain variety, whereas six had "normally" shaped skulls and 47 others could not be evaluated. (The above figures include both subadults and adults.)

The situation in Preclassic Seibal shows the early presence of Tabular head shaping in three individuals (one each of Tabular Oblique, Tabular Erect, and Tabular of uncertain variety) with one instance of slight lambdoid flattening and two individuals who could not be evaluated. Classic and Postclassic Seibal provides 12 examples of Tabular Oblique, five Tabular Erect, one Tabular of uncertain variety, one moderate lambdoid flattening, and six "normals." Nineteen others could not be evaluated.

Dental decoration The Maya were not content just to shape their children's heads. They also occasionally decorated (we again avoid the more often used but "value-loaded" term, "mutilated") their permanent teeth by filing the occlusal edges of incisors (and sometimes canines) and/or drilling shallow "pits" for jadeite or hematite inserts in the labial (lip) surfaces of maxillary teeth. Dental decoration types found in Mexico and Central America have been classified by Romero (1970) according to location and type of decoration. Of the 22

dentitions that could be examined for this trait, only three showed signs of decoration – the other 19 showed no modification of the relevant teeth. Romero type C-2 or C-6 (symmetrical filing of both angles of the crown) was present in one male in the early Cocos mass burial and Romero type F-3 or F-4 (asymmetrical filing of both angles of the crown) was present in one male and one female, both Cocos. No inserts or drilled "pits" were noted.

Comparative The Preclassic Altarians included two individuals whose filed teeth represented Romero types A-4 and B-4. Eighteen Classic and Postclassic Altarians possessed filed teeth that included Romero types A 1,2,3,4; B 4, 5; and C 5, whereas three of the later inhabitants had Romero type E-1 inserts and one other had a combination of inserts and filing.

Seibal yielded one Preclassic individual with Romero type C-5 filing. Five Classic and Postclassic individuals had filed teeth, including Romero types A-3, C-2 and 5, and F-4. Five other later individuals had Romero type E-1 inserts plus in one case a G-13 insert.

Probable cut marks; red ocher

Pieces of the clavicle, mandible, and humerus of the Bladen (or possibly Lopez) phase burial 9, a fragmentary, robust MA male, show traces of what may be red ochre, and bits of red were found in the dirt inside the humerus. Probable old cut marks can be seen on the bottom of the left side of the "chin." There are no signs of healing. He also had lingual wear (+ +LSAMAT) on his maxillary incisors, plus labial chipping of an upper canine and premolar, and bowing (+ +) and swelling (+) of both tibiae.

Some of the cranial fragments of the pyramid burial 27, described in greater detail in "Decapitations," have a faint pinkish-purple cast, perhaps produced by the red plaster dome covering the grave.

The extremely fragmentary remains of an adult male, Cocos burial 109, also bear old cut marks with no signs of healing. At least five short (3–4 mm long) crosscuts have been made perpendicular to the deltoid tuberosity of a right humerus fragment. In addition, parietal fragments are scarred with longer cut marks which are certainly not the "grooving" caused by blood vessels.

All of the above cuts are definitely not fresh and cannot have occurred during excavations or cleaning, but cannot be definitely related to the cause of death, either.

DISCUSSION

Although often damaged post-mortem by root penetration and scouring, the Cuello burial sample (at 122 individuals one of the largest Preclassic samples known) has, after intensive reconstruction and examination, yielded useful information on a number of aspects of the ancient population.

Population composition

Subadults and older adults seem to be under-represented throughout. In the case of the former, this may relate to differential preservation of more fragile remains and/or preferential burial practices whereas in the latter case it is more likely a reflection of the rigors of life during the Preclassic period. Females are present in all culture phases although perhaps under-recognized within the unknown or uncertain sex category for adults.

The two mass burials are totally lacking in subadults and virtually lacking in females (only one probable female in the earlier group and no apparent females in the later group) with a seeming emphasis on younger adults (relatively few middle adults in both and only one old adult in the earlier burial). These skewed age and sex distributions for the mass burials in combination with the careful manner in which the burials were arranged are more suggestive of sacrificial deaths than epidemics.

Health

The presence of possible saber-shin tibia in at least 33 individuals at Preclassic Cuello suggests that treponemal disease has very early (and definitely pre-Columbian) roots in the New World (cf. Baker and Armelagos 1988). Increasing percentages over time of linear enamel hypoplasia, a lesion related to childhood illness, suggest that overall nutritional and health conditions were better during the earlier than later phases. This appears to be true in regard to the mass burials as well, and both mass burials also show a higher frequency for this lesion than the rest of the population.

The virtual absence (present in only three individuals, not present in 38) of spongy or porotic hyperostosis cranii, a lesion that seems to be associated with iron deficiency and similar anemias, is noteworthy inasmuch as it is common elsewhere in the Maya Area. This could be related to nutritional and/or cultural as well as environmental differences at Cuello. Poor preservation precluded a complete examination for the ossified subperiosteal hemorrhages (OSPH) that in association with periodontoclasia (PDC or alveolar degeneration) suggest the presence of vitamin C deficiency or scurvy (possibly present at Altar and Seibal). Only six examples of OSPH (four in association with PDC) were found, of which four seemed to be quite small and insignificant whereas the other two were more extensive. Of these latter, one was associated with pronounced PDC whereas the other, being part of a mass burial, could not be associated with a specific dentition.

Common dental problems included the previously mentioned periodontoclasia, abscesses, and dental caries or decay, often a contributing factor to PDC, as is the frequently noted presence of dental calculus, an accretion associated with a high carbohydrate diet and lack of "brushing." Dental attri-

tion or tooth wear is common at Cuello as it is elsewhere in the Maya Area owing to the grinding of maize, etc., between stones that then add their "grit" to the preparation. However, we have not previously recognized lingual surface attrition of the maxillary anterior teeth (LSAMAT) with no corresponding diagonal wear of the mandibular anterior teeth. Found in 25 males and females of the 40 evaluable adults, this lack of sexual limitation suggests a causal association with the eating of a basic local food item. Enamelomas or dental pearls, an essentially normal variation, were found in three individuals.

Five healed fractures (two upper extremity and three lower extremity) were found at Cuello whereas very few have been found elsewhere. This may be a function of sample size. A few additional instances of trauma (cranial) such as "erosions" (? = "dents") and healed grooves and perforations were noted, while other features noted during excavation could not be evaluated owing to the condition of the remains.

Miscellaneous disorders included spondylolisthesis, a vertebral column lesion so distinctive it could be diagnosed from a fingertip-sized fragment of a superior articular process; osteoarthritis (DJD), which was present in at least nine individuals, but could not be examined for in others owing to poor preservation; an example of a neurofibroma of the inferior alveolar nerve located within the mandibular canal (open in this instance), a lesion that we have not previously noted in the Maya Area; two possible examples of osteoid-osteomas or benign bone tumors (on a femur and on a humerus of different individuals), and at least two individuals with probable maxillary sinusitis.

Stature

Since only one male femur and one female tibia were sufficiently intact for direct measurement, we hesitantly estimated femur length for 18 additional males and females, using proportional comparisons of fragmentary femora with intact bones from Cuello and other Maya groups. The resultant stature estimates based on femur length estimates are suggestive of a decline in male and possibly female stature over time (as noted at Altar) but the opportunities for error inherent in our methodology preclude firm conclusions.

Cultural modifications

Most (14) of the 32 individuals who could be evaluated for head shaping showed no signs of intentional modification, although two may have had some tumpline deformation and one of these, along with ten others, showed lambdoid flattening of the sort associated with the use of a cradleboard in infancy. Only six individuals showed signs of intentional shaping (including both Tabular Erect and Tabular Oblique varieties). Probable cut marks were found on the bones of two individuals, and red ocher may have also been present on one of these.

Of the 22 dentitions that could be evaluated for dental decoration, only three showed intentional modification (including Romero filing types C-2 or C-6 and F-3 or F-4). No inserts or drilled "pits" were noted.

APPENDIX

MASS BURIALS (Tables 7.3, 7.4)

Both mass burials are described elsewhere (Chapters 3, 10) in detail, and the difficulties inherent in deconstructing such complex rituals and their components are clear. Throughout our analysis an attempt has been made to link fragment to fragment and bone to bone in order to "build" as complete an individual as possible from the "bundles" and assorted bits and pieces found in each mass burial. However, the condition of the remains, both when interred and after considerable post-burial erosion, often made this impossible. Therefore, the number of individuals in each mass burial can only be approximated (minimum number in a particular patch) and pathology can usually only be noted in relation to the fragment examined.

Early Cocos Mass Burial 1, phase V (400–300 B.C.)

This burial (Table 7.3), contained the skeletal remains, in whole or part, of approximately 32 adult individuals, with a M:F:? ratio of 26:1:5 (see burial 30 below for comment on the uncertain sexual assignment of this one possible female). Some individual burials appeared to be relatively complete and isolated; others, although not isolated, could be separated out to one degree or another; and still other sections contained what has been described as "bundles" of probably excarnate bones and/or otherwise commingled assorted body parts.

Burial 29 [F31] consisted of the very fragmentary cranial (including mandible), postcranial (right and left tibia, femur, humerus, radius, and ulna; pelvis; vertebrae; etc.) and dental (20 teeth, no LEH, no LSAMAT) remains of a robust Y/MA male.

Burial 30 [F33] contained the fragmentary, eroded remains (including both femora and an unsided radius) of an unusually small adult – either a very small female or abnormally small male (nothing to support dwarfism is apparent). This burial may have cut through an earlier burial of a probable male adult represented by a few more robust (and more eroded) long bone fragments. Four teeth (wear consistent with young adult) could have belonged to either individual but most likely were part of the more complete individual.

Burial 32 [F148], a probable male young adult, was represented by skull fragments, two teeth (LEH present), and a few scraps of the left hand (a deciduous incisor, obviously from somebody else, was also present).

Burial 33 [F165], one incisor (LSAMAT present) and scraps of ulna (left), tibia (left), fibula (right?), femur (unsidable), and pelvic (and other) bits, was a Y/MA male.

Burial 34 [F171] was relatively complete and well preserved; this is the 55 to 59-year-old male described earlier, with "parry" fractures (Fig. 7.8), arthritis, unusual grooving of a canine (Fig. 7.7), sinusitis, etc.

Burial 35 [F172] was unsexable, although the postcranial scraps available appear to be adult.

Burial 36 [F173] – a few long bone fragments and nine teeth (slight LSAMAT present, no LEH) – was classified as Y/MA based on tooth wear.

Burial 37 [F175] extremely scanty remains could only be identified as an adult.

Burial 38 [F178], made up of robust, unduplicated shaft fragments from femora (right and left), tibiae (right and left), humerus and fibula appears to be an adult male.

Burials 39–40 [F179] contained the highly fragmented, incomplete postcranial and dental remains (30 teeth, LEH present) of a minimum of two YA males.

Burials 41–44 [F180] are a confusing conglomeration of pieces of a minimum of four adults (one a YA, based on wear of the single tooth found. LEH present): two robust males (including tibia and femur fragments, left radius, left ulna, left hand plus another ulna fragment) and two smaller unsexable individuals (legs and lower arms of one, left leg and lower arm of the other).

Burials 45–46 [F182] consist of at least two males, with dental wear suggesting that one is a MA and another a YA. The upper central incisors of the YA are filed in Romero C-2 or C-6 style (no LEH). Moderate (+ +) LSAMAT (without LEH) is present in the teeth of the MA, plus periodontoclasia (+ + +). The rest of [F182] consists of left and right femur fragments, left tibia fragments, two left humerus fragments (one slightly larger than the other), a very few cranial fragments with open sutures, plus other assorted fragments of rib, pelvis, etc.

Burials 47–49 [F183] and [F186] were linked by matching femora (left and right) bearing identical lesions suggestive of ossified subperiosteal hemorrhages, and contain the fragmentary parts (including cranial, vertebral, long bone, left foot, patella, teeth) of at least three probable males, one YA and two Y/MA (tooth wear). Most of the long-bone fragments bearing OSPH were found in [F183]. LEH is present in one Y/MA. At least one person in the group probably suffered from arthritis, as a fragmentary cervical vertebra and a foot phalanx show lipping on their articular surfaces.

Burials 50–60 [F188], [F189], and [F203] are almost inextricably tied together, with the first two being a double primary burial and [F203] the "bundles" of bones at their feet and in their laps.

Burial 50 [F188] appears to be a Y/MA male (older and more robust than [F189]) represented by fibula, tibia, femur, left radius and ulna, right radius and ulna, right and left humeri, mandible, and skull (all very fragmentary), and 13 teeth. Moderate (+ +) periodontoclasia and LSAMAT (+ +) are evident, as well as LEH on two molars and the single canine. There are also two extra teeth, LEH present, which probably are part of [F203].

Burial 51 [F189] is a YA male (younger and smaller than [F188]). His long-bone fragments are all from the left side – humerus, radius, ulna, femur. In addition, fragments of the left and right acetabulum, mandible, skull, clavicle, and 29 teeth were found (plus ten extra teeth, again probably part of [F203]). His molars and premolars show signs of LEH and slight (+) LSAMAT.

Burials 52–60 [F203] contain the fragmentary, "bundled," cranial, postcranial and dental remains (partial, anyway) of at least nine male adults – four robust, two medium, three gracile. Tooth wear indicates that at least one was a MA and at least one a YA. A partial list of fragments includes:

Femur – 1 pair matching robust and 1 pair matching medium
Tibia – 4 left and 4 right
Forearms (radius and ulna) – right and left of 1 robust individual, right and left of 1 smaller individual
Humerus – right of 2 robust and 2 smaller individuals, left of 3 (or 4) individuals
Scapula – 2 left and 1 right
Right foot
Hand – 2 large right and 1 smaller left
Cranial remains include right and left temporal bones from 2 different individuals plus other miscellaneous bits and teeth. Of special note is the skull (plus a few teeth) of the MA male with the "hole" described earlier.
Pathology found in [F203] includes arthritic lipping of a thoracic vertebra, spondylolysis (Table 7.6), and a broken toe.

Late Cocos Mass Burial 2, phase XI (*c.* A.D. 100)

This mass burial [F128] (Table 7.4), containing at least parts of approximately 15 adult individuals with a M:F:? ratio of 13:0:2, is described as beginning with two seated individuals, (1318) and (1352), into whose "laps" were placed "bundles" of probably excarnate bones, (1319) and (1320) respectively. Another burial, (1143), was found in the fill. Miscellaneous teeth and bone fragments (1187) were scattered throughout the fill.

Burial 70 (1318): What appears to be the primary individual is a robust YA male with LEH, periodontoclasia (maxillary, not mandibular), maxillary sinusitis, slight bowing and swelling of tibiae, and probable arthritis of toe phalanges. Although fragmentary, this individual is represented by cranial, dental and postcranial remains.

The partial remains of a smaller, unsexable MA were also found in (1318), and may actually be a part of the "bundles" in the "lap" of the primary burial. These remains include bits of clavicle, fibula and right hand, plus five molars (LEH present).

Burial 79 (1352): The probable primary individual in this section is again a robust YA male, again fairly "complete" and represented by cranial, dental, and postcranial fragments. The pathology evident is LEH and the healed fractures of left distal radius ("Colles" fracture), left capitate, lunate and navicular described earlier.

In addition to the primary burial above, this burial also includes the very fragmentary, very partial remains of at least two more, including: fragments of femur, humerus, and occipital bone of an adult male plus fragments of the right tibia and left radius of a very small male or female adult. The dental remains of an additional YA and a Y/MA (LEH present) were also found. Again, these additional bits may come from the "bundles" in the "lap" of the primary YA male.

Burials 71–74 (1319): These consist of the "bundles" in the "lap" of C1318, containing the postcranial remains of a minimum of three adult males, one very robust, one robust, and one smaller but nevertheless a male. A partial list of fragments includes:

Femur – 2 robust pairs (one very robust) plus 1 smaller left femur
Tibia – 1 left and 1 right which could be a pair
Humerus – 2 right and 1 left (all robust), plus 1 very robust left humerus
Ulna – 1 pair (left and right), plus 1 left ulna
Radius – 1 pair (left and right), plus 1 left radius
Fibula – 1 left and 1 right
Clavicle – 1 left and 1 right
Dental remains include the teeth of 3 adults plus a partial but toothless maxilla: 2 Y/MA (LEH present in one) and 1 YA (large teeth, definitely male, also with LEH present).

Burials 75–78 (1320): These "bundles" from the "lap" of (1352) contain the cranial and postcranial remains of at least three adults – two robust males and one very small male or female (whose fragments are scattered in several places in [F128] and counted in (1352) only). A partial list includes fragments of:

Cranial – thick fragments including right and left temporal and frontal
Femur – 2 left and 1 right (all robust), plus 1 very small but mature right femur
Tibia – unsided
Right foot
Humerus – right and left (medium to large size with possible osteoid-osteoma on right), plus 1 unsided very small but mature humerus
Radius – left
Ulna – left
Left hand
Dental remains include the teeth of 2 adult males: a MA with periodontoclasia, LEH and extreme (+ + +) lingual wear of the upper incisors (leading to exposure of the pulp cavity of one of them and the subsequent "root canal" appearance described earlier), and a YA with LEH.

Burials 68–69 (1143): This was found in the fill of [F128] and contains the partial cranial and postcranial remains of at least two adult males, one slightly larger than the other. The partial bone fragment list includes:

Femur – 2 right, 1 left
Tibia – 1 right
Fibula – 2 right, 1 left
Radius – 1 right, 1 left
Metacarpals and phalanges, probably left
Cranial – assorted bits, including mastoid area
Dental remains include the loose teeth of at least 2 individuals, a YA and a MA, with LSAMAT (+ +) on one upper incisor, and a mandible containing 6 teeth (a YA male with severe (+ + +) periodontoclasia and an asymmetric chin).

It is possible that (1143) represents a primary burial with "bundled" or scattered extra parts, but the condition of the fragments makes it impossible to sort out.

(1187): Assorted bone fragments and teeth found in the fill were given this number and may (or may not) belong to any or all of the above sections of [F128]. Two right scaphoids (one robust, the other very robust) give us a minimum of two males represented by postcranial scraps. Right and left metatarsals and foot phalanges show the signs of arthritis also seen in (1318). Eight loose teeth belonged to at least three male individuals, two YA (one with LEH) and one Y/MA.

Chapter 8 CRAFT TECHNOLOGY
AND PRODUCTION

INTRODUCTION

The artifact inventory of Maya sites is usually classified by the raw material and technological process employed into such categories as chipped stone, ground stone, polished stone, bone, shell, and pottery objects; sometimes such categories are divided, that of chipped stone into chert (flint) and obsidian (Willey, 1978), sometimes conflated, as with Willey's subsumption of jades into the Seibal ground-stone industry, while Garber (1989) makes them first-order separate industries. A further criterion can be applied, however, that of source of raw material and locus of manufacture: some classes of artifact will be made of microlocally available raw material, obtained within the few kilometres' normal daily range of a sedentary farmer, and inferentially created within the consuming community. Others will be of materials available within the region, and obtainable by local residents with some effort, but also acquirable within local exchange networks such as markets: such artifacts may be part of the subject community's craft production, but may equally be part of an intraregional interdependence such as that modeled by Siverts (cf. Hammond, 1988: Fig. 3.13). A third category consists of exotic raw material, unobtainable regionally: this may have arrived in the locality either in finished artifact form, or as partly processed raw material awaiting final finishing, either by local craftspersons or by traveling specialists. Choosing between these alternatives is often a matter of common sense: in the Maya Lowlands, for example, *metates* of volcanic stone from the highlands are unlikely to have been shipped in any form other than finished goods because of their weight and relatively low value, while obsidian is likely to have been shipped as prismatic cores because of the fragility of the finished blades. Jade, initially perceived as the most exotic of goods, is nevertheless a low bulk/high value commodity which could have been worked to final form at either source or destination: often classed purely as an import, its forms may well have been locally decided.

This discussion of the crafts and imports at Cuello

(Chapters 8 and 9) follows such a division: those classes of material which were, or could plausibly have been, worked within the Cuello community are discussed in terms of craft production, while those of apparent exotic origin are seen as trade items, with consumption but not production functions in the local system. Chipped stone tools of chert and chalcedony, ground stone implements of limestone, pottery vessels, and objects modeled from potters' clay or reworked from sherds are all plausibly of local material and manufacture, as are artifacts of human or animal bone and freshwater shell; some varieties of chert and limestone come from beyond the immediate locale, while marine shell, obsidian, jade and other greenstones are indubitably exotic, but may nevertheless be artifacts of local design and manufacture. Each of these materials is examined with this ambiguity in mind.

CHERT AND CHALCEDONY TOOLS
(Figs. 8.1–8.13 and Tables 8.1–8.11)

Rebecca McSwain
with a section on obsidian technology by
Jay K. Johnson

THE NATURE OF THE ASSEMBLAGE
The Cuello Preclassic stone tool assemblage consists of 2,135 chert and chalcedony items, products and byproducts of community chipped stone industries. There are also some 360 fragments of obsidian, most of them prismatic blade sections which will be discussed separately.

There is no evidence for any great degree of specialization or of mass production of stone tools at Cuello and we argue that for the most part individuals made tools for their own use, or that each family or kin group perhaps had one or two skilled members who made chipped stone implements for the whole group. It is also possible that, in addition to locally produced tools, by the Late Preclassic some tools were imported ready-made from the chert workshops at Colha, 27 km to the southeast (Shafer and Hester 1983; see also Chapter 9).

Raw materials for tools are divided into two broad classes: one is a fine-grained brown or gray chert, occasionally banded (especially just underneath the cortex); the second consists of two raw material types: a rough white chert, and a translucent chalcedony of white, brown, or gray, sometimes coarse in texture and often flawed, occurring in small nodules or tabular blocks in the immediate vicinity of the Cuello site. This second group is hereafter referred to as "local material," while the fine cherts come from a chert-bearing zone running north–south over as much as 100 km, the nearest edge of which lies some 5–10 km to the southeast of Cuello (Hester 1980; Fig. 2). Because these cherts are quite similar in appearance to those

used at the site of Colha (which is located in an area of major outcrops of chert nodules along Rancho Creek), the fine-grained brown and gray cherts are here dubbed "Colha material."

Typology and chronology

The variety and number of formal types – tools made to a relatively invariant pattern – are rather limited at Cuello. The types that do appear are of some use for broad chronological distinctions: we can separate the Late Preclassic from the preceding Middle Preclassic and from the succeeding Classic period. Fig. 8.1 shows the sequence of formal tool types worked out for Preclassic Cuello, which can be compared with that for Colha (Shafer and Hester 1983: Fig. 4): the blades, stemmed macroblades, and T-shaped tool found at Colha in the Late Preclassic first occur at Cuello in Middle Preclassic times, while the large oval biface and the tranchet-bit tool are Late Preclassic at both sites. Further information from other sites in northern Belize will no doubt make possible the construction of a more complete regional chronology and typology (Hester 1982: 39).

Technology

Stoneworking techniques at Cuello do not seem to have changed much over time, and the technical ability demonstrated can be characterized as skilful but strictly limited in range. Fig. 8.2 shows a limestone hammerstone similar to percussion implements reported from the Colha workshops (Shafer and Oglesby 1980: Fig. 9); other hammerstones are cobbles and reused cores of both chert and chalcedony which show marked battering usewear. Shafer and Oglesby suggest that the biconical limestone hammers were used for later stages of biface reduction and thinning, while the other chert and chalcedony hammers (which are largely unshaped) were used in the initial reduction of blanks or "in removing problem areas on a blank during the process of thinning" (1980: 203).

There is evidence of a good level of control over all raw material used: flaws are avoided, disparately shaped broken pieces are retouched to new working edges which are almost identical to one another, and platforms are sometimes extensively prepared. Certainly the part-time stoneworkers at Cuello knew exactly what they were doing from the earliest days of the community's existence. There is, however, no detectable increase in the degree of skill through time, although tools made to a strictly formal pattern appear only in the late Middle and Late Preclassic, and some of the last may have been brought in from Colha rather than made locally.

From the technological point of view, the Cuello tools can be seen as the products of a two-level interrelated system. The

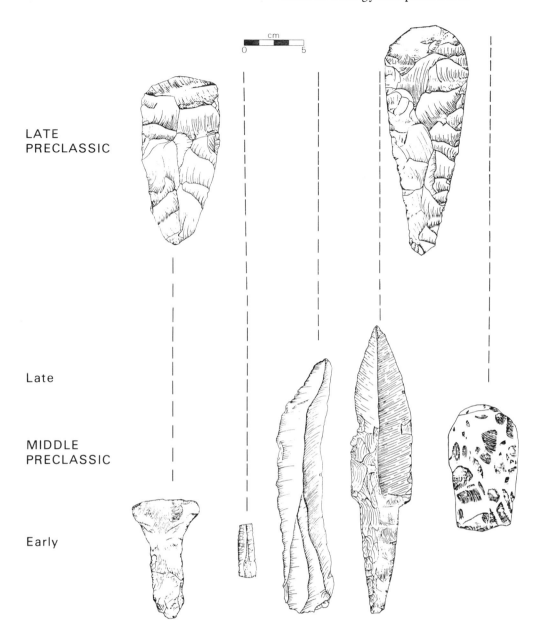

cm
0   5

LATE
PRECLASSIC

Late

MIDDLE
PRECLASSIC

Early

Fig. 8.1 Chronological sequence of chipped stone tool types at
Cuello.

first level is the primary industry, consisting of complete
examples of formal bifaces, formal unifaces, and blades which
are the final products of standardized reduction sequences,
and are found altered only by use or by resharpening of the
original edge or edges. The second level is the secondary
industry, made up of (1) recycled tools from the primary
industry, (2) tools made using non-standardized reduction
techniques – mainly flake tools, but also including core tools
such as hammerstones and pounders; and (3) the recycled
byproducts of tool manufacture such as flakes and decortica-
tion debris. No particular locus of manufacture is implied for
these industrial levels.

Although most products belonging to both industries were
probably produced at Cuello, it is possible that during the
Late Preclassic the primary industry became linked to an
intersite distribution system, bringing certain formal tool
types (especially the large oval biface and the tranchet-bit
tool) into the community as finished products. However, if
relative numbers of tools are taken as indicative, the local
primary industry and the secondary industry seemingly
remained most important in the economic life of the Cuello
community.

Fig. 8.2 Limestone hammerstone.

Functional groups

From the functional standpoint, about half the Cuello lithics
were placed into three broad tool groups based loosely upon
distribution within the site, form, and imputed function. (The
portion of the assemblage that was not so classified is composed of byproducts such as cores, flakes and amorphous
pieces, and of broken items.) First, there is a large group of
small implements, commonly found within houses, in subfloor fill and in middens, presumably used for such tasks as
food preparation, making clothing, and perhaps kitchen-
garden cultivation; these comprise the "domestic toolkit."
Secondly, there are heavy-duty tools assumed to have been
used in a variety of agricultural and architectural jobs (Hester
1982: 46–7; Shafer 1982: 175–9). Finally there may be a group
of ceremonial lithics, although it is difficult to isolate any
distinctively ceremonial types from the Cuello collections.
The stemmed macroblade or "dagger" has been cited in the
Maya Area and elsewhere as a ceremonial item (Clark and Lee
1979), and in fact at least five examples of this type were found
in burials or caches at Cuello. That from [F140] of phase VII,
the deer-jawbone cache in the center of the plaza floor in front
of the pyramid, is illustrated in Fig. 8.3. These "daggers" also
appear in ordinary trash at Cuello, however, as they do at
Cerros (Mitchum, personal communication; Hester 1982: 47).
Furthermore, most of the lithics found in burials and caches at
Cuello are indistinguishable from those in quotidian contexts.
There are two possible fragments of eccentrics, one from
rubble possibly associated with child burial 23[F50], the other
from the *chultun* [F87]; neither the contexts nor the objects are
convincingly ceremonial, and the latter may simply be oddly

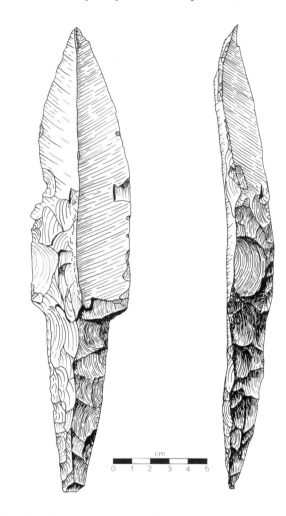

Fig. 8.3 Chert stemmed macroblade from [F140].

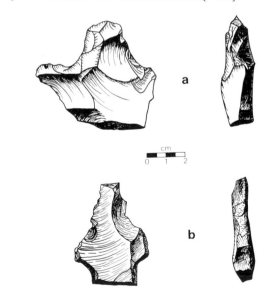

a

b

Fig. 8.4 Chert "eccentrics".

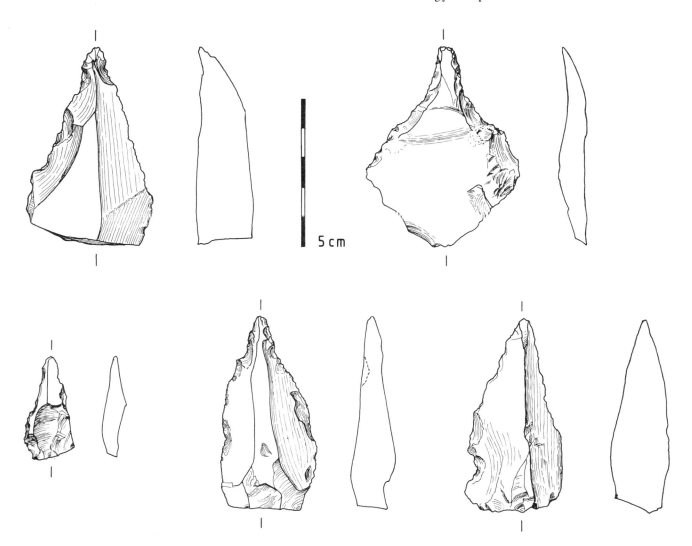

5 cm

Fig. 8.5 Pointed tools.

shaped tools or fragments (Fig. 8.4). The class of "ceremonial" lithics is thus created rather *a priori*: there does not seem to have been a special lithic production system focused on religious items.

Five rather loosely formulated tool types which occur in quantity and consistently through the sequence make up a group identified as a domestic toolkit. These are small pointed tools or "drills," "scrapers," blades, a small T-shaped plano-convex tool, and small (< 100 mm long) bifaces. The pointed tools have a variety of shapes and retouch patterns, but have in common a retouched drill- or awl-like point; examples are shown in Fig. 8.5. Scrapers are broadly defined as having steep retouch and a plano-convex section; most are unifacially retouched but some are bifacial. Many examples show macroscopic edge damage suggestive of scraping use. In outline, scraper form is variable; clearly these tools were often made of whatever suitable material was readily available, including

scraps of broken tools and amorphous debris from manufacturing byproducts. In other cases, scrapers are more carefully made, for example on large flakes and as formal unifaces. No doubt these implements were used for a great variety of tasks, not just "scraping"; Fig. 8.6 shows the range of sizes and shapes included in the category of "scraper." Fig. 8.6a is bifacially retouched, of fine brown chert, with traces of cortex on one face; this kind of item was probably made on a piece of debris or on a large, very thick blade or flake. Fig. 8.6b shows a scraper made on a cortical flake of gray chalcedony, and Fig. 8.6c recycled sharpening flakes from large bifaces of fine-grained brown chert, perhaps large oval bifaces; the upper example has a high-gloss polish on the exterior face, perhaps from agricultural use of the original tool. Fig. 8.6d is a "thumbscraper" made on a scrap of fine-grained brown chert; retouch is minimal and the form amorphous, a tool made casually on a manufacturing or sharpening byproduct.

Throughout Preclassic times, the generalized scraper form is the most frequently occurring kind of tool in the Cuello

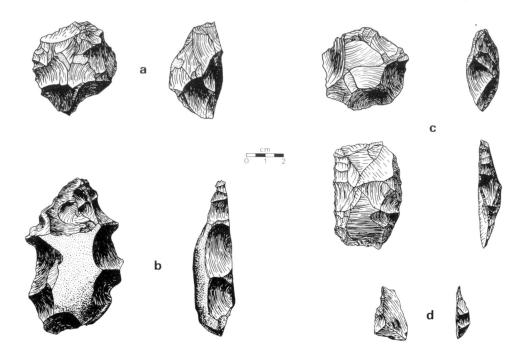

Fig. 8.6 Scrapers (a) bifacial, fine brown chert; (b) unifacial, gray chalcedony; (c) recycled flakes of fine brown chert; (d) "thumbscraper".

assemblage (in apparent contrast to the Barton Ramie collections, in which only eight to ten items identified as scrapers come from Preclassic contexts, out of a total assemblage for all periods of 524 chert and chalcedony items (Willey *et al.*, 1965: 437–8).

Another kind of tool assigned to the "scraper" group is the T-shaped tool (Fig. 8.7). This is a relatively rare type, and one of only two formal types identified among the scrapers. Although no use-wear studies have been done on the Cuello specimens as yet, the T-shape may have been used for small-scale building work.

The second formal type identified among the scrapers is the pointed and notched tool (McSwain 1982: Fig. 2e). In terms of form, this is an unusual implement in that the overall form of the tool is highly variable, sometimes made on a broken blade and often plano-convex in section, but the working edge is very consistent: a dull point, sometimes showing macroscopic traces of wear, flanked by deep notches apparently created with a single blow, also occasionally showing flakescars indicative of use damage. It is on the basis of the edge morphology that this tool is defined.

The chert and chalcedony blade collection from Cuello includes a great diversity of sizes and manufacturing techniques. There are some macroblades, often retaining large areas of cortex; two examples are shown in Fig. 8.8a–b. Additionally, there are medium-length blades (80–100 mm

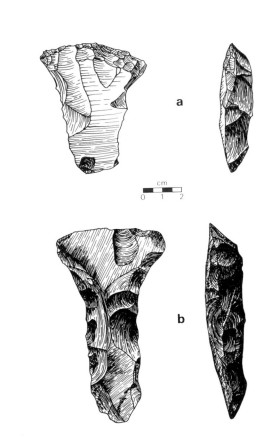

Fig. 8.7 T-shaped tools.

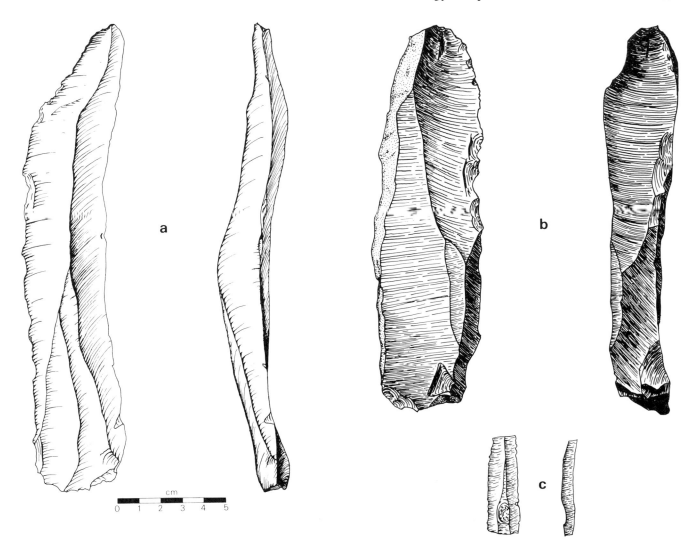

Fig 8.8 Blades: (a) fine brown chert, with retained cortex; (b) fine brown chert, minimal retouch; (c) fine brown chert, little or no retouch.

long), usually without cortex and often retouched thoroughly just along the edges. Finally there are small blades, rather delicate and usually found only as fragments, with neither retouch nor cortex (Fig. 8.8c). Blades are always considered part of the primary industry; though some are certainly recycled, it is difficult to distinguish flakescars which are the result of retouch for shaping or reshaping from those which are the result of edge damage from use.

Several kinds of tools in the Cuello assemblage are made on blades, and it is possible that the blade forms we have are simply tool blanks. Shafer and Oglesby (1980: 215) note the presence of macroblades in a Colha workshop, and suggest that they were blanks brought in in that form, the initial removal from the core having taken place at the quarry.

Potter (1982) has noted the occurrence of macroblades in a likely Middle Formative domestic context in Op. 2012 at Colha, and suggests that the blades were used both as tools in their original form and as blanks to be reduced to make other, bifacial tools. A similar set of processes probably occurred at Cuello in a domestic/ceremonial context perhaps not very different from that at Colha.

Small bifaces are, like scrapers and blades, persistent throughout the Cuello sequence, and show some variation in size and form (Fig. 8.9). There are no consistent patterns of wear or breakage, and it is likely that these were multipurpose tools. They are, like scrapers, often casually or roughly made, possibly on blade blanks (Potter 1982: 113). Some small bifaces are probably recycled from larger bifacial or unifacial tools, and are thus part of the secondary industry – but in most cases it is not possible to separate specific examples of these recycling products from other small bifaces.

The "heavy-duty" tools are rare in the Cuello sequence.

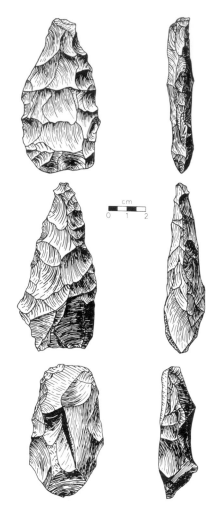

cm
0 1 2

Fig. 8.9 Small bifaces.

Shafer (1979: 55) and Shafer and Oglesby (1980) have identified two large-tool types manufactured at Colha, the large oval biface and the tranchet-bit tool, and these heavy-duty tools are found also at Cuello (Fig. 8.10a–b; see also McSwain 1982). Also found at Cuello is the sharpening flake from the tranchet-bit tool (Shafer 1976; dubbed by Wilk (1975) and Hammond *et al.* (1979) the "orange peel" from its distinctive biaxial curvature); the flake is as rare as the tool itself, there being only a half-dozen in the Cuello assemblage.

Another form in the heavy-tool category is a chipped and polished tool, thick and ovoid in section, the pointed (presumably working) edge ground or polished almost smooth, with a sharp edge, and the thicker distal and retaining more, and less-smoothed, flakescars. One example shows bilateral edge crushing or grinding, suggesting that the tool may have been hafted, and there is both crush and flakescar damage on the bit end (Fig. 8.11). There may be a similar tool from Colha (Eaton 1981: Fig. 6). A final formal type placed in the heavy-duty

category is the large biface, 100 mm or more long; bifaces in this category are those that do not have the characteristic shape of the large oval biface discussed above.

The rarity of all these large tools may be due to the uses to which they were put and the nature of the Cuello excavation locus: if this is one in which some combination of household and ceremonial activities took place – that is, the center of the community – we would not expect to find many agricultural tools there. Rather, they would be carried to and from fields or forest, and many would be lost or broken well away from the community. Broken pieces brought back would often be recycled, so that the original tool type would be obscured; there are enough broken fragments of the large tools to suggest that this type of reuse occurred quite often. Shafer (1983) and McAnany (1986) have seen considerable reworking of this sort at the Pulltrouser Swamp sites northeast of Cuello. In addition, large-scale architectural work would be infrequent, especially given the modest construction overall at Preclassic Cuello, and tools relevant to such heavy tasks would be concomitantly infrequent in the archaeological record. Some building work, such as repairs to walls or plaster surfaces, would be done more frequently but might require smaller and less specific tools, such as the T-shaped tool described above.

The heavy-duty tools all belong to the primary industry, being clearly the products of systematic, consistently patterned reduction sequences, some of which have been described by Shafer and Oglesby (1980).

To summarize the technological and functional analysis of the Cuello chert and chalcedony chipped stone tool systems, Fig. 8.12 shows in schematic fashion the nature of the Cuello lithic assemblage, considered as a set of technological or manufacturing options (primary industry/secondary industry; biface/uniface/blade), and as a set of functionally significant end products (heavy-duty tools/domestic toolkit/ceremonial lithics). Note that bifaces can feature in both the primary and secondary industries, as can unifaces. The domestic toolkit includes items from all technical categories of both primary and secondary industries, with slightly more unifaces than bifaces, far fewer blades, with the secondary industry contributing slightly more tools overall. Ceremonial lithics (the various kinds of lithics found in caches, burials, and other special deposits) lie within the domestic toolkit in terms of form, with the possible exception of bifacial eccentrics and stemmed macroblades. The spaces outside the recognized functional groups represent lithic items in the collection which could not be convincingly fitted into any functional group, even given the flexible and speculative nature of those groups.

THE DEVELOPMENT OF THE CUELLO STONE TOOL SYSTEMS: TYPOLOGY, TECHNOLOGY, AND USE
In the discussion that follows, the lithic assemblage is des-

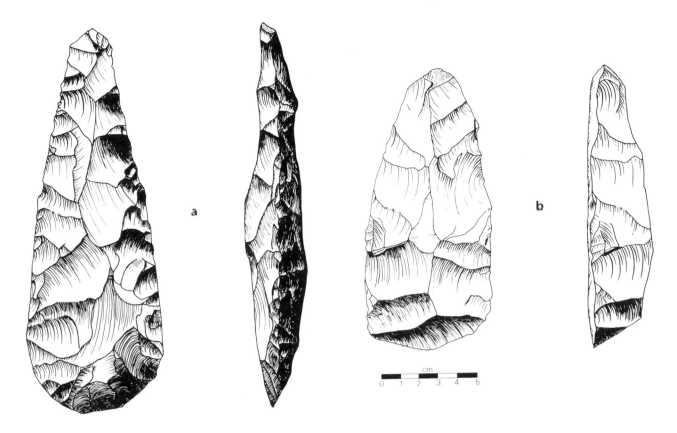

Fig. 8.10 Heavy-duty tools: (a) large oval biface; (b) tranchet-bit tool.

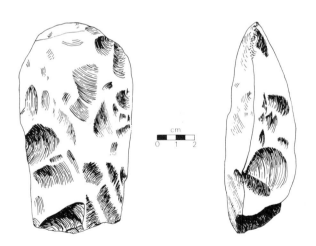

Fig. 8.11 Chipped and polished tool.

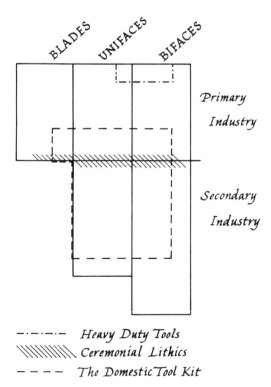

Fig. 8.12 Interrelationships of Cuello lithic industries and types.

Table 8.1 *Cuello lithics: early Middle Preclassic functional groups (n = 221)*

Group/type	Raw material	
	Colha-like	Other
Heavy-duty tools		
Large biface	1	1
Domestic toolkit		
Drill/pointed tool	6	28
Scraper	38	87
Pointed/notched	1	4
T-shape	0	4
Blade	31	7
Small biface	12	7
Ceremonial lithics		
Stemmed macroblade	2	1
Total	90	131

Table 8.2 *Cuello lithics: late Middle Preclassic functional groups (n = 192)*

Group/type	Raw material	
	Colha-like	Other
Heavy-duty tools		
Large biface	3	0
Chipped and polished tool	0	1
Domestic toolkit		
Drill/pointed tool	11	47
Scraper	18	69
Pointed/notched	0	3
T-shape	4	1
Blade	8	4
Small biface	17	9
Ceremonial lithics		
Stemmed macroblade	1	0
Total	62	130

cribed for each period as defined by the associated pottery. For each period the assemblage is examined in two ways: from the technological standpoint, the assemblage is composed of two related industries, the primary and the secondary, while from the functional standpoint, that assemblage is composed of three groups of tools: heavy-duty tools, the domestic toolkit, and ceremonial lithics. The technological and functional categories overlap, as noted above, but in general more items were able to be classified as to technological category than functional, and thus for each period the number of items in the primary and secondary industries is greater than the number of items in the functional groups.

Swasey and Bladen phases 0–IIIA (early Middle Preclassic) The lithics from these two earliest periods have been considered as one group, because the number of items from each is rather small, about 300 together, and there do not on initial inspection seem to be any significant changes from one period to the next. There are 329 lithic pieces classified into the primary and secondary industries, and 221 into functional groups. Table 8.1 summarizes the early Middle Formative lithic data by functional groups.

The only heavy-duty tool present is the large biface, one of Colha-like chert and one of other material. Scrapers are made predominantly of chalcedony and coarse white chert (70 percent), but small bifaces are less emphatically of local material, while brown and gray cherts are clearly the preferred material for blades (79 percent) and for small bifaces (71 percent). The T-shaped tool and pointed and notched tools are present, most of them made of local materials. Two

fragments of stemmed macroblades, both of fine brown chert, come from subfloor fill of this period.

In Swasey/Bladen times, 42 percent of the lithics are products of the primary industry. Tables 8.4–8.5 show that 56 percent of the primary industry and 70 percent of the secondary industry are of local raw materials.

Lopez Mamom phases IV–IVA (late Middle Preclassic) The tool collection from this period is smaller than from the others, totaling only 311 items in the technological groups and 192 in the functional. Table 8.2 shows the composition of the functional groups. Again the large oval biface and tranchet-bit tool are absent. There are three large bifaces, all of Colha-like cherts. The chipped and polished axe is first found in Mamom, made of local material. With the exception of the T-shaped tool, scrapers are more frequently made of white chert and chalcedonies (80 percent). Most of the T-shaped tools are of Colha-like chert, contrary to the situation in the Mamom assemblage as a whole, where only 35 percent of the primary industry and 17 percent of the secondary are made from brown and gray cherts (Tables 8.4–8.5); but 66 percent of blades are of Colha-like chert as well as 65% of the small bifaces. One stemmed macroblade fragment, in fill, is of gray chert.

Tables 8.4–8.5 show that the Lopez Mamom primary industry is similar to that of the preceding Swasey and Bladen phases, in that it uses mostly local raw materials; the amount of brown and gray chert is in fact reduced somewhat from earlier periods. The secondary industry shows an even greater reduction in percentage of these cherts during this period.

Table 8.3 *Cuello lithics: Late Preclassic functional groups*
(n = 641)

Group/type	Raw material	
	Colha-like	Other
Heavy-duty tools		
Large biface	34	17
Large oval biface	5	0
Tranchet-bit tool	5	0
Chipped/polished tool	2	6
Domestic toolkit		
Drill/pointed tool	21	44
Scraper	119	207
Pointed/notched	13	8
T-shape	1	6
Blade	72	27
Small biface	49	21
Ceremonial lithics		
Stemmed macroblades	7	2
Eccentrics	3	0
Total	317	324

Cocos Chicanel phases V–XIV (Late Preclassic) The Late Preclassic at Cuello is marked by an increase in sheer numbers of lithics, and by the appearance of several tool types for the first time. There are about 1,300 lithics in the primary and secondary industries from Late Preclassic contexts, with 641 classified in the functional groups. Table 8.3 shows that identifiable specimens of the large oval bifaces and tranchet-bit tools occur, albeit rarely, for the first time, all made of fine-grained brown and gray cherts. There are many large bifaces, with a marked preference for the Colha cherts as raw material. The chipped and polished axe is found in numbers approximately equal to the other heavy-duty tools, but is usually made from white chert or chalcedony. In the domestic toolkit there is a tendency for the T-shaped tool to be made of Colha chert also. About 53 percent of the domestic toolkit is of local materials, including 65 percent of scrapers, while 74 percent of blades are of Colha-like chert, continuing the basic functional group distributions of raw material seen in the Middle Preclassic. Colha-like chert is used for 70 percent of small bifaces.

The possibly ceremonial lithics also increase in numbers, with a marked preference for brown and gray cherts, although five macroblade fragments are either of local material or so burnt that the raw material cannot be determined. The Chicanel stemmed macroblades occur in a variety of contexts,

as noted above: a few with burials or caches, such as the four in [F80], and the rest in fill or rubble.

Table 8.4 shows some interesting changes in the primary industry in Chicanel times: the raw material distribution of the previous periods is reversed, with 55 percent of the primary industry now made from brown and gray cherts. This change occurs because of shifts in the raw material proportions for formal bifaces and formal unifaces; the material distribution for blades remains similar, and even shows a slight decrease in the amount of brown and gray chert. At the same time, the primary industry as a whole is more important than previously, constituting 61 percent of the Chicanel tool assemblage.

It is also noteworthy that the secondary industry shows an increased proportion of brown and gray chert to other material from earlier periods; this is probably simply a function of the increase seen in primary tools, especially bifaces, of the same material, since more of it would be available for recycling from broken bifaces, sharpening flakes, and debris. When the number of brown/gray chert bifaces increases 15-fold from late Middle Preclassic to Late Preclassic times, it is no surprise that the number of recycled bifaces increases 19-fold over the same period. These increases are much more impressive than those seen for bifaces of all materials together: bifaces overall increased roughly ninefold from early Middle Preclassic through Late Preclassic times, and recycled bifaces of all materials increased eightfold.

OBSIDIAN: A TECHNOLOGICAL ANALYSIS
The assemblage (12 flakes, 4 blade cores, 225 blades, and 12 biface fragments) comprises all of the obsidian recovered at Cuello during the 1978, 1980, and 1987 seasons; the 1979 obsidian (114 blades) was not available for study. The small size of the collection is itself informative in light of the volume of deposit excavated at the site.

The earliest obsidian comes from late in the Bladen phase (IIIA): one of the two early pieces is retouched and incised (Fig. 8.13: SF 1899). Four blades of the sample (9 percent) are from Lopez Mamom contexts, while 38 blades (86 percent) and one biface fragment are from Cocos Chicanel contexts, paralleling the tremendous rise in overall lithic numbers due partly to the larger volume of excavated deposit from this period. Source characterization of obsidians is discussed in Chapter 9.

The obsidians are part of the primary industry, although some recycling is likely; in terms of function, obsidian blades probably fall within the domestic toolkit, with their presence in burials and caches suggesting a ceremonial function also. At least seven of the obsidian blades are from caches or burials, making this class of lithic item the only one apart from chert stemmed macroblades found with any regularity in ritual contexts; but, like the macroblades, obsidian is also found in

Table 8.4 *The primary industry (n = 935)*

Period	Early Middle Preclassic		Late Middle Preclassic		Late Preclassic	
Material	Colha	Other	Colha	Other	Colha	Other
Bifaces	29	47	33	47	299	219
Unifaces	10	27	8	41	24	63
Blades	21	3	7	2	42	13
Total primary industry	60	77	48	90	365	295
	(44%)	(56%)	(35%)	(65%)	(55%)	(45%)

Table 8.5 *The secondary industry (n = 982)*

Period	Early Middle Preclassic		Late Middle Preclassic		Late Preclassic	
Material	Colha	Other	Colha	Other	Colha	Other
Recycled bifaces	4	8	1	4	74	29
Other secondary tools	53	127	29	139	180	334
Total secondary industry	57	135	30	143	254	363
	(30%)	(70%)	(17%)	(83%)	(41%)	(59%)

Fig. 8.13 Retouched and incised obsidian blade segment (Bladen).

all other kinds of contexts, including rubble and *chultun* fill.

Unfortunately, nearly half of the obsidian (5 flakes, 4 cores, 102 blades) came from contexts which were either mixed or yielded no diagnostic ceramics. Those which can be plausibly dated on the basis of the latest ceramic phase represented range from the early Middle Formative, Bladen phase, to the Terminal Classic. The Early Classic, Nuevo Tzakol phase, followed in frequency by the Late Classic, Santana Tepeu I/II, yielded the largest amounts of dated obsidian; the Late Formative phases are also well represented (Table 8.6). One context (Q3033) yielded 24 Swasey/Bladen phase sherds and two obsidian blades while another (Q3032) yielded a single blade of Bladen date. These, with SF 1899, represent the earliest documented obsidian from the Maya Lowlands so far reported. Two blades came from contexts which yielded

sherds assigned to the Bladen phase but, in both cases, later, Lopez Mamom, sherds were also recovered. Mixing, however, is not a big problem in the ceramic phase assignment for the obsidian: 18 percent of the dated blades are from single phase contexts and 78 percent are from proveniences with sherds and representing three or fewer phases. It is therefore possible to search for chronological patterning in spite of the relatively small size of the collection.

The first and most obvious conclusion to be reached on the basis of the 12 obsidian flakes is that obsidian production activities which produced flakes were relatively unusual at Cuello, the more evident in that half of the flakes show facets on their dorsal surface indicating that they were derived from (presumably exhausted) blade cores. This is in line with the generally battered condition of the cores from Cuello (see below). One of the flakes derived from a blade core shows the exaggerated compression rings which are characteristic of bipolar reduction, and all of the flakes are small enough to have come from blade cores (Table 8.7). On the other hand, two of the flakes without blade scars show small patches of what may be cortex on their dorsal surfaces, suggesting that they were derived from nodules.

None of the four blade cores was recovered from a context which could be dated. Although they are relatively large

Table 8.6 *Obsidian artifacts broken down by phase assignment*

Phase	Blades	Flakes	Cores	Biface
Swasey	3			
Bladen				
Lopez Mamom	3			
Cocos Chicanel	19	3		
Terminal Cocos Chicanel	19	1		
Freshwater Floral Park				
Nuevo Tzakol	41			
Tepeu I	8			
Santana Tepeu I & II	23	3		
Rancho Tepeu III	7			
No assignment	102	5	4	1

Table 8.7 *Obsidian flake dimensions (in mm)*

Dimension	n	Mean	Standard deviation
Length	5	20.40	9.15
Width	12	15.00	4.43

Table 8.8 *Obsidian blade core dimensions (in mm)*

Dimension	n	Mean	Standard deviation
Length	2	54.50	0.71
Width	4	18.75	2.99
Thickness	4	15.75	1.71

Table 8.9 *Platform preparation techniques by time period*

Period	Plain platform	Ground edges	Ground platform	Rejuvenated platform
Middle Formative		1		
Late Formative	1	6		
Early Classic	1	9	1	3
Late Classic	4	17		1

(Table 8.8) and would not be considered exhausted on the basis of size, all show step fractures, hinge fractures, or edge collapse – blade removal failures which would have made them useless for further blade production. Two of the cores show evidence for platform rejuvenation in that some of the blade scars lack negative bulbs of force, i.e., they were derived from a platform which was removed to make the ultimate platform; however, no rejuvenation flakes were recovered.

One of the cores retains evidence that the last blade was removed improperly and took off the end of the core. The average width for the last successful blade to be removed from each core, as measured from the blade scar, is 8.75 mm with a standard deviation of 0.96. This is considerably less than the 10.75 mm average width for the blades from Cuello. All of the cores were battered following their rejection as blade sources. There is no particular pattern to the destruction of the cores and little skill was involved. Flakes were removed at random angles and, in some cases, the cores were split both parallel and perpendicular to the long axis using crude percussion techniques.

As in most lowland Maya sites, prismatic blades make up the largest proportion of the collection of obsidian and offer the greatest opportunity for detecting changes through time in production and utilization. About a third (80) of the blades from Cuello are proximal fragments and this allows techniques of platform preparation to be observed. Preclassic blades show individual platform preparation, relatively large

bulbs of percussion with occasional large eraillure scars, occasional ventral platform lipping, and some platform crushing, all suggesting a percussion technique of blade removal from the core although in other respects the Cuello blades are quite similar to the prismatic blades described from Chalchuapa (Sheets 1978: 11–14). It has been suggested the production of prismatic blades by percussion rather than pressure is a pan-Mesoamerican Preclassic trait (Clark 1982: 373).

Edge grinding is most common, followed in frequency by plain platforms with no preparation, rejuvenated platforms, and ground platforms (Table 8.9). Only one of the ground platforms falls within the subset which can be dated and is assigned to an Early Classic phase. This had been considered a Late Classic or Postclassic time marker (Rovner 1974; Johnson 1976) but recent research has shown it to occur as early as the Late Formative (Sheets 1978; Dreiss 1988).

Lengths of complete blades range from 70 to 122 mm, thickness from 2 to 4 mm, and widths from 9 to 19 mm. The mean width for the entire collection of blades from Cuello is 10.75 mm. This is similar to the blade width for a generally later collection of obsidian from Palenque (Johnson 1976) and comparable to other lowland Maya samples, confirming a general observation that non-source regions tended to use their obsidian more intensively (Rovner 1975).

Working on the same assumption, that blade width will reflect intensity of utilization and relative access to obsidian, blade width at Cuello was broken down by time period (Table 8.10). There is no apparent pattern. Of course, technological factors may have intervened. The few cores from Cuello do not suggest a great deal of skill in recovering from platform

Table 8.10 *Obsidian blade width (mm) by time period*

Period	n	Mean	Standard deviation
Middle Formative	5	10.20	2.68
Late Formative	38	11.16	2.80
Early Classic	41	10.66	2.54
Late Classic	38	10.95	2.38

Table 8.11 *Sherd to obsidian ratio by time period*

Period	Sherd count	Blade count	Ratio
Middle Formative	319	3	106.3
Late Formative	4,531	35	129.5
Early Classic	4,028	25	161.1
Late Classic	1,232	4	308.0

failures, a necessity if cores are to be exhaustively utilized, thereby producing narrow blades.

Relative availability of obsidian in the Maya Lowlands has been measured a number of ways in order to examine the dynamics of exchange across time and space. Sidrys (1979) used the volume of excavation to adjust obsidian counts and Rice (1987) based her study on the number of obsidian artifacts per operation. Both techniques are problematic in that they fail to take into account overall variability in artifact density from excavation to excavation. Rathje (1973) plotted the amount of obsidian per burial and used it to examine obsidian availability. This measure is based on a standard unit which must have had reality to the Maya. However, the factors which dictate the composition of grave goods may have had little to do with resource availability. Moholy-Nagy (1976) and Johnson (1976) used obsidian to chert ratios on the assumption that if obsidian was not readily available, chert would be substituted. At sites like Tikal and Palenque, where chert is locally available, this ratio showed patterning which could be interpreted in terms of differences in spatial and temporal access to obsidian.

It would be interesting to apply the obsidian to chert ratio to the Cuello material, but unfortunately chert was recorded in a way that makes such a study impossible. As an alternative, a sherd to obsidian ratio was examined. A significantly different set of assumptions underlies this measure of obsidian "density": it is based on the argument that sherd counts reflect relative differences in the amount of domestic refuse in the fill of each excavation unit. Insofar as obsidian is considered by many Mayanists to have been used primarily in utilitarian contexts, this ratio should respond to differences in the relative intensity of this use. Of course, not all potsherds are domestic refuse; neither was all obsidian utilitarian in the narrow sense: still, the ratio may have value. When examined across time, the 67 obsidian blades from dated contexts for which sherd counts are available show some variation (Table 8.11). However, except for the Late Formative and Early Classic, the number of examples in this reduced sample is so small as to render the differences suspect. The numbers of sherds per blade for the Late Formative and Early Classic are very close, suggesting little changes in obsidian availability through these periods.

The final artifact category in the obsidian sample from Cuello to be discussed is represented by a single small (9 mm wide, 16 mm long, 3 mm thick) biface. The tip is broken off and the base is pointed. Shallow side notching occurs about half-way between the base and fractured end. The bifacial flaking does not completely obscure the fact that it was made on a blade. It cannot be dated by ceramic association.

In summary, not a great deal that is remarkable can be said about the Cuello obsidian. The sample suggests that most of the obsidian reached Cuello in the form of polyhedral cores. Prismatic blades were the primary product and there is some evidence for rejuvenation although not as much as might be expected given the distance to the upland obsidian sources. Cores were discarded containing a good deal of usable obsidian had they been rejuvenated. Post-blade-removal flake-scars on the cores reflect relatively crude attempts to reduce them to smaller, unpatterned pieces. There are no apparent shifts in the composition or characteristics of obsidian use over the long span of access in the region, and the most important aspect of the Cuello assemblage is the evidence that obsidian blades were being used in limited numbers during the early Middle Formative, Bladen phase, placed by hydration dating early in the first millennium B.C.

DISCUSSION

The Cuello lithic industries show both continuity and change through the Preclassic sequence at the site. On one level there are continuities in production techniques as well as in the forms and occurrence of types probably related to daily activities in the community center. Thus, although the Late Preclassic marks a major increase in the numbers of lithics recovered, certain basic tools and the methods used to produce them remain roughly the same. On the other hand, this period also sees some changes in the kinds of tools found, with new types appearing, and in the raw materials used for the primary industry. The importance of bifacial tools of all kinds increases, from 50 percent of the Swasey/Bladen primary industry to 72 percent of the Cocos Chicanel primary industry. It has been noted that the percentage of the lithic assemblage identified as the domestic toolkit decreases in the Late Preclassic.

The impressive standardization of a few large tools suggests a higher level of organization for tool production in the Late Preclassic than before. At the same time, there is no evidence for specialization in toolmaking at Cuello, and these large standardized tools are rare. (It appears that the shift in organization indicated by their introduction was not a community one, but at regional level. In terms of the production and procurement of stone tools, Cuello apparently joins a higher-level organization, centred on (and perhaps controlled by) Colha, while retaining its established intra-community and relatively non-specialized level of toolmaking.)

CERAMICS (Figs. 8.14–8.15 and Tables 8.12–8.14)

Laura J. Kosakowsky and Norman Hammond

The Cuello ceramic assemblage consists of about 250,000 sherds and 150 whole vessels from the four ceramic complexes defined in Chapter 3, from which all the vessels and about 60,000 sherds were closely analyzed. The quantity of pottery recovered at Cuello suggests local manufacture, and thin-section analysis of some 50 sherds by Dora Barlaz (n.d.) indicates a similarity of paste that also suggests use of local clays, yet no identifiable ceramic production areas were located nor dumps of firing rejects.

The absence of documented production areas for ceramics at Cuello is less disturbing when considered within the context of other Preclassic Maya sites, which also lack them, and ethnographic research among modern Maya (the Kekchi of southern Belize; Hughes Hallett 1972; Kosakowsky, field notes 1979–80) provides a possible explanation. The Kekchi produce small quantities of undecorated pottery for domestic use, usually to store boiled corn or as *incensarios* for their household altars: pots are usually fired one or two at a time directly on the earthen floor inside the house (to avoid a bad burn if it rains). When firing is completed the only tangible remains besides the pots themselves are scorch marks on the floor. Similar marks on some plaster floors at Cuello could be evidence of such domestic firing. Kekchi pottery firing also takes place outside the house in the yard, on the ground surface under a small bonfire of dry corncobs and wood, which again leaves only a scorch mark soon obscured by human and animal traffic.

Possible exceptions to the apparent absence of more elaborate firing technology at Cuello are a few of the "firepits" (see Chapter 3): while most of these are small bowl-shaped depressions lined with clay and/or pottery, some of those in the late Cocos Chicanel phase XIII such as [F119] (Fig. 8.14) may use stone slabs and large sherds as heat baffles, in a way

Fig. 8.14 Possible pottery firing area [F119] of phase XIII, *c*. A.D. 200, showing lining of large sherds at two stages in excavation, and vertical stone slabs set on one side of the firepit area, perhaps as a heat baffle. (Scales in cm).

that would protect vessels from direct heat and thus prevent rupture (Reina and Hill 1978; Rye 1981).

Bruhns (1987: 127) suggests that some of the contents of *chultun* [F87] at Cuello are "debris identifiable as being remains of pottery making activities." Among these are "quantities of very large sherds, many of them remains of nearly whole vessels with no particular signs of wear ... large and varied enough to suggest that some of them were wasters from firing." While there is no direct evidence to support this thesis, the high proportion (49.6 percent) of Society Hall Red varieties in the [F87] assemblage, against 25–35 percent from other coeval contexts, is unusual. While the high wastage rate in traditional firing methods might account for the quantity of material if this is a waster dump, the thickness of Society Hall Red vessel walls is likely to explain the large sizes of the sherds.

Bruhns also identifies "two clay balls ... approximately 5 cm in diameter" as the raw material for making clay coils; but the form of these is modern, resulting from their recovery in the flotation sample (C.H. Miksicek, personal communication), and analysis shows them to contain only about 20 percent clay, too low to be prepared potters' clay.

A third class of material from [F87] that Bruhns (1987: 127) associates with pottery manufacture is

the extremely large quantity of fragmentary sheets of incompletely oxidised clay, the remains of low-fired clay sludge or slip. This is precisely the sort of material one would expect from open firing on the floor of a yard or patio in which construction of vessels was also done, the floor being swept from time to time to rid it of pieces of half-fired clay, sherds, leftover fuel, ashes and other trash. The incomplete oxidation, resulting in quantities of hardened, blackened, thin sheets of ceramic-like material, is indicative of the low temperatures at which these ceramics were fired: clays with a high calcium carbonate content cannot be fired at much over 750°C or they will spall and collapse (Rye 1981: 114). The black colour is indicative of high organic content, due either to the source of the clay, or perhaps to the addition of organic materials as an aplastic ("temper") to make the clay easier to work.

In Bruhns's opinion, therefore, [F87] has yielded wasters, large sherds for protective baffles (such as those found in [F119], and low-fired sludge which are good evidence of the area from which the *chultun* contents derived having been used for pottery manufacture. She also (1987: 127–8) identifies a complete vessel (Fig. 8.15) from [F87] as being a *molde*, a tournette or revolving base into which a pancake of clay can be fitted to form the bottom and lower sides of a vessel. The walls are then built up through coiling or other techniques, while the *molde* is turned with the hands or feet to facilitate formation of the vessel body, which may be of any size. The device is similar to the *kabal* noted by R.H. Thompson (1958) in Yucatan.

The Cuello example has walls of variable thickness of a heavily tempered oxidized clay; Bruhns (1987: 127) considers

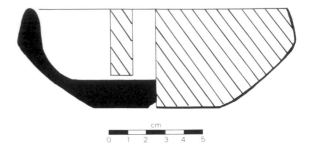

Fig. 8.15 Bowl from *chultun* [F87] with conical depression in base, possibly used as a *molde* or *kabal* in pottery manufacture.

it to be unslipped and with a scraped surface with no further smoothing, while one of us (LJK) observes a very thin interior and exterior slip, and provisionally assigns the vessel to the Sierra Red type. Bruhns observes "heavy rotary wear marks' on the flat bottom and some signs of wear in the rim, and the "other (whole) vessels from this site and context did not have wear patterns like these" (1987: 127); one of us (LJK) finds this wear pattern commonly on other Late Preclassic bowls, and does not believe that it gives any specific clues as to use. The burning of the vessel, with fire clouds on interior and exterior, may be related to either use or disposal.

The most unusual feature of the vessel is the conical depression in the center of the bottom. It was scraped or drilled into the finished vessel, and while Bruhns (1987: 128) regards it as "enigmatic," if the object in question was used at some point as a *molde* or *kabal* it might have served to locate a peg holding the device in place while it rotated on a base. Whether the vessel was originally made for such a purpose remains doubtful, given the fairly common occurrence of this form of bowl at other Late Preclassic sites in northern Belize as well as at Cuello; but the possibility that at some point in its use-life it was utilized in the making of other vessels cannot be excluded.

All the Cuello pottery was made using a coil technique, and some 90 percent of the assemblage shows evidence of smoothing to mask coil attachment, with about 50 percent exhibiting further burnishing. Slip colours are remarkably consistent from sherd to sherd within ceramic type classes, suggesting that the Cuello potters enjoyed continuous access to similar clay and pigment sources, and had expert control of firing techniques. There is a definite standardization in vessel form, especially in the Late Preclassic, but little evidence that techniques of manufacture changed much over the millennium and a half of occupation at Cuello.

TYPOLOGICAL AND STYLISTIC CHANGE
The successive ceramic complexes and their constituent types and varieties were noted in Chapter 3. Although such type classes are most useful for constructing a relative chronology

Table 8.12 *Median dimensions of Swasey and Bladen vessel-form classes*

Form class	Median diameter (cm)	Median neck height (cm)
1 Wide-mouth jar		
1–1 Short neck	24	1.5
1–2 Long neck	28	3.8
2 Narrow-mouth jar	14	1.4
3 Bottle	2.7	—
4 Incurved-recurved bowl		
4–1 Small capacity	18	—
4–2 Large capacity	28	—
5 Incurving bowl	20	—
6 Tecomate	16	—
7 Incurving bowl with collar	19	—
8 Outcurving bowl or dish		
8–1 Small capacity	20	—
8–2 Large capacity	35	—
9 Vertical to flaring bowl		
9–1 Small capacity	22	—
9–2 Large capacity	32	—

Table 8.13 *Median dimensions of Lopez vessel-form classes*

Form class	Median diameter (cm)	Median neck height (cm)
1 Wide-mouth jar		
1–1 Short neck	22	2.1
1–2 Long neck	30	4.8
2 Narrow-mouth jar	16	4.8
3 Bottle	3.2	—
4 Outcurving dish or plate		
4–1 Small capacity	21	—
4–2 Large capacity "platter"	42	—
5 Incurving bowl	20	—
6 Tecomate	12	—
7 Vertical to flaring dish	22	—
8 Composite silhouette bowl or dish		
8–1 Recurving	24	—
8–2 Medial angle	24	—

within the site, and for cross-dating between sites, they are much less helpful for other kinds of analyses such as the examination of intrasite variability of ceramics (Kosakowsky 1983). Frequency distributions of ceramic types between contexts at Cuello show little variation, and what little there is has been ascribed to different pottery-using activities.

The use of vessel form to delimit function, although difficult, is easier than simply assuming functions for specific type-classes, since analysis of form can utilize ethnographic studies of vessel-form use by modern Maya (Thompson 1958; Hughes Hallett 1972; Reina and Hill 1978), and such studies also remind us that pottery probably constituted only a part, and perhaps a small part, of the total range of containers used by a prehistoric Maya household. Baskets and gourds and other perishable materials were probably used (and occasionally survive in archaeological contexts), so that not all activities will be represented in the ceramic assemblage. Thus the ceramic vessel-form classes described below may provide some clues to functional variability in containers at Cuello, but will not encompass the entire range of uses and behaviors enjoyed by the Preclassic Maya inhabitants.

Swasey and Bladen vessel forms

The continuity of forms from Swasey into Bladen, and the similar frequencies of both types and shapes, together with the relatively small sample, suggest a composite analysis. Table

8.12 lists the nine shape classes and their median rim dimensions. A range of wide- and narrow-mouthed jars, narrow-necked bottles, and bowls ranging from the restricted orifice of the tecomate to the outcurving and flaring walls of the open forms suggests a set of domestic storage and service uses, with gradations of function too subtle to be discerned without ethnographic observation.

Lopez Mamom vessel forms

After *c.* 600 B.C. the most dramatic change is in the emphasis on outcurving side-dishes or plates at the expense of bowl forms (Table 8.13). This is not confined to Cuello, but seems to occur in the later Middle Preclassic at most lowland Maya sites. The introduction of "platters" of large capacity is most striking, and if these were, as is often assumed, used for the service of food, then either portions were larger, or the group being served from a single vessel was more numerous.

Cocos Chicanel vessel forms

By 400 B.C., although there are still eight basic form classes, their internal variability has become greater, and the outcurving-side dishes and plates that were popular in the preceding period virtually disappear (Table 8.14). There is an emphasis on large-capacity bowls, some of the diameters exceeding 60 cm: while the techniques of potting remain unchanged, the expertise needed to produce such vessels successfully is greater than for small bowls, and the degree of standardization also increases. Modification of vessel walls by flanging and

Table 8.14 *Median dimensions of Cocos Chicanel vessel-form classes*

Form class	Median diameter (cm)	Median neck height (cm)
1 Wide-mouth jar		
1–1 Short neck	24	1.4
1–2 Long neck	32	4.0
2 Narrow-mouth jar		
2–1 Short neck	16	1.8
2–2 Long neck	18	4.0
3 Outcurving or flaring bucket	32	—
4 Outcurving bowl or dish		
4–1 Small capacity	20	—
4–2 Large capacity	32	—
5 Incurving bowl	28	—
5–1 Unmodified	28	—
5–2 Labial ridge or flange	28	—
5–3 Medial ridge or flange	28	—
5–4 Basal ridge or flange	28	—
6 Tecomate	14	—
7 Flaring bowl or dish		
7–1 Small capacity	24	—
7–2 Large capacity	32	—
7–3 Miniature	14	—
8 Composite silhouette bowl		
8–1 Recurving	28	—
8–2 Medial angle	32	—
8–3 Cuspidor	22	—

ridging becomes popular, and intersite uniformity of design reaches its peak in this period. While the evidence does not allow us to identify craft production of ceramics as a specialized activity at Cuello, it does not preclude it, either.

CERAMIC, BONE, SHELL, AND GROUND STONE ARTIFACTS
(Figs. 8.16–8.53 and Table 8.15)

Norman Hammond

CERAMIC ARTIFACTS

Apart from these pottery vessels, all except one import apparently of local manufacture and most probably made within the Cuello community, numerous fired-clay objects were recovered in the excavations. These fall into two major classes: those made from recycled sherds of broken vessels, and those modeled from clay.

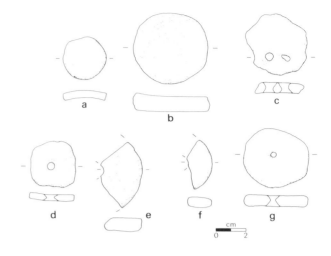

Fig. 8.16 Reworked sherds (a), (b) sherd disks (SF 1319, 1327); (c) sherd pendant (SF 1192); (d)–(g) perforated sherd disks (SF1157, 1994, 1273, 1195).

Reworked sherds (Fig. 8.16) The most numerous category of sherd-based artifacts is that of plain pottery disks (n = 51; Fig. 8.16a, b); two of these were of Late Classic date from superficial deposits, the others occurred throughout the Preclassic sequence. The largest disks were *c*. 90 mm in diameter, the majority 40–60 mm, but two were small (28–31 mm) and four very small (13–22 mm): clearly, a range of functions was encompassed, with the largest disks being suitable for pot lids or even beehive stoppers, and the smallest for not much more than tokens or gaming pieces. The size range was similar to that reported by Garber (1989: 73–77) for Late Preclassic Cerros domestic contexts, but Cuello lacks the large numbers of large disks with a modal diameter of *c*. 100 mm (Garber 1989: Fig. 26), found in non-domestic contexts and suggested by Garber to have functioned as lids for "beer mug" vessels used in ritual acts.

Pottery disks were also centrally perforated, usually by scraping away the fabric from one side or both (Fig. 8.16d–g); sometimes the perforation was abandoned part-done. Of the 17 perforated disks found, three were of Classic date; the size range lay within that of plain disks, and while some of the small examples could have been used as *ad hoc* spindle whorls, the large ones had some other function, perhaps as beehive doors like the perforated limestone disks (see below).

Sherds, usually of monochrome red slipware, were also worked into decorative forms: small find (SF) 814 is a fragment of Swasey/Bladen date carved into a roughly human shape with incised eyes, waist, and legs; it was found in a Cocos context, and may be no earlier. Sherds of Lopez phase Joventud Red, with its waxy slip, were used as the vehicle for incised designs of some complexity (Fig. 8.17a: SF 909), as the Cocos phase Sierra Red was on occasion, for example the

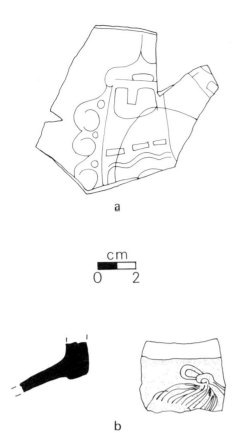

a

cm

0   2

b

Fig. 8.17 Reworked sherds, with incised decoration (a) Joventud Red sherd with complex design (SF 909); (b) Sierra Red sherd with human head and topknot (SF 817).

graffito of a human head and topknot (Fig. 8.17b (see reconstruction in Hammond 1982b: 136): SF 817) but in most cases reuse was simple, including a pendant with two suspension holes (Fig. 8.16c: SF 1192), a domino-like rectangle with eight scraped pits (SF 746), and notched *mariposas* thought to have been net-weights for fishing (SF 329, 1116, 1885); these last are found from Bladen times onwards. Some sherds had smoothed edges but had not yet been shaped (SF 339, 756, 824), further indication of the local nature of the reworked potsherd industry. The range of forms and functions is similar to that documented by Garber (1989: 77–86) at Cerros, although at that coastal site it is not surprising to find *mariposas* as the most common type.

Modeled clay artifacts These come in a variety of forms, all small and all apparently personal in function, although such functions apparently range from the decorative to the ritual. The earliest in occurrence are *human figurines*, which appear from Swasey times onwards (SF 1150, 2033); the fragments are of torsos with arms attached: in at least one instance (Fig. 8.18a: SF 2033) the body is a hollow cylinder and may have

been an effigy ocarina or flute, a type known in later Maya prehistory. The earliest figurine head, SF 1996 of Bladen date (Fig. 8.18b), has an amygdaloid punched hollow with a circular pupil punched deeper still, the ear a plain projecting flange, and the hair shown at front, side, and back by a raised margin and semi-parallel incisions; similar details are shown on one highland example from Chalchuapa of the Kulil Figurine Complex of 1200–600 B.C. (Dahlin 1978: Fig. 2b2, Vilanova Naturalistic: Vilanova Variety). SF 1966 is a fragment 45 mm high and wide, suggesting a rather large figure overall if the body was in proportion, and at least 250 mm high by analogy with the later Barton Ramie specimen no. 1771 (Willey et al. 1965: Fig. 256a–b), which is an almost complete seated figure 126 mm high with a head half the scale of the Cuello example. Large human figures may have been made in Lopez times also: the possible arm fragment SF 675 (Fig. 8.18e) is 80 mm long. Other examples are smaller, however: SF 676 (Fig. 8.18d) is only 72 mm high from crotch to shoulder and was a seated figure. The similar BR1771 has a torso the same size as the Cuello example, arms set away from the body (cf. Cuello SF 675; see Willey et al. 1965: Fig. 256f,h, for other examples, of possible Preclassic date), breasts, and a coiffure or headdress. The Cuello torso has the nipple marked in a position suggesting that a breast is intended, unlike SF 821 of Cocos date (Fig. 8.18c) where the torso is broad and flat and the nipples, as well as an apparent upper chest ornament, simple conical pits. Hammond (1989) has argued that the contrast is between female (SF 676) and male (SF 821) figurines, and that on this basis SF Q4091.03.01 (Fig. 8.19) is clearly male; he also suggests that the headband or diadem and earflares may identify this example as a ruler portrait, although the similar traits on BR 1771, apparently female, would not support this.

Figurines with attributes are rare at Cuello; the only clear Preclassic example, apparently of Bladen date, is SF 640 (Fig. 8.20), the upper part and mouthpiece of an effigy ocarina. The human figure is missing: the only remaining attributes are a headdress or helmet in the shape of a bird head, and a circular object, perhaps a shield or fan, held up by the right hand. The best analogies are much later, from the Late Classic period (Joyce 1933: Plates I, 15; II, 1, 3, 4, 13), and the presence of such a sophisticated design in the Middle Preclassic is surprising. Both the fabric and the stratigraphic context (35/35[124]) support this date, however.

Other human figurine fragments were found at Cuello (SF 819, 1124, 1140, 1642) from early Bladen through Chicanel times: such objects were in continued, though not common, use for almost the entire Preclassic period at the site. Human faces also appear on pottery vessels (Figs. 3.37, 8.22c).

Animal effigies make their first appearance in late Bladen times: the bird-shaped ocarina (Fig. 10.1: SF 1734) from the

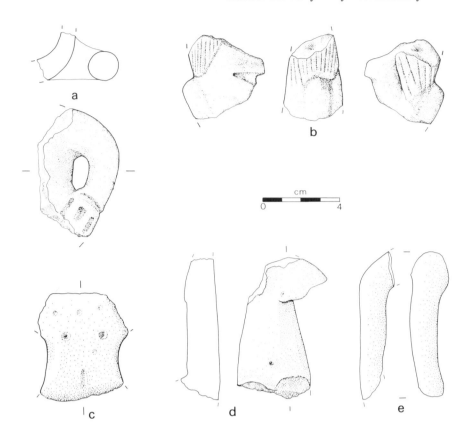

Fig. 8.18 Modeled pottery figurines: (a) Swasey phase tubular
(?flute) body with attached arm and hand (SF 2033); (b) Bladen
phase head fragment with double-punched eye and incised coiffure
(SF 1996); (c) torso, apprently male, with nipples, navel (?), and
possible chest ornament (SF 821); (d) torso of seated figure with
modeled left breast and shoulder (SF 676), (e) arm (?) (SF 675).

understood, although a clear possibility is that many were
children's toys; Healy (1988) suggests that those of the Classic
period were made for, used in, and discarded after funerary
rituals, but even though SF 1734 was from a burial, it is the
only example at Cuello not from a trash or fill context.

child burial [F219] is the earliest from a primary stratigraphic
context (and is surprisingly similar to SF 891 (Fig. 8.21a),
from an Early Classic fill context; another fragmentary bird-
ocarina (SF 1334) is of Chicanel date. A hollow feline head
fragment (Fig. 8.21b: SF 1657) is of Lopez date and an
armadillo (SF 568) and saurian effigy ocarina are from Cocos
times. Numerous animal- and bird-head adornos are also
known from pottery vessels, and include what appear to be
duck (from the spatulate bill, or a vulture from its curve in
profile), monkey (Fig. 8.22a–b), turtle, and dog among identifiable species. Most of these also appear in the diet (Chapter
4), although duck or vulture bones are lacking and the ceramic
representation (if that is indeed what Fig. 8.22a is) is among
the earliest evidence of Maya use of the birds.

Whistles or ocarinas are commoner at Cuello than the few
effigy examples, but most of the fragments are of mouthpieces
only (SF 820 (late Bladen), 1142, 1256 (both Cocos), and 311,
763 (undated)), and could be from either effigy or plain
instruments. The social function of instruments remains little

Roller stamps with a molded or excised continuous design are
found from late Bladen times onwards (Fig. 8.23a: SF 641;
also SF 1882), although most come from Cocos contexts (Fig.
8.23b–c: SF 1881 and the similar 1882; Fig. 8.23d–e: SF 1841,
and SF 183 with a basic design close enough for the former to
be a fragment of it); they could have been used for applying a
design to flesh or fabric. Willey *et al.* (1965: Fig. 258*l*) call a
very small specimen a "cylinder seal," but a sealing or
marking-of-ownership function seems unlikely for the larger
Cuello roller stamps; Ricketson and Ricketson's (1937: 221)
"might have been large beads but were more probably textile
stamps" or Longyear's (1952: 103) "served to extend designs
on cloth or hide" are better guesses. The Ricketsons' (1937)
Fig. 145*d–f* and Plate 78*a*1–3 show several parallels to Cuello
specimens, including the openwork technique (Plate 78*a*3)
and bold excision of the background (Fig. 145*d,f*), and the
latter is present on a Preclassic specimen from Copan (Longyear 1952: Fig. 83*a*). One Uaxactun specimen (Ricketson and
Ricketson 1937: Fig. 145*e*, Plate 78*a*1) shows a woven mat

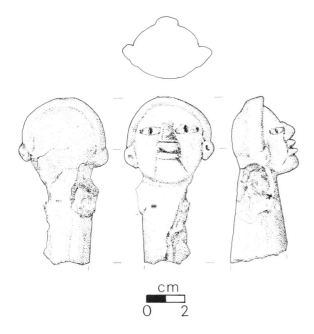

cm
0   2

Fig. 8.19 Head and partial torso of apparently male figure, Lopez phase (SF Q4091.03.01).

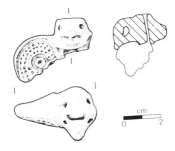

cm
0   2

Fig. 8.20 Bird headress and flanking circular object; fragment of an effigy ocarina, Bladen phase (SF 640).

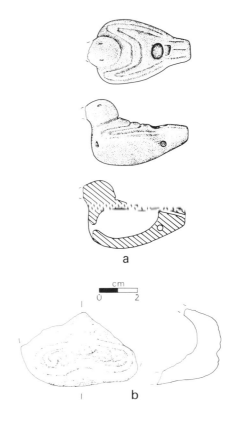

a

cm
0   2

b

Fig. 8.21 (a) Bird-effigy ocarina, Early Classic or earlier (SF 891), (b) hollow feline figure, Lopez phase (SF 1657).

pop motif similar to the Cuello carved bone tubes (Figs. 8.35–8.38).

Flat stamps could have marked ownership, although again decoration of the body or of textiles seems more likely. A number of these, mainly from Cocos deposits, have designs ranging from simple parallel lines or rows of dashed lines (Fig. 8.24a: SF 833) or hollow circles (SF 833, 916, 1122, 1125) through concentric circles (SF 1641) to cruciforms (SF 1115, 2059) and finally to elaborate three-part designs (Fig. 8.24b: SF 1954; also SF 1032, 1033) on three stamps from the sacrificial burial 27 (Fig. 10.8) in Structure 352. Of these SF 1032 has a clear bar and four dots, the Maya coefficient for 9, and SF 1954 has three dots in a U-bracket in the same central section. Dating to *c*. A.D. 100, this evidence of numeracy at

Cuello accords with examples of bar-and-dot notation from other lowland sites of this date. A flat stamp from Uaxactun Group E (Ricketson and Ricketson 1937: Fig. 145*b*) is of similar form to the Cuello examples, but with a simple spike handle instead of a flat perforated one; the double-U design on it is similar to the small Cuello limestone stamp in Fig. 8.52. Closer parallels in their subrectangular shape, although still with imperforate handles, are found at Chalchuapa from the Late Preclassic onwards (Sheets 1978: 65–6) and in the Preclassic at Copan (Longyear 1952: 103 and Fig. 83*e*).

Both kinds of stamp give us an idea of Middle and Late Preclassic design that is usually missing from pottery vessels, and are among the more elaborate modeled clay artifacts from Cuello. Also well made are ribbed or segmented beads (Fig. 8.25: SF 624, 338), like miniature roller stamps but lacking designs. Cruder are two cylinders with modeled ends which may be phalli (Fig. 8.26a: SF 560), a slab with four nubbin feet which could be a toy *metate* (SF 1118), and plain pottery rings (Fig. 8.26b: SF 697), these last from as early as the Lopez phase. Spindle whorls include one decorated early Cocos example (SF 1120), but eight of the nine were from superficial deposits and may well be of Classic period date.

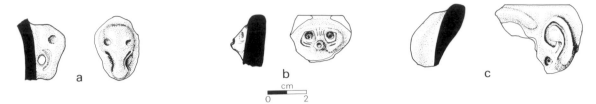

Fig. 8.22 Effigy adornos from Cocos phase bowls: (a) duck or
vulture (?) head (Q687); (b) spider monkey (SF 822); (c) human
ear and eyebrow (SF 918).

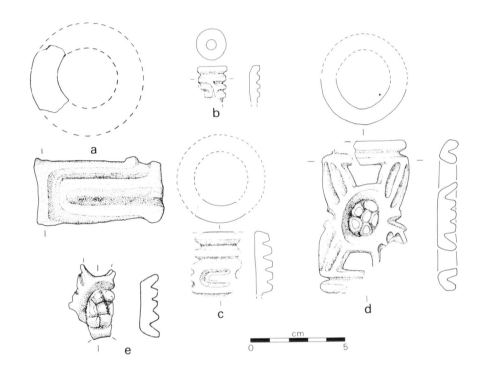

Fig. 8.23 Roller stamps (a) Bladen phase (SF 641); (b)–(e) Cocos
phase (SF 1881–2, 1641, 813).

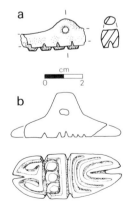

Fig. 8.24 Flat stamps, Cocos phase: (a) with two rows of dashed
lines (SF 833); (b) with a complex three-part design possibly
including the coefficient for 3 (SF 1954).

BONE ARTIFACTS (Figs. 8.27–8.38)
A modest number of objects was found at Cuello made from
human and animal bone. The former was rarely used (or at
least rarely identified) as a raw material, but five bone disks
have been identified by Frank P. Saul as being made from
human crania (SF 433–435, 1296–1297). The first three, one
represented only by fragments, were of c. 49 mm diameter and
5–6 mm thick, the others much smaller (Fig. 8.27: SF 1296).
The most closely datable, SF 434–435, are of mid-Cocos date,
c. 100 B.C., although another drilled skull fragment (SF 437)
comes from Bladen phase context.

Most bone artifacts are sufficiently altered from the raw
material that the species cannot be identified, even where the
work was not completed, as with a cut and beveled long-bone
fragment (SF 1752). One of the commoner categories is that of
beads, ranging from the simple perforated tooth-pendant (SF
532) to small bone disks and squares some 5 mm in diameter
(SF 1086, 1087) and long-bone sections either plain (SF 1043,

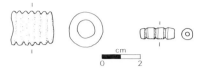

Fig. 8.25 Ribbed/segmented pottery beads, Cocos phase: (a) ribbed type (SF 624); (b) segmented type (SF 338).

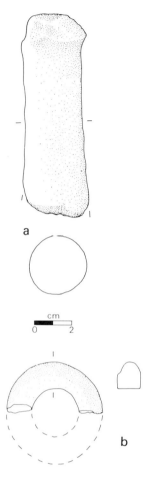

a

Fig. 8.26 (a) Pottery cylinder with expanded end, possibly phallic (SF 560); (b) pottery ring (SF 697).

b

Fig. 8.27 Bone disk made from human skull (SF 1296).

Fig. 8.28 Long bone segmented by grooves, perhaps for bead making or in a preliminary stage of carving like Figs. 8.35–38 (SF 471).

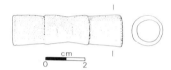

Fig. 8.29 Bone ear-ornament with expanded central section (SF 1281).

1803–4) or segmented (Fig. 8.28: SF 471). Other personal ornaments include a rectangular pendant 37 mm long (SF 1089), a minuscule globular pendant only 3 mm across (SF 1985) of Lopez date, and what seem to have been tubular ear-ornaments with an expanded central section (Fig. 8.29: SF 1281) or center and end (Fig. 8.30: SF 2066), of Cocos date. A biaxially perforated phalange, possibly human (Fig. 8.31: SF 2070) could have been a pendant or perhaps a whistle.

Made for practical use were awls polished down from long-bone splinters and 83–144 mm long (Fig. 8.32: SF 2024, also Fig. 8.33 upper), and eyed needles (Fig. 8.33 lower: SF 1825) from 43 to 105 mm long. Two deer metapodials, 120 and 148 mm long (SF 1959–60), had their ends carved into hooks, (Figs. 8.34, 10.2c) that may have been intended for netting or basketry, although the final use of the objects may have been to fasten a textile shroud around burial 123. Two bone picks (SF 1969, 2067) 102 and 91 mm long may also have been weavers' or basketmakers' tools.

Most striking of the Cuello bone artifacts are a series of bone tubes, made from the long bones of deer-sized animals

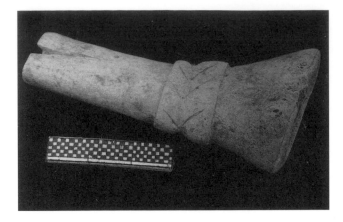

Fig. 8.30 Bone ear-ornament with expanded end and chevron-decorated central section (SF 2066). (Scale in cm).

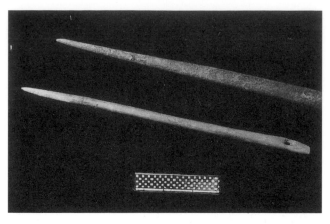

Fig. 8.33 Medium-sized awl, 100 mm, and eyed needle, 102 mm (SF 1825). (Scale in cm).

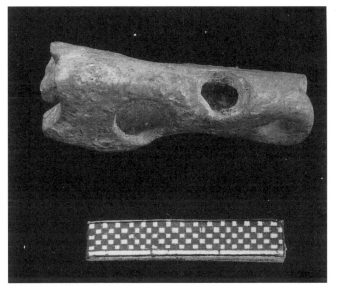

Fig. 8.31 Phalange, biaxially perforated, perhaps as a whistle (SF 2070). (Scale in cm).

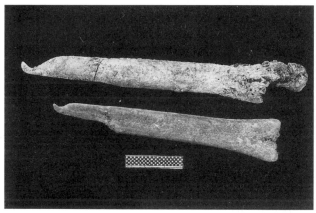

Fig. 8.34 Deer-metapodial bone hooks, 120 and 148 mm, perhaps for netting or shroud pins, found with burial 123 (SF 1959–60). (Scale in mm).

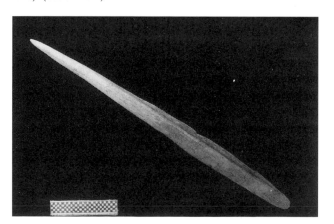

Fig. 8.32 Large awl made from a long-bone splinter, 137 mm (SF 2024). (Scale in cm).

and found accompanying the phase V Mass Burial 1 of 400–300 B.C. (Figs. 10.4–5). All six were carved in low relief with complex designs (Fig. 8.35): four (SF 1493, 1594–5, 1597) bore an interwoven motif, the *pop* symbol of rulership in Classic Maya art (Fig. 8.36). The other two (SF 1596, 1650) are more elaborate: SF 1650 bears a set of volute scrolls around a focal double disk (Fig. 8.37), and SF 1596 a serpentiform design against a background including more volutes (Fig. 8.38).

Willey *et al.* (1965: 494–9 and Figs. 30.5–7) discuss 32 bone tubes, both plain and decorated, from Barton Ramie, mostly with Late/Terminal Classic contexts and none of Preclassic date; some of those reported from Uaxactun Group E by Ricketson and Ricketson (1937: 206–8) are from buried plaza deposits probably of Chicanel date.

Three long-bone sections, possibly similar decorated tubes in the process of manufacture (SF 1154, 1707, 2030), or

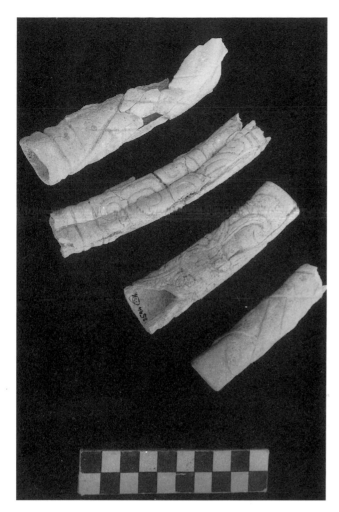

Fig. 8.35 Four of seven carved long-bone tubes found with Mass Burial 1: the upper and lower have woven-mat (*pop*) designs, the central two more complex iconography (see Figs. 8.36–38). The bones were probably from deer. (Scale in cm).

perhaps blanks for wide-bore beads (Fig. 8.28), date from phase VI and later at Cuello. While their end product is uncertain, they show that boneworking was carried on at Cuello, and that, whatever the function of the decorated tubes, their art may well be that of the community (see Chapter 10). Thus the entire bone industry of Cuello, from the quotidian tools and simple jewelry to the ritually import-ant objects deposited with Mass Burial 1, is most likely to have been the work of local craftspersons.

The same appears to be the case at Seibal, where Willey (1978: 168–71) reports worked bone scrap, mainly long-bone sections or discarded epiphyses of deer with annular or longitudinal cut marks, as well as awls, bone tubes, raspers, beads, pendants, and pierced animal teeth. Few of the Seibal artifacts have a firm Preclassic context, however, and most are likely to be Late/Terminal Classic in date. At Cerros the

converse is true: most of the bone artifacts described by Garber (1989: 51–9 and Figs. 16–19) are of Late Preclassic date, but like those of Cuello share the same range of formats and functions as the Altar de Sacrificios (Willey 1972: 229–39), Seibal, and Barton Ramie bone industries. Such crafts show a limited range but impressive continuity of techniques and uses from Middle Preclassic thought Terminal Classic times across the central and southern Maya Lowlands.

SHELL ARTIFACTS (Figs. 8.39–8.46)
With the exception of *Crassostrea* (114 specimens, all prob-ably weathered out of the limestone), and some 1,300 shell beads of unidentifiable species, 106 marine shells and shell artifacts were recovered at Cuello and identified as to species by Lawrence H. Feldman. These can be divided into two classes, "small marine" (n = 43), including *Mulina*, *Mytilop-sis*, *Turbonilla*, *Aequipecten*, and a number of tiny species of no cultural significance and "large marine" (n = 63), including *Anadara*, *Diodora*, *Lucina*, *Melongena*, *Oliva*, *Olivella*, *Ostrea*, *Prunum*, *Turbinella*, *Spondylus*, *Strombus*, and large unidenti-fied marine shell fragments (the presence of several fragments of the same species from any context is considered to represent one individual unless more than one hinge, columella, etc., is present).

Not all of even this small number of marine shells are the result of human activity: the lime encrustation and size of some of the "small marine" category (fragments of *Aequipec-ten*, and shells of *Turbonilla*, *Cerithidea*, *Mulinia*, and *Myti-lopsis* – all both rare and tiny) suggest that they too are weathered from rock, although there is one possible *Aequipec-ten* artifact and three possible ones of *Cerithidea virginica*.

There are thus 65 marine shells identifiable as to species, and a further 14 large marine shell fragments or artifacts worked too much for the species to be distinguished. The most common species is *Strombus gigas* (11 specimens), followed by *Melongena* (8), *Turbinella* (8), *Prunum* (3 species) (8), *Spondylus* (3 species) (4), and *Olivia* (3). Other species are present as one or two specimens. Very few are of Pacific origin (e.g. *Spondylus calcifer*, 1 specimen), and all of these come from Classic period deposits. The Preclassic marine shells are all of Caribbean origin, as might be expected given the relative closeness of the coast. Some species, such as *Strombus gigas* and *Turbinella angulatus*, occur as artifacts in all periods from Swasey onwards; those with an apparently more restricted temporal distribution also have a small sample size, but the presence of at least 11 species in Swasey phase deposits suggests that a range of marine shells was imported to Cuello from the beginning. The species commonest at Cuello are also common at Middle Formative and later sites closer to the coast, and may well have been collected by their inhabitants before being exchanged inland.

Of some 1,340 shell artifacts recovered in the Cuello

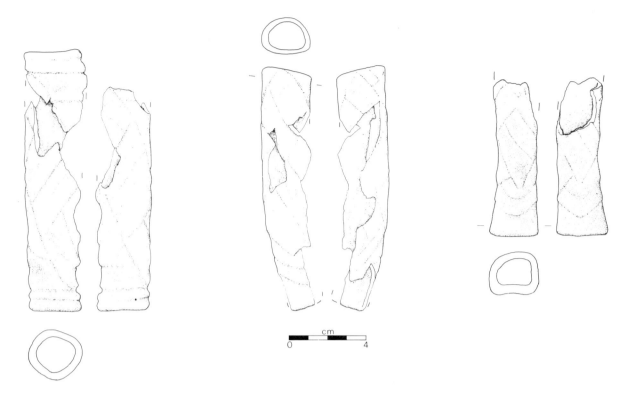

Fig. 8.36 Three of four carved bone tubes from Mass Burial 1 with the *pop* motif, which in Classic Maya times symbolized rulership (SF 1493, 1597, 1594). SF 1493 has double moldings at each end of the tube.

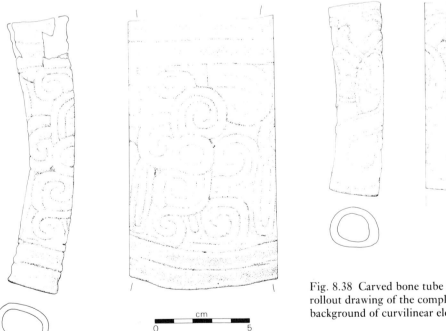

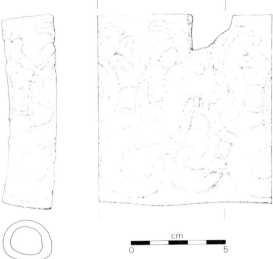

Fig. 8.38 Carved bone tube (SF 1596) from Mass Burial 1, with rollout drawing of the complex design of a serpentiform against a background of curvilinear elements

Fig. 8.37 Carved bone tube from Mass Burial 1 (SF 1650) with rollout drawing of the multiple-volute design panel between double moldings.

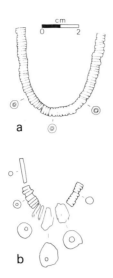

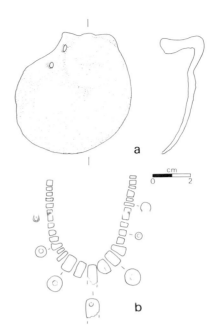

Fig. 8.39 Shell bracelets accompanying burial 114: (a) 76 matched disk beads from the left wrist (SF 1709); (b) assorted bead shapes from the right wrist (SF 1697).

Fig. 8.40 Shell grave goods of child burial 102 (a) *Spondylus* valve probably from pelvic region (SF 1517); (b) necklace (?) of 29 shell beads and a central greenstone pendant (SF 1515–6).

excavations, just over 1,300 were small beads, found either singly or in necklaces and bracelets accompanying burials. About half were very small disk beads of 3.5–5 mm diameter, made by chipping and grinding from marine shell of undeterminable species, while the remainder were larger (*c.* 10 mm), more roughly made flat beads chipped from the shells of the freshwater molluscs *Pomacea flagellata* and *Pachychilus pyramidalis*. It seems highly likely that the latter were locally made, while the small quantity of other shell artifacts and paucity of waste marine raw material (there are two cut discards) suggest that some of the better-made beads and most other shell goods may have been imported. In Cocos times a coastal community such as Cerros (Fig. 1.1) could have been a supplier, since although a surprisingly small number (n = 160; Garber 1989: 61–71) of shell objects was found there, many have close parallels at Cuello. Some 57 percent of the Cerros shell industry was in the form of beads, of which 57 percent in turn were of the disk form common at Cuello (Garber 1989: Table 11). Unexpectedly, stone beads outnumbered shell at Cerros, unlike the Cuello inventory, where stone, pottery, and bone beads, although isomorphous with the shell examples, were rare.

Marine shell beads were being brought to, or possibly made at, Cuello well before the foundation of Cerros *c.* 300 B.C., since they occur in Swasey phase deposits (SF 970, 989, 1064; n = 31). Bladen and Mamom deposits yielded well over 500 beads, including large numbers from flotation of midden deposits. Freshwater *Pomacea flagellata* beads were made from early Bladen times onwards (SF 973), and marine species such as *Melongena* and *Ostrea* were also being imported by then. The bead assemblage accompanying the terminal Bladen burial 114 is a useful example of shell artifact variability at

Cuello by *c.* 600 B.C.: it includes a bracelet of 76 small disk beads around the left wrist (Fig. 8.39a: SF 1709), 23 other beads around the pelvis, probably from clothing, and a bracelet on the right wrist comprising at least two *Nephronaias* rings, one greenstone bead, two small marine univalves, one *Melongena melongena* spire, one *Dentalium* shell, and 19 small disk beads (Fig. 8.39b: SF 1697); see also Fig. 9.8 (row 4, lower left) for a jade from this burial. Burial 123, also of terminal Bladen date (see Fig. 10.2), was accompanied by a bracelet of 107 beads, including some made from the freshwater *Nephronaias*. The Cocos phase child burial 102 had a necklace of 29 graduated disk beads and a central greenstone pendant (Fig. 8.40b: SF 1516–7) as well as a *Spondylus* valve (Fig. 8.40a: SF 1517).

A few beads were made from the red inner shell of *Spondylus americanus* (e.g. SF 529), but this bivalve was more often found in the form of complete valves with the hinge, spines, and outer layer stripped away to reveal the red interior, perforated by two (on one example four) holes to form a pendant. Six of these were found at Cuello, all in Cocos deposits (SF 654, 767, 1274, 1343, 1517, 1761: Fig. 8.41); the position of two of them, in child burials 86 and 102, suggests use as a pubic shield. Also made of *Spondylus* shell, but from an Early Classic fill context, is a frog or toad effigy (Fig. 8.42). A single *Spondylus* disk bead was included in the phase IVA cache [F190] together with 24 jade beads (Chapter 10).

Few other shells are as easy to identify once worked into artifacts, but some remained close to their original form, having only small portions removed or perforations made, or

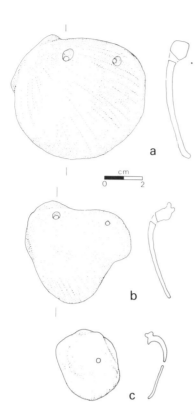

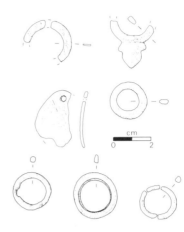

Fig. 8.44 *Nephronaias* nacre artifacts: rings (from top left) SF 1333, 1295, 1294, 1262 [3], pendant (SF 1277). SF 1294–5 were found with the Classic period burial 130.

Fig. 8.41 *Spondylus* valves with the red inner layer exposed: (a) from child burial 86 (SF 1343), (b) SF 1274; (c) SF 1761.

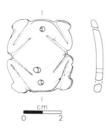

Fig. 8.42 Frog/toad effigy of *Spondylus* shell, Late Preclassic or Early Classic date (SF 1326).

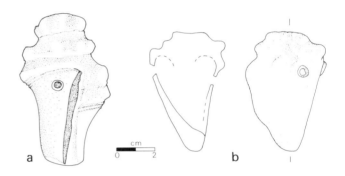

Fig. 8.45 (a) *Strombus gigas*, cut and perforated for use as a trumpet (SF 691), (b) *Strombus pugilis*, perforated as a pendant (SF 1158).

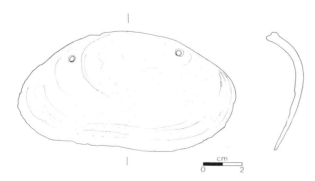

Fig. 8.43 *Nephronaias* valve perforated for use as a pendant or gorget, from burial 34 (SF 1427).

possessed salient characteristics such as the nacreous sheen of the freshwater bivalve *Nephronaias ortmanni*. This last was used as an entire valve 115 mm long perforated as a pendant (Fig. 8.43: SF 1427; cf. Willey *et al.* (1965): 504, 507 and Fig. 309*m* for Terminal Classic examples), or with two immature specimens forming a matched pair of pendants in a burial (SF 1358), or stripped to the nacreous interior and cut (Fig. 8.44) into pendants (SF 1277) or rings (SF 1262, 1294, 1295, 1333). An immature *Strombus gigas* (SF 931) was perforated for use as a pendant, and another (Fig. 8.45a: SF 691) had the spire removed as well as the lower portion, before being perforated, perhaps for use as a trumpet. One *Strombus pugilis* (Fig. 8.45b; SF 1158) was perforated for use as a pendant, while two others, perforated and with their spines removed (SF 829), were placed with burial 30, the only possible female in Mass Burial 1, along with a beige cowrie shell pendant of undetermined species (SF 794) (see Garber 1989: Fig. 22b,f for similar Cerros examples of *Strombus* artifacts). Another

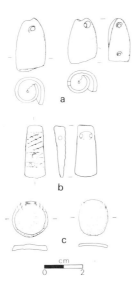

Fig. 8.46 (a) *Oliva* shells, trimmed and perforated, perhaps as tinklers (SF 1304, 1331); (b) shell pendant with cross-hatched decoration (SF 1704); (c) shell disks (SF 1211, 1258).

Table 8.15 *Raw materials for grinding stones at Cuello*

	Manos	Metates	Total	%
Limestone	63	58	121	81
Chert	4	2	6	<4
Granite/sandstone	0	6	6	<4
Andesite lava	1	0	1	1
Unidentified		16	16	11

unspecified bivalve perforated near the hinge (SF 785) was found in a Bladen phase context, the earliest use of a complete valve at Cuello. One specimen of *Turbinella angulatus* (SF 1429) was perforated and had its margin ground smooth, and one *Prunum apicina* was simply perforated. Several *Oliva* shells had their spires removed and were perforated for suspension (Fig. 8.46a: SF 1304, 1331: cf. Garber, 1989: Fig. 23e,f for Cerros parallels; Kidder 1947: 63–4 for Uaxactun examples from Mamom through Tepeu times).

Most of the non-bead ornaments made from unidentifiable shells were pendants, some plain like SF 781, others decorated with incised and cross-hatched designs (Fig. 8.46b: SF 1704, with a technically close and coeval parallel at Barton Ramie: Willey *et al.* 1965: 508 and Fig. 304*a*); a number of shell disks, some perforated, may be throatplates for earflares (Fig. 8.46c: SF 1211, 1258; cf. Garber 1989: Fig. 21e–j for Cerros examples) and date from early Lopez times onwards. At both Barton Ramie and Seibal a similar range of artifacts to those from Cuello was found, but dating mainly from Late/Terminal Classic times (Willey *et al.* 1965: 507–11; Willey 1978; 162–5), while at Tikal similar forms and a variety of social and ceremonial functions for shell artifacts have been documented by Moholy-Nagy (1985); Maya shell-working, like that in bone, seems to have been a fairly simple and stylistically conservative industry in most places.

The final category of worked marine material is that of stingray spines, two of which (SF 1090) were trimmed and placed in cache [F80] for the dedication of the earliest phase of Structure 352. One unmodified shark tooth of early Bladen date was found (SF 831), and a number of unmodified marine

shells (some of them fossils from the local limestone, as may be a few worked pieces). These are found from Swasey times onwards and may have been brought in as raw material for ornament manufacture; with the one piece of waste shell they are sparse evidence for a marine-shell industry at Cuello, but the manufacture of beads and pendants from freshwater shells shows that such a craft may have been practiced on a small scale, especially in Cocos times. Personal adornments were made from barely modified as well as extensively worked shells, and deposited in burials along with numerous beads, while stingray spines were the only marine materials used in cached offerings, and freshwater shell caches of the kind reported from Late Classic Lubaantun by Hammond (1975b: 384–5) were not found.

Tools and domestic implements made from marine shell were totally absent; but these were also rare at Cerros on the coast, where Garber (1989: Figs. 20n, 22e) reports a single shell axe and a scoop and notes that all extant examples of the latter are otherwise of Classic or Postclassic date. While shell was never a common artifact material at Cuello, the abundance of shell beads with burials of all ages, and the recovery of many other objects from trash and fill rather than burial or cache contexts, suggests that it was not seen as rare and precious so much as a desirable and obtainable regional product.

GROUND STONE
Grinding stones The commonest items in the Cuello ground-stone inventory of *c.* 200 were food-processing equipment, *manos* and *metates* for grinding maize (and perhaps other seeds or nuts such as cacao). Since maize kernels and cobs were recovered from the entire Cuello sequence from early Swasey times onwards (Chapter 4), it is not surprising to find these tools from the earliest times also. What is more unexpected is that the earliest examples, from a phase II fill of recycled midden (Fig. 9.7), are of a roseate metamorphosed sandstone from the Maya Mountains massif, some 150 km to the south: the early inhabitants of Cuello procured even basic tool resources from some distance.

The most frequent material used for *manos/metates* at Cuello was, however, limestone (Table 8.15). Of 150 speci-

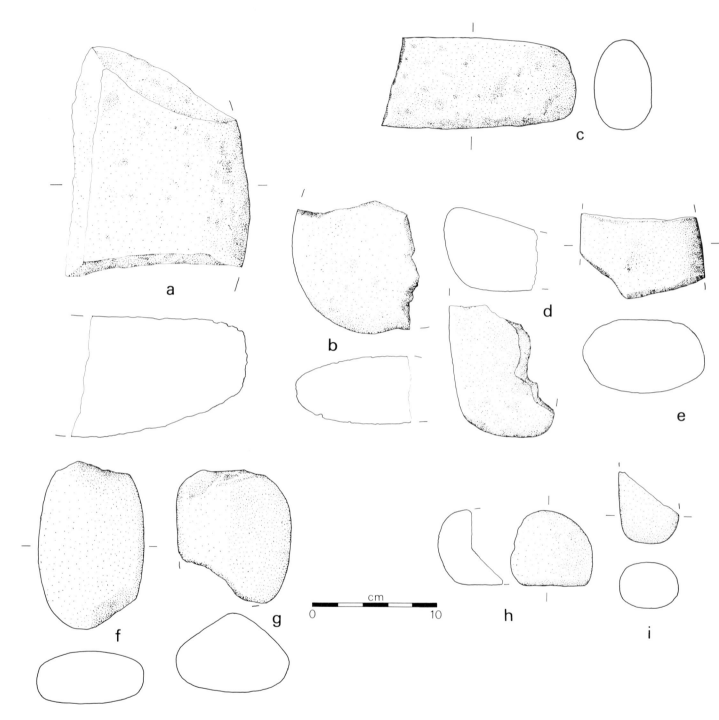

Fig. 8.47 Middle and Late Preclassic grinding stones: (c), (d), (f)
Lopez phase (SF 4141.01, 4004.01, 4004.02); all others Cocos
phase (SF 4059.01, 4078.01, 4104.03, 4073.02, 4073.03, 4075.04).

mens, almost all fragmentary, 43 *manos* and 33 *metates* were of a plain limestone that could have been quarried almost anywhere in the region, including the vicinity of Cuello (Fig. 8.47). Two *manos* and four *metates* were of a fine-grained limestone, also regionally available, and another 15 *manos*, (including a complete specimen 265 × 80 × 75 mm: SF 302), and 17 *metates* were made from a crystalline limestone of less common occurrence. (Willey (1978: 60) believes many of those identified as such at Altar de Sacrificios to be in fact of quartzite, an identification which he follows for the Seibal specimens and which is in turn followed, without independent petrological analysis, by Garber (1989: 15) for the Cerros material; it may be noted that examination of a large sample (n = 202) of *manos* and *metates* of Late Preclassic through Terminal Classic date from Nohmul, midway between Cuello and Cerros, by a professional geologist, found many of a silicified limestone but none of quartzite *sensu stricto* (Truebe n.d.). Truebe also found that 62.4 percent of the overall sample was of limestones from the central/northern Maya Lowlands and another 24.7 percent possibly from that zone, or from further south; only 12.8 percent were most probably from the southern lowlands, 10 percent probably from the Maya Mountains or similar igneous/metamorphic areas of Honduras, and 2 percent from the Motagua valley.)

Three *manos* were made from a quartz-rich rock, possibly non-local, three *metates* from a very porous limestone, and one from a porcellaneous limestone. In spite of the work of McDonald (see McDonald and Hammond 1985: 16) the microlocal limestone geology of northern Belize is still not well known, but it is clear that most varieties of limestone used for *mano* and *metate* production at Cuello were available within a relatively short radius, perhaps 15 km, of the site and that these tools, 81 percent of the total (n = 121), were the product of, if not intracommunity, at most intraregional craftspersons.

A further two *metates* and four *manos* were made from chert, available just east of the New River not more than 10 km from Cuello; two complete *manos* were 210 and 260 mm long, and 86 × 76 and 75 × 70 mm in cross section (SF 644, 167), although the latter may be of Classic period date. These bring the percentage of regionally made food-processing tools to 85 percent. Of the remaining 14 percent, 11 percent (n = 16) were *manos* and *metates* of unidentified raw material: many of these were burnt fragments, and some were probably of local materials.

Imported *manos* and *metates* constituted the remaining 4 percent (n = 7) and are noted as trade goods in Chapter 9. Most of the 150 implements were found in trash or fill contexts (Garber (1989: 22) suggests that this may have been votive behavior rather than just rubbish disposal), but two *metate* fragments (Fig. 8.48: SF 911) were used to cover the child burial 23, itself placed in construction fill and possibly dedicatory.

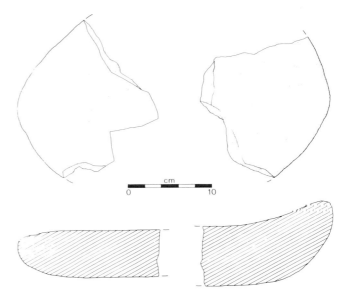

Fig. 8.48 Two limestone *metate* fragments (SF 911) used to cover the Cocos period child burial 23.

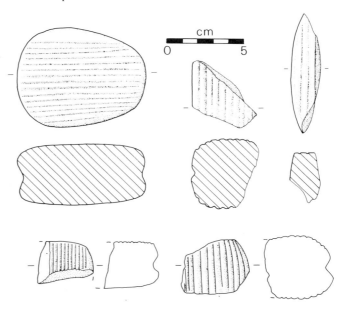

Fig. 8.49 Barkbeater (SF 517) and fragments of four others (SF 2065, 000, 907, 1667); those in the bottom row are of Bladen phase date, and the others are Cocos or later.

Barkbeakers Ten of these parallel-grooved objects were found, all of limestone and probably of local if not community manufacture. One example (Fig. 8.49: SF 517) was complete, 84 mm long and 62 × 39 mm in section, with a circumferential groove to hold a withy handle. The nine fragmentary examples were all of the same general form; two (SF 907, 1667) are of Bladen date and one (SF 2063) of early Cocos, while the

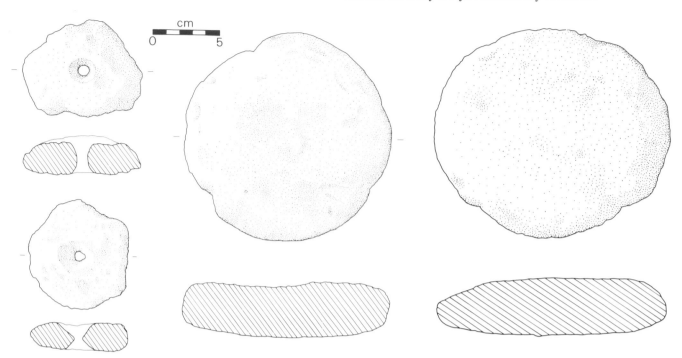

Fig. 8.50 Limestone disks, perhaps log beehive stoppers, and perforated rough disks.

Fig. 8.51 Perforated rough limestone disks. (Scale in cm)

remainder are from later Cocos or uncertainly datable contexts. The complete example may be no earlier than Early Classic from its context.

The identification of barkbeaters, and hence inferentially of barkcloth or bark paper, the raw material from which Maya codex books were made, as far back as the early Middle Preclassic, is of some interest: Uaxactun had no Preclassic examples, at Barton Ramie barkbeaters could be assigned a date no earlier than the terminal Preclassic Floral Park phase,

while one at Altar de Sacrificios was of Late Preclassic date and one at Seibal of late Middle Preclassic (Willey 1978: 55, 80). Neither of the two from Cerros is datable (Garber 1989: 34).

Limestone disks Twelve of these carefully chipped but roughly finished objects were recovered, with diameters ranging from 95 to 195 mm and a mean of 133 mm; seven others were found with a central perforation, the largest example being 125 mm across (Figs. 8.50–8.51). Several come from late contexts (SF 127, 139, 519, 634), but others are well stratified (e.g. SF 492, 903, 1986) in early Cocos times. The most plausible use for the unperforated disks is as stoppers for hollow-log beehives (summarized by Andresen 1986), and the perforated ones could as easily be entrance slabs for the hives. Garber (1989: 26–9, 31–2), discussing a much larger sample of 101 plain disks and 27 perforated ones from Cerros, reviews earlier explanations including use as digging-stick weights (now with some confirmation from Cerén in El Salvador) and suggests that at least some of the Cerros perforated examples were elements in architectural sculpture, and plain ones used as pot rests. The contextual data from Cuello neither support nor refute these suggestions.

Other limestone objects A small number of other limestone artifacts were found, including two polishers (SF 728, 2091) 82 and 78 mm long, shaped like miniature *manos*, three hammers, including a spindle-shaped soft-hammer (Fig. 8.2: SF 1604) found cached with two chert blades possibly made using it; and at the level of personal possessions a seal-like

Fig. 8.52 Polished limestone cylinder with U-shaped incised design on one end (SF 164).

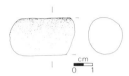

Fig. 8.53 Stick of prepared red ocher (hematite and goethite; SF 1332).

cylinder 13 mm long (Fig. 8.52: SF 164) with a U-shaped design incised into one end, and what may be a blank for making two others, 28 mm long with a groove cut midway (SF 171).

Possibly non-local objects A siltstone mano or polisher of Cocos date (SF 1474) may be of stone from southern Belize, but could be of north Belizean origin, as perhaps could be a travertine/tuff-like *mano*. The same must be said of ten pieces of red and yellow ocher (hematite and goethite: Michael Carr, X-ray diffraction results, personal communication 1986), some of it apparently ground to powder and reformed into pigment sticks (Fig. 8.53: SF 1332; Karen O. Bruhns, personal communication 1980). Red ocher lumps (SF 1417, 1418) were found in burial 79, the young adult male in the eastern part of Mass Burial 2 of phase XI (Fig. 10.6d), and in prepared form in the Bladen phase burial 116 (SF 1756; see Fig. 10.1). These are all red ocher, as are SF 698, 1008–9, 1858 and 1976; yellow ocher is found alone in SF 1757 and mixed with red in SF 1810. Ocher is a naturally occurring substance in limestones, and while uncommon in northern Belize cannot be positively identified as an import to the region; its use at Cuello runs from at least late Bladen times onwards.

Chapter 9

EXTERNAL CONTACTS
AND TRADE AT CUELLO

INTRODUCTION

Although Cuello was a small and unimportant community for
its entire existence, with a population of less than 2,500 at its
height and a political reach of only a few kilometers, it was not
isolated: from the Swasey phase onwards there is evidence of
the procurement of basic resources from beyond the settlement's exploitation territory of agricultural land and the local
forests, wetlands, and mineral sources. Those resources
arguably obtained in the course of forays from Cuello into the
surrounding area, and brought back for processing within the
community, have been considered in Chapter 8: while some of
the goods may have been acquired in zonal intersettlement
exchange of the sort modeled by Hammond (1973: Fig. 1),
such transactions are at present archaeologically undetectable.
In this chapter we examine the clearer evidence for contact
outside the immediate site exploitation of territory of Cuello,
which we take to have had a maximum radius of 10 km. Such
contacts take two forms: stylistic borrowings, and actual
imported goods of exotic raw materials.

CHERT TRADE

Rebecca McSwain

Interpretation of the lithic materials from Cuello (and from
everywhere in northern Belize and adjacent regions) must be
undertaken with reference to the important chert workshops
at Colha, 27 km southeast of Cuello (Wilk 1975; Hester 1979;
Shafer and Hester 1983): it has been suggested that Cuello and
other sites in the region were "consumer communities" for
the products of the Colha craft specialists, especially in the
Late Preclassic when Colha "virtually monopolizes chert
production" (Shafer 1982: 35). Shafer (1982: 35) has also
suggested that Colha administrators controlled the sources of
fine brown and gray chert during the peak periods of stone tool

production. The questions of whether completed tools were distributed from the Late Preclassic workshops at Colha, whether stone tools of the brown and gray cherts were produced outside Colha, and whether access to chert sources was restricted in the Late Preclassic to Colha knappers, relate to more abstract questions about conditions and causes of socio-economic complexity in the Maya Lowlands before the Classic period.

As noted in Chapter 8, formal tools very similar to those described from Late Preclassic Colha are found at Cuello in the Cocos Chicanel period, although there are few complete examples. It is not clear, however, where these tools were made: as noted in Chapter 8, large bifaces, blades, stemmed macroblades, and small bifaces of Colha-like material are found at Cuello from early Middle Preclassic times onwards, before the florescence of Colha as a chert-working community and possibly even before its earliest known occupation in the Bolay phase (900–500 B.C.), coeval with Bladen and early Lopez at Cuello.

There can be no doubt that the Late Preclassic Colha workshops produced massive quantities of tranchet-bit tools and large oval bifaces; the case for large-scale production of other items is perhaps less clear. As Shafer and Oglesby (1980: 215) put it with reference to one Late Preclassic workshop, "the major production systems include the large oval bifaces and tranchet-bit tools, while minor production systems include the macroblades, tapered-stem bifaces, and eccentrics."

The evidence from Cuello suggests the possibility that, although tranchet-bit tools and large oval bifaces were being made exclusively at Colha for regional distribution in the Late Preclassic, other kinds of tools were being made within other communities at the same time, utilizing the same brown and gray cherts used for the major production systems at Colha as well as locally available coarser white cherts and chalcedonies. Shafer and Hester (1983: Fig. 1) note that although the zone of occurrence of chert nodules is as much as 20 km southeast of Cuello, there is a zone of chert-bearing soils extending to within about 5 km of the site.

Thus it may be that the fine brown and gray cherts appear in the Cuello lithic assemblage through two separate economic subsystems: on the one hand, tranchet-bit tools and large oval bifaces were brought in during the Late Preclassic as finished tools; they were used, resharpened, and finally either discarded or recycled into other tool forms; on the other, brown and gray chert was also brought in as raw material (although not as whole nodules) for the manufacture, by Cuello residents, of blades, bifaces, and unifaces.

Evidence for the import rather than local manufacture of the two major Colha tool types is in part negative. There is no evidence that these tools were being made at Cuello: no collection of manufacturing failures and no significant accumulation of characteristic debris (such as the tranchet

Table 9.1 *Occurrence of cortex on all lithic tools (n = 2,134)*

	Early Middle Preclassic		Late Middle Preclassic		Late Preclassic	
Cortex	Colha	Other	Colha	Other	Colha	Other
Absent	99	155	64	163	570	513
Present	27	93	17	88	95	250

flakes). On the positive side there is ample evidence for large-scale production of these (and other) tool forms at Colha (Shafer 1979). It is possible that the tranchet-bit tools and the large oval bifaces are the result of the "mass production of a series of items sensitive to the demands of consumers operating in a shifting ecological adaptation" (Shafer and Oglesby 1980: 215), and that in the Late Preclassic Cuello was indeed on the "consumption end of the Colha industry" (Shafer 1982: 36) with regard to the two major tool forms produced by that industry.

However, it is also possible that the existence of the large oval biface and tranchet-bit tool in the Cuello community results from a mechanism or mechanisms other than the "producer-consumer" model presented by Shafer and Hester (esp. 1983): for example, these types at Cuello could be elements in a Late Preclassic lithic style shared by residents of Colha, Cuello, and other northern Belize communities.

The occurrence of manufacturing debris in the Cuello lithic collection shows that many stone tools were being made within the community throughout the Preclassic period, using both locally available and Colha-type brown/gray cherts. Pieces retaining cortex on more than 10 percent of exterior surface are, in some cases, products of early stages of reduction in stone tool manufacture; as Table 9.1 shows, such pieces are found from early Middle Preclassic through Late Preclassic times, and in the latter period 28 percent of these items are of the Colha-like cherts, while among tools of Colha-like cherts, 14 percent retain some cortex.

Blade production seems to have been particularly important: there are large pieces of debris from Cuello, trapezoidal or triangular in section, with dorsal ridges and 50 percent or more exterior surface retaining cortex, which may represent steps in core preparation for the removal of large blades. There are no blade cores as such from Cuello, but such cores are also absent from Colha (Shafer and Oglesby 1980: 215). These blade-like pieces of debris may have been brought back to the Cuello community from a quarry site for use as *ad hoc* tools, and many of them show retouch or edge damage along one or more edges. They range in size from 44 mm long and

Table 9.2 *Occurrence of cortex on flake tools of Colha-like chert from ceramically dated contexts (n = 167)*

| Period | Cortex | | n |
	Absent	Present	
Early Middle Preclassic	27 (69%)	12 (31%)	39
Late Middle Preclassic	12 (71%)	5 (29%)	17
Late Preclassic	87 (88%)	24 (22%)	111

Note:
Chi-square = 1.55; df = 2; p = 0.46

Table 9.3 *Occurrence of cortex on flake tools of other raw materials from ceramically dated contexts (n = 515)*

| Period | Cortex | | n |
	Absent	Present	
Early Middle Preclassic	78 (58%)	57 (42%)	135
Late Middle Preclassic	74 (62%)	45 (38%)	119
Late Preclassic	167 (64%)	94 (36%)	261

Note:
Chi-square = 1.46; df = 2; p = 0.48

24 mm wide to 149 by 46 mm, and are almost exclusively of the Colha-like cherts. Andresen (1976: Fig. 6) has recorded large blades which he calls "tool blanks" from various northern Belize sites; two of those illustrated retain cortex and all very much resemble some of the Cuello examples.

Flake tools are also present in the Cuello assemblage, and Table 9.2 shows the occurrence of flake tools of the Colha-like cherts that retain cortex. The percentage of these flake tools retaining cortex decreases slightly through time, but a chi-square test does not suggest that there is significant variation in the occurrence of cortex over time.

Table 9.3 shows, for purposes of comparison, the occurrence of cortex on flake tools of other raw materials. Again, there is a slight decrease over time, which is not statistically significant.

Another kind of byproduct representing tool manufacture at Cuello is flakes. A study of 107 flakes from the Late Preclassic *chultun* [F87] shows that 18 percent of brown chert flakes and 15 percent of gray ones retain cortex, as do 23 percent of chalcedony flakes (McSwain 1982: Table 3). There is nothing to show what the end products were of the initial reduction steps represented by these flakes, but it is clear that materials of all kinds were brought into the community in unprocessed or minimally processed form.

It is interesting to compare the result of the *chultun* study with an analysis of debitage from three workshops at Colha, one dating to the Preclassic, another to the Postclassic, and a third which may be at least partly Late Preclassic, judging from the tool types found (Nash 1980). The sample from Colha is several times larger than that from Cuello, and the Colha study is much more detailed, but certain similarities are noteworthy. One is that in both samples there are more flakes of brown and gray chert than of other materials, 98.5 percent at Colha, 77 percent at Cuello. The second similarity is that in the Colha workshops 16 percent of brown and gray chert flakes have some cortex; at Cuello there is cortex on 16.5 percent of such flakes. In addition, 24 percent of amorphous

(chunky, without retouch) pieces from the Cuello *chultun* were of brown and gray cherts, and of these 23 percent retain some cortex (McSwain 1982: Table 5). It should also be noted that the *chultun* contained a large crude biface of brown chert which may be a tool blank.

Indeed, postulating other explanations for the presence of the Colha-type tools at other sites in northern Belize may lead in turn to other models of the Late Preclassic economic situation in the region. A shared stylistic sphere for chipped-stone tool types might indicate a shared cultural tradition; disappearance of the shared lithic styles might signal dissolution of that cultural unity. Alternatively, the morphology of these tools might have strictly functional significance; in that case, their similarity in form across northern Belize might indicate a narrowing of possibilities for subsistence throughout the region, such that many communities were following identical agricultural strategies. These strategies, and the acquisition of tools with which to pursue them, could be entirely voluntary, not the result of control of trade or agriculture from Colha. Again, the distribution of either raw material or finished tools could be controlled, but from another, more important, regional center such as Nohmul.

In summary, there may have been, in Late Preclassic northern Belize, a chert distribution system involving the exportation of at least two tool types, the tranchet-bit tool and the large oval biface, from the Colha manufacturing center to smaller communities very possibly engaged in large-scale intensive agriculture, as Shafer (1982) and others have suggested. It seems likely, however, that residents of the smaller communities also obtained, either through a Colha-controlled distribution or through independent procurement efforts in the chert-bearing zone (which extends well north of Colha), unprocessed or minimally processed brown and gray chert for the manufacture of other tools within their own communities. Evidence from Cuello points to blades of all sizes as a major component of these local industries using brown and gray cherts; however, the production of unifaces and small bifaces (at least some made on the blades) was also probably import-ant, utilizing both locally available materials and cherts brought from a few kilometers away (see Table 8.4–8.5). Given the variety of forms in which the fine brown and gray cherts appear in the Cuello assemblage and the increasing presence of those materials at Cuello through time, it seems unlikely that access to chert sources was controlled by Colha, although the best-quality material may have been appro-priated by Late Preclassic Colha specialists interested in mass production and tight control of product quality.

The stemmed macroblade or "dagger" is a special case deserving brief mention in this context. This item was probably among those manufactured at Colha, and has been reported, made of brown chert like that from northern Belize, from several sites in Mesoamerica and the Caribbean (W.R. Coe 1957; Moholy-Nagy 1976: 96; Clark and Lee 1979). It is likely, given the occurrence of macroblade fragments and tool fragments in the collection, that stemmed macroblades were made at Cuello also, where they appear in early Middle Preclassic times, and possibly at Cerros (Beverly Mitchum, personal communication). Moholy-Nagy suggests that the stemmed macroblades at Tikal were imported as finished goods, but it is also possible that macroblades were imported and subsequently reduced to "dagger" form by the Tikal knappers, as was probably the case in the Middle and Late Preclassic communities of northern Belize.

CERAMIC TRADE

Laura J. Kosakowsky

There are few identifiable ceramic trade items in any of the Formative phases at Cuello. Local clays are available for the fabrics and slips of pots, and there are local sources for tempering materials; no ceramic workshop areas have been located at Cuello, although worked clay and a possible *molde* for pottery manufacture were found in the fill of *chultun* [F87] (see Chapter 8) and thin-section analyses of Cuello ceramics show only local tempering materials. It seems likely that Cuello ceramics were on the whole locally produced and used.

During the Swasey phase of the early Middle Formative there are no identifiable ceramic trade pieces at all, although since little is known from other sites of this period this is not surprising. In the succeeding Bladen phase there are a few small sherds of a hard-fired, fine paste gray ware with specular hematitic fugitive paint, that are probably of exotic origin because they are unlike any other Bladen ceramics in either paste or decoration, and are similar to material found in the highlands at sites such as Chalchuapa. There is one sherd, unfortunately a surface find, which might also be exotic: it

Fig. 9.1 Black-rimmed white bowl, probably Bladen phase, possibly an import; surface find.

Fig. 9.2 "Mushroom stand" fragment, red-slipped with fingernail incised ornament, Lopez Mamom complex.

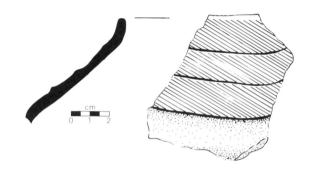

Fig. 9.3 Fine-paste gray ware, narrow-necked bowl or jar, with fugitive red pigment on upper portion of early Cocos Chicanel date.

comes from an incurving side bowl with a cream-slipped exterior, brown-slipped interior, and black-smudged rim band (Fig. 9.1). Although the slip texture and colors are within the range of variation exhibited in Bladen ceramics, the rim treatment and cream slip are reminiscent of early lowland Gulf Coast pottery (Coe and Diehl 1980: Fig. 156).

In the Lopez Mamom ceramic complex of the late Middle Formative there are four or five sherds from "mushroom stands" (Fig. 9.2), a form represented in the Joventud Group at Altar de Sacrificios (Adams 1971: Fig. 13D), and although they are probably of local manufacture at Cuello, their similarity to the Altar material may indicate contact continu-ing from that between the Bladen and late Xe or early Mamom spheres.

Similar minor suggestions of contact occur in the early part of the Cocos Chicanel complex, with pieces of a fine paste gray ware (Fig. 9.3) with fugitive red paint similar in form and decoration to material from Chalchuapa (Sharer 1978a: 134–5). By late in Cocos there are two sherds of local imitation

Fig. 9.4 Imitation Usulutan bowls with red-on-buff trickle decoration, of late Cocos Chicanel date.

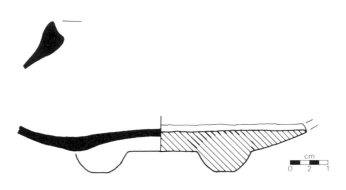

Fig. 9.5 Olocuitla Orange Usulutan bowl of highland origin, from a Cocos Chicanel mass burial.

Fig. 9.6 Three-pronged *incensario* fragment, of late Cocos Chicanel date.

Usulutan, with red wavy trickle lines on a buff ground (Fig. 9.4), similar to other lowland Maya imitations from Tikal (Culbert, personal communication 1981), Cerros (Robertson-Freidel 1980: 406–14), Colha (Adams and Valdez 1980: 21–3), Nohmul (Pring 1977a: 302–3), Barton Ramie (Gifford 1976: 116–9), and further north in the Yucatan Peninsula (Ball 1977: 48–52). There is also one vessel of genuine Usulutan resist ware, identified by Arthur Demarest (personal communication 1981) as Olocuitla Orange Usulutan; it is unfortunately fragmentary (Fig. 9.5) and thus of unknown form, although probably an incurving side bowl with four small nubbin supports, a dimpled concave base, and an unusual interior-thickened rim with the lip both grooved and beveled outwards. Although sherds from it were found all the way up from rubble (1195) of phase VA to burial [F128] in phase XI,

the vessel is believed originally to have been buried with the phase VA mass burial, and broken by the intrusion of [F128]; alternatively, it could have been interred with [F128] broken, and some of the sherds sifted down through the rubble. The temporal persistence of Olocuitla Orange polychrome is sufficiently long that either explanation is possible (Demarest and Sharer 1982). So far, this is the only indubitable trade piece at Cuello.

In other late Cocos deposits are a number of fragments of three-pronged *incensarios* (Fig. 9.6), a form identified by Borhegyi (1951) as being mainly of highland manufacture, although lowland copies are also known (Borhegyi 1959), from Uaxactun, San Jose, and Holmul.

The entire Formative sequence at Cuello is thus marked by the absence of identifiable ceramic trade items, except for the Usulutan vessel, although it is clear that the inhabitants were well aware of the ceramic styles produced in other areas. Ceramic contact throughout the lowlands, and between the lowland and highland zones, is likely to have occurred on a larger scale than is actually documented at Cuello, although imitation probably played at least as large a part as importation.

TRADE IN GROUND STONE
Norman Hammond

Apart from the roseate sandstone *mano* and *metate* fragments from Swasey phase contexts (Fig. 9.7) already noted in the discussion of ground-stone implements in Chapter 8, there were four granite *metate* fragments from Maya Mountains sources (SF 150, 520, 1202, 1934), the first two of pink granite, the second two of gray (possibly discolored). All were of turtleback form, the earliest (SF 1934) of Cocos date and two (SF 150, 1202) from superficial deposits and thus perhaps as late as the Classic period. A single gray vesicular lava *mano* fragment came from topsoil, and is almost certainly of Late Classic or even Postclassic date, given the known temporal distribution of this material (sometimes described as "andesite" or "basalt") in the Maya Lowlands. The only other

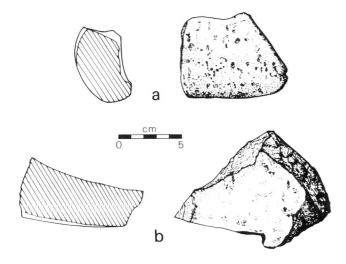

Fig. 9.7 *Mano* (a) and *metate* (b) fragments from Swasey phase deposits, both of roseate metamorphic sandstone from the Maya Mountains massif 150 km south of Cuello.

object (apart from obsidian) from the volcanic highlands of Guatemala was a loaf-shaped piece of pumice (SF 623) 58 mm long, perhaps used for grinding pigment on a miniature slab like SF 387; since pumice is found along the coast of Belize, brought down from the highlands by the Motagua and other rivers, the object itself could have been locally fabricated at Cuello. These exotics, 86 percent of Maya Mountains origin, constitute only 4 percent of the total grinding-tool inventory at Cuello.

Equally rare by comparison with locally made tools of similar function are imported small axes or celts, mostly made from a dark metamorphic greenstone that may come from the Maya Mountains but is more likely to originate in the northern highlands of Guatemala. Similar axes are abundant at Motagua valley sites such as Quirigua, and import along the same coastal route as Ixtepeque obsidian seems likely. Of the ten specimens, one (SF 1097) is from an early Bladen phase context, two others (SF 754, 1096) from Lopez contexts, and one (SF 1449) from the early Cocos Mass Burial 1. A fragment of ?inlay (or a chip from a fine axe: SF 811) is early Lopez in date. Three other greenstone axe fragments (SF 19, 168, 1178) came from superficial contexts, and three other axes (SF 1415, 1416, 1849) are of non-greenstone metamorphic or volcanic rocks. None of the Cuello greenstone specimens is complete (like the eight Cerros specimens: Garber 1989: 46), but the cross-sections and butt sizes of the measurable fragments suggest that none would have been over 15 cm in length, and most less than that. One similar celt of light gray polished stone from burial 33 of early Cocos date (SF 1415: see Robin 1989: 223) is complete at 92 mm. Given the abundance of chert and chalcedony biface axes at Cuello (Chapter 8) and the

availability of the raw material, these imports must have had an other than purely practical function.

OBSIDIAN TRADE

Norman Hammond

Obsidian is one of the most easily recognized and traced exotic materials found in lowland Maya sites; while in early excavations it was treated as relatively unimportant, and sometimes not even tabulated (Ricketson and Ricketson 1927: 187), a realization of its importance in reconstructing prehistoric trade patterns has resulted in precise quantification and elaborate analyses, as with the 3,670 pieces from Colha discussed by Dreiss (1988) in the most recent broad examination of Maya obsidian trade. While the complementary inland-riverine and coastal route networks proposed by Hammond (1972) and modified by Neivens *et al.* (1979: Figs. 1–5) and Hammond *et al.* (1984: Fig. 1) still seem to be valid, their synchronous and competing use for the distribution of El Chayal and Ixtepeque obsidian respectively can now be seen as an over-simple model operative, if ever, only for a short period in the Late Classic. Instead, a succession of sources has emerged as principal suppliers to the lowlands, beginning with the San Martin Jilotepeque (Rio Pixcaya) source in Middle Preclassic times, with El Chayal becoming dominant in the Late Preclassic through Late Classic periods, and Ixtepeque developing as the major Terminal Classic and Postclassic source of supply (Neivens *et al.* 1979; Nelson 1985; Dreiss 1988). All three major sources continued to operate throughout the Late Preclassic through Terminal Classic period, however, and the overall pattern of exchange seems to have been a complex one.

The Cuello obsidian forms a sample useful for studying the earlier end of this trade: a Bladen phase III specimen from the Rio Pixcaya source (SF 1899) is the earliest stratified obsidian in the Maya Lowlands to date, and has a hydration date of 1209–1047 B.C. (Mohlab 165–2019), the equivalent of a radiocarbon date of *c.* 980 b.c. Two obsidians from the 1976 excavations, from phase IVA and X contexts, were also sourced to Rio Pixcaya and have hydration dates of 1067–895 and 952–760 B.C. (JKW-302, 304), the equivalents of *c.* 880 and 740 b.c. in radiocarbon years. All three pieces were from secondary contexts, and the dates show how much upward mixing has occurred, something that must be considered when evaluating source attributions without hydration dates to calibrate them.

From the overall Cuello inventory of some 362 cores, flakes, bifaces, and blades, most of them fragments (Chapter 8), a sample of 102 pieces from the 1980 field season (94 percent of

Table 9.4 *Obsidian trade at Late Preclassic Cuello*

Sample size: 109		Ixtepeque	42 (38.5%)	
El Chayal	45 (41.3%)
Unsourced	22 (20.2%)

Settlement area sample, unphased:		38 (35%)	
Platform 34 sample, phased:		71 (65%)	
Phase XIV:			16 (15%)
Phases IVA–XIII:			55 (50%)

Phase no.	IX	EC	U	Total
XIV	6	9	1	16
XIII	2	2	1	5
XII	1	0	0	1
XI	3	2	2	7
X	0	1	2	3
IX	2	0	0	2
VIII	4	3	1	8
VII	2	1	2	5
VI	1	2	0	3
VA	8	4	5	17
V	2	1	0	3
IVA	1	0	0	1
Total: incl/XIV:	32 (45%)	25 (35%)	14 (20%)	71
w/o XIV:	26 (47%)	16 (24%)	13 (24%)	55

the total of 109) and seven from 1987 (100 percent) was selected for analysis, using proton-induced X-ray emission (PIXE). The analyses and comparison with source samples from Ixtepeque and El Chayal were carried out by Gene Hall at Rutgers University with the assistance of Eric Marshall. PIXE was intended as a low-cost rapid method of clustering artifact samples with one (or none) of the two major source obsidians; further analysis of uncharacterized or equivocal specimens using instrumental neutron activation analysis (INAA) is in progress. Further hydration dates are also being obtained.

Of the 109 Cuello samples, 22 (20.2 percent) were not sourced (Table 9.4); 42 (38.5 percent) were characterized to the Ixtepeque source and 45 (41.3 percent) to El Chayal including 11 to the San Jose Pinula outcrops at the southern end of the source area, which are distinguishable. The sample spans all periods from the end of the Middle Preclassic to the Late Classic, however, and 38 specimens (35 percent) came from the 1980 settlement area test excavations where chronological control was not as fine-grained as in the Platform 34 excavations.

The other 71 (65 percent) were from Platform 34 and could be phased, although 16 (15 percent) were attributed to the

very long phase XIV embracing the Early Classic construction of Structure 35 and subsequent sporadic occupation of the platform through the twelfth century A.D. This group comprised nine obsidians from the El Chayal source, six from Ixtepeque, and one from an unknown source (Table 9.4).

The remaining 55 obsidians, 50 percent of the analyzed sample, were from tightly stratified deposits in Platform 34 which ranged from phase IVA through phase XIII, or roughly 400 B.C. through A.D. 250 in date with each of the 11 phases averaging 60 years in length. Occurrence was fairly well spread through the period, with a mean of five samples per phase, although phase VA had the highest number of samples (n = 17) and phases IVA and XII the lowest (n = 1). Although the upward-mixing phenomenon noted above must be taken into account, the sealing of pre-phase V deposits by the construction of Platform 34 and the periodic reflooring of the plaza spanning the entire excavated area suggests that for this period it was not serious.

Sixteen (29 percent) of the 55 obsidians were attributed to the El Chayal source, 26 (47 percent) to Ixtepeque, and 13 (24 percent) to unknown sources. Thus the Ixtepeque source provided a third more of the Late Preclassic obsidians stratified in Platform 34 than the El Chayal source, although a quarter of the total came from sources other than those two dominant suppliers. As Table 9.4 shows, the plurality of Ixtepeque obsidians occurs through the entire period. If the phase XIV samples from Platform 34 are included there is little alteration in the Cuello proportions: Ixtepeque supplied 45 percent, El Chayal 35 percent, and other sources 20 percent, a relative ordering maintained even when the settlement area samples are factored in.

This pattern is strikingly different from the regional one for northern Belize at this period adduced by Dreiss (1988: 62) from a sample of 33 obsidians from six sites (26 being from Cerros and Colha) in which Ixtepeque supplied 21 percent, El Chayal 64 percent, and Rio Pixcaya 15 percent. A sample of unspecified size from the New River–Rio Hondo basins (Dreiss 1988: Fig. 10) yielded a Late Preclassic pattern of Ixtepeque 17 percent, El Chayal 66 percent, and Rio Pixcaya 17 percent.

The Cuello pattern of Ixtepeque dominance is not found in the Late Preclassic in any of the areas analyzed by Dreiss (1988: Figs. 10–18), although Colha and Kichpanha at this time have a 60:40 proportion of Ixtepeque to Rio Pixcaya obsidian with an absence of El Chayal material, and the Belize coastal sites achieve a 3.5:1 ratio of Ixtepeque to Chayal obsidian by the Late Classic, presaging a greater dominance in the Postclassic.

The size and stratified nature of the Cuello sample leads us to suggest that the regional pattern presented by Dreiss (1988: 62, 83–4) obscured sharp differences between different zones of northern Belize in their procurement pattern of obsidian.

JADE AND GREENSTONE TRADE

Norman Hammond

Some 110 objects of jade or jade-like greenstone – all apparently considered "jades" by their users and the latter designated "social jade" by Hammond, Aspinall, *et al.* (1977: 61) – were recovered in the Cuello excavations (Hammond 1980b). Colors ranged from bright through pale green and from green-blue to blue, many with light patches of albite or other minerals (Salati n.d.; this study also has Munsell color codes for jades). The vast majority were small oblate to spherical beads with biconical perforation, ranging in size from 3 mm to about 20 mm diameter and in weight from 0.1 to 10.4 gm (e.g. Fig. 9.8a–1). A number of others were tubular beads, also biconically perforated (e.g. Fig. 9.8, m, o, q), the largest of 31.26 gm.

A few were of irregular form. Among these were the claw-shaped pendant and the fragmentary pendant with a duck-billed head (see Hammond 1988: Fig. 9.30), both from burial 9 of terminal Bladen or early Mamom date, and the "spangle"-shaped pendant of blue jade-like stone from burial 114, of late Bladen date (Fig. 9.8n). These jades and a blue tubular bead from the late Bladen phase burial 116 [F219] (see Fig. 10.1), all dating to around 700–600 B.C., are the earliest at Cuello. Another blue bead with edge-perforation (Fig. 9.8p: SF 808) from a non-burial context may also be early. A fragment of a greenstone celtiform object (SF 1097) of early Bladen date, *c.* 900 B.C., is the earliest stratified "jade," but its mineralogical identity has not yet been ascertained.

Jades remain uncommon (n = 25) at the site through the Lopez Mamom period (phases IV–IVA), although burial 5 yielded two very small disk beads of bright green jade (see Hammond 1988: Fig. 9.30). A number of jades were chips or fragments of beads, apparently buried in that condition. There was no evidence for jade-working at Cuello, and we assume that all the objects were imported as finished pieces, although breakage may have occurred during use, or as part of ritual disposal (Garber 1983, 1989).

The first large group of jades are the 22 small beads in cache [F190], set into the patio floor of phase IVA immediately prior to the burial of the Lopez Mamom patio group under Platform 34; these were of many different sizes and colors, and clearly had been gathered together for the offering rather than being already assembled as a necklace or wristlet (although Bishop *et al.* (n.d.:21) note the presence of jades from different sources in a single necklace and in a mosaic mask from Altun Ha). In [F190], as in several other contexts, they were associated with a bead of red *Spondylus* shell, suggesting that the latter had a value to the Preclassic Maya more or less equal to that of jade.

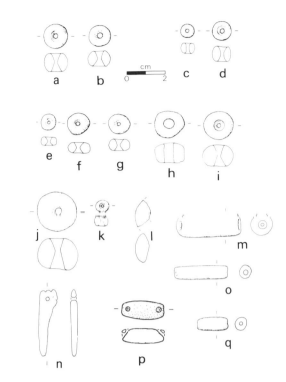

Fig. 9.8 Jade beads from burial and other contexts (a), (b) SF 1260, from cache [F131], phase XI; (c) SF 1161, phase XIII; (d) SF 1346, from Mass Burial 2, phase XI, (e), (f) SF 1265, from cache [F11], phase XIII, (g) SF 1303, from stela cache [F136], phase XI, (h) SF 1177, from cache [F113], phase XIV; (i) SF 1335; [j] SF 1348 and (k) SF 1357 from Mass Burial 2; (l) SF 1298, from cache [F133], phase XI; (m) SF 1045 (cylindrical), phase XIII; (n) SF 1203 (irregular), from burial 114, phase IIIA; (o) SF 1354 (cylindrical), from Mass Burial 2, phase XI; (b) SF 808 (ovoid, edge-perforated), phase IV; (q) SF 1353 (cylindrical), from burial 88, phase XI.

During the Late Preclassic (phases V–XIV) jades (n = ~70) were found offered singly or in pairs (these usually matching in color and texture: Salati n.d.), most often between lip-to-lip cache vessels. The largest collocation was in [F6], where the 92 vessels yielded some two dozen beads, while a total of 44 came from stratified contexts in the Main Trench, with eight or fewer per phase. The latest stratified jades came from the phase XIV skull burial in the top of Structure 35 [F18].

Source analysis

A sample of 46 jades was selected for compositional and structural characterization by the Maya Jade and Ceramics Project (Bishop *et al.* n.d.), along with similar samples from many other lowland Maya sites and geological sources of jadeitite in the Motagua valley. These sources included most of those analyzed by Hammond, Aspinall, *et al.* (1977), and

Table 9.5 *Analyzed jades by stratigraphic phase, with small finds, context and analytical laboratory reference numbers, and source group, if any*

Phase	SF no.	Context	Form	BNL no. (JA-)	Group
IIIA	1703	[F215]	Spangle	478	NG[1]
IV	C908	76/124	Bead	359	MG[2]
IV	C916	76/127	Bead	356	CH[3]
IV	C916	76/127	Bead	355	[CH]
IV	C933	76/137	Bead	059	NG
IV	C933	76/137	Bead	060	MG
IV/IVA	C992	76/247	Claw	049	NG
IV/IVA	C992	76/247	Duckbill	050	NG
IVA	C894	76/81	Bead	357	MG
IVA	1525-b	[F190]	Bead	476	MG
IVA	1525-c	[F190]	Bead	506	MG
IVA	1525-f	[F190]	Bead	473	NG
IVA	1525-h	[F190]	Bead frag.	474	MG
IVA	1525-j	[F190]	Bead	477	NG
IVA	1525-k	[F190]	Bead	509	NG
IVA	1525-m	[F190]	Bead	507	NG
IVA	1525-t	[F190]	Bead	508	NG
IVA	1525-w	[F190]	Frag.	475	NG
V	428	35/30(109)	Frag.	212	NG
V	429	35/30(109)	Frag.	220	NG
IXA	37	35/30(35)	Bead	171	NG
XIII	C844	[F124]	Frag.	358	
XIII	159	[F6]	Frag.	222	CR[4]
XIII	452-a	[F6]	Bead frag.	218	NG
XIII	452-b	[F6]	Bead frag.	292	NG
XIII	452-c	[F6]	Bead frag.	293	NG
XIII	452-d	[F6]	Bead frag.	309	NG
XIII	453	[F6]	Bead frag.	219	NJ[5]
XIII	454	[F6]	Bead frag.	211	NG
XIII	455	[F6]	Bead frag.	221	CR
XIII	456	[F6]	Bead frag.	213	CR
XIII	457	[F6]	Bead	166	NJ
XIII	459	[F6]	Bead	172	CR
XIII	460	[F6]	Bead frag.	169	CR
XIII	461	[F6]	Bead	176	CR
XIII	462	[F6]	Bead	163	ML[6]
XIII	463	[F6]	Bead frag.	215	[CR]
XIII	162	[F11]	Bead	174	NG
XIII	470	[F11]	Bead	224	MG
XIII	282	[F12]	Bead	168	NJ
XIII	283	[F12]	Bead	167	NJ
XIII/XIV	318	60/55(2)	Bead frag.	225	MG
XIV	465	[F18]	Bead frag.	226	NG
XIV	431	20/30(1)	Frag.	173	NG
LP	388	40/15(112)	Bead	170	NG
LP	332	30–40/0–15	Bead frag.	216	NG
LP	467	20/20–25/30	Bead frag.	214	ML
LP	504	50/15(82)	Bead	125	NJ

Note:

[1] Non-grouped specimens
[2] Maya Green Reference Group
[3] Chichén Green Reference Group
[4] Costa Rican Light Reference Group
[5] Non-jade greenstones
[6] Motagua Light Reference Group

Table 9.6 *Oxide concentrations for analyzed jadeitite specimens belonging to reference groups*

BNL no.	Na₂O pct	Sc₂O₃ ppm	Eu₂O₃ ppb	Lu₂O₃ ppb	Yb₂O₃ ppm	HfO₂ ppm	Cr₂O₃ ppm	Fe₂O₃ pct	CoO ppm
Motagua Light Reference Group									
JA163	12.7	0.62	74.8	37.4	0.207	0.81	16.7	0.776	5.45
JA214		1.14	61.0	52.8	0.242	1.79	92.3	1.679	7.46
Chichén Green Reference Group									
JA356		5.16	94.2	57.8	0.332	0.337	670.	1.330	6.27
Maya Green Reference Group									
JA060	11.3	4.30	0.106	61.4	0.444	0.154	< 0.173	1.05	5.44
JA224	11.4	3.39		93.3	0.575	0.485	0.079	1.48	7.82
JA225	11.8	2.22		84.3	0.619	0.349	0.061	1.22	6.24
JA357		7.48	< 0.131	109.9	0.583	0.311	0.235	1.30	5.73
JA359		1.98	< 0.118	64.6	0.393	0.212	0.057	1.12	5.40
JA474		3.12	0.149	116.9	0.547	0.317	0.072	1.23	7.35
JA476	11.3	5.05	0.206	139.0	0.766	0.661	< 0.111	1.51	10.09
JA506	10.9	2.95	0.154	95.3	0.755	0.321	0.65	1.18	8.20
Costa Rican Light Reference Group									
JA169	14.5	5.22	0.551	325.8	1.400	5.26	3.69	1.84	3.37
JA172	14.0	5.37	0.472	302.0	1.321	5.11	4.24	1.85	3.39
JA176	14.4	5.14	0.508	302.0	1.349	5.04	3.53	1.82	3.30
JA213 +	11.8	6.49	0.218	102.1	0.482	1.52	25.29	1.70	4.09
JA221 +	11.2	3.75	0.220	98.6	0.630	1.84	15.89	1.32	3.15
JA222 +	11.4	1.21	< 0.127	61.4	0.318	1.65	3.06	1.32	2.22
Non-grouped specimens									
JA049	6.6	2.78	184.9	60.4	0.383	0.45	728.	1.71	11.51
JA050	10.0	10.21	193.2	144.9	0.836	0.77	1180.	1.65	9.48
JA059	9.7	11.51	140.0	134.9	0.703	0.59	938.	1.52	10.69
JA164	12.8	0.61	52.4	26.6	0.131	0.36	16.	0.68	3.91
JA170	6.9	20.61	143.9	23.9	0.093	1.72	3532.	0.29	0.46
JA171	6.7	51.05	238.8	154.2	0.693	0.12	3828.	1.85	12.11
JA173	11.6	1.71	158.9	78.3	0.290	4.18	78.	0.43	2.40
JA174	12.9	0.25	17.3	15.3	0.069	1.10	27.	0.50	4.95
JA211		1.42	166.0	58.7	0.272	1.59	2.	1.42	2.30
JA212		8.04	34.0	22.3	0.023	0.37	1119.	0.79	0.79
JA215	11.9	5.57		29.1	0.229	2.45	10.	1.66	6.87
JA216		26.12	899.5	96.6	0.598	4.28	2291.	0.40	0.66
JA218	11.6	0.65	119.1	94.2	0.511	0.72	9.	1.36	7.69
JA220		22.08	487.5	74.8	0.339	1.00	1271.	0.40	0.37
JA226		3.57	77.4	38.0	0.209	0.38	154.	0.68	0.37
JA292	13.0	0.77	130.9	99.3	0.587	1.19	14.	1.38	8.26
JA293	10.9	0.86	138.0	121.1	0.671	0.72	15.	1.39	8.38
JA309		0.71	103.0	89.7	0.447	2.83	11.	1.26	7.00
JA355		1.78	92.9	67.9	0.371	0.63	143.	1.34	6.37
JA473	12.1	1.84	121.1	72.9	0.383	7.60	357.	1.21	8.36
JA475	13.9	2.83	28.2	23.7	0.117	0.24	349.	0.41	1.77
JA477	20.6	2.00	114.0	85.1	0.430	2.20	147.	1.39	7.67
JA507	12.4	1.83	89.5	65.8	0.357	26.79	50.	1.10	5.87
JA508	12.4	1.87	73.6	58.7	0.324	7.89	149.	1.14	6.17
JA509	10.6	13.30	115.1	90.8	0.455	0.74	652.	1.54	8.32

Table 9.7 *Analyzed jades in [F190] context 25/35 (1400) of phase IVA*

S.F. no.	BNL no. (JA-)	Form	Group
1525-b	476	Bead	MG
1525-c	506	Bead	MG
1525-f	473	Bead	NG
1525-h	474	Bead frag.	MG
1525-j	477	Bead	NG
1525-k	509	Bead	NG
1525-m	507	Bead	NG
1525-t	508	Bead	NG
1525-w	475	Frag.	NG

Table 9.8 *Analyzed jades in [F6], context 25/50 (2) of phase XIII*

S.F. no.	BNL no. (JA-)	Form	Group
159	222	Frag.	CR
452-a	218	Bead frag.	NG
452-b	292	Bead frag.	NG
452-c	293	Bead frag.	NG
452-d	309	Bead frag.	NG
453	219	Bead frag.	NJ
454	211	Bead frag.	NG
455	221	Bead frag.	CR
456	213	Bead frag.	CR
457	166	Bead	NJ
459	172	Bead	CR
460	169	Bead frag.	CR
461	176	Bead	CR
462	163	Bead	ML
463	215	Bead frag.	[CR]
464	164	Bead	NG

Bishop *et al.* also used Instrumental Neutron Activation Analysis (INNA) for trace-element analysis.

About one-third of the total sample of artifacts examined by Bishop *et al.* could be correlated with the Motagua valley source groups. Two of these were from Cuello (Late Preclassic: phase XIII), which together with one Late Preclassic "bib-head" pendant from the neighboring site of Nohmul were assigned to the "Motagua Light Reference Group"; this also contained two fragments from the Late Classic Terzuola workshop site in the Motagua valley, suggesting that the source was not far distant. Fifteen of the Cuello jades were placed in other reference groups which could not be correlated with known geological sources of jade: these are listed in Tables 9.5–9.6, and include one of the 34 members of the "Chichén Green Reference Group" (late Middle Preclassic: phase IV); also in this group are two fragments from the Terzuola workshop and four artifacts and one unworked jade rock sample from the site of San Agustin Acasaguastlan nearby.

Eight Cuello specimens (late Middle Preclassic: phase IV-2; phase IVA-4; terminal Late Preclassic phase XIII/XIV-2) fell into the "Maya Green Reference Group," which included artifacts from as far apart as Chichén Itzá and Monte Alto on the Pacific Coast, and which matched no source or workshop samples, although Bishop *et al.* (n.d.) remark on the relative homogeneity within the group and suggest that the same source was exploited from Preclassic through Postclassic times.

Six Cuello specimens (all terminal Late Preclassic: phase XIII) were in the "Costa Rican Light Reference Group," the majority of members of which came from Costa Rica, and none of which, again, matched any source material. Bishop *et al.* (n.d.:23) note that one Cuello specimen "is questionable, for it has the basic mineralogical components of the Motagua-focused specimens; it is included in the Costa Rican Light

group, however, based on its probability of membership in the group."

Twenty-five specimens from Cuello were ungrouped (the largest single category defined by Bishop *et al.*), although one (of phase IVA) was given a "probable" attribution to the Chichén Green group and another (of phase XIII) to the Costa Rican Light group. Finally, six of the analyzed Cuello specimens were not of jade, but of other greenstones with too low a sodium content to be considered part of the jadeite–albite system.

Several of the jade reference groups established by Bishop *et al.* were not represented in the Cuello sample, including Motagua Dark, Motagua Exceptional, Albite Light, Albite Dark, and Costa Rican Dark. Of these, the two albite groups contained mainly archaeological specimens from Honduras (although the light group was represented at Altun Ha in central Belize and also in the Motagua valley workshop sites), and the Costa Rican group consisted entirely of specimens from that country. Motagua Exceptional comprised only modern source specimens without archaeological correlates, but the Motagua Dark group included jades from Altun Ha, Cerros, Holmul, and Santa Rita in the eastern lowlands as well as from Copan, and also both source and workshop samples from the Motagua valley.

Nine (of 22) beads or fragments from the earliest jade cache [F190] were analyzed (Table 9.7): three fell into the Mayan Green group and six were ungrouped. Sixteen (of 24) beads or fragments from the latest major cache [F6] were also analyzed (Table 9.8); six were of the Costa Rican Light group, and one other probably of this group, one bead was from the Motagua Light group that could be correlated with known source material, six were of ungrouped jade, and the remaining two were of non-jade greenstones.

The Cuello jades are characteristic of the general pattern of source composition elucidated by Bishop *et al.*: only two are in the same reference group with known sources in the Motagua valley, and only three with the Terzuola workshop site there. Cuello artifacts fall into the same groups as those from Altun Ha, Cerros, Holmul, and Santa Rita Corozal, suggesting the same broad pattern of jade procurement over time, which Bishop *et al.* (1989) feel is essentially from the Motagua valley, but Cuello is unusual in having six specimens in the Costa Rican Light group (Cerros has two, also of Late Preclassic date).

Most of the 17 grouped Cuello jades are from Late Preclassic contexts: only six (including three from the [F190] cache and two others) in the Mayan Green group, and one from Structure 317 in the Chichén Green group came from late Middle Preclassic contexts. None of the earliest (phase IIIA) blue-green jades were selected for analysis by Bishop *et al.* for reasons that included size and irregular shape. Thus the sources of the Chichén Green and the Mayan Green compositional groups are the earliest documented at Cuello, *c.* 400 B.C., while neither the Motagua Light nor the Costa Rican Light groups appears there before *c.* A.D. 200. The non-jadeitite specimens are also of this late date, suggesting that "social jade" became more acceptable towards the end of the Late Preclassic period, perhaps as demand began to press upon supplies of real jadeite.

Chapter 10

RITUAL AND IDEOLOGY

BURIAL PRACTICES

Cynthia Robin and Norman Hammond

INTRODUCTION

A total of 142 individuals were excavated at Cuello, of which 124 date to the Preclassic period: 11 to the Swasey and Bladen phases, 1200–600 B.C.; 10 to the Lopez Mamom phase, 600–300 B.C.; and 103 to the Cocos Chicanel phase, 300 B.C.–A.D. 250, comprising the largest known sample of Preclassic lowland Maya burials (see p. xxi). The Cuello burials form an important primary and comparative source for the study of Preclassic Maya funerary practices and their underlying social implications (Robin 1989). The burial customs of a society provide an important basis for the study of social structure and the rôles played by individuals; behind this assertion is the assumption that the burial practices of a society are non-random and relate to the social structure and ideology of that society, reflecting or inverting various aspects of society, a notion supported by studies of Maya burials (Ricketson 1925; Ruz 1965, 1968; Rathje 1970; Welsh 1988; Robin 1989) and ethnohistoric sources (Tozzer 1941).

Since the present study focuses on the Preclassic community at Cuello the four burials dating to the Nuevo Tzakol phase, A.D. 250–600 (Robin 1989: 120–3 and Appendix A, burials 13, 14, 65, 67) and the 14 individuals excavated in 1980 as part of a settlement sampling program (see Chapter 6), none definitely of Preclassic date (Robin 1989: 16 and Appendix A, burials 129–142), are excluded from this analysis. The 124 Preclassic Cuello burials are examined here with a consideration of (1) patterning of the physical format of the burial and grave, e.g. skeletal position, azimuth, grave type, etc., and (2) the social, ritual, and ideological mechanisms that may underlie these patterns.

Early endeavors to relate Maya funerary patterns to social structure were greatly hindered by the lack of properly excavated and recorded burials (Ricketson 1925; Ruz 1965, 1968). At Cuello, a uniform burial record was implemented from 1978 onwards: a field sheet included data on location, relationship to important features or other burials, grave type, grave goods, skeletal position and orientation, comments on condition of the grave and the skeletal remains, the relative survival of various body parts, a tentative age and sex assessment, stratigraphic phasing, and references to relevant plans, photographs, and site-book pages (Spriggs and Van Bueren, 1984).

This information on the 124 Preclassic burials at Cuello, augmented by the Sauls' final skeletal assessments (see Chapter 7), provided the data set used here; previous studies by Gerhardt (1985, 1988), Pyburn and Kosakowsky (n.d.), and Truncer (n.d.) used preliminary age, sex, and phase assessments on different parts of the burial inventory, and are superseded by Robin (1989), where in Appendix A a complete catalogue of data sheets, burial plans, and illustrations of grave goods can be found. Terminology used in this chapter is defined by Robin (1989: Chapter 2).

EARLY MIDDLE PRECLASSIC BURIALS: SWASEY/
BLADEN PHASES, 900 + to 600 B.C.

Eleven individuals in ten graves date to the early Middle Formative Swasey and Bladen phases, of which only one (burial 62) is unequivocally of Swasey date (Chapter 3). Of the 11, four are male – three middle adults, and one young/middle adult; five are female – three young adults and two adults; one is possibly a female adult; and one is a juvenile aged 1–4 (Robin 1989: Tables 1–8).

The early Middle Formative saw the development of a predominantly domestic patio group at Cuello (phases II–IIIA) out of initial occupation on low platforms constructed directly on the old ground surface (phases I–IA). The platforms surrounding the Middle Formative patio are considered to have domestic functions, and the phase I–IA cobble surface and phase II–IIIA patio floors are pitted with clay, stone, and ceramic lined pits, which suggests that this area is the focus of domestic activity such as cooking and washing (Chapter 5; also Gerhardt 1985, 1988; Hammond and Gerhardt 1990).

Nine of the eleven early Middle Preclassic interments were in graves cut into house platform floors (Robin 1989: Table 1). These burials were placed in house platforms during initial construction, use, and at abandonment, indicating opportunistic placing of domestic burials and continued use of the platform afterwards. The remaining two interments were probably also domestic-linked burials, although placed outside the house platforms themselves. Adults of both sexes and juveniles were interred in Swasey/Bladen house platforms, indicative of family-type residential burials as Haviland (1985) demonstrated for small Classic period residential groups at Tikal. Nine of the ten Swasey/Bladen phase graves were simple and all contained male and female adults. Only one grave (burial 116) is a cist, and a haphazard one at that, containing a juvenile aged 2–4 (Fig. 10.1). This data suggests

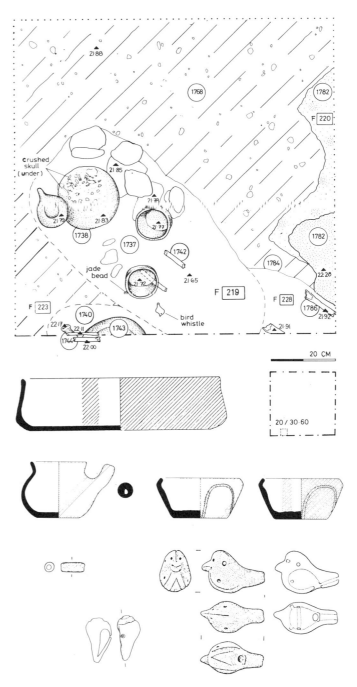

Fig. 10.1 Bladen phase burial 116 [F219], a 2–4-year-old child in a haphazard stone crypt in Structure 323 of phase III, accompanied by four pottery vessels, a marine shell pendant, a blue jade bead, and five-note ocarina in the shape of a bird. The vessels are drawn at one-half the scale of the other artifacts; ceramic types are, from top left: Chicago Orange: Nago Bank variety bowl, diameter 31 cm (inverted over skull); Chicago Orange: Nago Bank variety "chocolate pot"; two Cotton Tree incised: Cotton Tree variety bowls.

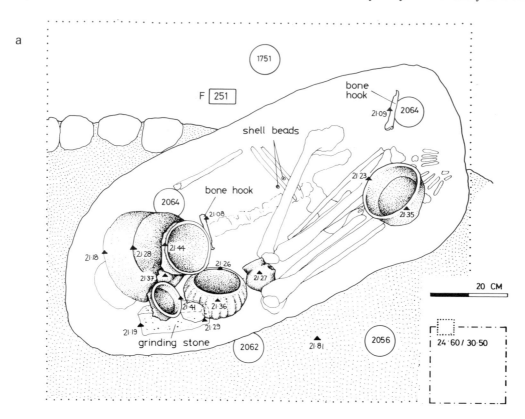

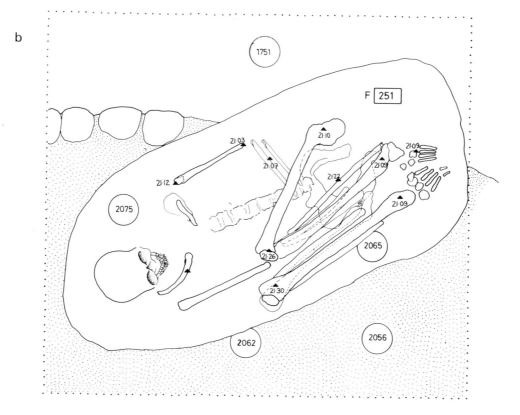

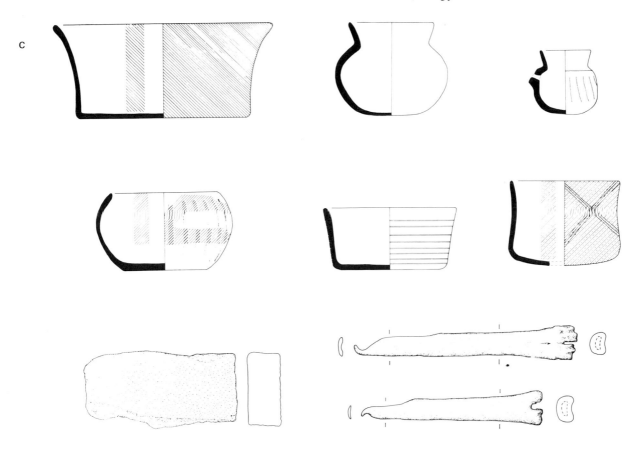

Fig. 10.2 Bladen phase: burial 123 [F251] in Structure 323 of phase IIIA, a young/middle adult male in a flexed supine position, with two deer-metapodial bone hooks perhaps used to fasten a shroud, a whetstone of exotic rock, six pottery vessels, and a shell-bead bracelet on the left wrist, (a) as excavated, (b) with grave goods removed, exposing skeleton, (c) grave goods. The vessels are drawn at one-half the scale of the other artifacts; ceramic types are, from top left, Consejo Red: Estrella variety bowl, diameter 29 cm (inverted over skull); Chicago Orange: Nago Bank variety jar; Copetilla Unslipped: Gallon Jug variety "chocolate pot"; Quamina Group: variety unspecified bowl with orange clouding on cream ground; two Cotton Tree Incised: Cotton Tree variety bowls.

that simple graves are the predominant grave type in the early Middle Preclassic, but shows that cists also occur.

Extended, flexed, seated, and disarticulated skeletal positions occur in the Swasey/Bladen phase (Robin 1989: Table 2). Among the extended and flexed burials, supine (3) is more common than lying on the left side (1). Extended (2) and flexed (3) positions are more common than seated (1). Male burial 9 is the only Middle Preclassic example at Cuello and other lowland Maya sites of the seated position. Even with the small sample size, this concurs with Ruz's (1968) findings that at Uaxactun in the Middle Preclassic both flexed and extended positions were the most common, without a preference for either one. There is no clear relationship between age

and sex or context and skeletal position in the sample of Swasey/Bladen individuals.

Five Swasey/Bladen phase interments have a known azimuth, with north, east, southeast, and west represented in the sample and no preference for any one direction and no association between age and sex, skeletal position, or location and azimuth (Robin 1989: Tables 3–4). None of the Swasey/Bladen phase residential platform burials are axial. In all cases the azimuth of the individual is the same as the axis of the grave (where grave cut is discernible), but which was the controlling factor cannot be determined from the archaeological evidence. No relationship between location and azimuth of a platform and that of burial is seen in the Swasey/Bladen phases.

Except for the Cocos Chicanel phase, the Swasey/Bladen phase grave good assemblage is the most diversified and least consistent at Cuello (Robin 1989: Tables 5–6). Types of grave goods found in the Swasey/Bladen phase are local pottery; a ceramic bird whistle (Fig. 10.1); jade beads (Fig. 10.1) and pendants; greenstone beads; shell rings, beads, pendants, necklaces/bracelets, and unprovenienced bead groups; bone hooked tools (Fig. 10.2); chert tools; and ground stone. The presence of jade and greenstone in the burial assemblage by the end of Bladen indicates the procurement of long-distance trade items for sumptuary use from as far as 350 km away in the Guatemalan highlands; a utilitarian long-distance trade item, a pink sandstone whetstone associated with male burial 123 (Fig. 10.2), was procured from about 150 km away in the Maya Mountains.

Only two of the eleven Swasey/Bladen interments had no grave goods: one was the female secondary burial (8), consisting of leg bones only, accompanying female burial 7 associated with four grave goods. The other is the female primary burial 120, whose grave was only partially excavated as it extended outside the excavation area: this could have had grave goods in the unexcavated portion.

Ceramic and shell objects were the only grave goods found frequently in the Swasey/Bladen phase grave goods assemblage. All other grave goods with the exceptions of jade, found thrice, and red ocher, found twice, occurred only once in the assemblage; no consistent age/sex association of grave goods is possible. Pottery vessels were the most common grave good in Swasey/Bladen phase burials: eight of the eleven individuals had them, six with two or more vessels, all locally made and associated with both sexes and the one juvenile (Figs. 10.1–10.2). For seven of the individuals the location of the vessels is known: six had one medium- to large-sized bowl inverted protecting the skull. This supports Ruz's (1965, 1968) and Welsh's (1988) conclusions that this was a prevalent association among the lowland Maya; its origins in the early Middle Formative are demonstrated by its high frequency in the Cuello Swasey/Bladen phase sample.

One other ceramic object, a five-toned bird ocarina, was associated with the juvenile burial 116 (Fig. 10.1). This is the only ocarina found in the Cuello burial assemblage, and its association with a juvenile supports the hypothesis of Ruz (1965, 1968) and Welsh (1988) that ceramic effigy whistles are found only with juvenile burials in the lowland Maya area. Shell objects were slightly more commonly associated with female adults (three of five) than male adults (one of four); the juvenile burial also contained a shell object.

Jade, a luxury long-distance trade item, was associated with one male, one female, and the one juvenile. One jade object associated with adult female burial 114 is of particular interest. It is a blue jade spangle pendant, one of few blue jades found at Cuello (Fig. 9.8n). The source for this blue jade is unknown but, as it resembles blue jade spangle pendants from La Venta, it is possible that it originated in the Gulf Coast/Isthmus of Tehuantepec region some 600 km to the west of Cuello (Hammond 1980b). Neither jade nor greenstone was found in the buccal cavity, noted by Landa as being a common practice among the contact-period Maya (Tozzer 1941: n.606) and found with some frequency in the Classic period also. The Cuello beads were placed on the body and most likely functioned as adornment.

Individuals of all ages and both sexes even in this small sample seem to have had access to both local and long-distance trade items. Where both local and non-local grave goods occurred in at least three different graves (i.e. ceramic vessels, shell ornaments, and jade ornaments) they are associated with both sexes and the one juvenile. Only when grave goods are unique, or in the case of red ocher occurring twice, are they unavoidably restricted in apparent age/sex association. This suggests that use of grave goods was eclectic and cut across age and sex boundaries in the Swasey/Bladen phase.

Contrary to Ruz's (1965, 1968) Preclassic sample, the early Middle Preclassic burials at Cuello were all fairly well furnished. Individuals in the Swasey/Bladen sample had a range of zero to nine grave goods, with about two-thirds (7/11) having three or more, but nobody having six. The four individuals having between seven and nine grave goods are a juvenile aged 1–4 (Fig. 10.1), a female adult, and two males – one middle adult and one young/middle adult (Fig. 10.2). These four individuals are also the only ones with long-distance trade items included in their graves. Thus, access to both many grave goods and long-distance trade items cut across age and sex boundaries. If generalizations on social structure could be based on eleven individuals, the distribution of grave goods in the Swasey/Bladen phase suggests some social differentiation not based on age or sex.

Of the 11 Swasey/Bladen phase individuals, only five had skulls which were adequately enough preserved for the presence or absence of cranial deformation to be determined (Robin 1989: Table 7). Of these five, only two individuals, burial 2, a female young adult, and burial 123, a male young/middle adult, definitely had normal skulls. Two female skulls exhibit unintentional types of cranial deformation due either to the use of a cradleboard in infancy or a tumpline to carry heavy loads. Only one skull of a male individual, burial 118, exhibits an intentional cranial deformation of the Tabular Oblique variety. He had two grave goods, supporting Romero's (1970) hypothesis that intentional cranial deformation is not linked to grave wealth and status, rather than the reverse. There are no examples of dental decoration in the Swasey/Bladen phase sample.

Though single primary inhumations (nine cases) are the norm in the early Middle Preclassic, two secondary mutilations in two females may indicate human sacrifice at Cuello beginning then (Robin 1989: Table 8). Burial 7, a female primary inhumation with four grave goods, was accompanied by a secondary mutilated female (burial 8) without grave goods and consisting of leg bones only, perhaps indicative of the "personal" sacrifice of one individual, a relative, child or slave, to honor/accompany another individual in death as observed by Landa (Tozzer 1941: 129–30).

Possible sacrifice by severe mutilation is also indicated by burial 2, cut into the third plaster floor of the western Structure 321, interpreted by Gerhardt (1985, 1988) as a

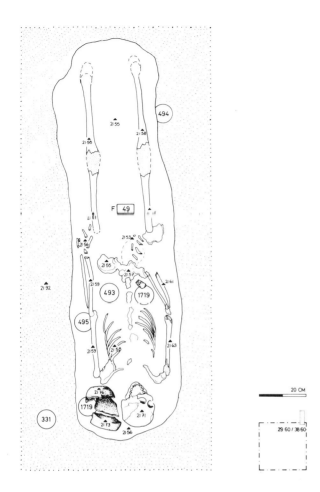

Fig. 10.3 Lopez phase: burial 22, a middle/old adult male of robust build interred in the center of the phase IV patio, perhaps as a focus of ancestor veneration.

house platform. Though not initial to this structure, it may be dedicatory to subsequent reconstruction and enlargement. If the secondary mutilations of burial 2 do indicate sacrifice, one must consider the possibility of a public/ceremonial function for Structure 321 as well as a domestic one (see below).

LATE MIDDLE PRECLASSIC BURIALS: LOPEZ MAMOM PHASE, 600–300 B.C.

Ten individuals in ten graves dated to the late Middle Preclassic Lopez phase, of which six were adults (four males, one female, and one of unknown sex) and four were juveniles (Robin 1989: Tables 9–15). Of the four males, one was a middle/old adult, one a middle adult, one a young adult, and one an adult of unknown age. The female was a young/middle adult, as was the individual of unknown sex. Three of the juveniles were aged 10–14 and one 5–9.

By Lopez times the patio floor was less the locus of domestic activity. Gerhardt (1985, 1988) compares the growth of the

Cuello patio group in the Lopez phase to that of Group B at Altar de Sacrificios in the Late San Felix phase (500–300 B.C.): Smith (1972) suggests a ceremonial function for Group B at this time. There are only two pits of postulated cooking or washing function cut into the earliest Lopez phase patio floor (IV). Burial 22, of a male middle-to-old adult (Fig. 10.3), located in the center of the patio, may be evidence of the use of the patio area for communal ritual activity in the form of ancestor veneration, a practice more common in the Late Preclassic at Cuello. The subsequent Patio Floor V contained no pits associated with domestic use: all domestic activity was relegated to ancillary platforms. Patio Floor V was cut by one jade cache [F190], though by no burials.

Eight of the ten Lopez phase interments were situated in houses or ancillary structures, one in an occupation surface associated with a domestic platform, and one, as noted above, was located in the center of the patio floor (Robin 1989: Table 9). As in the preceding Swasey/Bladen phases, adults of both sexes and juveniles were interred in domestic platforms. The predominant grave type (9/10) in the Lopez phase continued to be simple. Only one individual, a male middle adult buried in a house platform (burial 5) had a cist grave. Small sample size precludes correlation of grave type, age/sex, and grave good wealth.

Sixty percent (6/10) of the Lopez burials were extended; 50 percent (5/10) were supine (Robin 1989: Table 10). With the exception of burial 20, excavated only from the waist up and thus undetermined, all adult Lopez phase burials were extended. Males and unsexed individuals were supine and the one female individual was extended lying on her left side. Three of the juveniles had a known skeletal position: one was supine extended and two were flexed.

There seems to have been a preference for extended positions over flexed in the Lopez phase sample. The extended position, both supine and prone, was also predominant at Barton Ramie in the Middle and Late Preclassic (Willey et al. 1965: 531). However, at Uaxactun in the Mamom phase both extended and flexed burials occurred fairly equally and in the Chicanel phase the flexed position becomes predominant (Ruz 1965). There was no prevalent orientation in the Lopez phase burials: azimuths of north, east, southeast, south, southwest, and west occurred; no two individuals of the same sex or age had the same azimuth, supporting Ruz's conjectures of a lack of constraint on burial orientation in the Preclassic (Robin 1989: Tables 11–12). None of the Lopez phase residential platform burials was axial, and in all recorded cases the orientation of the skeleton was on the axis of the grave, as in the Swasey/Bladen phases.

The mortuary assemblage of the Lopez phase was sparser than that of Swasey/Bladen (Robin 1989: Tables 13–14). It included local pottery, jade beads, shell beads and necklaces/bracelets, chert and hematite. Jade was the only certain long-distance trade item found in Lopez mortuary contexts, since hematite nodules occur in lowland limestone.

Five individuals (burials 6, 108, and 124, apparently lacking grave goods, and burials 20 and 115, with three and five grave goods respectively), were only partially within excavation limits, and more grave goods may have been deposited than recovered. One must remember that many of the Lopez phase buildings lay only partially within the excavation when assessing the apparent decrease in total number and complexity of the Lopez phase mortuary assemblage compared to the preceding Swasey/Bladen phase assemblage.

Six out of the seven Lopez phase burials with grave goods, males, females, and juveniles, had pottery vessels, three of them with a bowl inverted over the skull. One of the three individuals lacking this association (burial 1) had a block of tabular chert replacing the missing head. All seven of the Lopez phase individuals with grave goods had some kind of shell ornament: shell beads were associated with males, juveniles, and the unsexed adult; shell bracelets/necklaces were found with males, females, and juveniles; and groups of shell beads with males and females. One shell bead was found in the mouth of burial 115.

Other grave goods, chert, hematite, and jade, were less common. Two jade beads were associated with males, a young and a middle adult, and were found only by the elbows or in association with shell jewelry. Individuals of all ages and both sexes had access to a range of local goods; only males had long-distance trade items (jade) but since there was only one female in the sample, this may not denote increased importance of males.

The number of grave goods associated with an individual ranged from zero to seven. There was greater differentiation in Lopez between individuals with and those without grave goods than in the Swasey/Bladen sample. Seventy percent of the Lopez phase burials had at least three grave goods, and the majority of those with grave goods had three to five items. The two males with five grave goods were the only individuals associated with long-distance trade items. The single secondary, possibly sacrificial burial (1) with seven grave goods, was unsexed and with no long-distance trade items. Though these burials were not on the whole as well and diversely furnished as the (Swasey)/Bladen phase ones, they do not conform to Ruz's picture of scarce and poor assemblages. Certainly pottery vessels were not lacking.

Of the nine Lopez phase burials with skulls, all males, only three were preserved adequately enough to determine cranial shaping: one young adult had a normal skull, one middle adult had unintentional lambdoidal flattening, and one middle/old adult had intentional Tabular shaping, of uncertain variety (Robin 1989: Table 15). There were no occurrences of dental decoration in the sample.

All ten Lopez phase interments were single inhumations,

nine primary; burial 1 lacked the skull, possible evidence of decapitation. It was interred in the western platform, Structure 317, and it is interesting that the only other Middle Formative single possible sacrificial burial also lay in this western structure. Functionally, this is considered a ceremonial platform in the Late Preclassic and Early Classic (Chapter 5): in Structure 352 (phases ?VI–IXA) a secondary/sacrificial adolescent burial was axially placed and in phase XIV a secondary juvenile skull-only burial was placed at the top midpoint of the final pyramid, Structure 35. Thus only secondary burials are known from the western platform throughout the Formative and Early Classic, while all other Middle Preclassic platforms contained only primary burials (except for secondary burial 8, considered a "personal" sacrifice for burial 7), although no great architectural distinctions are apparent between the western platforms and those on the other sides of the patio.

Adult secondary mutilated individuals, either single or multiple (but not in association with a primary individual), were found in public/ceremonial locations (i.e., ceremonial platforms, temples, household shrines, and plazas), at Mountain Cow, Baking Pot, Uaxactun, Altun Ha, Dzibilchaltun, Altar de Sacrificios, Seibal, Copan, and Tonina (Ricketson and Ricketson 1937; Smith 1950; Smith 1972; Andrews and Andrews 1980; Welsh 1988). This suggests a connection between secondary mutilated adults and public ritual sacrifice, though secondary mutilated adult burials have been found in residential contexts at Altun Ha and Dzibilchaltun (Andrews and Andrews 1980; Pendergast 1982).

LATE PRECLASSIC COCOS PHASE BURIALS: 300 B.C.– A.D. 250

The largest number of burials, 103 individuals comprising 82 percent of the total Cuello sample, date to the Cocos phase (Robin 1989: Tables 16–52). The large size of the sample and an excavation strategy exploring all Cocos phase contexts on Platform 34 suggest that it is representative of the population buried on Platform 34 in this period. As Platform 34 was the focus of the Late Preclassic ceremonial precinct at Cuello, the burial practices were perhaps most representative of those of the élite segment of the population.

Both sexes and all age groups from infancy to old age are represented in the Cocos phase sample. It is clear from Table 10.1 that the 48:1 ratio of men and women (44:1 if M?'s and F?'s are included) does not represent a normal population distribution, but a population where male individuals were non-randomly selected for.

CONTEXTS (Robin 1989: Tables 17–19).

Early in Cocos times (phase V) the Lopez patio group was buried by limestone rubble over a meter deep. A sacrificial mass burial (Mass Burial 1: burials 29–60; Robin 1989: Tables

Table 10.1 *Age/sex distribution of Cocos Chicanel skeletal population*

Age	Sex					
	Male	Male?	Female	Female?	?	Total
OA	1	—	—	—	—	1
MA	8	3	3	2	2	18
Y-MA	9	2	5	1	3	20
YA	18	6	2	—	2	28
A	12	3	—	1	4	20
15–19	—	—	—	—	1	1
Total adult	48	14	10	4	12	88
10–14					2	2
5–9					6	6
Birth–4					7	7
Total juvenile					15	15

44–5) of ~ 32 individuals was placed in a depression measuring approximately 5 m N/S by 4 m E/W located in the center top of the rubble fill (Fig. 10.4). In the center of this group the two main individuals (burials 50 and 51), both primary males, one young adult and one young/middle adult, were the first to be placed in the depression (Fig. 10.5). In their laps and by their feet lay body bundles of nine severely mutilated male young/middle adult individuals (burials 52–60). Vessel fragments were stuck between the disarticulated bones of this bone pile and the other body bundles of the mass burial in such a way that the bones must have been at least partly fleshed prior to burial. Around this central group were placed 21 more individuals: just to the south of the central group along the left side of burial 50 lay burial 37, a single primary adult of unknown sex. Further south lay a row of four more individuals: the double burial 39 and 40, both primary possibly male young adults; burial 32, a single primary possible male middle adult, and burial 33, a single primary male young/middle adult. To the southwest lay burial 34, a single primary male old adult, and beyond him burial 35, a single primary unsexed adult. To the west and at the feet of burials 50 and 51 lay a body bundle of three severely mutilated individuals (burials 47–49), all possible males, of which one was a young adult and two were young/middle adults. Further west lay a single primary unsexed young/middle adult and body bundle burials 41–44, which consisted of an upper layer of dismembered body parts and a lower layer of possibly partly articulated body parts.

To the north of the central individuals was a double burial (30 and 31) of a primary possible female adult and a secondary possible male adult, and a single primary burial (29) of a male young/middle adult. To the east lay a single primary burial

(38) of a male adult, and southeast a double burial (45–46) of two primary interments, one male young adult and one possible male middle adult. With the exception of burial 30, all sexable individuals in the mass burial were males, ranging in age from young adult to old adult; not all of them were necessarily members of the Cuello community. This holocaust marked the construction of Platform 34 and a change in architectural layout from the Middle Preclassic patio group to the broad open platform of the Late Preclassic.

Successive plaza floors were constructed on Platform 34 in phases VA to XIV, and in phase XI the plain Stela 1 was erected in the center of Plaza Floor VI above the locus of the mass burial (Figs. 5.22, 10.19–10.20). The erection of the stela is dated to 100 A.D. ± 50 on stratigraphic evidence (Hammond 1982a).

In phase XI another sacrificial mass burial [F128] (Mass Burial 2: burials 68–79; Robin 1989: Tables 46–47), containing 12 male individuals, was inserted into Plaza Floor VII directly above the earlier mass burial and east of Stela 1 (Fig. 10.6). Two single primary burials, a double secondary burial, and two body bundles, containing eight secondary interments, make up Mass Burial 2. The two body bundles resemble those of the earlier Mass Burial 1 both physically in their age range of young to middle adult, and in their location in the laps of the two central individuals.

In the uppermost layer of Mass Burial 2 is a double secondary burial containing two possible males; the younger, burial 68, only partly disarticulate, the older, burial 69, completely so and also incomplete, lying mostly to the east of burial 68. The grave goods lie around burial 68, possibly indicating that burial 69 is a sacrifice related to honoring burial 68, in addition to being part of the mass sacrifice (cf. burials 30–31 in Mass Burial 1). Only the two central individuals in Mass Burial 2 were primary. Their youth suggests that they, like the other members of this mass burial, were sacrificed.

Neither individuals nor grave goods were randomly dispersed within the mass burials, indicating that these mass burials were constructed in a meaningful, non-random way. In both cases two individuals were the first to be placed in the mass burial (Figs 10.5, 10.6c). These pairs were the central focus of each group, and in each case both central figures had human body bundles in their laps. The remaining interments were located around the central pair: in Mass Burial 1, single and double interments lay around the central figures, while in Mass Burial 2, the remaining interments lay vertically above them. Not only are the central pair the focus of each mass burial, they also possess the most grave goods: such patterning suggests that the two individuals were not just the physical focus of the group, but also its social focus. The exact significance of the mass burials is unknown, but they clearly played a major symbolic role in validating structural and

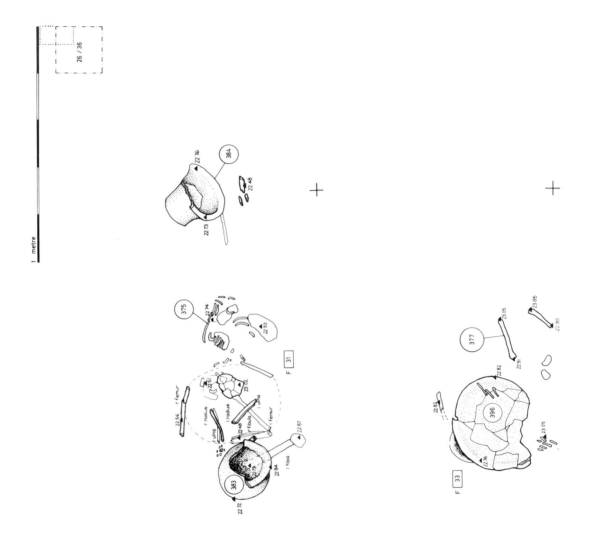

Fig. 10.4 Cocos phase: Mass Burial 1 of phase V (400–300 B.C), comprising some 32 individuals, mostly disarticulated and all except one probably male, deposited in the rubble fill of Platform 34. For ceramic grave goods, see Fig. 3.39; for the carved bones see Figs. 8.35–8.38.

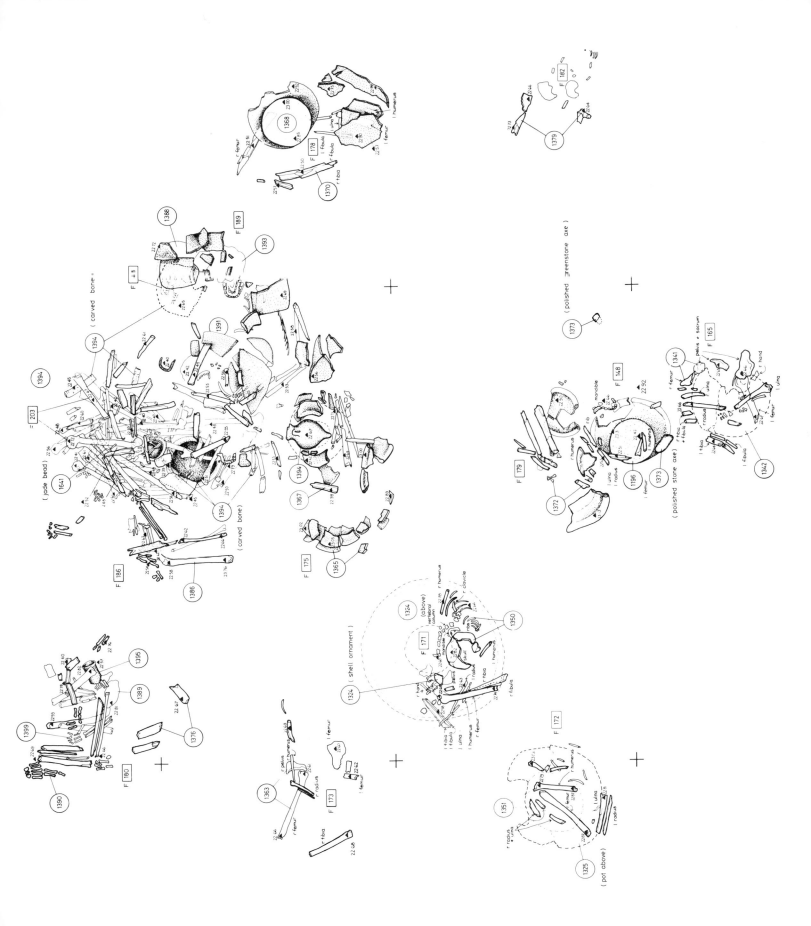

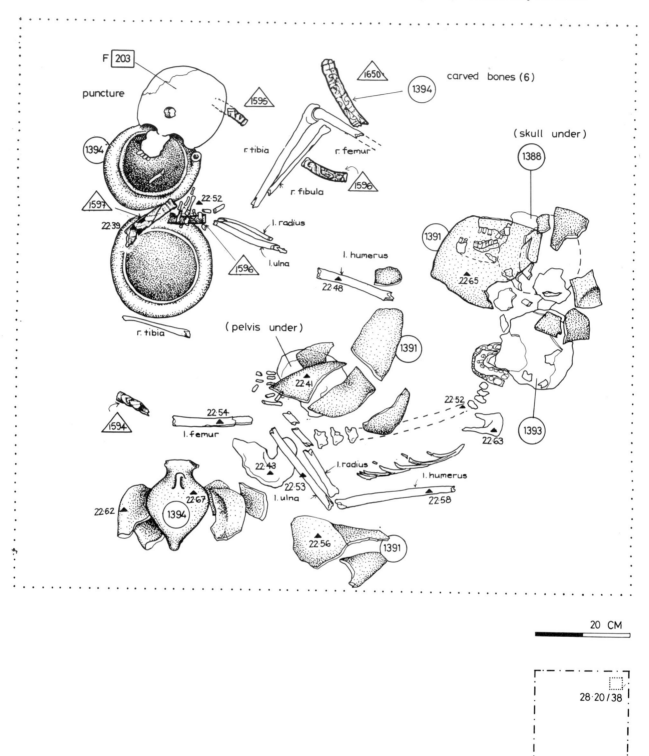

Fig. 10.5 Cocos phase: the central area of Mass Burial 1, showing the two primary individuals (1388, 1393) and their grave goods, including six carved bone tubes, four with the *pop* motif denoting rulership (see Fig. 8.36).

ideological changes in the function of Platform 34, and also perhaps the power of a ruling lineage or individual.

Seven other burials seem to have been sacrifices associated with the construction of Platform 34: three (burials 10–12) in the thick layer of recycled midden (context 69/109 and 4003) overlying the phase V rubble fill, and four in early extensions of the north side. Burials 10 and 12 were both decapitated young/middle adults, one male and one ?female, lying parallel to each other but on opposite orientations, their skulls and mandibles standing upright some little way from their natural position (Fig. 10.7); burial 11 consisted of the teeth of another individual accompanying the male burial 10. The four slightly later sacrifices comprised: burial 126 127 of two young children, one decapitated with a pot over the stump of the neck; burial 125, of a partly disarticulated young/middle adult male sprawled in construction fill, belonging to the first two northward extensions of Platform 34 in phase VA; and the young adult male burial 121, sprawled at the base of a north-facing wall probably of the second extension, and thus covered by the fill of its successor.

On the western side of the plaza in phases VI–XIV stood a succession of apparently ceremonial buildings of which the earliest, Structure 352, was a raised platform and the later ones stepped pyramids (Structures 351, 350, 35). An axial burial of an adolescent (Fig. 10.8: burial 27), decapitated and with scattered disarticulated ribs and upper vertebrae, possibly indicating sacrifice, was placed in the final phase of Structure 352, the first western ceremonial structure. This is the only burial in these western structures in the Cocos phase, an area where only secondary burials have been found throughout the Preclassic.

Only the buildings on the north side of the Late Preclassic plaza are known: those to the south and east, if any, are unexcavated and overall layout of the plaza group is not known. On the north side of the first plaza floor (phase V) stood a single house platform (Structure 312) spanning the width of the main excavation trench. In phases VI–XI two domestic (residential or ancillary) structures lay side by side in this location. Phases XII–XIV saw the incorporation of the two structures into one larger structure again (Chapters 3, 5).

Burials were placed in every Cocos phase residential platform except possibly the phase VI ancillary platform, Structure 311. This structure had only one construction phase and its surface did not survive: consequently, it is impossible to tell if any features, including burials, were originally cut from its surface. Thus, the evidence suggests that burials were placed in all residential structures and there were no special funerary structures (Robin 1989: Tables 17–18).

As in the Middle Preclassic burials were placed in initial, intermediate, and terminal platform layers, indicating continued opportunistic placement of domestic burials and use of structure after burial. This opportunistic placement of domestic burials contrasts with the purposeful placement of the two mass burials and the two ceremonial platform interments, burial 27 in Structure 352 and burial 17 in the apsidal platform [F19] just north of the pyramid. Burial 119, in the plaza floor, lies parallel to the front of ceremonial platform Structure 302.

It is clear that strikingly different populations were buried in the public plaza area and the residences on the northern edge of the plaza. If one considers only definitely sexed individuals, the ratios of males to females and adults to children are 28:0 and 47:0 in the public plaza area. In residential platforms (house and ancillary included) the ratio is 16:10 and 31:11. Males were selected for public burial, implying their importance in public activity (including sacrifice) in the Cocos phase. Within the residential sector the ratio of men to women to children suggests the same family-type burial grouping seen in the Middle Preclassic patio residences.

Similarly, the male:female ratio in each of the northern platforms considered separately is fairly equal (slightly favoring males in the northwestern platform), and juveniles were about one-third of the buried population in both northern platforms. This age/sex distribution clearly fits a family-type residential burial pattern for both of the northern platforms.

BURIAL FORMAT

Fifty-two graves (including the two large mass burial graves) contained the 103 Cocos phase interments (Robin 1989: Tables 19–20). The predominant grave type, 41/52 (80 percent), was still simple. Simple graves had single, double and triple, primary and secondary interments; also both mass burials were in simple graves. All ages and both sexes were in simple graves; six cist graves were found, with both sexes and one juvenile present, and four crypt graves. Two were simple crypts containing a possible male young adult (burial 17) and a male young adult (burial 119). The other two were plaster crypts: one contained a double burial (15 and 16) of two primary individuals, one female young/middle adult and one male middle adult; and the other held an adolescent aged 15 to 19 (burial 27). More elaborate types of graves do not seem to be sex-associated though they were more used for adult than juvenile burials. Seven were located in residential platforms, one was located in the plaza floor (just in front of ceremonial Structure 302) and both ceremonial structure graves were crypts. No association between grave wealth and grave type is apparent.

The predominance of simple graves and the occurrence of cist graves confirms Ruz's (1965, 1968) observations for this period, but he makes no mention of crypt graves in the Late Preclassic.

Extended, flexed, seated, semi-reclining, disarticulated, and skull-only positions occurred in the Cocos phase (Robin 1989: Tables 22–25). The seated position (Fig. 10.9) was the

a

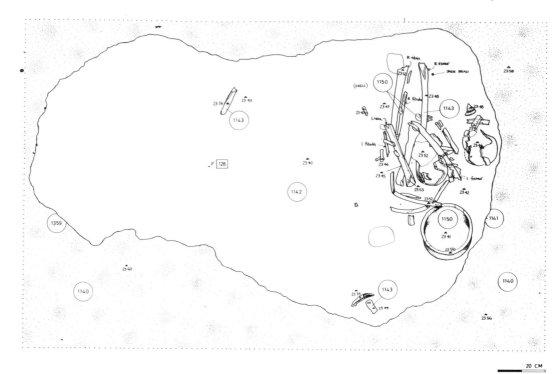

20 CM

b

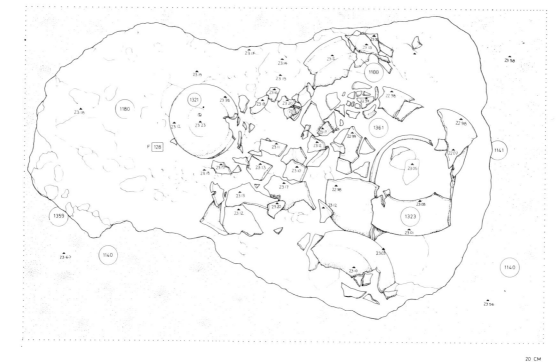

20 CM

28 20 / 37 20

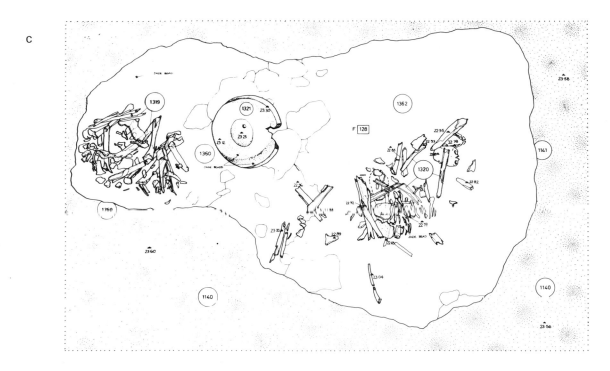

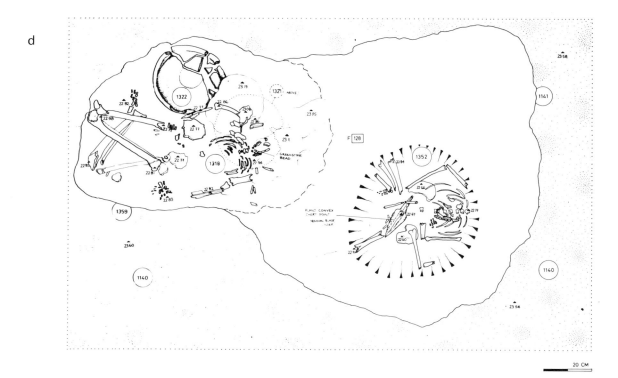

Fig. 10.6 Cocos phase: Mass Burial 2 of phase XI, containing remains of at least 12 male individuals (*c*. A.D. 100): (a) secondary burials 68 and 69 above the eastern primary burial; (b) pottery vessels smashed above the eastern primary burial; (c) secondary burials above the two primary interments; (d) primary burials 70 and 79 and their grave goods. For grave goods, see Fig. 3.42.

(b) pelvic area of burial 10, showing crossed and possibly tied hands

Fig. 10.7 Cocos phase: sacrificial burials 10 and 12 of phase VA, (a) burial 10: note location and orientation of skull

most common articulation (43 percent), while 28 percent of individuals were flexed (Fig. 10.10), 17 percent extended (Fig. 10.11) and 12 percent were semi-reclining. The fact that 31 percent (32 individuals) of all Cocos burials were disarticulated reflects on the large number of individuals (24) contained in body bundles in the two mass burials.

Males and females had a similar distribution of skeletal positions, both with extended, flexed, seated, and semi-reclining positions, and about two to three times as many occurrences of the most common, seated, position as the others. Juvenile burials were extended, flexed, or seated. The prevalence of the seated position among both sexes and all ages suggests that in the Cocos phase this hitherto rare position became standard, at least in the segment of the population buried in the Platform 34 residences.

Among extended and flexed burials the supine position was slightly the more common: nine were supine, four prone (Fig. 10.11), four were on their right side and six on their left. Complete disarticulation was exclusively associated with male adult burials in the Cocos phase: 42 percent of all male burials were disarticulated, reflecting the large numbers of males in sacrificial body bundles. Only three examples of completely disarticulated positions were found outside the public plaza locus. Otherwise, there is no apparent correlation between skeletal position and context and no specific association between skeletal position and grave type, although seated and semi-reclining burials were generally found in subcircular graves and extended and flexed burials in subrectangular graves, with the graves of flexed usually smaller than those of extended burials. Thus skeletal position reflects grave shape or vice versa.

Fifty-seven Cocos phase individuals had a known orientation: every cardinal and intercardinal direction is represented (Robin 1989: Tables 26–33). West (25 percent) had the most

(c) burial 12: note that the torso lies on the right side, while the skull stands upright. (Scales in cm).

occurrences but south and southeast (approximately 16 percent each) are not significantly different. There is no indication that any particular orientation was prevalent in the Cocos phase. Males lay just about evenly in every direction with slightly more oriented west. Females lay in every direction but east and juveniles to the north, southeast, south, and west with slightly more west orientations. An extended or flexed body followed the axis of the grave and there was no correlation between azimuth and grave type or skeletal position in the Cocos phase. None of the residential platform burials were axial and, as in the Middle Preclassic, no association between location or azimuth of a residential structure and skeletal azimuth existed.

Within the plaza, though every cardinal and intercardinal direction was represented except northwest, 54 percent (seven individuals) were oriented west. The correlation between plaza burials and a predominantly western or towards-the-pyramid orientation may also signify the importance of these burials in public/ceremonial rituals.

MORTUARY ASSEMBLAGE

The Cocos phase mortuary assemblage was the most diversified in the Preclassic phases at Cuello (Robin 1989: Tables 21, 34–40). Types of grave goods found in the Cocos phase include pottery vessels (one imported), ceramic ring (one), carved bone tubes (seven), jade beads (nine), greenstone beads (two), shell (beads, seven; pendants/ornaments, nine; bracelets/necklaces, three; groups of beads, two), obsidian blades (two), chert tool (one), ground stone metates (two), ? mica (or nacre) (one) and red ocher (two). Continuation of Middle Preclassic trade routes between Cuello and both the Guatemalan highlands and the Maya Mountains is illustrated by the presence of jade, greenstone, obsidian, metamorphic stone, and possibly mica. Contact between Cuello and the eastern Maya Highlands is illustrated by the presence of an Olocuitla Orange Usulutan tetrapod bowl (Fig. 9.5), the only imported vessel found at Cuello, in the burial assemblage. This type is dated by Demarest and Sharer (1982) to 400 B.C.–A.D. 100.

In the Middle Preclassic the mortuary assemblage did not differ from the domestic assemblage, and in the Late Preclassic also the absence of a specific mortuary assemblage is noted, although burials often included large examples of generally used vessel forms (Pyburn and Kosakowsky, n.d.). There were a few grave good types unique to mortuary contexts in the Cocos phase, including seven carved bone tubes (Figs. 8.35–8.38) which could have functioned as handles for feather fans or bloodletting implements, mica (or nacre), an Usulutan vessel, and an amphora-shaped jar of Society Hall Red: Society Hall variety. All were found in mass burial assemblages, where the body bundles of disarticulated remains might also be considered as "human grave goods."

Seventy-seven percent (61 individuals; body bundle individuals have been excluded from the grave good analysis) of the Cocos phase interments have grave goods. Sixty-nine percent (55 individuals) had at least one ceramic vessel and 23 percent (19 individuals) had some type of shell object. The remaining Cocos phase grave goods were only occasionally found. Pottery vessels were associated with adults of both sexes and all age groups. Within domestic contexts (houses and ancillary platforms) males (1.05) and females (1.09) had roughly the same mean number of pots per individual, and juveniles had a mean 0.73 pots. Males within public/ceremonial contexts had a higher mean number of pots than either males, females, or juveniles buried in other contexts at Cuello. Males within Mass Burial 1 had a mean of 3.00 pots per individual, those in Mass Burial 2 a mean 2.25 pots.

Vessels were either placed in the grave whole (Figs 10.9–10.10), or ritually smashed over the body; whole vessels were more common but 13 individuals, of both sexes and juveniles, had one or more smashed vessels. Ritual smashing of vessels was associated with both pairs of central individuals in the two mass burials (Fig. 10.6a), but was also found in household

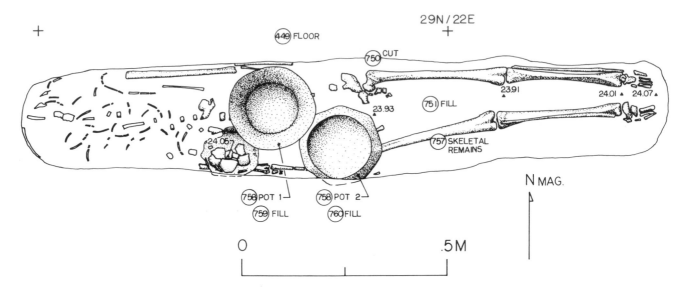

Fig. 10.8 Cocos phase: burial 27, a gracile adolescent interred, decapitated, below a plaster dome on the axis of Structure 352, a precursor of the western pyramid on Platform 34 dating to *c*. 200 B.C.

burials containing no other grave goods aside from the smashed pot. This suggests that the ritual smashing of ceramic vessels was a fairly common Cocos phase custom unrestricted by age, sex, or context.

As 55 Cocos individuals had ceramic grave goods, the pattern of placement of vessels around the body is well documented (Table 10.2). The pot (generally a bowl) over skull association seen in the Middle Preclassic remains the most common association: 64 percent (35 individuals) had at least one vessel, whole or smashed, inverted over their heads (or bodies). Thirty of them had bowls inverted over their heads, three have buckets (Fig. 10.9), one has a "chocolate pot," and another a jar. In addition, one individual had a bowl upright over the head, one a bowl and a bucket covering the back of the head and the face, and one had a bowl upright below the skull. It seems that bowls were selected for mortuary use to cover/protect the head or body of the deceased. Another vessel position, not found previously, was common in the Late Preclassic: 14 individuals (25 percent) had a vessel upright in their lap and two others had a bowl smashed/inverted in the lap. Several vessel types including bowls, ollas, buckets, and "chocolate pots," are found in the lap. The upright position of the vessel in the lap suggests its possible use as a food storage container. The pot-in-lap position was most commonly found with seated burials, perhaps explaining why it was not used until the Late Preclassic.

Shell objects were found with 19 individuals with no apparent correlation with age or sex although no definite

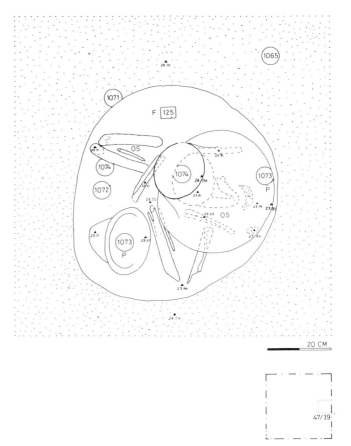

Fig. 10.9 Cocos phase: burial 66, a seated robust middle adult male with a bucket inverted over his head and a bowl in the right hand. A detailed drawing of the skeleton is shown opposite.

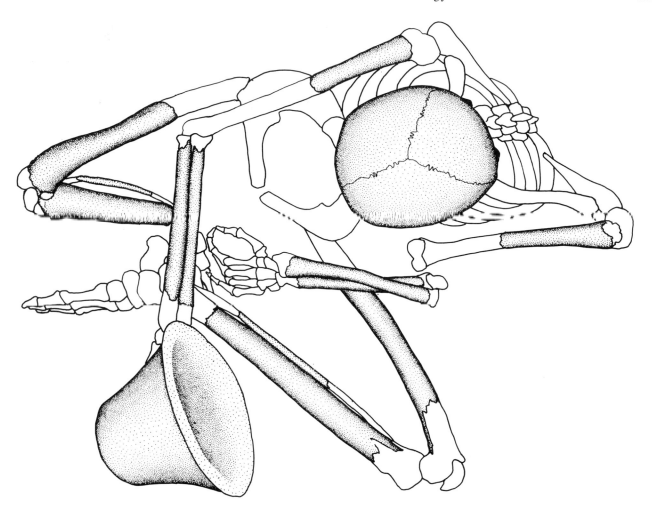

females were found with shell objects. Shell grave goods were found in both public and domestic burials. Three individuals had shell ornaments over the pelvic region; one is a male old adult and the others are juveniles, aged 1–4 and 5–9. The location of these objects suggests that they may have been pubic shields. A male young/middle adult had two single jade beads placed over his pelvis, and two male young adults with pot-in-lap arrangements had the pots inverted, which may indicate use as pubic shields, not as containers.

Long-distance trade items including both utilitarian (ground stone and obsidian) and luxury (jade, greenstone, and ?mica) items were found occasionally in Cocos burial contexts: 11 of the 17 long-distance trade items were found in one of the two mass burials and three with two individuals in a triple sacrifice (burials 10, 11, and 12) in phase V. The only long-distance trade items attributable to definite females and juveniles are found in residential burial contexts.

Jade was associated with adult male burials insofar as sex can be specified; only one (burial 70) had a jade bead placed in his mouth: all other jade beads were found around the body, suggesting their use as jewelry. The less valuable greenstone was associated with females and juveniles, suggesting that the Maya could distinguish real jade from "social jade" (Hammond, Aspinall et al. 1977).

Though all ages and sexes had access to long-distance trade items, they were much more commonly associated with public/ceremonial burials of males, certainly the case if one only considers definitely sexed individuals. In contrast to the Middle Preclassic, where access to long-distance trade items was associated with high overall total numbers of grave goods, in the Cocos phase, long-distance trade items were found with individuals possessing no other grave goods, as well as with those possessing many.

The total number of grave goods associated with an individual ranged from zero to ten; 23 percent of the Cocos phase individuals had no grave goods, 41 percent had one, 16 percent two, 9 percent three, and only a few had more than three; there is no age/sex correlation between simple presence

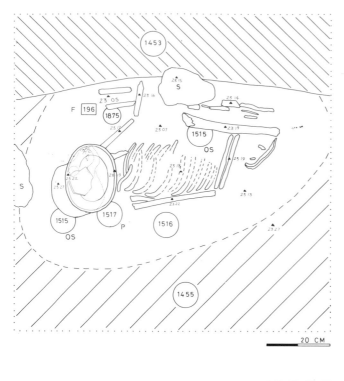

Fig. 10.10 Cocos phase: burial 104, a gracile young/middle adult male lying flexed on his left side and facing north. A medial-flanged bowl covered the skull.

or absence of grave goods. The mean number of grave goods per Cocos phase individual is 1.92: almost all the interments fall within two standard deviations of the mean.

Only five individuals, those with seven or more grave goods, fall beyond this: four (burials 50, 51, 70, and 10), were male, two young adults and two young/middle adults, and one was ?female (burial 30). She (?) is an anomalous case, not just because of the high number of grave goods – five pots, three marine shells, and a jade bead (the highest number of grave goods for a definite female is three), but in ?her inclusion in Mass Burial 1, an otherwise male burial locus. Burial 10 is also anomalous in terms of our analysis: his grave goods comprise merely eight beads, placed in separate locations on the body and thus listed as individual goods, but are far fewer in total number than the bead bracelets and necklaces found with other burials.

All five of these individuals were sacrificial burials, four from the mass burials, and one in a triple sacrifice in phase V. Thus, whether the grave goods of these individuals marked

individual wealth or the importance of the ritual activity in which they played a part is difficult to say, but certainly "wealth" in terms of total grave goods was concentrated in public/sacrificial burials in Cocos times.

In residential burial contexts 25 percent (eight individuals) had no grave goods and little variation in total number of grave goods (0–3: mean = 1.33) was observed among residential platform burials or between the two functional types, house and ancillary platforms (mean for house platform burials = 1.30, ancillary platform burials = 1.41); neither was there much differentiation in terms of grave goods between the northeastern and northwestern structures on Platform 34 (northeastern structure mean = 1.40, northwestern structure = 1.50). The same lack of age/sex differentiation in total number of grave goods observed in the Middle Preclassic continued into the Late Preclassic, in residential contexts: the mean number of grave goods per male was 1.14, per female 1.36, per adult, 1.28, and per juvenile 1.18.

Individuals buried in public contexts had significantly more grave goods than those buried in domestic contexts. The two mass burials (excluding body bundles) comprised nine males, five ?males, three unsexed adults and one ?female; they had a mean number of 3.10 grave goods per individual, much higher than the domestic burials, but even so 25 percent (five individuals) had no grave goods, roughly the same proportion as in domestic burials. Males within the mass burials had a mean number of 4.66 (3.13 including ?males) grave goods.

Twenty-three Cocos phase individuals had skulls which were adequately preserved for the presence or absence of cranial deformation to be noted (Robin 1989: Table 41). Eleven of these skulls were normal, eight had unintentional deformation, and four exhibited intentional deformation. Three of these had Tabular Erect shaping, two males and one ?female; one male exhibited Tabular shaping of uncertain variety.

The first examples of dental mutilation, in the form of filing, were in the Cocos phase, three male and one female; one male young adult had both cranial deformation and dental filing. As in the Middle Preclassic, individuals with such cultural modification had a range of grave goods, including none, but lacked high numbers of them. This supports Romero's (1970) and Smith's (1972) hypotheses that cranial deformation and dental filing are not linked to wealth and status, as does the fact that all individuals with intentionally shaped heads or dental decoration were interred in simple graves. One individual with unintentional lambdoidal flattening was in a cist grave, all other individuals with unintentionally shaped heads in simple graves. Small sample size precludes conclusions on the age/sex distribution of cranial shaping and dental decoration, but the absence of juveniles from the sample of intentionally modified skulls/teeth should be noted.

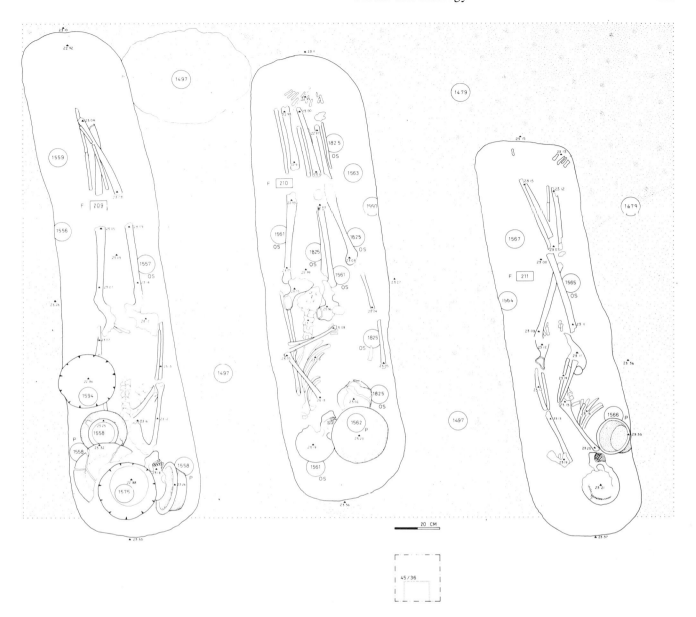

Fig. 10.11 Cocos phase: burials 110–113, three parallel graves containing prone extended interments, two males flanking a female accompanied by the fragmentary remains of a 10–14-year-old child. The graves lie within Structure 312, and appear to be coeval.

Of all Cocos phase interments 39 percent were secondary, including 42 percent of all males, no definite females, and 33 percent of all juveniles (Robin 1989: Tables 42–43). Whether there was any association between secondary interment and age among adult burials is impossible to tell because of the high number of secondary burials whose age could not be defined more precisely than adult (> 20 years), since the fragmentary nature of many secondary burials makes precise aging difficult. Four secondary interments occurred in

domestic contexts, but the majority of secondary burials came from non-residential contexts: there were 18 secondary interments in Mass Burial 1, with three body bundles containing nine, four, and three severely mutilated individuals each (Robin 1989: Table 44). Two other secondary interments in Mass Burial 1 were the skull and hand phalanges of a ?male middle adult, and the disarticulated leg bones of a ?male adult accompanying a ?female adult (burial 30). Whether this honored burial 30 in particular, or was just part of the mass burial is impossible to tell. Apart from the mass burials, 14 secondary burials are found in the Cocos phase exhibiting four types of mutilation: severed skull (or teeth fleshed from a skull), decapitated body, disarticulated complete body, and disarticulated leg bones only (Robin 1989: Tables 48–51).

Table 10.2 *Arrangement of ceramic vessels in Cocos Chicanel burials*

One vessel (35 cases)
1. Inverted over head or body (19 cases, 16 are bowls)
2. Upright in lap (8 cases)
3. Other:
   (a) upright by skull or over shoulders (3 cases)
   (b) beside body (3 cases)
   (c) under body (2 cases)

Two vessels (10 cases)
1. One inverted over skull and another upright in lap (4 cases)
2. One over skull or body and one by skull or over shoulder (3 cases)
3 Other:
   (a) both over skull
   (b) one over skull and the other by the feet
   (c) upright on stomach and upright on right side of lap area

Three vessels (6 cases)
1. On over skull and two in lap (2 cases)
2. Other:
   (a) one over body, one in lap, and one behind body
   (b) all over head or body (2 cases)
   (c) two covering back and front of skull, one upright over shoulder

Four vessels (1 case)
1. All over skull

Five vessels (2 cases)
1. All over body
2. Three over head, two in lap

Seven vessels (1 case)
1. Three over head, three beside body, and one in lap

Secondary mutilations indicative of human sacrifice were found, however, throughout the Cuello sequence: the earliest three instances date to the Bladen phase and one to Lopez. In the Bladen phase severe mutilation of a single body (two cases) and disarticulated leg bones accompanying a primary individual (one case) were noted: these mutilated femurs of a female accompanying the primary female suggest the sacrifice of the first individual for the "personal" honor of the second. In the other two cases, the severely mutilated individuals were single interments in residential platforms; if these mutilations do indeed indicate sacrifice, they may have been dedicatory sacrifices. In the Lopez phase one type of secondary mutilation was observed: the removal of the head. A male young adult buried in the western residential platform had his head replaced by a block of tabular chert. This may indicate ancestor veneration rather than human sacrifice, but the youth of this individual makes the latter more likely. If this muti-

lated burial and the Bladen mutilated burial, both in the western platform, were sacrificial, a public/ceremonial as well as residential function for this building as early as Bladen times must be considered possible.

In the Late Preclassic human sacrifice was exhibited in the number and condition of those interred in the mass burials, and also by four types of mutilation: severed skull, decapitated body, disarticulated complete body, and disarticulated leg bones only. Secondary mutilated skeletons were most common in public contexts, but three skull burials, perhaps dedicatory, in the northern residential structures indicate that these possibly had a public/ceremonial function sometimes as well as a domestic one.

All three instances (one Bladen and two Cocos phase) of double burial consist of a primary individual associated with disarticulated leg bones, suggesting that this sacrifice was made for the "personal" honor of the primary individual, who in each case was a female.

Severely mutilated individuals packaged into body bundles were unique to the mass burials. We suggest that they lost not only their physical identity as individuals, but their social identities as well, and can be interpreted as "human grave goods."

Although we cannot determine whether mutilation was the cause of death or part of post-mortem ritual, such secondary mutilated burials are our best evidence for Preclassic Maya human sacrifice, although sometimes the context of a primary burial will also indicate it. On the evidence to hand, individual sacrifice was practiced from the early Middle Formative onwards, persisting throughout the Cuello sequence, while mass sacrifice was introduced at the same time as monumental architectural construction begins to reflect the reality of political power at the beginning of the Late Preclassic around 400 B.C.

SOCIAL IMPLICATIONS OF PRECLASSIC BURIAL PRACTICES AT CUELLO
Throughout the Preclassic the inclusion of individuals of both sexes and juveniles in domestic platforms illustrates the family nature of these burials. Domestic burials show no age/sex differentiation of grave "wealth" in terms of type and number of grave goods or their absence. The association of juveniles with as many grave goods as adults could indicate hereditary wealth, or, equally likely, grave goods were personal equipment that did not function as "wealth." The presence of cranial deformation or dental mutilation is not correlated with burial locus or content.

Throughout the initial construction, use, reflooring, remodelling, and eventual abandonment or destruction of a building, burials were incorporated into its structural fills and floors, indicating opportunistic sepulture in residential contexts; often more than one burial was placed in a structure, contrasting with the contact period observation of Landa that a building was abandoned after the burial of an occupant (Tozzer 1941: 130):

They buried them inside or in the rear of their houses . . . Usually they abandoned the house and left it deserted after the burials, except when there were a great many persons in it, so that they with their society lost some of their fear which remained in them on account of the death.

In the Preclassic at Cuello the latter circumstance, of continued occupation, seems to have been the norm, although temporary abandonment is probably archaeologically undetectable (cf. Willey et al. 1965; Smith 1972). Though some Preclassic structures at Cuello lacked burials, none lay completely within the excavation, and unexcavated portions of these structures could hold burials. There is no evidence for specifically mortuary structures: those burials not in house platforms seem to have been dedicatory to ceremonial buildings at Cuello.

Mortuary assemblages were fairly consistent throughout the sequence, internally and in relation to refuse assemblages (Pyburn and Kosakowsky, n.d.); although some pottery types are known only from burials there is no indication that they were made only for sepulture, and where there was apparent selection, as for especially large dishes and bowls in some Cocos burials, there was also a clear practical function of protecting the corpse. Throughout the Preclassic at Cuello, ceramic vessels and shell objects, predominantly beads, were the most common grave goods. Jade was used from the end of the Bladen phase, and although obsidian occurred in refuse contexts at Cuello from Bladen onwards, it was not part of the mortuary assemblage until the Cocos phase. Chert tools were found throughout the Preclassic, bone tools only in Bladen burials, ground stone in both the Bladen and Cocos mortuary assemblages, and red ocher in Lopez and Cocos. The low frequency of many objects rather than true chronological differentiation probably causes this apparent association with certain time periods.

Throughout the Middle Preclassic (Swasey, Bladen, and Lopez phases) males, females, and juveniles were comparably furnished; in the Late Preclassic, residential burials continued to be so, but by this time the focus of elaborate burial activity had changed from the domestic/individual locus to the public/communal one. Males predominated in this activity, especially in the two sacrificial mass burials, with far "wealthier" grave assemblages and greater access to long-distance and unique items than either males or females and juveniles in residential burials. Whether this "wealth" represented individual lifetime possessions or the importance of the public burial rite is uncertain. The non-random patterning of grave goods in the mass burials suggests that the two central individuals in both mass burials were elaborately interred not

just as the foci of these mortuary rites, but also possibly as members of a perceived élite, either that of Cuello or that of the community from which the burial participants were drawn. If the former, the inclusion of the bone tubes with the *pop* motif suggests veneration of a ruling lineage; in either case, differentiation of nobility in death as in life. The mass burial of *c*. 400 B.C. is the earliest evidence of social ranking at Cuello, evidence corroborated by the architectural context of the interment. Such indications of developing social complexity accord with what is becoming known from other Preclassic Maya sites (Hammond 1986), although evidence from both Tikal (Laporte 1989: 298, Fig. 140) and Nakbe (Hansen n.d.) suggests that such processes were already in train at larger Maya centers during the latter part of the Middle Preclassic between 600 and 400 B.C. The overall burial record at Cuello demonstrates a peripheral community in which social differentiation and ranking were not present, or if present not reflected in mortuary ritual, at least until the Late Preclassic, and even then were only modestly celebrated.

OFFERTORY PRACTICES: CACHES

Norman Hammond and Juliette Cartwright Gerhardt

A total of 31 caches of deliberately deposited artifacts were found at Cuello, 26 of them in the Main Trench and pyramid excavations, four in Platform 34 outside the trench, and one in a residential group attached to the north side of the platform. Caches are generally differentiated from burials by the absence of skeletal remains, although three of the Cuello caches included detached skulls of children as part of the offering. All but one of the caches are definitely of the Late Preclassic phase at the site, and the exception [F190] is likely to fall at the very beginning of that period. All pottery vessels included in cache offerings are of the Cocos Chicanel ceramic complex, with the majority belonging to Sierra Red: Sierra variety and Society Hall Red: Society Hall variety, the two dominant ceramic types of the Late Formative. Most are flaring-side bowls, which when paired are set lip-to-lip.

The caches form three main groups: (1) dedicatory offerings for successive plaza floors on top of Platform 34; (2) dedicatory offerings for successive raisings of the buildings on the west side of the Platform 34 plaza, culminating in the Early Classic pyramid, Structure 35; (3) dedicatory and valedictory offerings for successive buildings on the north side of the plaza. The three exceptions to this are the earliest offering, [F190] of phase IVA, set into Patio Floor V but possibly linked to the infill of the patio and initial raising of Platform 34, with Plaza Floor I as its surface; the dedicatory cache of Stela 1 [F136], which is also connected with Plaza Floor VII of

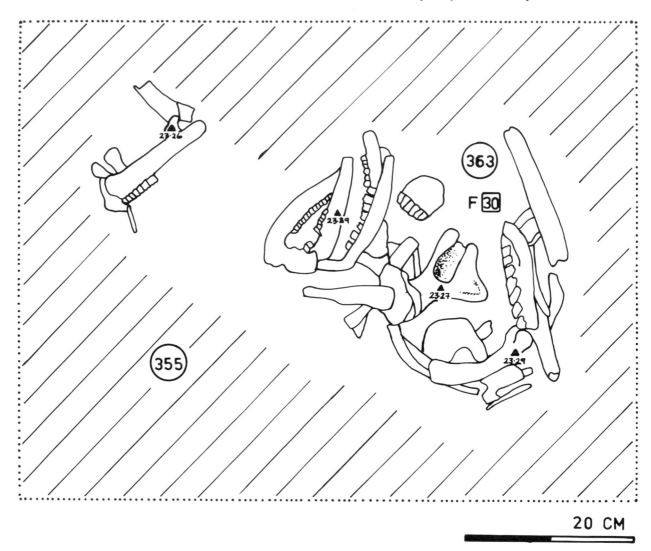

20 CM

Fig. 10.12 Cache [F30], one of two early Cocos offerings of deer jaws (and perhaps heads) in the center of the Platform 34 plaza.

phase XI; and [F5] below the patio floor of a plazuela group attached to Platform 34. Even the exceptional caches, therefore, seem to be associated with construction activity.

PLAZA FLOOR CACHES

The caches connected with the successive plaza floors of Platform 34 are varied in their context, but show a certain consistency in the artifacts offered, and an increase in the size and number of offerings through time. The earliest caches, associated with Plaza Floor III, consist of a pair of bowls set lip-to-lip [F181], and a concentration of deer (*Odocoileus virginianus*) mandibles [140] with a large tanged macroblade "dagger." The next oldest offering, [F30], is also a concentration of deer mandibles (Fig. 10.12), with upper molars and cranial fragments suggesting that entire heads may have been

offered, some two-thirds (20 out of a MNI of 30) of them juveniles (cf. Chapter 4; also Pohl 1983: 62–3), associated with Plaza Floor VI. Plaza Floor VII has three caches [F27, 131, 133], of a single bowl, a pair (containing two jade beads), and a pair plus a singleton, with one bead. Plaza Floor VIII has a single bowl.

Plaza Floor IX has three caches within the area of the Main Trench [F11, 122, 76/15], and eight others probably associated [F6, 12, 28, 47, 58, 60, 76, 83], although any one could be of an earlier phase. Two of those within the trench have multiple pairs of bowls, [F11] of three pairs running in a line north–south and [76/15] five pairs running east–west; each cache had two jade beads. The largest cache so far found [F6] (Figs. 10.13–14) contains 47 pairs of bowls, organized most often in groups of four pairs on a north–south alignment, with a total of 21 jade beads; [F12] has six pairs with three beads, running north–south (Fig. 10.15), [F28] three pairs and a singleton, [F83] four pairs, and the rest one pair. Thus a

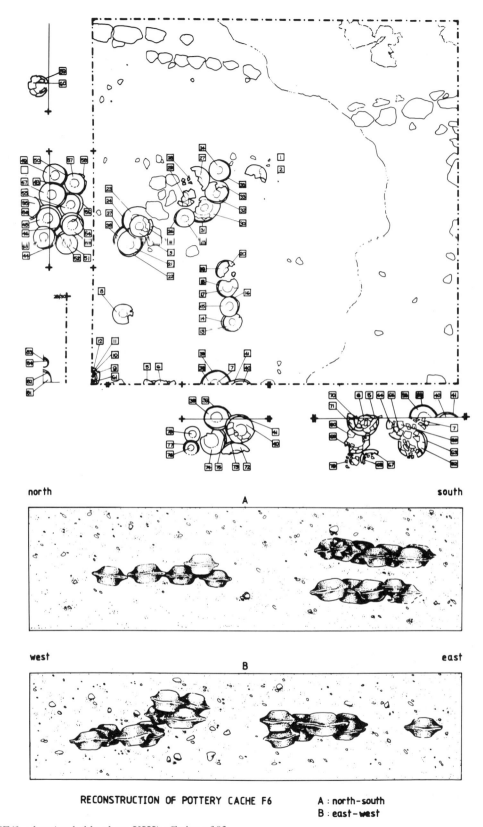

north   A   south

west   B   east

RECONSTRUCTION OF POTTERY CACHE F6   A : north-south
                                                B : east-west

Fig. 10.13 Cache [F6], a late (probably phase XIII) offering of 92
vessels in lip-to-lip pairs, set in clusters of up to eight pairs in the
5-m grid square 25/50. This 1978 plan shows the 84 vessels
recorded then; the remaining eight were found in 1979. North is at
the top of the diagram.

Fig. 10.14 Two clusters of vessels in [F6]: (a) the northern main cluster looking from vessels 21–22 northeast to vessels 33–34

(see Fig. 10.12); (b) the western cluster as first excavated in 1978, seen from the north: vessels 57–58 and 49–50 are in the foreground. (Scales in cm).

north–south orientation predominates where a group is linear: this may be facing the entire group towards (or away from) the pyramid on the west side of Platform 34. In addition seven of these caches have a north–south linear distribution (Fig. 10.16) along grid 50-52E, from [F83] on the north to [F60] in the south. Four caches, [F12], [F46], [F122], and (76/15), lie away from this alignment. The east–west orientation of (76/15) is parallel to, and equidistant between, Structures 302 and 303, while [F122] lies directly in front of Structure 302. The other two caches, [F12] and [F46], lie near the margins of Platform 34 and the former especially may be associated with a late reconstruction of the western retaining wall. Early in the history of Platform 34, two intact unused obsidian blades were thrust under the lowest course of its phase VI north retaining wall (4100); while not a formal cache, they seem likely to have constituted an offering.

[F190], a cluster of 24 jade beads and one *Spondylus* shell bead set into a plaster plug in Patio Floor V (phase IVA), with a central inner plug which may fill a small post hole originally holding a freestanding post in the patio, lies on the projected axis of Structure 316 and seems connected with its history (Fig. 3.8). The fact that it would probably have been disturbed if the patio had continued in use suggests that the cache was deposited as part of the phase V complex of rituals that included the stripping of the façade and burning of the superstructure of Structure 316, and the infilling of the patio with a mass of rubble, followed by deposition of the mass burial. The cache [F190] could be seen as both valedictory to Structure 316, and dedicatory to the beginning of the construction of Platform 34 over the courtyard group. Similar behavior may be indicated by the scatter of jade beads (76/127) in the scar left by the demolished front step of Structure 317 midway through phase IVA when it was replaced by Structure 314 (Figs 3.8–3.9). These two examples of termination, or combined termination–dedication rituals, contain only complete jade beads, in contrast to the smashed jades found marking such rituals in the Late Preclassic at Cerros (Garber 1989: 47–50): the practice of smashing jades as the buildings they were deposited in were themselves smashed may be an innovation of Late Preclassic times.

Fig. 10.15 Cache [F12] from the north. (Scale in cm).

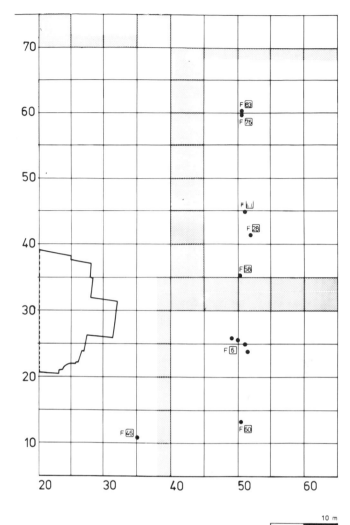

Fig. 10.16 Caches found in superficial levels (probably phase XIII) of Platform 34 outside the Main Trench: the seven offerings south from [F83] to [F60] form a line in front of and more or less at right angles to the pyramid.

PYRAMID CACHES

Five caches lie in the succession of buildings on the west side of Platform 34. The earliest [F80] is associated with Structure 352 (phase VI–VII), and consists of four chert macroblade "daggers," all unworn and of honey-colored/banded chert of the kind utilized at the Colha factory site 27 km to the southeast, and two stingray spines, all bundled together as though once wrapped, together with a very worn small igneous/metamorphic dark greenstone (?chloromelanite) axe (Fig. 10.17). All except the axe could have been used in bloodletting. It may be significant that Structure 352 is the first of the succession of west side buildings to be raised to any marked degree (Chapter 5), and possibly the first ceremonial rather than residential structure at that locus.

The succeeding Structure 351 (phase VIII?–XII), the first building of pyramid form, had two caches [F71, 100], each of a single bowl, and the succeeding Structure 350 (phase XIII) an offering [F57] of two unmatched bowls. The final pyramid, the Early Classic Structure 35, had an offering [F18] in its summit (Fig 10.18) of a ring-based bowl inverted over a child's skull, with two jade beads in the buccal cavity.

NORTH SIDE STRUCTURE CACHES

Eight caches below floors were found in the successive subcircular and subrectangular buildings on the north side of the plaza (Chapter 5), with none earlier than phase VIII. In that phase both Structures 306 and 308 had single-bowl caches [F177, 191]. In phase IX, Structure 307, succeeding 308, had a pair of bowls [F163] enclosing a child's skull, and Structure 305, which overlay 307 in phase XI, had a similar dedicatory offering [F143] of a child's skull under a single inverted bowl, as well as two valedictory caches, [F111] of a single bowl and [F162] of a pair of bowls containing a jade bead. Also in phase XI, Structure 304, built over 306, had a dedicatory offering [F259] of a pair of bowls. The latest cache

+
31N / 20E

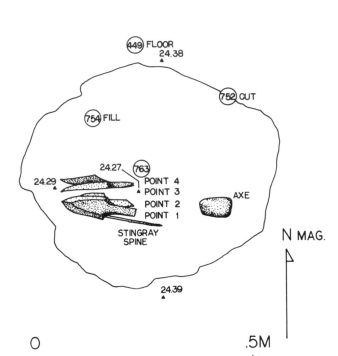

Fig. 10.17 Cache [F80], placed in a cavity dug into floor (449) as an offering prior to the construction of the final phase of Structure 352 above it. Four freshly made chert "daggers" and two stingray spines are bundled together, and a heavily worn axe blade lies to the east.

Fig. 10.18 Cache [F18] at the summit of Structure 35, a ring-based bowl inverted over a child's skull. (Scale in cm).

building (not fragments of Plaza Floor VI) and an apparently shaped piece of limestone. The stone and plaster could be considered debris used as fill rather than explicit cache items; the disposition of the items can be seen in Fig. 10.19, and the plain stela is shown in Fig. 10.20.

DISCUSSION

Absent from all these caches are any contents that the vessels might have held, apart from three with child skulls and those with jade beads. The provision of bloodletting equipment in [F80] reminds us that bloody paper could have been among these perishable offerings, as well as the foodstuffs often suggested. The parity of content between dedicatory offerings in the west side buildings, which are in form ceremonial, and those on the north side, suggests that the latter also might have had a ritual function, even though they were clearly lived in.

The mass of plaza floor caches shows that reflooring Platform 34 was not just a practical affair, but one accompanied by ceremony and offerings. While [F6] with its 94 vessels is among the larger Maya caches known, the vessels themselves and their imperishable contents were, like the grave goods found with the burials, modest in kind. The only vessels that might be seen as made for offertory purposes, being distinct from those found in middens, were those in the cache [F136] below Stela 1. Of the few non-ceramic offerings, the most unusual are the two collocations of deer mandibles [F30, 140]. This part of the animal does not carry much meat, so that they are unlikely to be the remnants of a ceremonial meal. Wing (Chapter 4) believes that the upper molars and cranial fragments present may indicate that complete heads were originally buried; the high proportion of juveniles (20 of MNI 30) in [F30] suggests selection. The significance of ritual faunas such as these deer-head offerings has been discussed by Pohl (1983).

The number of caches is low early in the Late Formative

in this part of the site, [F213], could have been dedicatory to either the structure capped by floor (1273) (phase XII) or to the overlying Structure 303 (phase XIII); its location in the north section and the erosion of (1273) above it made distinction between these alternatives impossible. One unusual offering consisted of a spindle-shaped limestone hammerstone (Fig. 8.2), a chalcedony flake, and a Colha-type chert tranchet-bit tool.

STELA CACHE

The Late Preclassic Stela 1 at Cuello has been fully published (Hammond 1982a), with an estimated date of A.D. 100. It was erected in phase XI and sealed by Plaza Floor VII; in the pit cut into Plaza Floor VI to receive the stela butt an offering of three vessels (Fig. 3.43) was made, including a trichrome open bowl, a monochrome red high-necked bowl, and an inverted bowl with a parrot effigy modeled over it. The cache also included a jade bead, a fragment of iron ore, possibly magnetite, five fragments of architectural plaster detached from a

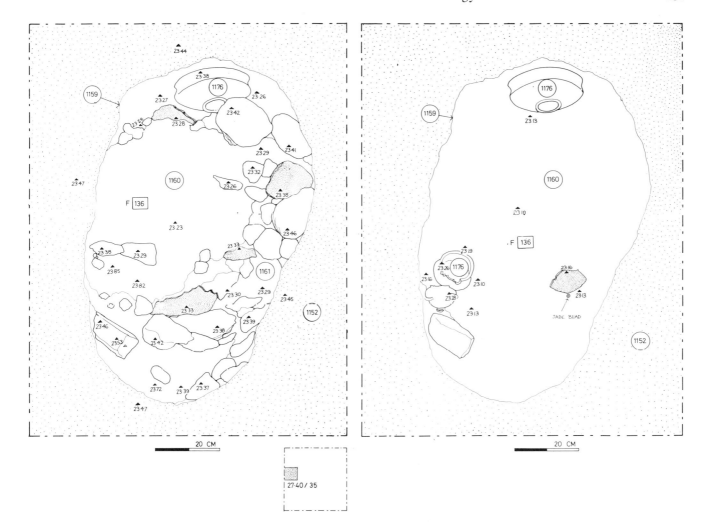

Fig. 10.19 Cache [F136] accompanying the erection of Stela 1: (a) after removal of the stela, exposing four pieces of plaster and one vessel at the north end of the pit; (b) after removal of the packing stones, showing the two other vessels and a (?) shaped stone in the southwest corner of the pit, and the jade bead with a fifth plaster fragment on the east.

(one to three per phase up to phase X, except for possibly four in phase VIII), rising to a maximum of eight in phase XI and with two to five in phase XII, four to five in XIII and two in phase XIV. This increase in offertory activity correlates with the move to ceremonial function of the buildings on the west side of the plaza, and with the erection of Stela 1 and then Structure 302 in the plaza center. The laying of Plaza Floor VII in phase XI, accompanied by the stela erection, the mass burial [F128], and the alignment of Structures 304–305 on a common front, as well as the high number of caches, suggests that a significant increase in the ritual status of the plaza took place in phase XI, c. A.D. 100, and was maintained through subsequent periods of use.

ART AND ICONOGRAPHY

Norman Hammond

The major media of Classic Maya art are free-standing stone sculpture in the forms of stelae and altars, and architectural sculpture in stone and stucco on public buildings. Both formats were used for the display of dynastic imagery and inscriptions, and were augmented at some sites by other media such as wood sculpture. While the earliest firmly dated lowland Maya monument is still Tikal Stela 29 at A.D. 292, the tiny "Hauberg" stela, looted from an unknown site, has been assigned an hieroglyphic date equivalent to A.D. 197 by Schele *et al.* (1990). Stelae appear at El Mirador towards the end of the Preclassic, but without firm dates; the small Altar 1 from Polol and a newly discovered stela at Nakbe both seem to be of mid-second century A.D. date, by comparison with Abaj Takalik Stela 5 of A.D. 126. Cuello Stela 1 dates, on archaeological grounds, to about A.D. 100 (Hammond 1982a) but is plain: its principal utility in the study of Preclassic Maya ideology is to show that the erection of the *te-tun* "stone tree"

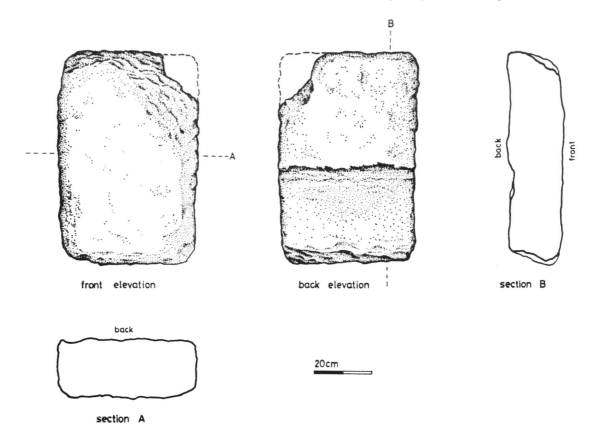

front elevation

back elevation

section B

back

section A

20cm

Fig. 10.20 Cuello Stela 1.

as a marker, presumably of time (Justeson and Mathews 1983), precedes its adoption as a vehicle for dynastic imagery and history.

In the Late Preclassic, architectural sculpture is known from around the second century B.C. onwards at El Mirador (Matheny 1986), the later second and first centuries B.C. at Tikal (Coe 1965) and Cerros (Robertson and Freidel 1986), and rather later at Lamanai (Pendergast 1981), Uaxactun (Ricketson and Ricketson 1937; Valdés 1986), and probably Kohunlich, in the form of giant masks flanking pyramid stairs. These masks were often painted in polychrome, red and black on a cream ground being the usual palette, and mural painting of the period from 100 B.C. to A.D. 150 is also known at Tikal (Coe 1965: Figs. 9, 12–13).

While Cuello lacks both carved stelae and architectural sculpture, the stair risers of Structure 350 retained traces of painted designs in black with red infill, over the cream plaster base (Fig. 10.21). The designs, though much eroded, seem to have been bilaterally symmetrical, with a set of concentric whorls at each side which may be the eyes of a supernatural face. The baluster edge of each riser was also marked in red, as

was the base of the wall of the superstructure on top of Structure 350; this had stone walls one course thick (~ 20 cm), of which only a scar on the floor plaster remained after demolition for the building of Structure 35, and cannot have supported more than a thatched or flat pole-and-plaster roof (Fig. 5.28).

The major arts (Clancy 1985: 58) are otherwise absent from Cuello, and our knowledge of the iconography of the Preclassic community comes from the minor arts of modeled clay, pottery vessels, and carved stone, bone, and shell, many items of which were clearly personal adornments. Among the objects in these media there is, moreover, relatively little decoration or imagery, but certain trends can be discerned.

SWASEY AND BLADEN PHASES

The Swasey phase has few decorated vessels, apart from pattern-burnishing on a few unslipped ?bottles (Fig. 3.29) and circumferential lines below the rim on pottery bowls. In modeled clay there is one example of a human effigy, of which the arm and hand modeled on to a tubular torso survive (Fig. 8.18a) from the tenth century B.C. A greater range of life forms appears in Bladen after 900 B.C. and these are the first naturalistic images at Cuello: they include human figurines, some apparently quite large and with stylistic parallels to

0   10   20 CM

Fig. 10.21 Polychrome painting on stair riser of Structure 350: color conventions as in Fig 3.25.

coeval figures in the highlands (Fig. 8.18b: compare Dahlin (1978) Fig. 2*b*2), and carefully observed but stylized birds, such as the ocarina from burial 116 (Fig. 10.1). Human and bird images are combined (although the former is missing) in the helmeted figurine in Fig. 8.20. Abstract designs in the Bladen phase include the first roller stamps (Fig. 8.23a), while cross-hatched incision and dichrome red-on-cream patterning (Fig. 3.32) appear on pottery bowls; more complex treatments including organic resist decoration are of final Bladen or even Lopez date (Fig. 3.33). Bladen phase jades include several irregular forms, including the spangle-shaped pendant of blue jade from burial 114 (Fig. 9.8n) and the claw-shaped and bird-head jades from burial 9 (Hammond 1988: Fig. 9.30) which may be of Lopez date.

LOPEZ MAMOM PHASE

Lopez pottery after 600 B.C. includes the use of red-on-cream technique combined with modeling and incision to create human visages with evidence for facial decoration, as in the spotted cheekbone and striped chin shown in Fig. 3.37; in modeled clay the figurine style remains similar, although attributes such as earflares and a ?diadem have been added (Fig. 8.19) and the male body apparently distinguished by a flat chest, while the female has explicit breasts (Fig. 8.18d). Animal effigies are still rare, although the feline muzzle in Fig. 8.21b shows a naturalism and scale surprising at this date. Graffiti on pottery, both on complete vessels (Fig. 3.38) and on sherds (Fig. 8.17a) are quite complex and reflect a sense of line and detailing that is simple neither stylistically nor iconographically. Jade and shell jewelry are plain, and bone artifacts likewise show no evidence that they were vehicles for

imagery, although this is somewhat at odds with what appears in the next period.

COCOS CHICANEL PHASE

With the dramatic architectural changes in phase V, a greater range of imagery appears: the seven carved bone tubes from Mass Burial 1 (Figs. 8.35–8.38) of 400–300 B.C. exhibit a mature technique using multiple overlapping layers (up to four on SF 1596: Fig. 8.38) to create a sense of depth and a secondary parallel modeling line similar to that used in some Izapa (e.g. Stela 2) and Maya highland (e.g. Kaminaljuyu Stela 10) sculpture of a later date. The double scrolls on SF 1650 (Fig. 8.37) are also paralleled in later Preclassic Izapan sculpture, and appear in the Maya Lowlands on Uaxactun Structure H-sub-10 (Valdés 1986: Figs. 5–8) where they co-occur with panels of the *pop* motif in monumental stucco sculpture and persist into Classic Maya art on such monuments as the masks of Tikal's Early Classic Structure 5D-23-2nd. The five tubes with the *pop* motif seem to be the earliest firmly provenanced instances of this symbol of authority in the Maya Lowlands, and suggest that from the fourth century B.C. onwards the effective exercise of power was accompanied and advertised by an iconography that developed into a greater Classic complexity.

The paucity of human figurines noted elsewhere for the Late Preclassic is relieved at Cuello by a few examples (e.g. Fig. 8.18c) from Cocos contexts (although possibly redeposited from Lopez times, since none are from burial or cache contexts). Human features appear modeled on bowls (Fig. 8.22c), and animal-head adornos are quite common (e.g. Fig. 8.22a–b), including the complete reorientation of a bowl as the body of a parrot with head and wings attached (Fig. 3.43b). Graffiti such as Fig. 8.17b show an acute sense of the human figure and its idiosyncrasies much less formal than that **found** in monumental art, even in the rare cases (such as **Tikal** Structures 5D-Sub-10-1st and burial 166) where humans are portrayed at this period.

The corpus of art from Preclassic Cuello is thus rather limited, in monumental media almost wholly absent and in the minor arts small in quantity. The human figure and visage do appear in a fairly naturalistic form from Swasey times onwards, however, and equally realistic bird and animal effigies occur from Bladen times on. Other kinds of ornament become more complex and detailed through time, as with the designs on roller stamps and flat stamps, and the decorative repertoire used on pottery vessels where both designs and techniques for creating them progress from simple incision to three-dimensional modeling, dichrome and trichrome painting, and the use of organic resist. Materials such as shell and bone, which in the Middle Preclassic are used to make plain simple objects, become in early Cocos times used for pieces not necessarily more elaborate in form, but which act as vehicles for an art style, which is plastic and sophisticated in some of its formal concepts.

Chapter 11   CUELLO CONSIDERED:
SUMMARY AND
CONCLUSION

Norman Hammond

The preceding chapters describe the investigations at Cuello between 1975 and 1987, the ideas that lay behind them, and the methods by which they were carried out. In Chapter 1, the nature of Maya civilization is briefly outlined, together with the state of Maya scholarship when the project began in 1975, and important developments in the field of Preclassic studies that took place during its progress. In this final section, the results of the work are summarized and considered further.

Chapter 2 outlines the changing concepts and developing methods that guided the work at Cuello. The site was discovered during site survey, carried out as part of the Corozal Project, a regional study of the prehistory and human ecology of northern Belize (Hammond 1974); the projects avowed emphasis on the Preclassic led to test excavations at Cuello in 1975 and to more extensive work from 1976 onwards, and field methods and recording systems evolved to accommodate the broadening scope of the investigation.

A stratigraphic terminology of "context" and "Feature" was adopted for descriptive and analytical purposes, to which interpretive terms such as "Structure," "Burial," "Cache," and "firepit" were added. Relationships between contexts were illustrated on a modified Harris Matrix, in a format which itself changed substantially over the years (Hammond 1991a) to include interpretation as well as observation of the sequence. Single-context planning, heavily labor- and material-intensive unless a computer is available in the field, was not used during the work described here except for site notes, but was fully implemented at Cuello in 1990. A second economical procedure, the extraction, tabulation, and discard of uninformative sherds and chert fragments in the field laboratory before the rest of the collections were shipped to the base laboratory for full analysis, was discontinued in 1990 to remove possible bias from the results; study of debitage convinced McSwain (personal communication) that information on the early stages of lithic reduction sequences was lost in the winnowing, and that the extent of intracommunity chert working had thus been underestimated.

Contextual analysis, a literal description of the process of analyzing the constituent matrix and material culture within a sampled context, is a term that has been widely and differently used since it was first defined and applied at Cuello in 1978. As Wilk and Kosakowsky describe in Chapter 2, it involved the deconstruction of the sample and the evaluation of its history of development (see Fig. 2.10). Its value lay not only in defining single-component *in situ* deposits, from which accurate dating of their time of deposition might also be obtained, but in rendering the almost ubiquitous "mixed" deposits useful, not for chronology but for an understanding of site formation processes. As a result, the extensive suite of radiocarbon dates from Cuello can be evaluated for the chronological utility of each determination, although this by no means solves all of the problems.

Chapter 3, on the stratigraphy, chronology, and development of the Preclassic sequence at Cuello, ties together the results of excavations over six seasons between 1975 and 1987, ranging from modest test pits to area exposures; the results of the 1990 season, carried out while this book was in press, do not change the basic picture (Hammond 1990). Fourteen major phases of construction, embracing 22 subphases and spanning some 1,500 years between 1200 B.C. and A.D. 300, are ordered by a chronology based on more than 80 radiocarbon dates and a few obsidian hydration measurements. The dates are given, in the text and in Table 3.1, as they were initially judged in terms of acceptability, although the "long" chronology originally proposed on the basis of the 1975–76 excavations (Hammond *et al.* 1976; Hammond, Donaghey *et al.* 1977) has undergone drastic revision as the result of further assays. Among these are a further series of conventional radiocarbon dates on charcoal, from the 1978–80 and 1987 excavations, which suggest a much later span for the Swasey and Bladen phases than first proposed (Andrews and Hammond 1990), and a number of AMS dates on the collagen of human bone from burials. In the latter case we are dating the ancient Maya themselves and not just their debris, and this technique has, as in several other areas of prehistoric archaeology, led to a drastic shortening of the timescale. The possibility of a preceramic occupation at Cuello in the third millennium B.C. producing some or all of the charcoal yielding the earliest dates remains, although there is no other evidence for it; but the sedentary, farming, pottery-making Preclassic Maya occupation of the Swasey and subsequent phases cannot, on present evidence, be placed earlier than about 1200 B.C.

In the discussion of stratigraphy which forms the bulk of Chapter 3, the data are laid out as an excavation report: discussion of the successive buildings uncovered is left until Chapter 5, as is consideration of architectural development and innovation at Cuello (see also Hammond and Gerhardt 1990). Since the chapter was compiled, the 1990 season has revealed the rear parts of the earlier Lopez and latest Bladen buildings (Structures 315, 320 of phases IV and IIIA) on the north side of the Middle Preclassic courtyard, and those of the early Cocos and final Lopez phases on the south side. In both instances the frontages were excavated in previous seasons, and are reported in Chapter 3: the major new evidence is for a succession of low platforms in phases VI–VIII facing on to the south side of the plaza on top of Platform 34, and a number of Middle Preclassic burials (Hammond 1990).

The concept of the Feature, defined in Chapter 2, is applied in Chapter 3 to a range of stratigraphic collocations, from complete buildings to simple caches and hearths. Redundancy is present in the designation of certain Features as Structures, if they formed part of a building, as burials if they contain formally deposited human remains (Chapter 10; see also Robin 1989), or as caches if they are other formal deposits of artifacts: in these cases the utility of a *stratigraphic* designation, the Feature, which is not culturally interpretive, outweighs the disadvantages of redundancy.

One type of Feature where interpretation is still uncertain is the "fire-pit"; these depressions, lined with clay, stones, sherds, or any combination of the three, are often (but not always) heat-hardened and reddened or blackened; their contents often (but not always) include concentrated trash, including charcoal, animal remains, and sherds. They were initially interpreted as hearths, and their burnt contents as the remains of fires, smothered by household rubbish. The widely disparate radiocarbon dates obtained for firepits within the same phase (Table 3.1) cast doubts on this. The existence of unbaked linings, as in [F293] excavated in 1990, suggests that other functions were also possible, including soaking and washing (see Chapter 5); some firepits, especially those found in the Late Preclassic, may have served to fire pottery, however (Fig. 8.14).

The ceramic sequence which forms the basis of the relative chronology at Cuello and comparison with the sequences at other sites is correlated with the occupational and architectural stratigraphy. Because the sequence has been the subject of two previous monographs (Pring 1977a; Kosakowsky 1987) and a number of other papers, only an outline of the four successive ceramic complexes and their characteristics is given in Chapter 3.

The first, and most controversial, of these is the Swasey complex, known at present only from Cuello, and on the basis of the dates available still, even on the short chronology used here, the earliest pottery in the Maya Lowlands. Kosakowsky's splitting of Pring's original "Swasey" complex into Swasey and Bladen complexes has removed many of the ambiguities and problems, including extremely early dichrome and organic-resist modes, and vessel forms closely related to the later Middle Preclassic Mamom sphere. Swasey *sensu novo* is dominated by simple vessel forms and only three ceramic groups, unslipped or with red glossy, orange low-gloss or matt slips, comprise 96 percent of the inventory. Groove-incision is the commonest decorative mode, although others are present, including pattern-burnishing and rare dichromes. Bladen pottery includes the consistent use of double slips, making the Consejo Red group more tonally consistent and by slip reservation creating the Tower Hill Red-on-cream type which then persists into Lopez Mamom times. Plain cream-slipped pottery also appears for the first time, as does an orange-brown ware, and there are innovations in forms which distinguish Bladen from Swasey vessels. Organic-resist decoration on monochrome or dichrome vessels appears late in the Bladen phase.

One result of the 1990 excavations has been the demonstration that many Bladen types continue to be made and used in early Lopez Mamom times after 600 B.C., occurring in middens and occupation deposits in the same fresh condition as Lopez pottery. Early Lopez burials include more Bladen types than might be expected, suggesting greater conservatism in ritual than in household use (Hammond 1990).

Bladen pottery is known from several other sites in northern Belize, including Santa Rita Corozal, Nohmul, San Estevan, El Pozito (Pring 1977a), Kichpanha, and Colha (Valdez 1987), where it forms the Bolay ceramic complex, dated to 900–500 B.C. This regional distribution has external links to the southwest, up the Hondo basin into northeast Petén, where there are parallels in the Eb complex at Tikal, and beyond to the Pasión basin, where specific type-level comparisons can be made with the Xe complex of Altar de Sacrificios. Such regional ceramic traditions, and links between them, are characteristic of later Maya times: the northern Belize material shows that this situation already existed early in the Middle Preclassic period.

In the succeeding Lopez phase, Mamom pottery is more uniform across the Maya Lowlands, with Cuello fitting into this pattern. The Lopez complex is, like its precursors, dominated by red slipped ware but the Joventud Red group is waxy rather than glossy, although less so than in the Petén. The red-on-cream Muxanal group accounts for nearly 20 percent of the inventory, and brings in an exuberant range of decorative motifs, while red-and-cream, brown-and-cream and other dichrome types proliferate.

Cuello has a transitional assemblage of pottery that combines the finish of Mamom fabrics with new forms characteristic of the succeeding Cocos Chicanel complex; the best example of this is the range of vessels associated with the phase V Mass Burial 1 (Fig. 3.39). Consideration was given to defining a separate ceramic complex, collateral with the Tzec complex at Tikal, but eventually the material was subsumed into an early facet of Cocos, extending the Late Preclassic back to 400 B.C. This accords with the subsequent decision by Valdez (personal communication) to place what had been the

Chiwa Mamom complex at Colha into an expanded Onecimo (Chicanel) complex spanning the period from 500 B.C. to A.D. 125.

Cocos at Cuello is a typical member of the Chicanel ceramic sphere, dominated by the Sierra (red) group. One type within this group, Society Hall Red, recognized as separate from Sierra Red by Kosakowsky (1983, 1987), has concentric rings of wiped slip that both suggest the use of a turntable in manufacture (see Chapter 8) and link Cuello with other sites showing this technique, in northern Belize and southwest through the Belize River valley and the northeast Petén to the Pasión valley. Characteristics of Classic period pottery, including hard, glossy slips, trichrome painting, and the basal-flange decorative mode, appear before the end of Cocos, together with the mammiform-tetrapod bowl form of the "Protoclassic" Holmul I style. Such apparently precocious Classic traits are most parsimoniously seen as evidence for the emergence of Early Classic ceramic style out of the preceding Late Preclassic, but the alternative, of developed Classic style impacting a backwater where Chicanel ceramics were still in vogue, must be considered. More precise dating of the late facet of Cocos at Cuello may resolve the question.

Occupation at Cuello continued into the Early Classic: the final pyramid at the Platform 34 locus, Structure 35, is dated to the fourth century A.D. by its dedicatory cache, and a number of the burials and other deposits encountered in the settlement survey (Chapter 6) are of this period; but the focus of community life at Cuello moved some 300 m northeast, to the new ceremonial precinct founded, so far as limited testing can tell, at the end of the Preclassic. Domestic and occasional ceremonial use of Platform 34 continued through the Late Classic into the Postclassic: debris of the eleventh to thirteenth centuries A.D. dates the final architectural embellishment of Structure 35, and an effigy *incensario* from the pyramid base may be even later. This latter millennium of occupation at Cuello does not, however, form part of this book, except for limited consideration in Chapter 6.

Overall, the ceramic sequence at Cuello from 900 B.C. onwards lines up beside those already established from other Preclassic sites in the southern lowlands such as Altar de Sacrificios, Seibal, Tikal, Uaxactun, Barton Ramie, and Becan, as well as with local sequences at Colha, San Estevan, and Nohmul. The pottery, and the dates, for the Lopez Mamom and Cocos Chicanel complexes fit into broad patterns of ceramic development in the late Middle and Late Preclassic. The Bladen complex has sufficient ties with other local sites, especially Colha, and with Tikal and Altar de Sacrificios, for its regional standing and time frame to be uncontroversial. The Swasey complex is acknowledged as antecedent to Bladen: a point of dispute is whether it has the status of a separate ceramic complex, as argued in this book, or whether it is better defined as an early facet of the same complex as Bladen, a view taken by Andrews (in Andrews and Hammond 1990: 579). This semantic issue is, however, irrelevant to the dating of Swasey, which, although the early second millennium b.c. placement argued most recently by Hammond (1984b) cannot now be sustained, still seems to be of late second and early first millennium B.C. date.

Chapter 4 examines the ecological background and economic infrastructure of the Cuello community. In the first part, Miksicek outlines the kinds of evidence recovered by flotation, a technique applied for the first time in Maya archaeology at Cuello. Well over 3,000 seeds, including those of forest trees and plants, and cultivated species such as maize, were recovered; some 1,150 maize cob and kernel fragments were identified, of which 141 cupules and 56 kernels were complete enough to be measured (Miksicek *et al.* 1981). Three types of maize appeared in Swasey/Bladen times, the smallest with a cob estimated to have been about 22 mm diameter, and "more like early types of maize [of the first millennium b.c.] from South America than any reported Mexican archaeological collections" (Miksicek *et al.* 1981: 57). The other two types resembled both early Mexican and Peruvian maize, and all three are as much like popcorn as more developed corn varieties. The Lopez Mamom corn from Cuello is much more like Mexican, and much less like South American, maize; one type is thought to be close to a primitive corn called locally "Dzit Bacal," the other to Nal Tel maize, both still grown in Belize. The bulk of the Cocos Chicanel sample came from one context, and probably one harvest, and is almost identical to Early Chapalote maize from Tamaulipas.

The Cuello corn thus fits generally into the pattern of Meso-american types, though with an interesting resemblance between the Swasey-1 and Cupisnique-3 and -4 types from northern Perú. The increase in cupule (Fig. 4.1) and kernel size through time suggests both increasing productivity (although Miksicek *et al.* (1981: 59) rightly urge caution), and selection by the Maya for a larger-cobbed plant.

Maize was abundant from the initial phases of occupation at Cuello, being present in 86 percent of samples of the early Swasey phase and 92 percent of the later, even while the general environment remained forested. It remains at this high level throughout the sequence, except for a decline in phase IIIA to 57 percent when the forest cover also expands again. Maize was the principal species recovered from the earlier of the two *chultunob* excavated, [F246], and the principal food plant from the later [F87]; these two sealed chambers, filled with trash when they ceased to be useful to the Maya, are the closest thing we have at Cuello to a short-term sample of plant remains. They also yielded mollusca suggesting, by their varying habitats, that the environment at Cuello had dried out significantly between 350 and 150 B.C., although from 600 to after 350 B.C. the water table had apparently risen steadily, something suggested also by subse-

quent work along the Rio Hondo (Bloom *et al.* 1983), and elsewhere in the Maya Lowlands (High 1975; Folan *et al.* 1983).

Among the mollusca from the *chultunob* were over 2,000 shells of *Pomacea flagellata*, an edible snail. Comparison of the size ranges of the shells with that of a modern arbitrary sample from the Rio Hondo indicates a strongly unimodal distribution for the ancient shells, suggesting collection at a perceived optimum size (Fig. 4.2), or even harvesting of a controlled resource.

The identification of tropical woods from their charcoal presented a number of problems, as Miksicek notes, but he developed an innovative digital code for anatomical description which enables the large number of species to be systematized. While many of the trees would have been used only for fuel, others are traditional construction materials, and many yield fruits or nuts of dietary value. The mix of species allows reconstruction of the local environment and of the degree of forest clearance and regrowth achieved (Hammond and Miksicek 1981): this can have surprising results, as where there seems to have been a revival of forest growth in phase IIIA (Fig. 4.3).

Miksicek uses a number of innovative approaches, some (like the experiments with *Pomacea* and with *chultun* storage) firmly in the experimental archaeology tradition pioneered in the Maya Area by Puleston (1971), some, like flotation recovery of plant remains, well established in archaeology elsewhere but not hitherto utilized in Maya research, and others, such as the digital taxonomy for tropical woods, being his own solution to the problems presented by the Cuello data set.

He charts environmental and subsistence trends through the Cuello sequence, noting how the combined evidence of vegetation and mollusca depict a landscape becoming cleared and adapted for agriculture on a long-fallow cycle. While maize was certainly cultivated, other food plants such as beans and chile peppers lie within the wild size range, as do tree crops including avocado, hogplum, and nance. Early Maya subsistence may have relied much more on wild plants, subsequently domesticated, than we have hitherto reckoned.

The second part of Chapter 4 deals with the procurement of protein from animals, and is based on Wing and Scudder's analysis of fragmentary faunal remains from excavation and flotation samples. They note the predominance of mammal remains (>77 percent) in all occupation, midden, and fill contexts, with a strong emphasis on the exploitation of white-tailed deer (*Odocoileus virginianus*) and dog (*Canis familiaris* or *Canis caribaeus*); that the latter also were used as food is suggested not only by their small size, as noted by Landa (Tozzer 1941: 203), but also by their diet: stable-isotope analysis indicates that maize formed *c.* 50 percent of the intake (N. van der Merwe, personal communication).

Given that the dogs were certainly domesticated, but that deer contributed significantly more to protein intake, the question of how the latter were obtained is worth further consideration. The traditional interpretation, following Landa's statement "that there are wonderfully many deer, but they are small and their flesh is good to eat" (Tozzer 1941: 204) and Classic period art like the Lubaantun figurines (e.g. Hammond 1988: Fig. 5.3), is that venison came from forest hunting of wild animals. That deer were tamable, if not domesticable, is also known from the ethnohistoric record. "They . . . raise other domestic animals, and let the deer suck their breasts, by which means they raise and make them so tame that they will never go into the woods, although they take them and carry them through the woods and raise them there" (Tozzer 1941: 127).

While domesticated herds of deer do not seem likely, and the faunal evidence from Cuello gives no support to any such interpretation either osteologically or statistically (Elizabeth S. Wing, personal communication), some kind of human–animal relationship which accounts for the plurality (and on occasion majority, in terms of either MNI or meat weight) of deer remains in Preclassic contexts at the site needs to be sought. Some form of loose- or close-herding such as practiced by the Lapps historically and by Upper Palaeolithic groups in northern Europe inferentially (Sturdy 1975) could have assured the Maya some of the protein they required.

In support of this one might also note that the other principal contributors to animal protein intake, the several species of mud and pond turtle could also come from controlled environments such as pens in the wetlands. The possible farming of *Pomacea* snails in wetland margins has been noted above, and although controlled wetlands (such as drained fields and their interstitial canals) do not exist within the community of Cuello, several small wetland areas exist on the ridge top within a few kilometers' radius, and clear evidence for Preclassic wetland exploitation in the Rio Hondo valley to the west is available (e.g. Bloom *et al.* 1983). Study of drained-field systems so far has not fully considered the possibility that cropping on the drained surfaces might well have been interdependent with the controlled raising of fish, turtles, and edible mollusca in the canals. The careful control of water flow, and perhaps species migration, within the Preclassic canal complex at Edzna (Matheny *et al.* 1983) is one piece of evidence in support of such an interpretation.

While it is clear from the list of mammal species represented by one or a few individuals in the Cuello assemblage (Tables 4.8–4.11) that hunting did play a serious part in protein procurement, such procurement may have been more carefully planned and less dependent on chance success in the forest than we have traditionally supposed.

As the Formative period progressed, the ratio of reptiles to mammals, and of turtles to deer/dog, rose steadily. At the same time the fish in the diet, in the Middle Preclassic overwhelmingly from freshwater sources, began in the Late Preclassic to come more from marine environments, including offshore and reef econiches that suggest expert, perhaps specialized, seafaring (something perfectly compatible with the coeval evidence for long-distance sea-trade in exotic goods such as obsidian: see Chapter 9). Wing and Scudder suggest that this broadening of the protein range resulted from over-exploitation of the local biome; I suggest that such stress could well have triggered attempts at controlled protein production to complement the greater procurement radius.

Wing and Scudder also raise the possibility that the scarce marine fish could have had a ritual, rather than purely dietary, significance, as could the concentration of toads (*Bufo marinus*) found in *chultun* [F87], of the second century B.C. Either their meat, or the toxin bufotenin in their parotid glands, or both, could have been the attraction; whether the creatures were bred in the chamber, lived there after its abandonment, or were introduced with the other trash used to infill it, remains moot.

Some animal remains were certainly deposited ritually, including the two caches of deer jaws and teeth, [F30, 140], in phases X and VII respectively, and the stingray spines in cache [F80]; unaltered or modified freshwater and marine shells also appear in cache and burial contexts.

Chapter 5 is the first of four sections detailing the architectural and artifactual remains of the Cuello community: it deals with the area identified as the Preclassic "site core," on and under Platform 34, which has also been the focus of excavation since 1975. While Platform 34 certainly seems to have been the largest single construction in use at Cuello during the Late Preclassic, prior to the foundation of the new ceremonial precinct to the northeast, there is no clear evidence that the Middle Preclassic courtyard group buried beneath it was of similar standing. Our interpretation of the courtyard as the focus of the community is based almost entirely on retrodiction from the Late Preclassic situation; on the basis of the survey and the test excavations described in Chapter 6 we can say only that no other substantial architecture prior to 400 B.C. is known.

The reconstruction of architectural development in Chapter 5 is extracted from the stratigraphic data summarized in Chapter 3. It indicates (so far as the limited area of 200 sq. m exposed can show) that a courtyard or plazuela layout did not develop until phase II, and that the earliest plaster-surfaced substructures for perishable buildings were little more than floors laid on the land surface with a thin fill of small limestone cobbling. Even when the courtyard layout was established, the substructures around it remained low, not exceeding 0.2 m in phase II. The apsidal plan, followed by that of the timber superstructure, and the overall dimensions closely resemble those of modern Maya houses in Yucatan (Wauchope 1938:

16–20, Fig. 11, Plates 3c, 6a), although features such as the internal T-shaped ramp of Structure 326 (Fig. 3.4) indicate a greater complexity of organization.

In phase III the overall organization of the courtyard became more formal, with Structures 321 and 323 both being increased in height, the former requiring an inset step for access. The patio floor had a defined edge at the northwest corner, and by phase IIIA firepits had been banished to the margins of the paved area. Techniques of construction for these low platforms were simple, with a core of earth and stones retained by rubble walls covered with plaster (Hammond and Gerhardt 1990). In spite of some architectural embellishments it is difficult to see other than a residential function for these buildings, even though Structure 323 was c. 11 m long by phase IIIA.

The partial demolition of buildings, and the reuse of the remaining stump as the core of a new structure, was characteristic of Middle Preclassic architectural practice at Cuello. Usually the walls were cut back, on all sides in the examples exposed so far, truncating burials on occasion and removing evidence of the outline of the superstructure (Structure 326 is an exception in having been interred virtually undamaged). In at least one instance, the demolition of Structure 317 in phase IVA, jade beads were scattered in the resulting scar, attesting to the ritual nature of the act. Burial in the center of the patio also occurred, in phase IV (burial 22).

The end of the Middle Preclassic saw the construction of the first rectangular-plan buildings (Structures 314, 315e) on the west and north sides of the patio, but whether any shift in function was involved is not known. The subsequent raising of successive squared buildings on the west side, culminating in the Terminal Preclassic Structure 350 and Early Classic Structure 35, with a ritual function at least plausible from the beginning of the Late Preclassic onwards in Structure 352, suggests that such a shift could have begun in phase IVA. The occurrence of only mutilated burials within the western building sequence (Chapter 10), beginning at the Bladen–Mamom transition around 600 B.C., suggests that it could have been earlier still.

Burial took place within the Middle Preclassic structures on all three excavated sides of the courtyard: the 1990 season documented supine interments of phase IV in Structures 320 and 315 on the north side, and flexed burial on the left side in all three of those of phase IVA in Structure 316. Whether this represents a systematic difference in funerary behavior between those living across the patio from each other can only be ascertained when the phase IV levels of Structure 316 are excavated in 1992.

The architecture of the core was transformed in phase V by the demolition of all the buildings around it, apparently with burning of the superstructures, and their replacement by the broad open expanse of Platform 34. This in turn was built

over, however, with the long Structure 312 on the north facing the projecting front platform of Structure 313 across a plaza 21 m wide – only a modest increase over the final dimensions of the Middle Preclassic courtyard. These structures were quite low, as was the (approximately) coeval Structure 353 on the west; only with the superimposition of Structure 352 did the western building become substantially higher than the others, maintaining this difference with the successive pyramids of Structures 351, 350, and 35.

On the north, however, the long Structure 312 was cut in half and a smaller round building created from its eastern exposed portion. A second round structure was then built to the west, set slightly back, and this pairing survived successive modifications and remodelings over several centuries. The numerous burials cut into the floors of both structures, of both sexes and all ages, suggests that they were family residences, even if families living atop Platform 34 were perhaps of the élite of Cuello. The mass of charred maize found behind the buildings in phase X, and interpreted by Miksicek as the result of a burnt corn-store, also suggests domestic activity.

On the south side of the plaza, only the very front of Structure 313 was known until 1990: the recent excavations revealed more of this and confirmed that superimposed later buildings, set slightly back to the south (Structure 331, 330), persisted through at least phase VIII, while anything at a higher level had been removed by erosion (Hammond 1990). It seems likely that the plaza was bordered by perishable buildings on low platforms on both the north and south sides throughout its history.

The east side remains largely unexcavated, although there is little in the surface contours to suggest substantial buildings there. At one point well before the end of the Late Preclassic, but not as yet firmly anchored into the Main Trench construction sequence, the 12.5 m square solid substructure of [F86] was constructed, with its center at approximately grid 50.00/45.00 and oriented on azimuth 28°; only fragments of [F86] have been revealed (unpublished plan 1979/77, Cuello archive), but it could well have faced the phase VA–VIII south side structures, or the Late Preclassic ramp (also unphased) that ascended the southern edge of Platform 34, forming at the same time an eastern limit to the plaza.

The plaza floor itself remained open for a long time, although offerings such as the deer-jaw caches [F140] of phase VII and [F30] of phase X were buried at its center. Only in phase XI, estimated to lie in the late first century A.D., did a focal point emerge with the erection of Stela 1. The deposition of Mass Burial 2 just east of the stela, and of dedicatory caches in Structures 307 and 304 on the north side of the plaza, suggest an increase in ritual function for the plaza, continued in phase XII when a single large building, Structure 303, was constructed on the north side, and a smaller one, Structure 302, in the center of the plaza adjacent to Stela 1 and facing the stairway of the pyramid. The burial of numerous multi-vessel caches, such as [F6], along the north–south axis of Platform 34 in phase XIII suggests that the entire area of the platform was now being treated as a single ritual unit.

In these late buildings of the third century A.D., including Structures 300, 302–303, and 350, well-dressed ashlar masonry was used for the retaining walls, albeit still covered by plaster, and the fill was massive, of limestone blocks or marl, instead of the earth and rubble mixture used hitherto. Building design at Cuello was for the first time unequivocally non-domestic (although such structures were already extant before 400 B.C. at Tikal (Laporte 1989: Fig 140), by 350 B.C. at Komchen (Ringle and Andrews 1988: 175–6), and at other major centers such as El Mirador and perhaps Cerros by the second century B.C. (Matheny 1986; Robertson and Freidel (1986)); prior to this time the materials and techniques had been undifferentiated, even where a ceremonial function could reasonably be posited. These changes in architecture, the increased investment required, and the coeval increase in deposition of exotics such as jade with burials in Platform 34 suggest that it was the seat of families forming part of the élite in the Cuello community.

What we know of that community comes from a different kind of archaeological probing, the random sampling of the Cuello settlement area by Wilk and Wilhite described in Chapter 6. Small test pits replace the broad exposures made on Platform 34, most of them not into visible mounds but into the open terrain between. The study was guided by the thesis that "non-mound occupation," of houses built directly on the old land surface, was as common a practice of Middle Preclassic Maya pioneer farmers as it is of their Kekchi collateral descendants in southern Belize today (Wilk 1983, 1984, 1988), and that such dwellings could be detected not only from their sparse remains, but also from the "toss zone" of trash that covered the surrounding area in a thin lens. Residential ephemerality is covariant with communal access to land, there being no motive for either permanence or investment.

Wilk and Wilhite argue that with increasing population density and increasingly intensive agriculture, residential mobility decreases, and the extended family becomes an important property-holding and transmitting unit more prone to invest in permanent housing and to advertise differential status by such investment. The construction of house platforms of stone, raising the superstructure, may in pre-Hispanic times have been the perquisite of only the upper levels of society, however, so that the "house mounds" which constitute the data from most settlement surveys in the Maya Lowlands may reflect a smaller population size and lower density than actually existed. The question of "hidden house-mounds," platforms so low that they were concealed by topsoil and leafmould, is one that has been addressed by

others, but the possibility that a substantial portion of the population never constructed any kind of basal platform for their houses, and thus remained archaeologically invisible, was first raised, and confirmed, at Cuello.

Both visible mounds and intermound spaces were sampled by a total of 81 test pits; many of those away from mounds nevertheless yielded high sherd densities, with a mean density of 283 per cubic meter but concentrated on the higher ridge areas where settlement might be expected. Seven pits also located very low platforms not noted in mapping.

Early Middle Preclassic pottery was found in 13 of the 81 tests (16 percent), ten of them in loci where Late Preclassic platform construction subsequently occurred. This may indicate that early settlers chose good house sites, or simply that later construction protected the evidence of prior occupation. This was of course the case at Platform 34, and the more substantial nature of the early architecture at that locus supports the contention that it was the core of the community from the early Middle Preclassic onwards.

Late Middle Preclassic sherds of the Lopez Mamom complex were found in 21 percent of the tests, including 65 percent of those with earlier material: the slight eminences and ridges of the site continued to be preferred house sites. For the Late Preclassic 77 percent of tests yielded evidence of occupation, including 93 percent of the mounds investigated, although in only ten cases (38 percent) was there coeval platform construction, and in only one of these cases was there great structural complexity. Wilk and Wilhite suggest that small pyramid-platform residential complexes were scattered among the more modest residences of the (presumably) lower social strata; they can be interpreted as the residences of lineage heads with accompanying foci for ancestor veneration. A similar typology and distribution has been observed at Seibal (Tourtellot 1988b: 277, 291). Most Late Preclassic houses were, however, like their precursors, perishable structures built at ground level.

While 55 percent of the tests yielded Early Classic material, the nature of the settlement pattern seems to have changed, with 78 percent of the platform construction at loci where only perishable buildings had existed before, and abandonment of some of the Late Preclassic platforms. Early Classic burials were quite frequently encountered in the settlement, while only two of Cocos date were found: the contrast with the plethora of Cocos burials in Platform 34 suggests that this area may have been preferentially used for sepulture in the Late Preclassic, although the domestic trash found around and behind the structures on Platform 34 contradicts any notion of their having been mausolea. Although some Late Classic burials were also found in the settlement, only 18 percent of the tests yielded pottery of this period, and Cuello seems to have been a community in decline.

From the evidence of their test excavations Wilk and

Wilhite propose that Middle Preclassic Cuello was a dispersed community with an egalitarian social structure, with social ranking emerging only during the Late Preclassic. Some evidence from the Platform 34 excavations, such as the large size of phase III–IV buildings, and the abundance of shell jewelry accompanying child burials, suggests, however, that ascribed status and ranking may have existed from late Bladen times onwards.

Estimates of population size are calculated from its relationship to refuse area, on the basis of ethnographic data from the Kekchi and the Maya Highlands. For the early Middle Preclassic, Wilk and Wilhite estimate a community of 53–66 households, each with a mean 5.6 persons (likely to be too low) and thus 296–370 people; for the late Middle Preclassic this yields 102–127 households and 571–711 people, and for the Late Preclassic a population of 2,200–2,600 in 335–419 households, a community the size of a small town rather than a village. In the Early Classic the population may have risen to nearly 3,400 before dropping in the Late Classic to just over 1,100. The Late Preclassic population expansion is one found at every site investigated in northern Belize, and many elsewhere, but the Early Classic continuation of this at Cuello is in contrast to the developmental trajectory of some other communities in the region. Three of the closest major centers, Nohmul, El Pozito, and Colha, all have diminished Early Classic populations, but some smaller communities, including San Antonio Rio Hondo and San Estevan, show a similar rise to Cuello. The demography and political geography of northern Belize clearly becomes more complex between the third and fourth centuries A.D.

In Chapter 7, Frank and Julie Saul analyze the population of Cuello as human beings, from their physical remains as preserved in burials. Our use of the term "burial" embraces any deliberate ritual disposal of human remains, whether of an entire articulated body or of some portion of it secondarily deposited: in this way each individual can be described and used for osteobiographical analysis (Saul 1972). Some "burials" in fact consist of partial remains interred in the same grave as a complete individual, from atavistic or other motives, while others, such as the skulls of children enclosed between two bowls, would also be considered as caches (see Chapter 10). In each of the mass burials, every individual has been given his or her own burial number to facilitate description and comparison, although for most of them only portions of the skeleton are present.

To the 122 individuals from Preclassic Cuello thus identified and considered in Chapter 7 must now be added the 14 excavated in 1990, of which 12 date to Lopez Mamom times (phases IV–IVA, bringing the total for this period from 8 to 20 individuals), one to the end of Bladen (phase IIIA), and one to early Cocos Chicanel (phase VIII). Three of these are provisionally identified as children, from less than a year to 7–8 years old, one is certainly and one probably an adult female, and the remaining nine are either adult males or adults of uncertain sex (personal communication from Saul and Saul cited in Hammond 1990). All but two are single burials; one female and the youngest child seem to have been buried together. No data are yet available to modify the evidence or conclusions about the Cuello population advanced in Chapter 7, although the high ratio of males to females in Lopez burials increases further; to the analysis of burial rite in Chapter 10 we must add the observations that (1) children were sometimes buried with more grave goods, especially shell adornments, than previously noted; and (2) there may be some differentiation in burial posture between graves on the north and south sides of the Middle Preclassic courtyard, or between early and late Lopez burials, or both: this question can be resolved only by further excavation.

Although the sex ratio in Swasey and Bladen times is fairly balanced, in Lopez there begins an emphasis on male burial in Platform 34 which continues into Cocos times, and is most dramatically illustrated by the two mass burials (although some or all of the men in these may have been outsiders).

The assessment of public health in Chapter 7 is based on the incidence of skeletal lesions and trauma, and on dental evidence; the many afflictions which mark only the soft tissue are archaeologically undetectable, as well as those for which good skeletal preservation is a necessary concomitant.

Among the most striking skeletal lesions is the evidence of treponemal infection, likely to have been syphilis or yaws; the former disease is certainly of pre-Hispanic origin (Baker and Armelagos 1988). the characteristic "sabering" and medullary thickening of the tibia have been identified in several Cuello burials, the oldest of Middle Preclassic date. This occurrence in the first half of the first millennium B.C. is the earliest documented in the Maya Area, and among the earliest in the Americas.

Cranial hyperostosis, an iron deficiency disease, was rare at Cuello, but those instances that do occur are in Cocos times. The Sauls speculate that ceremonial bloodletting could have contributed to the incidence. Subperiosteal hemorrhage and periodontoclasia are marks of vitamin C deficiency; they occur combined on four individuals, as early as the Bladen phase, and separately throughout the sequence. The stress marked by linear enamel hypoplasia, arguably the result of maternal protein withdrawal at weaning, increases steadily through the Cuello sequence, from an incidence of under 30 percent before 600 B.C. to 100 percent in late Cocos times. Dental caries is present from the early Middle Preclassic onwards.

Culturally caused dental changes include the curious diagonal attrition of the inner surface of the upper front teeth, the result apparently of a stripping action (like present-day artichoke consumption) which could be due to eating a fibrous food like manioc. Flat wear, caused by abrasion from mineral particles in the food – such as *metate* dust in maize dough – is very common. Cultural modifications such as head shaping and dental filing were present, but rare, at Cuello and do not seem to have had status associations.

Afflictions marking the skeleton include arthritis, neurofibroma, and spondylolisthesis; a number of traumatic injuries are documented, ranging from a parry fracture and dented skulls to broken limbs and phalanges. The most severe trauma, decapitation, was best evidenced by the separate placement or absence of the skull in burials.

The examination of craft production and exchange systems in Chapters 8 and 9 considers the factors of raw material acquisition, processing into artifacts, and function in the community. Some materials were local and locally worked, some exotic, but imported in raw or semi-processed form for local artifact production, and a few arrived as fully finished goods. Rebecca McSwain argues that the chert and chalcedony industry at Cuello was hybrid, with intracommunity chalcedony working, some processing of "Colha"-type cherts from the chert-bearing zone east of the New River (and possibly from the Colha outcrops themselves), but also importation of finished tools of "Colha" chert from that site. Such specialized forms she sees as increasing in quantity in Cocos times, as the Colha workshops increased their output of a restricted range of standard tool types. Some of these types occur at Cuello, however, earlier than they are presently known at Colha. The chertworkers at Cuello seem to have been competent craftspersons from the beginning, creating both a primary industry from raw materials, and a secondary one by recycling old tools into new forms. They had clear preferences for specific raw materials for particular tool types; the importance of "Colha" cherts and of the primary industry both increase through time.

The tools fall into three functional groups, the "domestic toolkit," heavy-duty construction and cultivation tools, and those of possibly ceremonial use. The domestic kit seems to have been used for a range of piercing, cutting, stripping, scraping, and light chopping activities, the heavy-duty tools for more onerous chopping. Some of the ?ceremonial forms, such as the stemmed macroblade "dagger," occur in caches and burials, but are also found in discard contexts suggesting a mixed utilitarian–ritual range of functions. Obsidian blades share such a range, although obsidian was scarce at Cuello and the few cores recovered do not suggest a thriving local industry; none of them comes from a clearly Preclassic context. The dimensions of blades suggest economical use of this exotic material throughout the history of Cuello.

Ground stone implements seem, like chert tools, to have been a substantially local industry: *manos* and *metates* for grinding, the largest category of finds, were most often of limestone, of varieties found within the region although not necessarily at Cuello itself; these comprised 81 percent of the total, while clearly exotic materials were used for only 4.8 percent, although including some of the earliest grinding stones known from Cuello. Barkbeaters and other ground stone objects were mostly made from limestone, and the few pieces of red and yellow ocher could as easily be of local origin as exotic.

Pottery manufacture seems to have been a local craft, and some evidence of its execution is described; there is a high degree of consistency in technique and finish, suggesting community norms and producer expertise in satisfying them. The range of forms is fairly steady through time, but there is an increasing emphasis on large-capacity bowls, as though more servings were required. The significance of this implied expansion of the gustatory group is unknown.

Ceramic artifacts include recycled sherds used as weights or lids, and modeled objects that include human and animal effigies, and stamps with designs that could be applied to skin, textile, or bark. Perforations that allowed the stamps to be worn or carried suggest that they may have been personal markers.

Bone was used to make personal adornments such as beads and pendants, for small tools like needles and awls, and for apparently ceremonial objects such as the relief-carved tubes from Mass Burial 1. Shell was also used mainly to create adornments, and the recovery of marine and freshwater shell scrap in the 1990 excavations shows that craft production was carried out within the Cuello community: the conclusion in Chapter 8 that the better-made beads were imports from the coast thus needs to be modified. A wide range of marine species was utilized, all from the Caribbean shore or cays; the inhabitants of Cuello could have obtained the shells directly, but acquisition through intermediaries fits the known regional distribution pattern better. The one marine item of purely ceremonial function is the stingray spine, used for bloodletting and found in an early Cocos cache.

The discussion of trade in Chapter 9 examines the regional impact of Colha on chert use at Cuello, and overlaps the topic of craft production and tool function examined in the previous section. Obsidian, a clear exotic, has been traced to its several sources in highland Guatemala by the use of PIXE analysis, and the pattern shows a surprisingly early and strong representation of the Ixtepeque source. Although Ixtepeque obsidian is known from Preclassic contexts elsewhere in northern Belize, its main presence in the lowlands has been felt to begin later in the Classic period (Neivens *et al.* 1979; Nelson 1985; Dreiss 1988). Although the Rio Pixcaya source (San Martin Jilotepeque) is the first to be represented at Cuello, in phase IIIA or earlier, both Ixtepeque and El Chayal obsidians are present from phase V onwards throughout the Late Preclassic, but with a predominance of the former which differs from patterns observed elsewhere for this period.

Jade was the other highland import subjected to source characterization: the inhomogeneity of the mineral compared with obsidian renders such analysis less successful. Less than half of the 46 Cuello jades analyzed by Bishop and his collaborators could be placed in reference groups; those that were fell into several different groups, along with jades from other sites across the Maya Lowlands. The correlation with sources and workshops that could be provisionally established suggests that at least some of the Cuello jades come from the middle Motagua valley area around San Agustin Acasaguastlan. The general pattern of jade procurement indicated at Preclassic Cuello is not significantly different from that at other sites in the eastern lowlands in the Classic through Postclassic periods; this suggests a fairly stable network of production and exchange from at least 400 B.C. onwards.

Jade was scarce at Cuello, and rare prior to Cocos times. The earliest occurrences are at the end of the Bladen phase, *c.* 600 B.C., and include small brilliant green beads and several blue ornaments; jade is used together with red *Spondylus* shell and white shell in bracelets at first, only later occurring by itself, but the earliest examples are also those of the highest quality, albeit tiny. Later jades include much albite, and some are only "social jade," greenstones containing no jadeite. It seems likely that pressure on sources had increased to the extent that manufacturers were seeking out and exploiting any other acceptable greenstone, several varieties of which exist in the Motagua valley. Association of these with female and juvenile burials in Cocos times, while true jade accompanied males, suggests that an appreciation of the difference existed.

Imported pottery was extremely rare: only one certain import, an Usulutan bowl, has been identified, although several Bladen phase sherds are of apparently non-local fabric and finish. Typological links with the northeast Petén and the Pasión basin show that ideas, if not actual vessels, were certainly arriving at Cuello from other regions.

Ritual behavior is examined in Chapter 10, including human burial, cache deposition, and the evidence of iconography. The section on burials discusses the same 122 individuals whose osteobiographies were analyzed in Chapter 7, plus two others: here again, "burial" refers to the interment of remains of a single human being, while the remains of more than one person may occupy a grave; the term "mass burial" is self-explanatory. We have used the term "mutilation" (following Robin 1989) to denote an individual only partly present in a burial, and "severe mutilation" when only one or two bones are present. This may represent a sacrifice to the principal occupant of the grave, or may in some cases (as with burials 148 and 151 (Hammond 1990)) simply be replacement of a burial disturbed by a later grave cut.

In the early Middle Preclassic, both sexes and all ages are represented in graves dug into house platforms before, during, and after their domestic occupation. A range of burial

positions was employed, with supine the most common and a single seated interment at the end of the period. Burials faced in all directions, and the grave good assemblage was diverse, with children as well equipped as adults; pottery vessels (one often inverted over the head) and shell bead bracelets were the most frequent offerings, but some late Bladen burials were accompanied by jades, as noted above. Exotics tended to occur in well-stocked graves, whatever the age or sex of the occupant, suggesting that differential access to goods was a matter of ascribed rather than achieved status.

Simple graves in house platforms, with supine burial predominating over flexed and a strong emphasis on adult males, marked the Lopez phase between 600 and 400 B.C. The additional 13 burials excavated in 1990 confirm this generalization, adding, however, the possibility that posture was determined by the locus of burial and hence perhaps by lineage affiliation. One grave of this period (burial 151) was marked by an upright stone projecting above the top of its fill. The first headless burials are noted in this period, one (burial 1) with a block of tabular chert in place of the head, the other (burial 152) with a bowl inverted over its position. The range of grave goods remained much the same as before, though less varied; the 1990 excavations showed that jade accompanied female as well as male burials.

By far the largest proportion (n = 103: 82 percent) of the Cuello burials excavated through 1987 were from the Cocos phase of 400 B.C.–A.D. 250, although almost half of these were in the two mass burials. The presence of mutilated remains accompanying primary burials, and of several children's skulls in bowls as apparent dedicatory caches, further reduces the number of separate graves, to 52.

A number of individual burials seem to have been associated with the overall program constructing Platform 34: in addition to Mass Burial 1, with its 32 mainly fragmentary skeletons, the beheaded burials 10 and 12 were laid in the upper fill, and the double child burial 126–127 marked the initial northward expansion of the platform. The adult male burials 21 and 125 accompanied further enlargments, and Mass Burial 2 the resurfacing of the platform in phase XI.

This purposeful and structured interment, much or all of it arguably sacrificial in nature and with a heavy emphasis on males, contrasts with the opportunistic placing of burials in the northern succession of buildings, where the male:female ratio of 16:10 and the adult:juvenile ratio of 31:11 seem likely to reflect a similar pattern of domestic sepulture to that discerned in the Middle Preclassic. There was, however, a change in fashion, with seated burial in a circular pit predominating (43 percent) over flexed and supine positions. Such changes in burial rite have sometimes been interpreted by archaeologists as denoting a new population, power structure, or ideology, but the degree of variability in Preclassic funerary behavior at Cuello, and the continuity in other aspects of activity and material culture, renders any such explanation implausible.

The Cocos mortuary assemblage is more varied than that of Lopez times, and the range of objects within each material category is larger: shell rings and pendants supplement the bead bracelets common since Bladen times, obsidian and *metates* occur as grave goods for the first time, and the variety of pottery vessels expands to include size and form variants uncommon in domestic contexts. The range of both pottery and other grave goods in Mass Burial 1 was greater than in the domestic burials. The number of vessels in these, around one per person on average, and their often worn condition, suggests that many were personal possessions rather than funerary ceramics *per se*; bowls, often found inverted over the head or body, may have been selected for their protective span, while vessels held upright in the lap may well have contained liquid or food. The smashing of pots, first noted in the early Lopez burial 22, is probably the Preclassic equivalent of the "killing" by basal perforation seen in many Classic burials. The mutilated individuals forming the "human grave goods" of the body bundles accompanying Mass Burials 1 and 2 could be seen as conceptually equivalent, although the alternative interpretation of their being venerated ancestral remains cannot yet be excluded. That Mass Burial 1 at *c.* 400 B.C. is the first strong evidence of social ranking at Cuello, as argued in Chapter 10, remains true, although the two richly ornamented child burials (burials 157–158: Hammond 1990) found in 1990 suggest that such wealth and status as was conferred by shell, and specifically *Spondylus*, jewelry was already heritable by 600 B.C.

The placing of dedicatory caches at Cuello was almost exclusively confined to Cocos times, with the construction of Platform 34 as a focus of ritual life. All of them appear to be construction-associated, accompanying either renewal of the plaza floor, or reconstruction of the surrounding building platforms; the intention may have been as much valedictory to the construction being buried (cf. Tourtellot 1988b: 449) as dedicatory to the new one. The form of some of the offerings, especially the circular setting of jade and shell beads in [F190], the four chert "daggers" and two stingray spines of [F80], and the two deer-jaw deposits [F30, 140], is unusual. Most, however, consist of pairs of bowls, some enclosing jade beads, with a few bowls containing children's skulls.

Architectural construction at Cuello lacked the rich sculptural adornment found at other Late Preclassic sites in recent years, the painted stair risers of Structure 350 being the only known decoration. Our knowledge of Preclassic iconography at Cuello comes perforce from the minor arts, and from objects which were probably personal possessions rather than public statements.

Swasey-phase art included the linear decoration of pottery vessels by grooving or incision, and linear pattern-burnishing.

Modeling is present, in the form of a tubular body (possibly from a musical instrument) with an attached arm and hand, and human effigies continue into the Bladen and Lopez phases with a degree of detail paralleling that of the more abundant figurines from highland sites such as Chalchuapa. Females are identified by their breasts, and males, arguably, by contrasting flat broad chests (Hammond 1989). Human faces appear modeled on pottery vessels, sometimes with painted decoration, and in Cocos times as graffiti also. Animal and bird forms appear first in Bladen times, with figurines later supplemented by adornos on the rims of bowls; dog, monkey, turtle, and a feline are among the animal species represented; a late Cocos bowl had the head, wings, and tail of a parrot attached to form a stylized effigy vessel.

Life forms were taken to abstraction, as with the avian outlined in organic-resist technique in Fig. 3.33, and non-figurative art persisted throughout the Preclassic at Cuello, becoming more elaborate with the development of cylindrical and flat stamps as vehicles for design, and with the multi-layered patterns on the relief-carved bone tubes from Mass Burial 1. Although ceramic surface decoration became more elaborate with the development of dichrome, trichrome, and organic-resist techniques, few vessels showed any elaboration of motif.

In general, little of the art of Cuello has transparent iconographic significance: only the *pop*-decorated bone tubes from Mass Burial 1 use a device with known meaning in Classic Maya times; the painted ornament on the Structure 350 stairway, the other carved bone tubes, the human and animal effigies, and the linear abstract designs are all still opaque to us as we try to understand the genesis of imagery in the Maya world. What little we do perceive links the development of public art with the emergence of iconographically defined rulership (Schele and Miller 1986; Freidel and Schele 1988), and it is possible that some earlier private art was also élite-oriented (Hammond 1989).

CONCLUSION

The fifteen centuries of Preclassic development embodied in the Cuello stratigraphy allow us to address a number of questions about the emergence of Maya lowland culture and its rise towards civilization, but the results of our investigation, summarized above, also place firm limits on the answers that can be obtained or expected. It is clear that Cuello was throughout its history a community which was never more than marginal to the emergence of a complex society in the Maya Lowlands. The discovery of that emergent complexity at sites such as El Mirador, Tikal, Komchen, Cerros, and Lamanai was discussed in Chapter 1, as was the fact that over the period of investigation at Cuello, from 1975 onwards, our whole view of the Preclassic Maya has been utterly changed. Instead of occupying only small villages, we know they raised impressive public buildings as early as 400 B.C., and by the second century B.C. these included the largest Maya structures ever erected. Literacy and numeracy, a developed art style, and a complex iconography all appeared during the final centuries of the Preclassic period, geared more to the cult of the ruler than to any economic purpose.

Only a little of this burgeoning complexity was apparent at Cuello, where the construction of Platform 34 reflected dimly major developments elsewhere, but the Middle Preclassic antecedents of this Late Preclassic florescence and the detailed process of development are, on the other hand, much better documented at the smaller site.

That Cuello *was* small is clear: even the surface mound population, most of it the result of Late Preclassic construction, and the evidence for non-mound occupation in the interstitial areas detected by Wilk and Wilhite (Chapter 6) do not indicate a community size much above 2,600, while the extrapolated figures for the test-pit sample suggest that the Swasey/Bladen phase village held 300–400 people and the Lopez community under a thousand. Middle Preclassic Cuello was yet another example of the "early Mesoamerican village" type defined by Flannery (1976), one which seems to have been the commonest community type throughout pre-history. As in some of the villages of highland Mesoamerica, some of the central buildings of Preclassic Cuello became aggrandized to the extent that a public or ritual function can be argued in addition to, or replacing, domestic use. House-sized and house-shaped buildings may have acquired extra-domestic functions by the early first millennium B.C, while the gradual evolution of the western structures into clearly ceremonial buildings, culminating in the succession of Late Preclassic pyramids that ended with Structure 35, may also document the emergence of a ritual focus within the community core (Hammond and Gerhardt 1990).

Certainly, architectural design and building technique evolved through the sequence at Cuello: while the basic raw materials of earth and rubble fill and lime-plaster coating were always used, the early very low platforms, barely more than pavings, had by 600 B.C. become both large in area and nearly a meter high. The quality of walling needed to retain the larger bodies of fill led to improved construction, and eventually to the use of dressed masonry in the Late Preclassic ceremonial buildings. Superstructures, of timber clad in daub for most of the community's history, began to be raised in coursed rubble by about 400–300 B.C., but stone vaults were not used at Preclassic Cuello in spite of their development at more advanced centers such as Tikal.

This architectural history fits into what we presently know about Preclassic Maya building, although a review of the entire corpus of data is now overdue. At sites such as Seibal and Komchen, Preclassic house platforms have been identified: similar in format to Classic dwellings, the quality of stonework used for retaining walls is rougher, something

noted also for large public buildings at El Mirador and Nakbe. The Cuello corpus provides a long developmental sequence of such domestic structures not so far matched elsewhere, and demonstrates the genesis of Classic and later Maya domestic architecture in the early first millennium B.C.

That Middle Preclassic Cuello was egalitarian in social structure is argued by Wilk and Wilhite on the basis of settlement data, and by Robin and Hammond (Chapter 10) from the mortuary evidence. While the range of Bladen and Lopez phase grave goods is wide, there is no indication that it is geared in any specific way to social rank. The presence of jade and shell jewelry in juvenile as well as adult burials might suggest ascription of status were the quantities of grave goods or the sample of burials from these phases larger. The 1990 excavations indicate that such an interpretation is plausible.

Where social layering does become apparent is at the beginning of the Late Preclassic, where the economic power and decision-making concentrated in the creation of Platform 34 is matched by the first overt rulership iconography. Even so, none of the individual burials of the Late Preclassic Cocos phase could be considered "chiefly" in its location or contents: if Cuello had rulers with distinctive burials, these were not placed in Platform 34, or at least in the parts of it so far investigated. Those households dwelling in the successive buildings on the north side of the plaza, arguably part of the social élite of Cuello from the location of their houses, had burials distinguished by neither age nor sex, and with grave goods restricted to a few personal possessions such as shell jewelry and pottery vessels.

Non-mortuary ceremonial behavior gives no further clues to social structure: a few offerings at the end of the Middle Preclassic are valedictory to particular buildings, but the number of Terminal Late Preclassic caches seems to form a pattern honouring the entire Platform 34/Structure 350 architectural complex; there is no especial focus except for the erection of Stela 1, in front of the pyramid and above the site of the mass burial of half a millennium earlier. The ideology of the Late Preclassic inhabitants of Cuello remains, like that of their ancestors, opaque, even in comparison with what is known of the belief systems of other coeval communities such as Cerros.

We are slightly better off in reconstructing the economic underpinnings of this society: Miksicek's data show how the first settlement at Cuello, already a maize-growing community with a crop successfully adapted to the tropical humid lowlands from its arid highland origins, was cleared from tropical forest – a typical pioneer community like those of modern Kekchi cultivators observed by Wilk in southern Belize. Tree crops from the forest were exploited by the inhabitants of Cuello, and they ranged southeast into the savannas of the "pine ridge" zone (which may have been closer then than now). Chert from the Colha beds in the same direction was also exploited from an early date, perhaps even before a permanent community became established at Colha itself, and other goods such as sandstone corn-grinding equipment were obtained from much greater distances to the south. Even the initial settlers were not isolated, but formed part of a network of interacting communities.

By early Bladen times, at latest, that network extended to the highlands of Guatemala, from where occasional pieces of obsidian came; by the end of the Bladen phase jade was also being imported, from the Motagua valley or the metamorphic highlands to the west of it; one blue jade spangle with close parallels at La Venta may document the easternmost reach of Olmec contacts *c.* 600 B.C., and together with several other blue jades from Cuello and elsewhere in the Maya Lowlands suggests Olmec–Maya interpenetration at the level of prestation and down-the-line trade rather than anything more elaborately directed. Demarest (1989: Fig. 13.2) proposes a lattice-like set of links between Middle Preclassic societies in Mesoamerica in which the Olmec heartland on the Gulf Coast of Mexico has strong connexions with the highlands and Pacific Coast of Guatemala and beyond them into Western El Salvador; much weaker ties join the Olmec to the northern Maya Lowlands, and the north to the southern lowlands and thence the highland zone. Links between the Olmec heartland and the southern Maya Lowlands are mapped as unproven, although Demarest (1989: 339) notes that a paucity of exposure of Middle Preclassic deposits in the Maya Lowlands is part of the cause.

Cuello seems, on Miksicek's evidence, to have undergone a diminution in size towards the end of Bladen times, with a decrease in maize and an increase in forest plants suggesting encroachment of the bush, but from Lopez times onwards the community flourished once again. The basis of the subsistence economy remained much the same throughout the history of Cuello, with white-tailed deer, domestic dog, and several species of turtle forming a major sources of animal protein. There was, however, significant input from local freshwater fish and mollusks: Wing and Scudder estimate that some 99 percent of the animal protein came from local sources, of which perhaps 2 percent was non-terrestrial; the remaining 1 percent was from marine species obtained from the coast 35 km away, and only began to be notable in the Late Preclassic. We may here have the beginnings of heavy exploitation of marine resources by inland communities which peaked in the Classic period, on the evidence of samples from Colha and from Lubaantun in southern Belize.

Given that the Cuello Project was explicitly directed towards recovering evidence for the earliest known occupation in the Maya Lowlands, it is ironic that the Late Preclassic community is by far the best known. As noted in Chapter 2, in order to expose the Middle Preclassic deposits it was necessary to excavate the later overburden carefully, and as a result we have a very detailed structural sequence for Platform 34, spanning phases VA–XIII and roughly 350 B.C–A.D. 250.

Over a hundred of the burials are of Late Preclassic date, and form one of the largest corpora of evidence for a population of this period. Demography and incidence of disease and trauma are all fairly well documented for the Cocos phase, while a sufficient sample for the Lopez and earlier periods is still lacking. Comparison of the patterns for the Middle Preclassic with that for the succeeding period is, however, informative: continuity in most features suggests a similar society, although treponemal disease does not seem to have been a serious problem until well into Cocos times.

The bulk of the evidence for craft production and trade is also of Late Preclassic date, and again shows informative continuities from the preceding phases. while small quantities of obsidian and jade were present in Middle Preclassic times, the increase after phase VA suggests that as Cuello developed into a larger and more complex community, so exotic goods found their way there more easily. Obsidian came more from the Ixtepeque source than from El Chayal, confirming that a distribution route down the Motagua and north along the Caribbean coast was in operation during the Late Preclassic as well as the inland–riverine network that supplied the Petén. Obsidian, like jade at Cuello, came from a number of different sources by differing trade routes. The supplies of marine shell, granite *metates*, Colha chert and other goods from more distant parts of the lowland zone all demonstrate a community bound into local, regional, and long-distance procurement networks: but these networks included, of necessity, many similar communities to those at Cuello – we are not dealing with an isolated center of population, but with one typical of hundreds, perhaps thousands, of Maya villages across the lowland zone.

Still unresolved is the question of lowland Maya origins: the Swasey settlers at Cuello already possessed distinctive craft traditions and an economy adapted to the tropical forest environment. While Andrews's thesis of a migration down from the highlands in the late second millennium B.C. fits the current dates for initial settlement (Andrews and Hammond 1990; Andrews 1990), it does not take account of either the period of gestation and adaptation necessary for the establishment of lowland society, nor the earlier radiocarbon dates from a number of sites, including Cuello, which suggest an earlier presence. Other material evidence for such a presence, apart from that of the putative preceramic sites summarized by Zeitlin (1984), is however absent, and the point must remain moot. The model of initial riverine penetration advanced by Puleston and Puleston (1971) similarly lacks confirmation; although some of the sites yielding early dates are on watercourses, others such as El Mirador are not, while Cuello itself is a ridgetop community some distance from the nearest river.

The major problem with placing Cuello into a broader context is a lack of exact comparanda: while other Middle Preclassic sites are known in the Maya Lowlands, few have been investigated by more than the lower levels of test pits, yielding a small sample of material evidence. There have been larger-scale exposures at Colha, where results comparable to those from Cuello are emerging (Potter *et al.* 1984; Potter, personal communications), but these are presently unpublished. At Tikal (Laporte 1989) and Nakbe (Hansen n.d.) the emphasis has been on large structures of the period from 600 B.C. onwards: the succession of domestic buildings excavated at Cuello from earlier in the millennium has no present parallel.

Similarly, the range of Middle, and to some extent even Late Preclassic material culture is difficult to match elsewhere in the Maya Lowlands, apart from the ceramic inventory of the Bladen and later complexes. The best published comparisons for the period prior to 400 B.C. are in other culture areas of Mesoamerica, at Chalchuapa on the Pacific slope of the Salvadorean highlands (Sharer 1978), at Chalcatzingo in Morelos (Grove 1987), and at San Lorenzo in the Olmec "heartland" of the Gulf Coast (Coe and Diehl 1980). The evidence of figurines, roller and flat stamps, other ceramic artifacts, and those of bone and shell suggests that Middle Preclassic Cuello, marginal both geographically and socially though it was, operated within a southern Mesoamerican *koine* of iconographic understanding and technical equiva-lence. As other first-millennium B.C. communities are excavated and published, the extent of, and regional variants within this communality will come to be better understood.

Perhaps the best lesson we can learn from the investigation of Cuello is that underlying the spectacular remains of Classic Maya civilization is an antecedent culture created by the ancestors of those same Maya, in the unprepossessing environment of the tropical lowlands of Mesoamerica. Unnoticed for over a century, as the great Classic cities were explored, and dismissed for several decades thereafter as a period of peasant villages lacking the cultural refinements of their successor communities, the Preclassic Maya have proved to be disturbingly developed in their adaptation to the environment, in their subsistence and production economies, and in their relationships with their near and distant neighbors. With a society visibly complex from the latter part of the first millennium B.C. onwards the Maya can now be seen as paralleling developments elsewhere in Mesoamerica, not just following them at several centuries' remove. The key to this process lies in the Middle Preclassic, in the centuries before 400 B.C., and after the initial village settlement of the Maya lowland zone: Cuello is one of the first, but undoubtedly not the last, of the sites of this crucial period to contribute to our understanding of the genesis of Maya civilization.

REFERENCES

Adams, R.E.W. 1971. *The Ceramics of Altar de Sacrificios*. Papers of the Peabody Museum of Archaeology and Ethnology, Harvard University, 63 (1). Cambridge, Mass.

1972. Maya Highland Prehistory: New Data and Implications. *Contributions of the University of California Archaeological Research Facility* 16: 1–21.

ed., 1977. *The Origins of Maya Civilization*. University of New Mexico Press, Albuquerque.

1982. The Origins of Maya Civilization in Northern Belize: Present Evidence. Paper presented at the 47th Annual Meeting of the Society of American Archaeology, Minneapolis.

Adams, R.E.W. and N. Hammond 1982. Maya Archaeology 1976–1980: A Review of Recent Publications. *Journal of Field Archaeology* 9: 487–512.

Adams, R.E.W. and F. Valdez, Jr. 1980. The Ceramic Sequence of Colha, Belize: 1979 and 1980 Seasons, in *The Colha Project. Second Season, 1980, Interim Report*. ed. T.R. Hester, J.D. Eaton, and H.J. Shafer, pp. 15–40. Center for Archaeological Research, University of Texas, San Antonio, and Centro Studie Richerche Ligabue, Venice.

Anderson, J.E. 1967. The Human Skeletons, in *The Prehistory of the Tehuacan Valley*, I: *Environment and Subsistence*, ed. D. S. Byers, pp. 94–111. University of Texas Press, Austin.

Andresen, J.M. 1976. Notes on the Precolumbian Chert Industry of Northern Belize, in *Maya Lithic Studies: Papers from the 1976 Belize Field Symposium*, ed. T.R. Hester and N. Hammond, pp. 151–76. Special Report No. 4, Center for Archaeological Research, University of Texas at San Antonio.

1986. Lowland Maya Beekeeping. Paper presented at the 51st Annual Meeting, Society for American Archaeology, New Orleans.

Andrews, E. Wyllys, IV 1965. Progress Report on the 1960–1964 Field Seasons, National Geographic Society–Tulane University Dzibilchaltun Program. *Middle American Research Institute, Tulane University, Publication* 31: 23–67. New Orleans, La.

Andrews, E. Wyllys, IV and E. Wyllys Andrews V 1980. *Excavations at Dzibilchaltun, Yucatan, Mexico*. Middle American Research Institute, Tulane University (Publication 48). New Orleans, La.

Andrews, E. Wyllys, V 1990. The Early Ceramic History of the Lowland Maya, in *Vision and Revision in Maya Studies*, ed. F. Clancy and P.D. Harrison, pp. 1–19. University of New Mexico Press, Albuquerque.

249

Andrews, E. Wyllys, V and N. Hammond 1990. Redefinition of the Swasey Phase at Cuello, Belize. *American Antiquity* 54: 570–84.

Arnold, J.E. and A. Ford 1980. A Statistical Examination of Settlement Patterns at Tikal. *American Antiquity* 45: 713–26.

Ashmore, W.A. 1981a. Precolumbian Occupation at Quirigua, Guatemala: Settlement Patterns in a Classic Maya Center. Ph.D dissertation, University of Pennsylvania, University Microfilms, Ann Arbor, Mich.

ed. 1981b. *Lowland Maya Settlement Patterns*. University of New Mexico Press, Albuquerque.

1981c. Some Issues of Method and Theory in Lowland Maya Settlement Archaeology, in *Lowland Maya Settlement Patterns*, ed. W. Ashmore, pp. 37–70. University of New Mexico Press, Albuquerque.

Ashmore, W.A. and R.R. Wilk 1988. Introduction: Household and Community in the Mesoamerican Past, in *Household and Community in the Mesoamerican Past*, ed. R.R. Wilk and W. Ashmore, pp. 1–28. University of New Mexico Press, Albuquerque.

Baker, B.J. and G.J. Armelagos 1988. The Origin and Antiquity of Syphilis: Palaeopathological Diagnosis and Interpretation. *Current Anthropology* 29: 703–37.

Ball, J.W. 1977. *The Archaeological Ceramics of Becan, Campeche, Mexico*. Middle American Research Institute, Tulane University, Publication 43. New Orleans, La.

Barlaz, D. n.d. Thin-section Analysis of Preclassic Maya Pottery from Cuello, Belize. MS (1978) on file, Cuello Project archive, Boston University.

Bass, W.M. 1971. *Human Osteology: A Laboratory and Field Manual of the Human Skeleton*. Missouri Archaeological Society, Columbia.

Becker, M.J. 1971. The Identification of a Second Plaza Plan at Tikal, Guatemala, and its Implications for Ancient Maya Social Complexity. Ph.D. dissertation, University of Pennsylvania. University Microfilms, Ann Arbor, Mich.

1979. Priests, Peasants, and Ceremonial Centers: The Intellectual History of a Model, in *Maya Archaeology and Ethnohistory*, ed. N. Hammond and G.R. Willey, pp. 3–20. University of Texas Press, Austin.

Berger, R., S. De Atley, R. Protsch, and G.R. Willey 1974. Radiocarbon Chronology for Seibal, Guatemala. *Nature* 252: 472–3.

Berger, R., V.R. Switsur, and N. Hammond 1979. A Second Millennium b.c. Radiocarbon Chronology for the Maya Lowlands, in *Radiocarbon Dating*. ed. R. Berger and H. Suess, pp. 83–8. University of California Press, Berkeley and Los Angeles.

Biddle, M. and B. Kjølbye-Biddle 1969. Metres, Areas, and Robbing. *World Archaeology* 1: 208–19.

Bishop, R.L., E.V. Sayre, and J. Mishara n.d. Compositional and Structural Characterization of Mayan and Costa Rican Jadeitites. MS (1989) on file, Conservation Analytical Laboratory, Smithsonian Institute, Washington, D.C.

Bloom, P.R., M.D. Pohl, C. Buttleman, F. Wiseman, A.P. Covich, C.H. Miksicek, J.W. Ball, and J. Stein 1983. Prehistoric Maya Wetland Agriculture and the Alluvial Soils near San Antonio Rio Hondo, Belize. *Nature* 301: 417–19.

Borhegyi, S.D. 1951. *A Study of Three-Pronged Incense Burners from Guatemala and Adjacent Areas*. Carnegie Institution of Washington Division of Historical Research, Notes on Middle American Archaeology and Ethnology 101. Cambridge, Mass.

1959. The Composite or "Assemble-it-Yourself" Censer: A New Lowland Maya Variety of Three-Pronged Incense Burner. *American Antiquity* 25: 51–8.

Bradbury, J.P., B. Leyden, M. Salgado-Labouriau, W.M. Lewis Jr., C. Schubert, M.W. Binford, D.G. Frey, D.R. Whitehead, and F.H. Weibezahn 1981. Late Quaternary Environmental History of Lake Valencia, Venezuela. *Science* 214: 1299–1305.

Brainerd, G.W. 1958. *The Archaeological Ceramics of Yucatan*. University of California, Los Angeles (Anthropological Records 19).

Bronson, B. n.d. *Vacant Terrain Excavations at Tikal*. MS (1967) on file, Tikal Project, University Museum, University of Pennsylvania, Philadelphia.

Brothwell, D.R. 1975. *Digging Up Bones*. British Museum (Natural History), London

Brown, K.L. 1980. A Brief Report on Paleoindian–Archaic Occupation in the Quiche Basin, Guatemala. *American Antiquity* 45: 313–24.

Bruhns, K.O. 1987. Ceramic Technology at Cuello, Belize. *Mexicon* 9: 126–9.

Bullard, W.R., Jr. 1965. *Statigraphic Excavations at San Estevan, Northern British Honduras*. Occasional Papers of the Royal Ontario Museum, 9. Toronto.

Campillo, D. 1977. *Palaeopatologia del Craneo en Cataluna, Valencia y Baleares*. Editorial Montblanc-Martin, Barcelona.

Carr, H.S. 1986. Faunal Utilization in a Late Preclassic Maya Community at Cerros, Belize. Ph.D. dissertation, Tulane University. University Microfilms, Ann Arbor, Mich.

Chase, D.Z. 1980. The Corozal Postclassic Project: The 1979 Excavations at Santa Rita and Nohmul. Paper presented at the 45th Annual Meeting of the Society for American Archaeology, Philadelphia.

1982. Gann'ed but not Forgotten: Santa Rita, Belize. Paper presented at the 47th Annual Meeting of the Society for American Archaeology, Minneapolis.

Clancy, F.S. 1985. Maya Sculpture, in *Maya: Treasures of an Ancient Civilization*, ed. C. Gallenkamp and R.E. Johnson, pp. 58 70. Harry N. Abrams, New York.

Clark, J.D. 1982. Manufacture of Mesoamerican Prismatic Blades: An Alternative Technique. *American Antiquity* 47: 355–76.

Clark, J.D. and T.A. Lee 1979. A Behavioral Model for the Obsidian Industry of Chiapa de Corzo. *Estudios de Cultura Maya* 12: 33–51.

Clark, R.M. 1975. A Calibration Curve for Radiocarbon Dates. *Antiquity* 49: 251–66.

Cliff, M.B. 1982. Lowland Maya Nucleation: A Case Study from Northern Belize. Ph.D. Dissertation, Southern Methodist University. University Microfilms, Ann Arbor, Mich.

1988. Domestic Architecture and the Origins of Complex Society at Cerros, in *Household and Community in the Mesoamerican Past*, ed. R.R. Wilk and W. Ashmore, pp. 199–227. University of New Mexico Press, Albuquerque.

Cobley, L.S., and W.M. Steele 1976. *An Introduction to the Botany of Tropical Crops*. Longman, London.

Coe, M.D. 1980. *The Maya* (2nd edn). Thames and Hudson, London.

1987. *The Maya* (4th edn). Thames and Hudson, London.

Coe, M.D. and R.A. Diehl 1980. *In the Land of the Olmec*. University of Texas Press, Austin.

Coe, W.R. 1957. A Distinctive Artifact Common to Haiti and Central America. *American Antiquity* 22: 280–2.

1965. Tikal, Guatemala, and Emergent Maya Civilization. *Science* 147: 1401–19.

Cohen, M.N. 1975. Archaeological Evidence for Population Pressure in Pre-Agricultural Societies. *American Antiquity* 40: 471–5.

Collier, G. 1975. *Fields of the Tzotzil*. University of Texas Press,

Austin.

Comas, J. 1960. *Manual of Physical Anthropology*. Thomas, Springfield, Ill.

Coon, C.S. 1965, *The Living Races of Man*. Alfed A. Knopf, New York.

Covich, A.P. 1983. Mollusca: A Contrast in Species Diversity from Aquatic and Terrestrial Habitats, in *Pulltrouser Swamp: Ancient Maya Habitat, Agriculture, and Settlement in Northern Belize*, ed. B.L. Turner II and P.D. Harrison, pp. 120–39. University of Texas Press, Austin.

Cowgill, U.M., G. Goulden, E. Hutchinson, R. Patrick, A. Pacec, and M. Tsukada 1966. *The History of Laguna de Petenxil*. Memoirs of the Connecticut Academy of Arts and Sciences 17, New Haven.

Culbert, T.P. 1988, Political History and the Decipherment of Maya Glyphs. *Antiquity* 62: 135–52.

 ed. 1991. *Classic Maya Political History: Hieroglyphic and Archaeological Evidence*. Cambridge University Press, Cambridge.

Dahlin, B.H. 1977. The Initiation of the Albion Island Settlement Pattern Survey. *Journal of Belizean Affairs, Special Publication* 5: 44–51.

 1978. Artifacts, in *The Prehistory of Chalchuapa, El Salvador*, ed. R.J. Sharer, vol. 2, pp. 134–211. University of Pennsylvania Press, Philadelphia.

 1983. Climate and Prehistory on the Northern Yucatan Peninsula. *Climatic Change* 5: 245–63.

Dahlin, B.H. and W.J. Litzinger 1986. Old Bottles, New Wine: The Function of Chultuns in the Maya Lowlands. *American Antiquity* 51:721–36.

Demarest, A.A. 1989. The Olmec and the Rise of Civilization in Eastern Mesoamerica, in *Regional Perspectives on the Olmec*, ed. R.J. Sharer and D.C. Grove, pp. 303–44. Cambridge University Press, Cambridge.

Demarest, A.A. and R.J. Sharer 1982. The Origins and Evolution of Usulutan Ceramics. *American Antiquity* 47: 810–27.

Donaghey, S., J. Cartwright, H.S. Carr, C.P. Beetz, P. Messick, J. Ward, and N. Hammond 1979. Excavations in Platform 34, Cuello, May-June 1978, in *National Geographic Society–British Museum–Rutgers University Cuello Project 1978 Interim Report*, ed. N. Hammond, pp. 20–44. Archaeological Research Program, Rutgers University (Publication 1), New Brunswick, N.J.

Dreiss, M.L. 1988. *Obsidian at Colha, Belize: A Technological Analysis and Distributional Study Based on Trace Element Data*. Papers of the Colha Project 4, University of Texas, Austin and San Antonio.

Dunsmore, F. n.d. Daub at Cuello. Ms (1987) on file, Cuello Project Archive, Boston University.

Dwyer, J.D. and D.L. Spellman 1981. A List of the Dicotyledoneae of Belize. *Rhodora* 83: 161–236.

Eaton, J.D. 1980. Operation 2011: Investigations within the Main Plaza of the Monumental Center at Colha, in *The Colha Project: Second Season, 1980 Interim Report*, ed. T.R. Hester, J.D. Eaton, and H.J. Shafer, pp. 145–61. Center for Archaeological Research, University of Texas at San Antonio.

Erasmus, C.J. 1965. Monument Building: Some Field Experiments. *Southwestern Journal of Anthropology*. 21: 277–301.

Esau, K. 1977. *Anatomy of Seed Plants*. John Wiley and Sons, New York.

Flannery, K.V., ed. 1976. *The Early Mesoamerican Village*. Academic Press, New York.

 ed. 1982. *Maya Subsistence*. Academic Press, New York.

Folan, W.J., J. Gunn, J.D. Eaton, and R.W. Patch 1983. Palaeoclimatological Patterning in Southern Mesoamerica. *Journal of Field Archaeology* 10: 453–68.

Freidel, D.A. 1979. Culture Areas and Interaction Spheres: Contrasting Approaches to the Emergence of Civilization in the Maya Lowlands. *American Antiquity* 44: 36–54.

Freidel, D.A. and V. Scarborough 1982. Subsistence, Trade and Development of the Coastal Maya, in *Maya Subsistence*, ed. K.V. Flannery, pp. 131–56. Academic Press, New York.

Freidel, D.A. and L. Schele 1988. Kingship and the Preclassic Maya Lowlands. *American Anthropologist* 90: 547–67.

Furst, P.T. 1981. Jaguar Baby or Toad Mother: A New Look at an Old Problem in Olmec Iconography, in *The Olmec and Their Neighbors: Essays in Memory of Matthew W. Stirling*, ed. E.P. Benson, pp. 149–62. Dumbarton Oaks, Washington, D.C.

Gann, T.W.F. 1918. *The Maya Indians of Southern Yucatan and Northern British Honduras*. Smithsonian Institute, Bureau of American Ethnology (Bulletin 64), Washington, D.C.

Garber, J.F. 1983. Patterns of Jade Consumption and Disposal at Cerros, Northern Belize. *American Antiquity* 48: 800–7.

 1989. *Archaeology at Cerros, Belize, Central America, Volume II: The Artifacts*. Southern Methodist University Press, Dallas, Tex.

Gerhardt, J.C. 1985. Preclassic Architecture at Cuello, Belize. M.A. thesis, Department of Anthropology, University of Texas, Austin.

 1988. *Preclassic Maya Architecture at Cuello, Belize*. BAR International Series 464, Oxford.

Gifford, J.C. 1976. *Prehistoric Pottery Analysis and the Ceramics of Barton Ramie in the Belize Valley*. Memoirs of the Peabody Museum of Archaeology and Ethnology, Harvard University, 18. Cambridge, Mass.

Goodrich, C. and H. van der Schalie 1937. *Mollusca of Petén and North Alta Verapaz, Guatemala*. University of Michigan Museum of Zoology (Miscellaneous Publication 34), Ann Arbor.

Grove D.C., ed. 1987. *Ancient Chalcatzingo*. University of Texas Press, Austin.

Gruhn, R., and A.L. Bryan 1977. Los Tapiales: A Paleo-Indian Campsite in the Guatemalan Highlands. *Transactions of the American Philosophical Society* 121: 235–73.

Hamblin, N.L. 1984. *Animal Use by the Cozumel Maya*. University of Arizona Press, Tucson.

Hammond, N. 1972. Obsidian Trade Routes in the Mayan Area, *Science* 178: 1092–3.

 1973. Models for Maya Trade, in *The Explanation of Culture Change*, ed. C. Renfrew, pp. 601–7. Duckworth, London and University of Pittsburgh Press, Pittsburgh, Pa.

 1974. Preclassic to Postclassic in Northern Belize. *Antiquity* 48: 177–89.

 1975a. Maya Settlement Hierarchy in Northern Belize. *Contributions of the University of California Archaeological Research Facility* 27: 40–55.

 1975b. *Lubaantun: A Classic Maya Realm*. Monographs of the Peabody Museum of Archaeology and Ethnology, Harvard University, No. 2. Cambridge, Mass.

 ed. 1975c. *Archaeology in Northern Belize: British Museum–Cambridge University Corozal Project 1974–75 Interim Report*. Cambridge University Centre of Latin American Studies, Cambridge.

 1977a. *Ex Oriente Lux*: A View from Belize, in *The Origins of Maya Civilization*, ed. R.E.W. Adams, pp. 45–76. University of New Mexico Press, Albuquerque.

1977b. The Early Formative in the Maya Lowlands, in *Social Process in Maya Prehistory: Studies in Honour of Sir Eric Thompson*, ed. N. Hammond, pp. 77–101. Academic Press, London.

1979. Introduction, in *National Geographic Society–British Museum–Rutgers University Cuello Project 1978 Interim Report*, ed. N. Hammond, pp. 6–19. Archaeological Research Program, Rutgers University (Publication 1), New Brunswick, N.J.

1980a. Cuello Project 1979: A Summary of the Season. *Belizean Studies* 8 (3): 33–44.

1980b. Early Maya Ceremonial at Cuello, Belize. *Antiquity* 54: 176–90.

1981a, Cuello-Projekt 1980. *Mexicon 3* (1): 7–10.

1981b. Settlement Patterns in Belize, in *Lowland Maya Settlement Patterns*, ed. W. Ashmore, pp. 157-86. University of New Mexico Press, Albuquerque.

1982a. A Late Formative Period Stela in the Maya Lowlands. *American Antiquity* 47: 396–403.

1982b. Unearthing the Oldest Known Maya. *National Geographic Magazine* 162 (1): 126–40.

1984a. Holmul and Nohmul: A Comparison and Assessment of Two Lowland Maya Protoclassic Sites. *Ceramica de Cultura Maya* 13: 1–17 (originally presented at the 42nd International Congress of Americanists, Paris 1976).

1984b. Two Roads Diverged: A Brief Comment on "Lowland Maya Archaeology at the Crossroads". *American Antiquity* 49: 821–6.

1985. Archaeological Excavations at the Early Maya Site of Cuello, Belize, Central America. *National Geographic Society Research Reports* 19: 255–67.

1986. New Light on the Most Ancient Maya. *Man* N.S. 21: 398–412.

1988. *Ancient Maya Civilization* (3rd. edn). Rutgers University Press, New Brunswick, N.J.

1989. The Function of Maya Middle Preclassic Pottery Figurines. *Mexicon* 11: 111–14.

1990. *Excavations at Cuello, 1990: A Preliminary Summary*. Department of Archaeology, Boston University.

1991a. Matrices and Maya Archaeology. *Journal of Field Archaeology* 18: 29–41.

1991b. Architectural Transformation in the Late Middle Formative at Cuello, Belize, in *Reconstructing the Past: Recent Studies in Maya Prehistory*, ed. D.M. Pendergast and A.P. Andrews, in press.

n.d. *Excavations at Cuello, 1975–1990*. BAR International Series, Oxford, in prep.

Hammond, N., A. Aspinall, S. Feather, J. Hazelden, T. Gazard, and S. Agrell 1977. Maya Jade: Source Location and Analysis, in *Exchange Systems in Prehistory*, ed. T. Earle and J. Ericson, pp. 35–67. Academic Press, New York and London.

Hammond, N., S. Donaghey, R. Berger, S. De Atley, V.R. Switsur, and A.P. Ward 1977. Maya Formative Phase Radiocarbon Dates from Belize, *Nature* 267: 608–10.

Hammond, N. and J.C. Gerhardt 1990. Early Maya Architectural Innovation at Cuello, Belize. *World Archaeology* 21: 461–81.

Hammond, N., C. Heighway, D. Pring, R. Wilk, and E. Graham 1973. 1973 Operations, in *British Museum–Cambridge University Corozal Project 1973 Interim Report*, ed. N. Hammond, pp. 34-74. Cambridge University Centre of Latin American Studies, Cambridge.

Hammond, N., L.J. Kosakowsky, A. Pyburn, J. Rose, J.C. Staneko, S. Donaghey, M. Horton, C. Clark, C. Gleason, D. Muyskens,

and T. Addyman 1988. The Evolution of an Ancient Maya City: Nohmul. *National Geographic Research* 4: 474–95.

Hammond, N. and C.H. Miksicek 1981. Ecology and Economy of a Formative Maya Site at Cuello, Belize. *Journal of Field Archaeology* 8: 259–69.

Hammond, N., M.D. Neivens, and G. Harbottle 1984. Trace Element Analysis of Obsidian Artifacts from a Classic Maya Residential Group at Nohmul, Belize. *American Antiquity* 49: 815–20.

Hammond, N., D. Pring, R. Berger, V.R. Switsur, and A.P. Ward 1976. Radiocarbon Chronology for Early Maya Occupation at Cuello, Belize. *Nature* 260: 579–81.

Hammond, N., S. Donaghey, D. Pring, R. Wilk, F. Saul, E. Wing, A. Miller, and L. Feldman 1979. The Earliest Lowland Maya? Definition of the Swasey Phase. *American Antiquity* 44: 92–110.

Hansen, R. n.d. Archaeological Investigations at Nakbe, Peten, Guatemala: 1989 Season. MS (1989) on file, Institute of Archaeology, UCLA.

Harris, E.C. 1975. The Stratigraphic Sequence: A Question of Time. *World Archaeology* 7: 109–21.

1977. Units of Archaeological Stratification. *Norwegian Archaeological Review* 10: 84–94.

1979a. The Laws of Archaeological Stratigraphy. *World Archaeology* 11: 111–17.

1979b. *Principles of Archaeological Stratigraphy*. Academic Press, London and New York.

Harrison, P.D. 1979. The Lobil Postclassic Phase in the Southern Interior of the Yucatan Peninsula, in *Maya Archaeology and Ethnohistory*, ed. N. Hammond and G.R. Willey, pp. 189–207. University of Texas Press, Austin.

Harrison, P.D. and B.L. Turner II, eds. 1978. *Pre-Hispanic Maya Agriculture*. University of New Mexico Press, Albuquerque.

Haviland, W.A. 1970. Tikal, Guatemala, and Mesoamerican Urbanism. *World Archaeology* 2: 186–98.

1972. Family Size, Prehistoric Population Estimates and the Ancient Maya, *American Antiquity* 37: 135–9.

1985. *Excavations in Small Residential Groups of Tikal: Groups 4F–1 and 4F–2*. Tikal Report 19. University Museum, University of Pennsylvania (Museum Monograph 58), Philadelphia.

n.d. Excavations in Residential Areas at Tikal: Non-elite Residential Groups Without Shrines. Tikal Report No. 23. MS (1975) on file, Tikal Project, University Museum, University of Pennsylvania, Philadelphia.

Hayden, B. and A. Cannon 1983. Where the Garbage Goes: Refuse Disposal in the Maya Highlands. *Journal of Anthropological Archaeology* 2: 117–63.

Healy, Paul F. 1988. Music of the Maya. *Archaeology* 41 (1): 24–31.

Hester, T.R., ed. 1979. *The Colha Project 1979: A Collection of Interim Papers*. Center for Archaeological Research, University of Texas at San Antonio.

1980. The 1980 Season at Colha, Belize: An Overview, in *The Colha Project: Second Season, 1980 Interim Report*, ed. T.R. Hester, J.D. Eaton, and H.J. Shafer, pp. 1–14. Center for Archaeological Research, University of Texas at San Antonio.

1982. The Maya Lithic Sequence in Northern Belize, in *Archaeology at Colha, Belize: The 1981 Interim Report*, ed. T.R. Hester, H.J. Shafer, and J.D. Eaton, pp. 39–59. Center for Archaeological Research, University of Texas at San Antonio.

Hester, T.R., J.D. Eaton, and H.J. Shafer, eds. 1980. *The Colha Project: Second Season, 1980 Interim Report*. Center for Archaeological Research, University of Texas at San Antonio.

Hester, T.R., H.J. Shafer, T.C. Kelly, and G. Ligabue 1981.

Observations on the Patination Process and the Context of Antiquity: A Fluted Point from Belize, Central America. *Lithic Technology* 11 (2): 29–34.

High, R.L. Jr. 1975. Geomorphology and Sedimentology of Holocene Coastal Deposits, Belize, in *Belize Shelf – Carbonate Sediments, Classic Sediments, and Ecology*, ed. K.F. Wantland and W.C. Pusey, III. pp. 53–96. American Association of Petroleum Geologists (Studies in Geology 2), Tulsa, Okl.

Housley, R.M., N. Hammond, and I.A. Law n.d. AMS Dating of Preclassic Maya Burials at Cuello, Belize. *American Antiquity* (submitted).

Houston, S.D. 1988. The Phonetic Decipherment of Mayan Glyphs. *Antiquity* 62: 126–35.

1989. *Maya Glyphs*. British Museum Publications, London.

Hughes Hallett, D.J. 1972. *Pottery and Related Handicrafts of San Antonio and San Pedro Columbia. Toledo District, Belize/British Honduras*. Centre of Latin American Studies, Cambridge University (Working Papers 5), Cambridge.

Hultin, H.O. and M. Milner 1978. *Postharvest Biology and Biotechnology*. Food and Nutrition Press, Inc., Westport, Conn.

Irish, J.D. and C.G. Turner II 1987. More Lingual Surface Attrition of the Maxillary Anterior Teeth in American Indians: Prehistoric Panamanians. *American Journal of Physical Anthropology* 73: 209–213.

Johnson, J.K. 1976. Chipped Stone Artifacts from the Western Maya periphery. Ph.D. Dissertation, Southern Illinois University, Carbondale. University Microfilms, Ann Arbor, Mich.

Joyce, T.A. 1933. The Pottery Whistle-Figurines of Lubaantun. *Journal of the Royal Anthropological Institute* 63: xv–xxv.

Justeson, J. and P. Matthews 1983. The Seating of the *tun*: Further Evidence concerning a Late Preclassic Lowland Maya Stela Cult. *American Antiquity* 48: 586–93.

Keeley, L. 1982. Hafting and Retooling: Effects on the Archaeological Record. *American Antiquity* 47: 798–809.

Kidder, A.V. 1947. *The Artifacts of Uaxactun, Guatemala*. Carnegie Institute of Washington (Publication 576), Washington, D.C.

Kosakowsky, L.J. 1982. A Preliminary Summary of Formative Ceramic Variability at Cuello, Belize. *Ceramica de Cultura Maya* 12: 26–42.

1983. Intrasite Variability of the Formative Ceramics from Cuello, Belize: An Analysis of Form and Function. Ph.D dissertation, University of Arizona. University Microfilms, Ann Arbor, Mich.

1987. *Prehistoric Maya Pottery at Cuello, Belize*. University of Arizona Anthropological Papers 47. University of Arizona Press, Tucson.

Kosakowsky, L.J. and F. Valdez, Jr. 1982. Rethinking the Northern Belize Formative Ceramic Chronology. Paper presented at the 47th Annual Meeting of the Society for American Archaeology, Minneapolis.

Kurjack, E.B. 1974. *Prehistoric Lowland Maya Community and Social Organization*. Middle American Research Institute, Tulane University, Publication 38. New Orleans, La.

LaMarche, V.C., Jr. 1974. Paleoclimatic Inferences from Long Tree-ring Records. *Science* 183: 1043–8.

Laporte M., J.P. 1989. Alternativas del Clasico Temprano en la Relacion Tikal-Teotihuacan: Grupo 6C–XVI, Tikal, Petén, Guatemala. Doctoral dissertation, Universidad Nacional Autónoma de México.

Law, I.A., R.A. Housley, N. Hammond, and R.E.M. Hedges n.d. Cuello: Resolving the Chronology through Direct Dating of Conserved and Low-collagen Bone by AMS. *Radiocarbon*, in prep.

Lewin, R. 1984. Fragile Forests Implied by Pleistocene Pollen. *Science* 226: 36–7.

Leyden, B. 1984. Guatemalan Forest Synthesis after Pleistocene Aridity. *Proceedings of the National Academy of Sciences* 84: 4856–9.

Linick, T.W. 1984. La Jolla Natural Radiocarbon Measurements X. *Radiocarbon* 26: 75–110.

Littmann, E.R. 1979. Preliminary Report on Plaster Floors at Cuello, in *National Geographic Society – British Museum – Rutgers University Cuello Project 1978 Interim Report*, ed. N.Hammond, pp. 86–99. Archaeological Research Program, Rutgers University (Publication 1), New Brunswick, N.J.

Longyear, J.M. III 1952. *Copan Ceramics: A Study of Southeastern Maya Pottery*. Carnegie Institute of Washington Publication 597, Washington, D.C.

Loten, H.S. and D.M. Pendergast 1984. *A Lexicon for Maya Architecture*. Royal Ontario Museum (Archaeology Monograph 8), Toronto.

Lowe, G.W. 1978. Eastern Mesoamerica, in *Chronologies in New World Archaeology*, ed. R.E. Taylor and C. Meighan, pp. 331–93. Academic Press, New York.

McAnany, P.A. 1986. Lithic Technology and Exchange Among Wetland Farmers of the Eastern Maya Lowlands. Ph.D. dissertation, University of New Mexico, Albuquerque. University Microfilms, Ann Arbor, Mich.

McDonald, R.C. and N. Hammond 1985. The Environment of Northern Belize, in *Nohmul: A Prehistoric Maya Community in Belize. Excavations 1973–1983*, ed. N. Hammond, pp. 13–42. BAR International Series 250, Oxford.

McNeish, R.S., S.J.K. Wilkerson, and A. Nelken-Terner 1980. *First Annual Report of the Belize Archaic Archaeological Reconnaissance*. Robert S. Peabody Foundation, Andover, Mass.

McSwain. R. 1982. Stone Tools in Secondary Refuse: Lithics from a Late Preclassic Chultun at Cuello, Belize. *Atlatl: Occasional Papers* 3: 1–20. University of Arizona Department of Anthropology, Tucson.

1989. Production and Exchange of Stone Tools Among Preclassic Maya Communities: Evidence from Cuello, Belize. Ph.D. dissertation, University of Arizona. University Microfilms, Ann Arbor, Mich.

Marcus, J. 1983. Lowland Maya Archaeology at the Crossroads. *American Antiquity* 48: 454–82.

1984. Reply to Hammond and Andrews. *American Antiquity* 49: 829–33.

Marquez Morfín, L. 1982. *Playa Del Carmen: Una Poblacion de la Costa Oriental en el Postclasico (Un Estudio Osteologico)*. Istituto Nacional de Antropologia e Historia, Centro Regional del Sureste, (Colleccion Cientifica 119), Mexico.

Matheny, R.T., ed. 1980. *El Mirador, Peten, Guatemala: An Interim Report*. Papers of the New World Archaeological Foundation 45, Provo, Utah.

1986. Investigations at El Mirador, Petén, Guatemala. *National Geographic Research* 2: 332–53.

Matheny, R.T., D.L. Gurr, D.W. Forsyth, and F.R. Hauck 1983. *Investigations at Edzna, Campeche, Mexico, Vol. 1 Part 1: The Hydraulic System*. Papers of the New World Archaeological Foundation 46, Provo, Utah.

Merbs, C.F. 1983. *Patterns of Activity-Induced Pathology in a Canadian Inuit Population*. National Museum of Man Mercury Series (Archaeological Survey of Canada Paper 119), Ottowa.

Miksicek, C.H., R. McK. Bird, B. Pickersgill, S. Donaghey,

J. Cartwright, and N. Hammond 1981. Preclassic Lowland Maize from Cuello, Belize. *Nature* 289: 56–9.

Miksicek, C.H., K.J. Elsesser, I.A. Wuebber, K.O. Bruhns, and N. Hammond 1981. Rethinking *ramón*: A Comment on Reina and Hill's Lowland Maya Subsistence. *American Antiquity* 46: 916–19.

Miller, R.R. 1966. Geographical Distribution of Central American Freshwater Fishes. *Copeia* 1966 (4): 773–802.

Minnis, P.E. and S.A. LeBlanc 1976. An Efficient, Inexpensive Arid Lands Flotation System. *American Antiquity* 41: 491-3.

Mitchum, B. 1982. Xaman Kiwik: Changing Functions in a Small Early Classic Community. Paper Presented at the 47th Annual Meeting of the Society for American Archaeology, Minneapolis.

Moholy-Nagy, H. 1976. Spatial Distribution of Flint and Obsidian Artifacts at Tikal, Guatemala, in *Maya Lithic Studies: Papers from the 1976 Belize Field Symposium*, ed. T.R. Hester and N. Hammond, pp. 91–108. Special Report No. 4, Center for Archaeological Research, University of Texas at San Antonio.

1978. The Utilization of Pomacea Snails at Tikal. *American Antiquity* 43: 65–73.

1985. The Social and Ceremonial Uses of Marine Molluscs at Tikal, in *Prehistoric Lowland Maya Environment and Subsistence Economy*, ed. M.D. Pohl, pp. 147–58. Peabody Museum of Archaeology and Ethnology, Harvard University (Papers 77), Cambridge, Mass.

Morley, S.G. 1946. *The Ancient Maya*. Stanford University Press, Stanford, Calif.

Morley, S.G., G.W. Brainerd, and R.J. Sharer 1983. *The Ancient Maya* (fourth revised edition). Stanford University Press, Stanford, Calif.

Nash, M.A. 1980. An Analysis of a Debitage Collection from Colha, Belize, in *The Colha Project: Second Season, 1980 Interim Report*, ed. T.R. Hester, J.D. Eaton, and H.J. Shafer, pp. 333–52. Center for Archaeological Research, University of Texas at San Antonio.

Nations, J.D. 1979. Snail Shells and Maize Preparation: A Lacandon Maya Analogy. *American Antiquity* 44: 568–71.

Neivens, M.D. 1976. El Pozito: A Late Classic Site, in *Recent Archaeology in Belize*, ed. R. Buhler, pp. 53–64. Belize Institute for Social Research and Action, Occasional Publication 3, Belize City.

Neivens, M.D., N. Hammond, and G. Harbottle 1979. Maya Obsidian from Northern Belize: Source Attribution Resulting from Neutron Activation Analysis. *Abstracts of the 19th International Symposium on Archaeometry and Archaeological Prospection, 1979*: 19. British Museum Research Laboratory and Institute of Archaeology, London University, London.

Nelson, F.W. 1985. Summary of the Results of Analysis of Obsidian Artifacts from the Maya Lowlands. *Scanning Electron Microscopy* 2: 631–49.

Netting, R. McC. 1982. Some Home Truths on Household Size and Wealth. *American Behavioral Scientist* 25: 641–62.

Parsons, J.R. 1971. *Prehistoric Settlement Patterns in the Texcoco Region Mexico*. Memoirs of the Museum of Anthropology, University of Michigan, 3. Ann Arbor.

Pendergast, D.M. 1979. *Excavations at Altun Ha, Belize, 1964–1970, Vol. I*. Royal Ontario Museum, Toronto.

1981. Lamanai, Belize: Summary of Excavation Results 1974–1980. *Journal of Field Archaeology* 8: 29–53.

1982. *Excavations at Altun Ha, Belize, 1964–1970, Vol. II*. Royal Ontario Museum, Toronto.

Pohl, M.D. 1981. Ritual Continuity and Transformation in Mesoamerica: Reconstructing the Ancient Maya *cuch* Ritual. *American Antiquity* 46: 513–29.

1983. Maya Ritual Faunas: Vertebrate Remains from Burials, Caches, Caves, and Cenotes in the Maya Lowlands, in *Civilization in the Ancient Americas: Essays in Honor of Gordon R. Willey*, ed. R.M. Leventhal and A.L. Kolata, pp. 55–103. Peabody Museum Press, Cambridge, Mass, and University of New Mexico Press, Albuquerque.

Pope, K.O. and B.H. Dahlin 1989. Ancient Maya Wetland Agriculture: New Insights from Ecological and Remote Sensing Research. *Journal of Field Archaeology* 16: 87–106.

Potter, D.R. 1982, Some Results of the Second Year of Excavations at Operation 2012, in *Archaeology at Colha, Belize: The 1981 Interim Report*, ed. T.R. Hester, H.J. Shafer, and J.D. Eaton, pp. 98–122. Center for Archaeological Research, University of Texas at San Antonio.

Potter, D.R., T.R. Hester, S.L. Black, and F. Valdez, Jr. 1984. Early Middle Preclassic Phases in Northern Belize: A Comment on "Lowland Maya Archaeology at the Crossroads." *American Antiquity* 49: 628–31.

Pring, D.C. 1977a. The Preclassic Ceramics of Northern Belize. Ph.D. dissertation, University of London. University Microfilms, Ann Arbor, Mich.

1977b. Influence or Intrusion? The "Protoclassic" in the Maya Lowlands, in *Social Process in Maya Prehistory: Studies in Honour of Sir Eric Thompson*, ed. N. Hammond, pp. 135–165. Academic Press, London and New York.

Pring, D.C. and M.G. Walton 1975. Survey and Excavation at Cuello, in *Archaeology in Northern Belize: British Museum–Cambridge University Corozal Project 1974–75 Interim Report*, ed. N. Hammond, pp. 138–51. Cambridge University Centre of Latin American Studies, Cambridge.

Pring, D.C., M.G. Walton, and R.R. Wilk 1975. Survey and Excavations at Colha, in *Archaeology in Northern Belize: British Museum–Cambridge University Corozal Project 1974–75 Interim Report*, ed. N. Hammond, pp. 152–83. Cambridge University Centre of Latin American Studies, Cambridge.

Proskouriakoff, T. 1960. Historical Implications of a Pattern of Dates at Piedras Negras, Guatemala. *American Antiquity* 25: 454–75.

Puleston, D.E. 1971. An Experimental Approach to the Function of Classic Maya Chultuns. *American Antiquity* 36: 322–35.

Puleston, D.E. and O.S. Puleston 1971. An Ecological Approach to the Origins of Maya Civilization. *Archaeology* 24: 330–7.

Pyburn, K.A. 1987. Settlement Patterns at Nohmul. a Prehistoric Maya City in Northern Belize, C.A. *Mexicon* 9: 110–14.

1989. *Settlement and Community Patterns at Nohmul, Belize*. BAR International Series 509, Oxford.

Pyburn, K.A. and L.J. Kosakowsky n.d. Burial Practices: Description of Ceramic Grave Goods [at Cuello]. MS (1982) on file, Cuello Project Archive, Boston University.

Rathje, W.L. 1970. Socio-political Implications of Lowland Maya Burials: Methodology and Tentative Hypothesis. *World Archaeology* 1: 539–73.

1973. Classic Maya Development and Denouement: A Research Design, in *The Classic Maya Collapse*, ed. T.P. Culbert, pp. 405–54. University of New Mexico Press, Albuquerque.

Reina, R.E. and R.M. Hill II 1978. *The Traditional Pottery of Guatemala*. University of Texas Press, Austin.

1980. Lowland Maya Subsistence: Notes from Ethnohistory and Ethnography. *American Antiquity* 45: 74–9.

Reynolds, P.J. 1979. *Iron-Age Farm: the Butser Experiment*. British

Museum Publications, London.

Rice, P.M. 1987. Economic Change in the Lowland Maya Late Classic Period, in *Specialization, Exchange and Complex Societies*, ed. E.M. Brumfiel and T.K. Earle, pp. 64–75. Cambridge University Press, Cambridge.

Ricketson, O.G. 1925. Burials in the Maya Area. *American Anthropologist* 27: 381–401.

Ricketson, O.G., Jr and E.B. Ricketson 1937. *Uaxactun, Guatemala: Group E – 1926–1931*. Carnegie Institution of Washington Publication 477, Washington, D.C.

Ringle, W.M. and E. Wyllys Andrews V 1988. Formative Residence at Komchen, Yucatan, Mexico, in *Household and Community in the Mesoamerican Past*, ed. R.R. Wilk and W. Ashmore, pp. 171–99. University of New Mexico Press, Albuquerque.

Robertson, R.A. and D.A. Freidel, eds 1986. *Archaeology at Cerros, Belize, Central America, Volume I: An Interim Report*. Southern Methodist University Press, Dallas, Tex.

Robertson-Freidel, R.A. 1980. The Ceramics from Cerros: A Late Preclassic Site in Northern Belize. Ph.D. dissertation, Harvard University. University Microfilms, Ann Arbor, Mich.

Robin C. 1989. *Preclassic Maya Burials at Cuello, Belize*. BAR International Series 480, Oxford.

Romero, J. 1970. Dental Mutilation, Trephination, and Cranial Deformation, in *Handbook of Middle American Indians*, gen. ed. R. Wauchope, Vol. 9 *Physical Anthropology*, ed. T.D. Stewart, pp. 50–67. University of Texas Press, Austin.

Roosevelt, A.C. 1980. *Parmana*. Academic Press, New York.

Rovner, I. 1974. Evidence for a Secondary Obsidian Workshop at Mayapan, Yucatan. *Newsletter of Lithic Technology* 3: 19–27.

1975. Lithic Sequences of the Maya Lowlands. Ph.D. Dissertation, University of Wisconsin. University Microfilms, Ann Arbor, Mich.

Rue, D.J. 1987. Early Agriculture and Early Postclassic Maya Occupation in Western Honduras. *Nature* 326: 285–6.

1989. Archaic Middle American Agriculture and Settlement: Recent Pollen Data from Honduras. *Journal of Field Archaeology* 16: 177–84.

Ruz, L.A. 1965. Tombs and Funerary Practices in the Maya Lowlands, in *Handbook of Middle American Indians*, ed. R. Wauchope, Vol. 2 *Archaeology of Southern Mesoamerica*, ed. G.R. Willey, pp. 441–68. University of Texas Press, Austin.

1968. *Costumbres Funerarias de los Antiguos Mayas*. Universidad Nacional Autónoma de México, Mexico City.

Rye, O.S. 1981. *Pottery Technology: Principles and Reconstruction*. Taraxacum Press, Washington, D.C.

Sabloff, J.A. 1975. *Excavations at Seibal, Department of Peten, Guatemala: Ceramics*. Memoirs of the Peabody Museum of Archaeology and Ethnology, Harvard University, 13 No. 2. Cambridge, Mass.

Salati, L. n.d. Data Recovery by Visual Analysis: Jade Material, Cuello Project 1980. MS (1981) on file, Cuello Project Archive, Boston University.

Sanders, W.T. 1965. *The Cultural Ecology of the Teotihuacan Valley*. Pennsylvania State University Department of Sociology and Anthropology, University Park.

Sanders, W.T., J.R. Parsons, and R.S. Santley 1979. *The Basin of Mexico*. Academic Press, New York.

Saul, F.P. 1972. *The Human Skeletal Remains from Altar de Sacrificios, Guatemala: An Osteobiographic Analysis*. Papers of the Peabody Museum of Archaeology and Ethnology, Harvard University 63 (2). Cambridge, Mass.

1977. The Paleopathology of Anemia in Mexico and Guatemala,

in *Porotic Hyperostosis: An Enquiry*, ed. E. Cockburn, pp. 10–18. Paleopathology Association (Monograph No. 2), Detroit, Mich.

Saul, F.P. and J.M. Saul 1984. La Osteopatologia de Los Mayas de las Tierras Bajas del Sur, in *México Antiguo, Tomo I, Historia General de la Medicina en Mexico*, ed. A. Lopez Austin and C. Viesca Trevino, pp. 313–21. Universidad Nacional Autónoma de México, Facultad de Medicina y Academia Nacional de Medicina, México, D.F.

1989. Osteobiography: A Maya Example, in *Reconstruction of Life From the Skeleton*, ed. M.Y. Iscan and K.A.R. Kennedy, pp. 287–302. A.R. Liss, New York.

Scarborough, V.L. 1983. A Preclassic Maya Water System. *American Antiquity* 48: 720–44.

1985. Late Preclassic Northern Belize: Context and Interpretation, in *Status, Structure and Stratification: Current Archaeological Reconstructions. Proceedings of the Sixteenth Annual Conference of the Archaeological Association of the University of Calgary*, pp. 331–44. Calgary, Alberta.

Schacht, R.M. 1981. Estimating Past Population Trends. *Annual Review of Anthropology* 10: 119–40.

Schele, L., P. Mathews, and F. Lounsbury 1990. *Redating the Hauberg Stela*. Texas Notes on Precolumbian Art, Writing, and Culture, No. 1 CHAAAC, University of Texas, Austin.

Schele, L. and M.E. Miller 1986. *The Blood of Kings: Dynasty and Ritual in Maya Art*. George Braziller, New York.

Schiffer, M.B. 1975. The Effects of Occupation Span on Site Context, in *The Cache River Archaeological Project: An Experiment in Contract Archaeology*, ed. M.B. Schiffer and J. House, pp. 265–9. Arkansas Archaeological Survey Research Series, 8, Fayetteville.

1976. *Behavioral Archaeology*. Academic Press, New York.

Schiffer, M.B. and R. McGuire 1982. *Hohokam and Patayan: The Prehistory of Southwestern Arizona*, Academic Press, New York.

Scott, R.F., IV 1982. Notes on the Continuing Faunal Analysis from the Site of Colha, Belize: Data from the Early Postclassic, in *Archaeology at Colha, Belize: The 1981 Interim Report*, ed. T.R. Hester, H.J. Shafer, and J.D. Eaton, pp. 203–7. Center for Archaeological Research, University of Texas at San Antonio.

Scrimshaw, N.S., M. Behar, M.A. Guzman, and J.E. Gordon 1969. Nutrition and Infection Field Study in Guatemalan Villages, 1959–1964, IX: An Evaluation of Medical, Social, and Public Health Benefits, with Suggestions for Future Field Study. *Archives of Environmental Health* 18: 51–62.

Sedat, D.W. and R.J. Sharer 1972. Archaeological Investigations in the Northern Maya Highlands: New Data on the Maya Preclassic. *Contributions of the University of California Archaeological Research Facility* 16: 23–35.

Selby, H. and A.D. Murphy 1982. *The Mexican Urban Household and the Decision to Migrate to the United States*. ISHI Occasional Paper 4, Philadelphia, Pa.

Seymour, D. 1980. The Maya Temper: A Study of Potsherd Damage from Preclassic Deposits at Cuello, Northern Belize. Senior Honors Thesis, Department of Anthropology, University of California at Santa Cruz.

Shafer, H.J. 1976. Belize Lithics: "Orange Peel" Flakes and Adze Manufacture, in *Maya Lithic Studies: Papers from the 1976 Belize Field Symposium*, ed T.R. Hester and N. Hammond, pp. 21–34. Special Report No. 4, Center for Archaeological Research, University of Texas at San Antonio.

1979. A Technological Study of Two Maya Lithic Workshops at

Colha, Belize, in *The Colha Project, 1979: A Collection of Interim Papers*, ed. T.R. Hester, pp. 28–78. Center for Archaeological Research, University of Texas at San Antonio.

1982. A Preliminary Report on the Lithic Technology at Kichpanha, Northern Belize, in *Archaeology at Colha, Belize: The 1981 Interim Report*, ed. T.R. Hester, H.J. Shafer, and J.D. Eaton, pp. 167–81. Center for Archaeological Research, University of Texas at San Antonio.

1983. The Lithic Artifacts of the Pulltrouser Area: Settlements and Fields, in *Pulltrouser Swamp: Ancient Maya Habitat, Agriculture, and Settlement in Northern Belize*, ed. B.L. Turner II and P.D. Harrison, pp. 212–45. University of Texas Press, Austin.

Shafer, H.J. and T.R. Hester 1983. Ancient Maya Chert Workshops in Northern Belize, Central America. *American Antiquity* 48: 519–43.

Shafer, H.J. and F.M. Oglesby 1980. Test Excavations in a Colha Debitage Mound: Operation 4001, in *The Colha Project: Second Season, 1980 Interim Report*, ed. T.R. Hester, J.D. Eaton, and H.J. Shafer, pp. 195–220. Center for Archaeological Research, University of Texas at San Antonio.

Shannon, C.E. and W. Weaver 1949. *The Mathematical Theory of Communication*. University of Illinois Press, Urbana.

Sharer, R.J., ed. 1978a. *The Prehistory of Chalchuapa, El Salvador* (3 vols.). University of Pennsylvania Press, Philadelphia.

1978b. Pottery, in *The Prehistory of Chalchuapa, El Salvador*, ed. R.J. Sharer, vol. 3, pp. 2–203. University of Pennsylvania Press, Philadelphia.

Sharer, R.J. and J.C. Gifford 1970. Preclassic Ceramics from Chalchuapa, El Salvador, and Their Relationships with the Maya Lowlands. *American Antiquity* 35: 441–62.

Sheets, P.D. 1978. Artifacts, in *The Prehistory of Chalchuapa, El Salvador*, ed. R.J. Sharer, vol. 2, pp. 1–133. University of Pennsylvania Press, Philadelphia.

Sidrys, R.V. 1979. Supply and Demand Among the Classic Maya. *Current Anthropology* 20(3): 595–6.

Sisson, E.B. 1970. Settlement Patterns and Land Use in the Northwestern Chontalpa, Tabasco, Mexico: A Progress Report. *Ceramica de la Cultura Maya et al.* 6: 41–54.

1976. Survey and Excavation in the Northwestern Chontalpa, Tabasco, Mexico. Ph.D. dissertation, Harvard University.

Smith, A.L. 1937. *Structure A–XVIII, Uaxactun*. Carnegie Institution (Publication 483, Contribution 20), Washington, D.C.

1950. *Uaxactun, Guatemala: Excavations of 1931–37*. Carnegie Institution (Publication 588), Washington, D.C.

1962. Residential and Associated Structures at Mayapan, in *Mayapan, Yucatan, Mexico*, ed. H.E.D. Pollock, pp. 165–319. Carnegie Institution (Publication 619), Washington, D.C.

1972. *Excavations at Altar de Sacrificios: Architecture, Settlement, Burials and Caches*. Papers of the Peabody Museum of Archaeology and Ethnology, Harvard University, 62 (2), Cambridge, Mass.

1982. *Excavations at Seibal, Peten, Guatemala: Major Architecture and Caches*. Memoirs of the Peabody Museum of Archaeology and Ethnology, Harvard University 15 (1), Cambridge, Mass.

Smith, R.E. 1955. *Ceramic Sequence at Uaxactun, Guatemala*. Middle American Research Institute, Tulane University (Publication 20), New Orleans, La.

Spellman, D.L., J.D. Dwyer, and G. Davidse 1975. A List of the Monocotyledoneae of Belize Including a Historical Introduction to Plant Collecting in Belize. *Rhodora* 77: 105–40.

Spriggs, J.A. and T.V. Van Bueren 1984. A Practical Approach to the

Excavation and Recording of Ancient Maya Burials. *The Conservator* 8: 41–6.

Steele, D.G. 1970. Estimation of Stature from Fragments of Long Limb Bones, in *Personal Identification in Mass Disasters*, ed. T.D. Stewart, pp. 85–98. National Museum of Natural History, Smithsonian Institution, Washington, D.C.

Stuiver, M. and P.J. Reimer 1986. A Computer Program for Radiocarbon Age Calibration. *Radiocarbon* 28: 1022–30.

Sturdy, D.A. 1975. Some Reindeer Economies of Prehistoric Europe, in *Palaeoeconomy*, ed. E.S. Higgs, pp. 55–95. Cambridge University Press, Cambridge.

Suess, H.E. 1965. Secular Variations of the Cosmic-ray Produced Carbon-14 in the Atmosphere and their Interpretations. *Journal of Geophysical Research* 70: 5937–52.

1967. Bristlecone Pine Calibration of the Radiocarbon Time Scale from 4100 B.C. to 1500 B.C. *Proceedings of the Symposium on Radiocarbon Dating and Methods of Low-Level Counting, Monaco*, pp. 143–51, I.A.E.A., Vienna.

Thompson, J.E.S. 1939. *Excavations at San Jose, British Honduras*. Carnegie Institution of Washington (Publication 506), Washington D.C.

1940. *Late Ceramic Horizons at Benque Viejo, British Honduras*. Carnegie Institution of Washington Publication 528, pp. 1–35 (Contributions to American Anthropology and History 35). Washington, D.C.

Thompson, R.H. 1958. *Modern Yucatecan Pottery Making*. Society for American Archaeology (Memoir 15), Salt Lake City, Utah.

Tolstoy, P. and S.K. Fish 1975. Surface and Subsurface Evidence for Community Size at Coapexco, Mexico. *Journal of Field Archaeology* 2: 97–104.

Tourtellot, G., III 1970. The Peripheries of Seibal: An Interim Report, in *Monographs and Papers in Maya Archaeology*, ed. W.R. Bullard, Jr., pp. 405–19. Papers of the Peabody Museum of Archaeology and Ethnology, Harvard University Vol. 61, Cambridge, Mass.

1982. Ancient Maya Settlement at Seibal, Peten, Guatemala: Peripheral Survey and Excavation. Ph.D dissertation, Harvard University. University Microfilms, Ann Arbor, Mich.

1988a Developmental Cycles of Households and Houses at Seibal, in *Household and Community in the Mesoamerican Past*, ed. R. Wilk and W. Ashmore. pp. 97–120. University of New Mexico Press, Albuquerque.

1988b *Excavation at Seibal, Department of Petén, Guatemala: Peripheral Survey and Excavations, Settlement and Community Patterns*. Memoirs of the Peabody Museum of Archaeology and Ethnology, Harvard University, 16. Cambridge, Mass.

Tozzer, A.M., ed. 1941. *Landa's Relacion de las Cosas de Yucatan*. Papers of the Peabody Museum of Archaeology and Ethnology, Harvard University 18. Cambridge, Mass.

Truebe, H.A. n.d. Petrography and Possible Sources of Ground Stone Artifacts Collected in 1983–1985 Field Seasons, Nohmul, Belize, Central America. MS (1986) on file, Nohmul Project Archive, Boston University.

Truncer, J.M. n.d. Early Lowland Maya Burial Practices with Reference to the Cuello Site, Belize, C.A. MS (1980) on file, Cuello Project Archive, Department of Archaeology, Boston University.

Turner, B.L., II 1983. *Once Beneath the Forest: Prehistoric Terracing in the Rio Bec Region of the Maya Lowlands*. Westview Press (Dellplain Latin American Studies 13), Boulder, Colo.

Turner, B.L., II and P.D. Harrison, eds. 1983. *Pulltrouser Swamp: Ancient Maya Habitat, Agriculture and Settlement in Northern*

Belize. University of Texas Press, Austin.

Turner, B.L., II, P.D. Harrison, R.E. Fry, N. Ettlinger, J.P. Darch, W. Johnson, H.J. Shafer, A. Covich, F. Wiseman, and C.H. Miksicek 1980. *Maya Raised Field Agriculture and Settlement at Pulltrouser Swamp, Northern Belize. Report of the 1979–80 University of Oklahoma–National Science Foundation Pulltrouser Swamp Project*. University of Oklahoma Department of Geography, Norman.

Turner, C.G., II and L.M.C. Machado 1983. A New Dental Wear Pattern and Evidence for High Carbohydrate Consumption in a Brazilian Archaic Skeletal Population. *America Journal of Physical Anthropology* 61:125–30.

Ubelaker, D.H. 1978. *Human Skeletal Remains: Excavation, Analysis, Interpretation*. Aldine Publishing Co., Chicago, Ill.

Valdés, J.A. 1986. Los Mascarones Preclásicos de Uaxactún: El Caso de Grupo H, in *Primer Simposio Mundial sobre Epigrafía Maya dedicado al Dr. Heinrich Berlin y a la memoria de Tatiana Proskouriakoff 1909–1985*, pp. 165–81. Asociación Tikal, Guatemala.

Valdez, F., Jr. 1987. The Prehistoric Ceramics of Colha, Northern Belize. Ph.D. dissertation, Harvard University. University Microfilms, Ann Arbor, Mich.

Valdez, F., Jr. and R.E.W. Adams 1982. The Ceramics of Colha after Three Field Seasons: 1979–1981, in *Archaeology at Colha, Belize: The 1981 Interim Report*, ed. T.R. Hester, H.J. Shafer, and J.D. Eaton, pp. 21–30. Center for Archaeological Research, University of Texas at San Antonio, and Centro Studi e Richerche Ligabue, Venezia.

Velasquez V., R. 1980. Recent Discoveries in the Caves of Loltun, Yucatan, Mexico. *Mexicon* 2 (4): 53–5.

Wauchope, R., 1938. *Modern Maya Houses: A Study of Their Archaeological Significance*. Carnegie Institution (Publication 502), Washington, D.C.

Welsh, W.B.M. 1988. *An Analysis of Classic Lowland Maya Burials*. BAR International Series 409, Oxford.

Wilk, R.R. 1975. Superficial Examination of Structure 100, Colha, in *Archaeology in Northern Belize: British Museum–Cambridge University Corozal Project 1974–75 Interim Report*, ed. N. Hammond, pp. 152–73. Cambridge University Centre of Latin American Studies, Cambridge.

   1983. Little House in the Jungle: The Causes of Variation in House Size Among Modern Kekchi Maya. *Journal of Anthropological Archaeology* 2: 99–116.

   1984. Households in Process: Agricultural Change and Domestic Transformation among the Kekchi Maya, in *Households: Comparative and Historical Studies of the Domestic Group*, ed. R. Netting, R. Wilk, and E. Arnold, pp. 217–44. University of California Press, Berkeley and Los Angeles.

   1988. Ancient Maya Household Organization: Evidence and Analogies, in *Household and Community in the Mesoamerican Past*, ed. R.R. Wilk and W. Ashmore, pp. 135–52. University of New Mexico Press, Albuquerque.

Wilk, R.R. and L.J. Kosakowsky 1979. The Contextual Analysis Sampling Program at Cuello, 1978: A Very Preliminary Summary, in *National Geographic Society–British Museum–Rutgers University Cuello Project 1978 Interim Report*, ed. N. Hammond, pp. 58–66. Archaeological Research Program, Rutgers

University (Publication 1), New Brunswick, N.J.

Wilk, R.R. and R.M. Netting 1984. Households: Changing Form and Function, in *Households: Comparative and Historical Studies of the Domestic Group*, ed. R. Netting, R. Wilk, and E. Arnould, pp. 1–28. University of California Press, Berkeley.

Wilk, R.R., D.C. Pring, and N. Hammond 1975. Settlement Pattern Excavations in the Northern Sector of Nohmul, in *Archaeology in Northern Belize: British Museum–Cambridge University Corozal Project 1974–75 Interim Report*, ed. N. Hammond, pp. 73–115. Cambridge University Centre of Latin American Studies, Cambridge.

Wilk, R.R. and W.L. Rathje 1982. Household Archaeology. *American Behavioral Scientist* 25: 617–40.

Wilk, R.R. and M.B. Schiffer 1979. The Archaeology of Vacant Lots in Tucson, Arizona. *American Antiquity* 44. 530–6.

Wilk, R.R. and H. Wilhite n.d. The Settlement Area Sampling Project at Cuello: Final Report. MS (1980) on file with the senior author, Indiana University.

Willey, G.R. 1970. Type Descriptions of the Ceramics of the Real Xe Complex, Seibal, Peten, Guatemala, in *Monographs and Papers in Maya Archaeology*, ed. W.R. Bullard, Jr., pp. 313–57. Papers of the Peabody Museum of Archaeology and Ethnology, Harvard University, 61, Cambridge, Mass.

   1972. *The Artifacts of Altar de Sacrificios*. Papers of the Peabody Museum of Archaeology and Ethnology, Harvard University, 63 (1). Cambridge, Mass.

   1973. *The Altar de Sacrificios Excavations: General Summary and Conclusions*. Papers of the Peabody Museum of Archaeology and Ethnology, Harvard University, 64 (3). Cambridge, Mass.

   1978. *Excavations at Seibal, Department of Peten, Guatemala: Artifacts*. Memoirs of the Peabody Museum, Harvard University 14 (1), Cambridge., Mass.

Willey, G.R., W.R. Bullard, Jr., J.B. Glass, and J.C. Gifford 1965. *Prehistoric Maya Settlements in the Belize Valley*. Papers of the Peabody Museum of Archaeology and Ethnology, Harvard University, 54, Cambridge, Mass.

Willey, G.R., A.L. Smith, G. Tourtellot III, and I. Graham 1975. *Excavations at Seibal, Department of Peten, Guatemala: Introduction: The Site and its Setting*. Memoirs of the Peabody Museum of Archaeology and Ethnology, Harvard University, 13 (1). Cambridge, Mass.

Wing, E. 1975. Animal Remains at Lubaantun, in *Lubaantun: A Classic Maya Realm*, ed. N. Hammond, pp. 379–83. Monographs of the Peabody Museum of Archaeology and Ethnology, Harvard University, No. 2, Cambridge, Mass.

Wing, E. and A. Brown 1979. *Palaeonutrition*. Academic Press, New York and London.

Wiseman, F.M. 1975. The Earliest Maya. Paper presented at the 40th annual Meeting, Society for American Archaeology, Dallas, Tex.

Wright, A.C.S., D.H. Romney, R.H. Arbuckle, and V.E. Vial 1959. *Land in British Honduras*. Her Majesty's Stationery Office (Colonial Research Publication 24), London.

Zeitlin, R.N. 1984. A Summary Report on Three Seasons of Field Investigations into the Archaic Period Prehistory of Lowland Belize. *American Anthropologist* 86: 358–69.

INDEX